THE LOEB CLASSICAL LIBRARY

FOUNDED BY JAMES LOEB 1911

EDITED BY

JEFFREY HENDERSON

EDITOR EMERITUS

G. P. GOOLD

REMAINS OF OLD LATIN

IV

LCL 359

REMAINS OF OLD LATIN

ARCHAIC INSCRIPTIONS

EDITED AND TRANSLATED BY

E. H. WARMINGTON

HARVARD UNIVERSITY PRESS

CAMBRIDGE, MASSACHUSETTS

LONDON, ENGLAND

First published 1940
Reprinted 1953, 1959, 1967, 1979, 1993, 2000

LOEB CLASSICAL LIBRARY® is a registered trademark
of the President and Fellows of Harvard College

ISBN 0-674-99396-9

Printed in Great Britain by St Edmundsbury Press Ltd,
Bury St Edmunds, Suffolk, on acid-free paper.
Bound by Hunter & Foulis Ltd, Edinburgh, Scotland.

CONTENTS

INTRODUCTION

Object and scope of this book.   The archaic period.

My main object in this fourth volume of *Remains of Old Latin* is to present and to translate a number of the older Latin inscriptions as being an important part of early Latin remnants; this book has, however, a wider scope, because it also introduces readers to the general subject of Latin epigraphy and, in a narrow sense, to the study of Roman numismatics. Epigraphy, which is a branch of palaeography or the study of ancient writing, deals with the lettering, language and subject-matter of inscriptions written on hard and durable material such as stone and metal; it includes inscriptions on coins, though this part of the subject is usually separated under the title of numismatics, and inscriptions on gems, which likewise are usually studied separately.

I have set the year 80 B.C. as the latest limit of the archaic period; but it must be noted at once that archaisms in the Latin language and spelling occur to a much later date, especially in official documents. In fact there are large records of a date later than 80 B.C. which in spelling [1] present an appearance just

---

[1] It should be noted however that the predominant surviving archaism or quasi-archaism is the spelling *ei* for *i* (for which see below). Cf. for example the *Lex Antonia* of 71 B.C. (*C.I.L.*, I, 2, 204); the so-called *Lex Iulia Municipalis* of 45 B.C. (*C.I.L.*, I, 2, 206); and the inscription on the arch of Augustus at Ariminum, of 27 B.C. (*C.I.L.*, XI, 365).

as archaic as many of the inscriptions given in this book and written before that year. Of some such, the date after 80 B.C. is indisputable. A good example of a doubtful one is the extant *Lex de Gallia Cisalpina* also called *Lex Rubria de civitate Galliae Cisalpinae* (not included in this book), *C.I.L.*, I, 2, 592. Though it is usually dated in 49 B.C., there is reason to believe that it was passed and inscribed before Sulla's time. In this book will be found some inscriptions beyond the given limit (*a*) which are of unknown date but contain archaisms in spelling, and (*b*) which are of known date but contain deliberate archaisms correct or false. Note also that there are inscriptions known to be earlier than 80 B.C. which show no archaisms at all. I have included most coherent inscriptions known to have been written before 80 B.C., except such as consist merely of letters, numbers, or names, or of one or two words only.

The interest of the archaic period regarding Latin studies.

Inscriptions are almost wholly pieces of writing which have come down to us each in its original and unique form,[1] if we except physical damage caused by the passing of time, and some deliberate alterations made during the ancient periods; they have, by their very nature, not suffered the changes which are produced in literary texts through frequent copying by hand. Thus through old Latin inscriptions we can get a closer picture of the Latin language in the making than we can from remains which have

[1] This statement does not apply so fully to coins, which were of course produced in the mass from mould or die.

come to us by tradition of manuscripts. The picture is, to be sure, very imperfect: we need many more old inscriptions than we have; again, since the subject-matter has an interest not less attractive than the language has, I have followed, without keeping equal pace with, an accepted division, based on Hübner's, of Latin inscriptions into classes and sub-classes, and have kept a roughly chronological order in each sub-class; in the chronology furthermore there is much that is guesswork. Still, what we have may be called early Latin straight from the workshop and throwing light on Roman and Italian public and private life.

The different kinds of Latin inscriptions.

There are two main classes of Latin inscriptions.

I. TITULI or INSCRIPTIONS PROPER, which are written on durable objects to show their special purpose. The great majority of them mention a person or persons or public authority, and their relation to the object. Some, however, lay down conditions relative to the object itself or to its purpose; these overlap into Class II described below. This first class—the class of TITULI—is sub-divided into the following sub-classes.

(i) *Tituli sepulcrales*, or *Sepulchral Inscriptions*, which are properly epitaphs; in the earliest times these gave only the dead person's name, and later, lists of names, where more than one person shared or was meant to share the sepulchre; later again, various details were added, even short laudatory pieces (' *elogia* ') of prose or verse, or details of careers, which in nature approach the sub-class (iii) called honorary

ix

as shown below. Further details added, like instructions about the proper use and preservation of the sepulchre, are in a sense *Instrumenta*, ' *Documents*,' of Class II given below. Details of the sepulchre's size and the deceased's age are supposed not to have been added on monuments dating before Augustus' time; but this is doubtful, and I have included some examples. I have included also certain inscriptions which refer to sepulchres but do not necessarily give actual epitaphs. In the Augustan age some sepulchral inscriptions overlap into the next sub-class by dedication of the sepulchre to the *dei Manes*.

(ii) *Tituli sacri* or *Dedicatory Inscriptions* on objects dedicated, that is, presented to a god or gods (not to a man); or on something attached to or connected with a dedicated object and announcing its dedication. Some of these overlap into sub-class (iii) when a statue of a man or representing a people, with ' honorary ' details, is devoted to a god, and when a dedicator is in some way ' honoured ' in the inscription; and into sub-class (iv) when the dedicated object is a public work such as a temple or part of a sacred building. Typical examples of dedicatory inscriptions name dedicator and deity.

(iii) *Tituli honorarii* or *Honorary Inscriptions*, in the Greek fashion, in honour of a man (rarely of a nation personified), never of a god, and mostly written on pedestals of statues, sometimes on busts or stone tablets. About Sulla's time the person honoured begins to be put in the dative case, but even so the statue, not being devoted to a god, is not ' dedicated.' The sub-class honorary inscriptions overlap into sub-class (i) when the ' honouring ' inscription is on a sepulchre; into (ii) when the statue is also dedicated

INTRODUCTION

(presented to a god), or an ' honouring ' inscription records a dedication also; into (iv) when the honouring inscription is written on a public work.

(iv) *Tituli operum publicorum* or *Inscriptions on and concerning Public Works*, especially buildings including temples, with overlapping here into sub-class (ii); also boundary-stones, milestones, bridges, roads, aqueducts. Many of the inscriptions overlap into sub-class (iii) because the official inaugurator or builder or giver of the work is ' honoured ' therein; and some of the works are inscribed with Instrumenta, ' Documents,' of Class II described below.

(v) *Instrumentum* (to be carefully distinguished from the Instrumenta of Class II) or *Equipment*. The word *instrumentum* is here used to indicate all kinds of movable objects made for use in public and especially private life, but not dedicated; and covers among others the following sorts: vessels and other articles of metal; earthen vessels; tiles; stamps and seals; tickets and tokens;[1] products of quarries and mines; leaden pipes; armour and missiles; weights and measures. The word *instrumentum* may be taken to include also any inscriptions on the articles, since the inscriptions are part, often a necessary part, of the articles, though they do not necessarily show, in their words, the purpose for which the articles were made. Coins likewise are *instrumentum*, and since their inscriptions belong to epigraphy, I have included some in this book, though as stated above, the subject

[1] Including such guest-tokens (recording pacts between man and man, or man and community) as were portable; some were not portable and are classed with *Instrumenta* or ' *Documents* '—see below, p. xii.

of coins is generally treated as a separate study Numismatics.

II. INSTRUMENTA (not *instrumentum* of Class I (v) above), also called ACTA, or DOCUMENTS, DEEDS, public and private. They are records written on durable stuff, normally bronze plates, for publication and preservation as long as required or as long as possible. The inscriptions of this class have no reference to the things on which they are written; the inscriptions are themselves the objects. They may be subdivided as follows, though I have not followed any strict order in giving the archaic examples.

(i) *Foedera* or *Treaties* made by Rome with other states. Akin to these are agreements of guestship or of patronage between any man and a community. But the examples in this book were portable, and so find their place in Class I among the inscriptions on *instrumentum*—see above, p. xi.

(ii) (*a*) *Leges Publicae Populi Romani* or *Leges Rogatae* or *Laws* (including *Plebiscita* or *Plebiscites*) passed as 'acts of parliament' by the Roman people.

(*b*) *Leges Coloniarum et Municipiorum* or *Laws issued to Colonies and Boroughs*. These are charters or constitutions granted to other communities by Roman officials having *imperium* (state authority of Rome). The constitutions are *Leges datae* or *Conditions granted*, issued by such officials in obedience to terms laid down by a general or particular *Lex Rogata* or by a decree of the Roman Senate (see pp. xiii, xl–xli). Under the empire, *Leges* of (ii) (*a*) became mostly mere 'archaisms,' but those of (*b*) continued more freely to be issued, as *leges*; those of (*a*) under the Empire took the form of decrees of the senate and imperial *constitutiones*.

INTRODUCTION

(*c*) *Leges dictae*, see below p. xl, or *Conditions prescribed* for public properties, all such in this book being written on sepulchres or public works of Class I above.

(*d*) *Locationes* or *Contracts* and the like. Nearly all which are found in this book are connected with a public work so closely that I give them as belonging to Class I (iv) above (*Tituli operum publicorum*). Indeed, the inscriptions recording *locationes* are often really a part of the work.

(iii) (*a*) *Senatus consulta* or *Decrees of the Senate* of Republican Rome (see p. xli). Most of the archaic examples occur only as reproduced by magistrates in their decrees of (iv) below, or in a Greek translation only.

(*b*) *Decrees* of similar bodies in Rome's colonies, in *municipia*, and in *pagi* (for these see below, pp. xxxvi–vii). The archaic examples in this book fall rather under other headings, that of *Pagus Herculaneus* (pp. 108–111) being classed in this book among dedicatory inscriptions, the *Lex parieti faciendo* (pp. 274 ff.) being rather a public *locatio* of sub-class (ii) (*d*) above. The public and private notices painted on walls—see (vii) below—for some definite purpose are generally classed here.

(*c*) *Decrees* of private *collegia* ' guilds ' (not colleges of priests or magistrates) and *sodalicia* ' associations.' See p. xlii.

(iv) *Decreta magistratuum* or *Decrees of magistrates* of Rome, and other Italian towns under Rome, sometimes in the form of letters. In a sense they are *leges datae*, sometimes even *leges dictae*—see p. xl.

(v) Various *Acta sacra et Acta publica* or *Deeds sacred and Deeds public* such as temple-laws; oracular

xiii

INTRODUCTION

replies; minutes of priestly *collegia* such as the Arval Brothers; *fasti* of magistrates; *acta triumphorum*; calendars.

(vi) *Acta privata* or *Private Deeds* of various kinds including curses, gifts, wills, accounts; but not including any of the next sub-class.

(vii) *Inscriptiones parietariae* or *Inscriptions* (public and private) *on walls* mostly at Pompeii; (*a*) painted: about local elections, lost property, property to let, announcements of shows, and so on; (*b*) ' *graffiti* ' or scratched on the wall; these consist of private scribblings of various kinds. (*a*) and (*b*) do not of course include inscriptions painted scratched or stamped on movable articles, since the latter are *instrumentum* —see Class I (v) above. Some of (*a*) are temporary *leges* or rather decrees private or public—see above (iii) (*b*).

[(viii) *Diptycha Consularia* tablets (of invitation?) of carved ivory on which are represented public shows; they are inscribed the names of high magistrates (whose portraits also are often included). But they date from A.D. 406–541 only. (ix) *Diplomata militaria*, recording privileges granted to veteran soldiers, date from A.D. 52 to A.D. 305.]

Dating of inscriptions.

Sometimes an inscription bears its own date; or mentions an event or conditions whose date or period is known from other sources; or reveals in other ways by its own subject-matter the time to which it must belong; or is mentioned or used by a literary source; again, the style of the lettering, the spelling of the words, and the way in which the meaning intended is expressed, are important though not precise evidence;

INTRODUCTION

even the material [1] on which inscriptions are written
should not be ignored.

Peculiarities of Older Latin. [2]

I have not concerned myself with the actual
facsimiles of inscriptions or the actual shapes of the
letters, nor with ligatures, monograms, or *apices* or
apexes denoting long vowels from Sulla's time
onwards, or single dots or marks separating words, or
signs used to express numbers, other than special
cases mentioned in the text and critical notes.
More important are archaisms in spelling and pronunciation which show the Latin language in its
progress from the primitive to the mature. I give
therefore next a few remarks about the Latin
alphabet and then a survey of the old spellings and
sounds and their changes, as they occur in the
inscriptions. When desirable I use capital letters
to indicate writings as distinct from pronunciation.
Section numbers are used for ease of cross reference.

§ 1. The Latin alphabet, derived from a Greek
alphabet that was neither Attic nor Ionic, [3] had no
use for the Greek aspirated consonants $\oplus = \theta = th$,
$\mathbb{O} = \phi = ph$, and $\mathbb{W} = \chi = ch$ (Latin had no
aspirated sounds), and kept them only as numerals;
soon it lost $\mathbb{I} = Z = dz$, though Z was retained in

---

[1] Cf. A. Gordon, on marble as a criterion for dating, in
Trans. and Proc. of the Amer. Philol. Assoc., 1934, xlii, xliii;
Univ. of California Publ. in Class Arch., I, No. 4, No. 5.

[2] This section has been thoroughly revised by the late
Roland G. Kent, to whom my thanks are due.

[3] A. Grenier, *L'Alphabet de Marsigliana et les Origines de
l'Écriture à Rome*, École Franç. de Rome. *Mélanges d'Archéo-
logie et d'Histoire*, XLI (1924), 3–41; R. Kent, *Sounds of Latin*
(eds. 2 and 3), § 12.

some non-Latin dialects to indicate *ts*. The letter
C, a form of $\Gamma = \gamma$, was at first used for the sound *g*
(as in Greek), but soon was used also as an alternative
for $K = k$; in the third century a new letter G,
formed out of C or of $\perp$,[1] was introduced, and about
234 B.C. was placed by Spurius Carvilius, a freedman
of the consul Spurius Carvilius Ruga, in the alphabet
where $\perp = Z$ stood in the Greek.[2] The letter K
now fell mostly into disuse, though it survived
regularly in K. = *Kaeso*, and also sometimes before
a in inscriptions, and even, for example in *Kaeso*,
Kalendae, in literary records; where also *Caius*[3] and
Cnaeus, always abbreviated *C.* and *CN.*, often survive
for *Gaius* and *Gnaeus*, always pronounced with *g*.
The complete Latin alphabet was thus for a time
like ours, but having I for both vowel *i* and consonant *j* (as in English *yet*), and V for both vowel *u*
and consonant *v* (as in English *we*), and lacking
W, Y, Z. Soon after the middle of the second
century B.C., *ph*, *th*, *ch* were introduced (cf. pp. 84–
86), and a little later also initial *rh-* (for Greek
initial $\dot{\rho}$-) and medial *-rrh-* (for Greek medial *-$\dot{\rho}\dot{\rho}$-*),
and Y and Z, in order to represent better the pro-
nunciation of words and names transliterated from
contemporary Greek.[4] Our *u* is of course always V

[1] Cf. Hempl, *Trans. of the Amer. Philol. Assn.*, XXX (1899),
24–41.

[2] This seems the best interpretation of Plut., *Qu. Rom.*, 59.

[3] Note that the *ai* in this word is two syllables *ăĭ*, not a
survival of the archaic diphthong *ai* which developed into *ae*
(cf. § 5).

[4] *ph*, *th*, *ch* were occasionally used in native words, such as
pulcher, perhaps through a fancied derivation from the Greek,
and in personal names such as *Cethegus*, to give a fashionable
Greek touch.

in old Latin, but I print *u* according to custom, where the V is a vowel.[1] " Capital " letters [2] only were used except in *graffiti* and other examples of rough writing or handwriting.

§ 2. The main archaisms in spelling and pronunciation (other than differences in length of monophthong vowel-sounds, some of which I here ignore), as found in the old inscriptions, are as follows.

§ 3. EI as real diphthong. In early Latin, *ei* was as true a diphthong in pronunciation as in spelling, being so used notably in ' root-syllables ' as in *deico* and other words; in the dative and ablative plural of the first declension (where it was from earlier *ai*): in the nominative, dative, and ablative plural of the second declension (here from earlier *oi*): and in the dative singular of the third declension. But even old Latin records show, by the substitution of *e* alone (until *c.* 200 B.C.) or of *i* alone, that the pronunciation

---

[1] J began in ordinary writing, and appears in inscriptions in the 2nd century A.D.; dotted *i* first appears about A.D. 500. U appears for both vowel *u* and consonant *v*, in the uncial style *c.* A.D. 200, and elsewhere later on. W is a late writing as a ligature of more than one letter. The distinctions (*a*) between vowel *i* and consonant *j* and (*b*) between vowel *u* and consonant *v* were not definitely made until some time after the introduction of printing.

[2] The official monumental style (*scriptura monumentalis*) of the alphabet, in very neatly shaped capitals cut by professionals, developed in the last three centuries of the Republic and reached its best under Augustus and the early Empire. Many of the more ordinary inscriptions have a smaller and simpler *scriptura actuaria* ; some are in ' handwritings,' *scriptura cursiva*, of which the *s. uncialis*, with rounded letters and decorative curves taken over from writing on papyri and parchments, appears in inscriptions after the middle of the 3rd century A.D.

tended to monophthongize sometimes into the sound
ē (in talk of the country), and sometimes into a sound
between *ē* and *ī*; and after *c.* 150 B.C., this latter
sound became *ī*, with I as the fixed spelling except
where remembrance of the older spelling or deliberate
archaism (correct or erroneous) was practised (see § 4),
though *ī* was the fixed pronunciation whatever the
spelling.

§ 4. EI as diphthong in spelling only. From about
150 B.C. or the beginning of the Gracchan period a
custom arose, influenced partly by recollection of
the older spelling and partly by attempts at archaism
(often mistaken), as well as by a desire to produce a
convenient distinctive spelling for different sounds,
of using EI to represent in writing the long *ī*-sound
in any words, whether these words originally had the
true diphthong *ei* or not.[1] Thus the spelling EI is
a false archaism or fanciful spelling when it is used
for the *ī* in the genitive singular of the second
declension; in the accusative plural and ablative
singular in the third declension (such as *omneis*,
fontei); in words like *ameicus*, *audeire*; and possibly
in the present infinitive passive. See for example
Popillius' milestone, pp. 150-1, where the *ei* is correct
in *fecei*, *poseivei*, *conquaeisivei*, *redidei*; false in
ponteis, *omneis*, *fugiteivos*; uncertain in *meilia*. Note
that in *conquaeisivei* the diphthong of the second
syllable was written -*aei*- as a compromise between
older *ai* and normal *ae*. In *mihei*, *tibei*, *sibei*, *nobeis*,
vobeis, *ubei*, *ibei*, *utei* there is good reason for *ei*, though
the pronunciation here, as in all these other words,

[1] For the opinions of Accius and Lucilius on the spelling
of *ei* or *i*, see *Remains of Old Latin*, Vol. II, xxii–iv; Vol. III,
114 ff.

was now *ī*.[1] Very rarely an EI of this kind was falsely used where the sound was properly long *ē*, and even where it was short *i* (as in *parenteis* for gen. sing. *parentis*) or short *ĕ*. About Sulla's time a tall *I* was introduced to express *ī*, whether from original *ī* or from original *ei*; this tall letter was sporadically used until late in the 2nd century A.D.

§ 5. AI, real diphthong (not two syllables as in *Gāĭus Achāĭa*; nor the two long syllables *āī* in the old genitive singular—see § 25). This, soon after 200 B.C., changed to *ae* to represent a slight change in pronunciation, in any kind of word or ending (in the dative and ablative plural first declension, it had previously changed to *ei* in very old Latin). In the dative singular of the first declension old Latin had *-ai*, and also occasionally *-ā*; both being from very old *-āi*,[2] which gave *-ăi* (later *-ae*) before a consonant, but *-ā* before a vowel. The nominative plural of the first declension ending in *-ā* is a dialectal form ending in *-ās*, with the final consonant dropped in writing. We sometimes find *e* for *ai* and *ae* in very old inscriptions of the country districts, and often in the language of the common people, especially after *c.* 100 A.D.

§ 6. OI, real diphthong, later changed, with slight shift in pronunciation, to *oe*; and then in most words to *u*, representing long *ū*, about 200 B.C.; though writings OI and OE continued to be used into the 1st

---

[1] But *mihi, tibi, sibi, ubi, ibi* got a short final *i* by Iambic Shortening unless the metrical ictus fell on the final vowel and required the length to be kept; we even find the inscriptional writing *sibei* in verse to represent two shorts.

[2] All diphthongs are long by nature, but some had the first part short (as in *ăi*) and others had the first part long (as in *āi*).

century B.C. Note that thus the original of some *ū*-syllables appears as *oe*; and that in the nominative, dative and ablative plural of the second declension, *oi* had become *ei* (whence later *ī*) in very old Latin.[1]

§ 7. The apparent diphthong *ou* was only a Greekish spelling for the sound *ū*, in early inscriptions (Greek *ου* was at that time pronounced *ū*); normally *ū* was written V, at all dates.

§ 8. The short vowel *ŏ* in certain inflexional endings became *ŭ* about *c.* 235 B.C.; but after a preceding V = *u* or *v*, the *o* was kept until the Augustan age, and sometimes a little later: so *equos, servos, suos, aevom*. An original *ŏ* that became *u* in classical Latin, appears in old Latin in many words before *l*, as in *consoluerunt* (p. 254). Initial *vo-* changed to *ve-* about 150 B.C., if followed by *r* or *s* plus a consonant, or by *t*. The writing *o* for *au* represents plebeian or countrified pronunciation *ō*, not an archaism.

§ 9. The combination *ŏv* became *u* in many words (for example *sŏvŏs* became *suŏs* and *sŭŭs*, § 8; *flovius* became *fluvius*, pp. 262–4); though *ov, vo, uo* remained usual until after the Augustan age to avoid the combination VV representing two different sounds in succession.[2]

§ 10. Old Latin similarly avoided the doubled II = *ĭĭ* and *jĭ*, the former by contracting the two sounds to one *ī* (so genitive singular always, until Catullus; forms of the perfect tenses sometimes) or

---

[1] All *i*-diphthongs remained before *i* plus a vowel, so that *maior, eius,* (old) *quoius, cuius* represent the pronunciations *mai-jor, ei-jus, quoi-jus, cui-jus* (*j* = English *y* in *yet*); note the occasional later spellings *eiius, cuiius*.

[2] For the same reason, the writing *fluio* = *fluvio* (p. 264).

by writing *iei* (*ei* here mostly for the original diphthong, §§ 3–4: second declension plural endings *-iei* and *-ieis*; perfect indicative 1st and 3rd singular *-iei* and *-ieit*—these are rarely contracted); the latter by omitting the consonantal *i* (the *y*-sound in our *yet*), for example *conjicio*, compound of *iacio* = *jacio*, was written *conicio* with first syllable long (pronounced *con-ji-ci-o*; there was also a pronunciation *co-ni-ci-o*, with first syllable short because of loss of the *j*), and names like *Gāĭus* and *Pompeius* (pronounced *Pom-pei-jus*) had genitives *Gai* (= *Gā-ī*) and *Pompei* (= *Pom-pei-jī*). Another old writing for *-ĭĭ-* was -IE- as in *adiese* = *adĭĭsse* (p. 256) and the like, to avoid -II- = dissyllabic *-ĭ-ĭ-*.

§§ 11–14. *Sounds not strongly pronounced, with a tendency to omission even in writing.*

§ 11. *s* final was often omitted in writing after a short vowel, in very old inscriptions; this omission ceases in inscriptions *c.* 130 B.C., except in careless writing, but it appears frequently in colloquial Latin later on. In literary poetry before Augustus' time, the *s* might fail to make position, even though it was written.

§ 12. *m* final gave a nasal sound to the preceding vowel, and was often omitted in old inscriptions; but after *c.* 130 B.C. it was not omitted except in careless writing, and in colloquial Latin of later times.

§ 13. *n* before *s* or *f* made the preceding vowel nasal, and was often omitted in old inscriptions; for example, COSOL became the regular spelling for *consul* in republican times.

§ 14. *t* final was sometimes omitted in very old inscriptions; this omission was perhaps limited to

dialectal or rustic language. When -*d* appears for
-*t* in the verb endings of the third person singular,
the -*d* represents an older ending which has been
replaced by -*t* in the later language.

§ 15. E for *i* in an unaccented syllable may be due
to a false archaism (for example, *tempestatebus dedet.
mereto*; see p. 4); cf. also § 10, end.

§ 16. *ŭ* and *ĭ* before *p, b, f*, or *m* plus a vowel varied
with each other in many words, such as *optumus* and
optimus, monumentum and *monimentum* (pp. 18 and 26),
pontufex and *pontifex*, until about Caesar's time, when
the spelling with *i* became standard in most of them,
but not in all. In the gerund and gerundive of the
third and fourth conjugations, -*und*- is the older
original formation, soon remodelled to -*end*- in
imitation of the -*ent*- of the present participle. The
endings seen in *Cererus* genitive singular for *Cereris*,
and *spatiarus* second singular present indicative
deponent for *spatiaris*, represent an older original
in -*os* (§ 8), perhaps used in country dialects; they
were crowded out by normal Latin -*is* from original
-*es*.

§§ 17–23. *Peculiarities of Spelling.*

§ 17. For *k, c, g, y, z, th, ph, ch, rh*, see § 1, on the
Latin alphabet; and for *ei*, §§ 3–4.

§ 18. Q, besides its standard use before consonantal *u* plus a vowel, stood alone for *qu* before a
vowel, in a few very old inscriptions; rarely, it stood
for *g* (p. 204); not infrequently it was used for *c*
before vowel *u*, as in *pequnia* (pp. 106–8), and
occasionally before *o* (p. 202).

§ 19. *xs* in the 2nd century B.C., especially the latter
half, was sometimes put for plain *x*, perhaps to

emphasise the fact that the letter represented two sounds, *-k-s-*. The writing *xs* became common again in Augustus' time and later.

§ 20. Consonants were not self-doubled in earliest Latin. Self-doubled consonants, that is, the same letter written twice in immediate succession, is a practice attributed to Ennius (239–169 B.C.), and are first found in an inscription (see p. 76) of 211 B.C., transliterating the Greek Ἔννα. In normal Latin they began some time afterwards;[1] from *c.* 195 to 135 B.C. instances of singles and doubles are roughly equal in number, then the doubles become commoner, and, from *c.* 115, normal—though singles also last on.[2]

§ 21. From about 175 to 75 B.C. mostly, we find in some inscriptions double *aa, ee, uu* for the long vowel sounds *ā, ē, ū* (once also *oo* for *ō*, page 80; never *ii* for *ī* in old Latin). These doubles were due to the rules formulated by Accius (170–*c.* 85 B.C.); they practically disappear after 75 B.C. (though there are exceptions, and there are late traces of *uu* in literature, as well as of *ii* for *ī* in manuscripts), an *apex* or acute accent ´ often appearing henceforth, until late in the 3rd century A.D., over the single letter to mark a vowel as long.

§ 22. Nominative singular *-ios* was often shortened to *-i*, so that not only the final *-s* was gone (see § 11), but the *-o-* also. This was either an abbreviation or,

---

[1] Similarly, in old Latin of the same dates, *ss* was used in transliterating Greek ζ in the middle of a word; ζ as an initial was expressed by a single *s*.

[2] The use of doubled consonants marks the consonantal sound as long, as in modern Italian *anno, petto*; in English only in compounds or in phrases, as in *cold day* compared with *coal day*.

so far as the -*o*- is concerned, an example of dialectal syncope.

§ 23. Joining of the preposition to the word following, and separation of the preposition in compound verbs from the verb, seem to be matters of personal preference only.

§§ 24–38. *Inflexions.*

§ 24. The following are the main peculiarities of formation, spelling, and punctuation in inflexions as they occur in old inscriptions, some being repeated from the general remarks already given.

§ 25. First declension: genitive singular in two long syllables—*āī* (not the diphthong *ai*—see § 5), which is used even by Virgil; still older genitive singular also in -*ās*, surviving into standard Latin in *pater familias* and *mater familias*; also in -*ais* or (from about 80 B.C. onwards in ' common ' or plebeian language) -*aes*. Dative singular in -*ai* or -*ā* (see § 5). Ablative singular in -*ād* until after 200 B.C. Nominative plural in diphthongal -*ai* (see § 5); also a rare older form in -*ās*, sometimes reduced to -*ā* (see § 5, also § 11). Genitive plural in -*om* or -*um* (rare), in imitation of the second declension form.

§ 26. Second declension: nominative singular in -*ŏs* or -*ŏ* (see § 11) and accusative in -*ŏm* or -*ŏ* (see § 12); plebeian and dialectal Latin show a rare nominative in -*is* (for -*ios*; also in -*i*—see § 22) and accusative in -*im* (for -*iom*). Ablative singular in -*ōd* until after 200 B.C. (*ud* in this declension being probably dialectic). Nominative plural in -*ei*, -*ē*, (classical) -*ī* (see §§ 3–4); also in -*eis*, -*ēs*, -*īs*, with -*s* transferred from the third declension. Genitive plural in -*om* (and -*o*, § 12) and -*um* (not a contraction

xxiv

of the following), and a later formation in -*ōrom* (also -*ōro*, § 12), classical -*ōrum*. Dative-ablative plural in -*eis* (§§ 3–4).

§ 27. Third declension: genitive singular -*ĕs*, becoming standard -*is*; also dialectal -*us* (from older -*ŏs*, see § 16). Dative singular -*ei* and -*ē* (see § 3); the latter disappearing *c.* 200 B.C., but surviving in the legal phrase *iure dicundo*, even in literary records. Ablative singular in -*īd* (-ED occurs twice, and may be either -*ēd* or -*ĕd*, but is an analogical form that did not spread) and rarely in -*ei* (for -*ī*, § 4). Nominative plural rarely in -*īs*, imitating the accusative. Accusative plural of *i*-stems properly in -*īs* (spelled also -*eis*, § 4) and of consonant-stems in -*ēs*, the two endings being confused with each other. Genitive plural -*om* (§ 8).

§ 28. Fourth declension: genitive singular in -*uŏs*, -*ī*, and (in literary records) -*uis*. Ablative singular in -*ūd*.

§ 29. Many forms ending in -*ē* in classical Latin originally ended in -*ēd*, seen in old Latin: thus accusative-ablative *med*, *ted*, *sed*, the preposition *sēd* and *sē* = ' sine ', adverbs such as *facilumed* (see p. 258); this -*d* is seen also in old forms of ablatives of nouns and pronouns and in imperatives which end in a long vowel. This final -*d* after a long vowel was lost in pronunciation about 200 B.C., after which time its use is an archaism. But the -*d* remains after a short vowel, and in *haud* if the next word begins with a vowel.

§§ 30–34. *Pronouns in old Latin inscriptions and literature* have the following forms not standard in classical Latin:

INTRODUCTION

§ 30. Forms of *qui, quis*: Nom. sing. masc. *qoi* (§ 18; p. 54), *quoi* (p. 242), *quei*. Gen. sing. *quoius* (= *quoi-jus*), *quius* (= *cui-jus*, § 18). Dat. sing. *quoiei* (= *quoi-jei*), *quoi*. Nom. plur. masc. *quei*, *quēs*.

§ 31. Forms of *is*: Nom. sing. masc. *eis* (p. 322), an error induced by *ei* in gen. *eius*, etc. Acc. sing. masc. *im, em*. Dat. sing. masc. *eiei* (= *ei-jei*; see § 10). Abl. sing. masc. and fem. *eōd, eād*, cf. classical *anteā, praetereā*, etc. Nom. pl. masc. *eeis, eis, iei, ieis*; dat. and abl. pl. *eieis* (= *ei-jeis*), *eeis, ieis, īs, ībus*.

§ 32. Forms of *hic*: Nom. sing. masc. *hĕc* (= *hic*; p. 4). Acc. sing. masc. *honc(e)*. Gen. sing. *hoius* (= *hoi-jus*). Dat. sing. *hoic(e)*. Loc. sing. *heic(e)*. Nom. pl. masc. *hei, heis(ce), hīs(ce)*. Dat. and abl. pl. *hībus*.

§ 33. Forms of *ille*: *olle, ollus*, etc.

§ 34. The personal pronouns: *eqo* = *ego* (p. 204; see § 18). Acc.-abl. sing. *mēd, tēd*, sing.-pl. *sēd*, for *mē, tē, sē* (see § 29).

§§ 35–38. *Verbal forms, including some differences in quantity*.

§ 35. Present subjunctive of *esse*: *siem, siēs, sied* (§ 14) and *siet, sient*.

§ 36. Imperatives active in *-tōd* (see § 29) and *-minō*; but *rogato, censento* seem to be passive imperatives, third person plural, with an original final *-r* dropped.

§ 37. Infinitive passive in *-ier, -ārier, -ērier, -īrier*.

§ 38. The perfect indicative: The 1st sing. goes back to *-ai* (seen in Faliscan *peparai*, Indog. Forsch. 32.84–6), whence *-ei* and later *-ī* (§ 3; Praenestine *-ī* on page 198 is an early dialectal development). The 2nd sing. had *-istei*, as in *gesistei* (p. 4; § 20); but *interieisti* (p. 22) has *-iei-* for *-ĭĭ-* to avoid a doubled vowel letter denoting two vowels (§ 10). The 3rd sing. went back to *-et* or *-eit*, and appears as *-ed* or *-et*, *-eit*, later *-it* (§§ 3–4). The 3rd pl. had *-ēre* (also once *-ēri*, p. 70; the *i* is only a careless writing) or *-ĕront*, which tended to be reduced in dialectal Latin to *-rot*, *-ro* (p. 62); standard Latin verse has *-ēre* and *-ērunt*, rarely-*ĕrunt* (a colloquial pronunciation).

§ 39. *Other archaisms* also occur in literary records; such others as occur in old inscriptions are mentioned in relevant footnotes to the text.

§ 40. *Direction of writing.* In some very old inscriptions, the writing runs from right to left, and in some in the two directions, in alternate lines or irregularly.

Abbreviations.

The following list contains such abbreviations, used by the original writers of the inscriptions included in this volume, as are not explained in the notes. I have spelt out the abbreviation usually into classical, not archaic Latin; and wherever advisable, I have added the relevant page. In spelling out proper names and *f. = filius* I mostly ignore oblique cases.

a. agris (*see* a.d.a.; a.d.a.i.; a.i.a.)
a. annos 22
a. ante (*see* a.d.)
a. asses 25
A. Aulus
act. actum
a.d. ante diem
a.d.a. agris dandis assignandis 296, 298, 316, 322, 324, 328, 332, 380, 382, 384
a.d.a.i. agris dandis assignandis iudicandis 174

adf. adfuerunt
aed. aedilis 8, 240; aediles 96, 184, 234
ag. agrum *or* agro
agr. agrum *or* agro 10, 30, 34
a.i.a. agris iudicandis assignandis 168, 170, 172
aid. aidilis 8, 144, 298, 316, 322; aidiles 64, 148, 184
alt. altum
an. annos *or* annis
ann. annos *or* annis

INTRODUCTION

arb. arbitratu
arf. arfuerunt
Arn. Arniensi (tribu)

b.f. bonum factum

O. Caiae (= Gaiae)
O. Caius (= Gaius) (*except* Claudiā, p. 36)
c. calendis 12
c. coeraverunt *or* curaverunt 148, 184, 192
c. consulto 84, 148, 174, 178, 194, 226, 230, 232, 234, 236, 238, 240, 380, 434, 448
C. Claudia (tribu) 36; *elsewhere* Caius
cal. calendis
cap. capitalis
cast. *or* castel. castellum (*acc. of* castellus)
cens. *or* ces. censor 94, 298, 322, 388; censores 184, 186, 428, 430
civ. civium
Cla. Claudia (tribu)
Clu. Clustumina (tribu)
Cn. Cnaeus (= Gnaeus)
coer. coeraverunt
coir. coiraverunt
Col. Collina (tribu)
col. ded. coloniae deducendae
concess. concessi
conlocā. conlocatus
cons. consuluit
contul. contulerunt
Oor. Corneliae
cos. consul 10, 78, 84, 86, 144, 146, 148–52, 182, 212, 240, 298, 316, 322, 398, 400, 432, 444; consule 134, 136, 158, 176, 178, 236, 402; consules 254, 304; consulibus 102, 104, 106, 108, 110, 118, 144, 208, 262, 268, 270, 274, 288, 374, 376, 380, 382, 384, 386, 388, 392, 394, 396, 398, 402, 410, 434, 444
cubā. cubat
cur. curatori 180, 182

cur. curulis 8, 144, 240
curar. curarunt

D. Decimus
d. dandis 296; dant *or* dederunt 64, 110, 112, 118, 120; dat *or* dedit 64, 70, 72, 90; datus 214; de 148, 180, 184, 186, 188, 192, 420. decreto 114, 116, 190, 196. decumanum 170. decurionum 116, 118, 180, 186, 190, 192. dicundo 178, 180, 190. diem *see* a.d. dolo 296, 298, 300, 322, 332, 334, 438, 440–2; dono *or* donom *or* donum[1] 64, 70, 72, 90, 110. duo 180
d.d. decurionum decreto 116, 118, 190
d.d. donum (*or* dono) dat (*or* dedit) 64, 70, 90
d.d. donum (*or* dono) dant (*or* dederunt) 64, 110, 112, 120
d.d.s. de decurionum sententia 180, 192
dec. decuriarum 36
dec. decr. decurionum decreto 188
ded. dedit 66
ded. deducendae 332
deder. dederunt
dic. dictator
d.m. dolo malo 296, 298, 300, 322, 332, 334, 438, 440, 442
don. donum *or* dono 72, 126
d. (*or* de) s. (*or* sen. *or* sena.) s. (*or* sen. *or* sent.) de senatus (*or* senati) sententia 148, 420, 442
d.s.p. de sua pecunia 184
d.t. dumtaxat
duovir, IIv. *see* v., vir
d.v. duo vir

e. eius 322, 400, 402, 430, 432; ei 422; eis 400
e. est 326, 328, 418; esse 400, 422
eid. eidus (= Idus) 14; eidibus (= Idibus) 415, 418
eid.que eidemque
eidu. eidus (= Idus) 14
e.l. ex lege

---

[1] Both *dono* and *donum* occur in full, in inscriptions and in literature, with *dare*: *dono* with *dare* may be dative or may have been regarded as such; but originally it may have been *dono(m)* with -m dropped (see p. xxi); we have also *donu* (which must be *donum* with -m dropped) *dat* in inscriptions.

r. rogatur *or* rogato(r) 322, 380, 400, 402, 430, 432

refic. reficiund.- *or* reficiend.-

restitu. restituit

rog. rogatam 386, 398, 400, 426, 428, 430

rog. rogavit 376, 388

r.p. re publica 402

S. Spurius, *passim*

s. scriptus 326, 328, 386; scriptum 300, 320, 384, 390, 394, 396, 406, 418, 420, 434; scripti (*nom.pl.*) 434; scriptae 420

s. semis 224; semissem 276

s. senatus (*or* senati) 84, 148, 174, 178, 182, 184, 188, 194, 226, 230, 232, 234, 236, 238, 240, 380, 420, 424, 434, 440, 442

s. sententia 180, 182, 184, 186, 188, 192, 234, 420, 424, 440, 442

s. servus 82, 90, 106, 110, 112, 120, 124, 126, 202, 210, 214; serva 110

s. sine 442, 444

s. sinistra 170

s. sua 50, 184, 442, 444

s. summa 194

s. sunt *see* s.s.s. *below*

s. supra 326, 328, 384, 386, 390, 394, 396, 420, 434

Sa. (Sal. 186) Salvius

sac. sacram

sacr. sacrum

s.c. senatus (*or* senati) consulto 84, 174, 178, 194, 226, 230, 232 236, 238, 240, 380, *etc.*

sc. (plebei) scitum 404; scito 374, 376, 386, 396, 406; scita 404; scitorum 404

sc. scribendo 254

scr. scriba 10, 36

scr. scribendo 260

scr.adf. scribendo adfuerunt 260

sc.arf. scribendo arfuerunt 254

s.d. sinistra decumanum 170

sen. senatus (*or* senati) 156, 176, 186; senatum 260

sen. sententia 86

sena. senatus (*or* senati)

sent. *or* sentent. sententia 156, 176, 186, 194

Ser. Sergia (tribu)

Ser. Servius

ser. servus 94, 192

serv. servus 202

Sex. Sextus

s.f.s. sine fraude sua

sing. singulos

sl. iudik. slitibus iudicandis

soc. sociorum

solv. solvit

s.p. sua pecunia 50, 184

sp. *or* spect. spectavit 214

s.s. senatus (*or* senati) sententia 182, 184, 234; 440, 442, 448

s.s. supra scriptum 396, 384, 390, 394; supra scriptus 386

s.s.e. supra scriptus est 326, 328

s.s.s. supra scripti (434; scriptae 420) sunt

St. *or* Sta. Statius

Ste. Stellatina (tribu)

T. Titus

t. templum

t. (*in* d.t.) taxat

Ter. Teretina (tribu)

testam. testamento

Ti. Tiberius

tr. tribunus 6, 8, 296, 298, 316, 322, 324, 328, 332, 364, 372, 374, 376, 380, 388, 406; tribuni (*gen.*) 52

Tro. Tromentina (tribu)

u. ultra

urb. urbanus 156; urbanum 134, 298, 300, 302, 450; urbano 180, 182

usq. usque

V. Vibius

v. verba 260

v. vir 180; virum 286; viri 190

v. vivit 32

Vel. Velina (tribu)

v.f. verba fecistis 260

vi. vivit

viat. viator

viator. viatori

vic. vicesima

vir. viro 18; viri 174, 180, 186, 188, 190, 192, 274, 438; viros 438; virorum 278; viris 110, 112

-vir. -viratum 34

vix. vixit

INTRODUCTION

Editorial.

The Latin text of the inscriptions in this book is in modern form. Though coincidences and intentional exceptions occur, the general arrangement of each inscription, the spaces, the punctuation, brackets, strokes, dots, arrows, the size of the letters, the capitals, the letter *u*, the paragraphs, and the lines of printed type, are editorial. The stroke |, always editorial, indicates the end of a line in the inscription, and is always used where such end of a line does not coincide with the end of a line in the printed type. Dots . . . indicate (i) a part of an inscription now lost and unknown and of which I have not given in the text any modern guess at filling the gap, such dots giving no indication of the size [1] of the gap; (ii) an extant or once known part of an inscription, which part is purposely omitted by me, the fact and nature of the omission being clear or indicated at each point. Ligatures, monograms, dots or other marks which merely divide words from each other, long letters I and apexes (see above, pp. xix, xxiii) are not reproduced except in a few cases and in critical notes. The text of an inscription as it now stands or is known to have stood once, or so much of it as I have given, and the translation of its text, have their modern style of 'roman' type. In my Latin text of an inscription modern 'italic'[2] type, of the same size as the 'roman' type, indicates letters and

---

[1] This is especially true in the case of the big gaps in the great laws *Lex Acilia* and *Lex Agraria*, pp. 316 ff.

[2] No italic type is used in presenting the inscriptions on coins, because where the inscription is missing from any particular specimen, it is supplied from other specimens of like issue.

words which do not appear in the inscription as we
now have it or as it was once known to exist. Excepting a number of certainties, I have enclosed such
' italic ' type in square brackets [ ]. It represents
mostly letters and words supplied [1] by deduction and
guesswork of modern scholars—above all, of Mommsen—as having been in fact written by the original
writer of the inscription, and unless otherwise stated,
the supplements are mostly Mommsen's [2]; in long
supplements the archaic spelling is generally not
used. But words or letters were sometimes put
wrongly or added needlessly by the original writer
of the inscription ; they must be corrected or omitted
from consideration ; italic type has again been used
for modern corrections of original errors in the
Latin, and words or letters which are still left in the
text but are to be omitted from consideration are
enclosed in brackets ⟨ ⟩.[3] Letters which are partly
gone now or can be seen but dimly are assumed to
be whole or clear, except when they are very doubtful. In such cases a dot is printed under each letter.
Letters or words enclosed in round brackets ( ) are
simply editorial spellings out of abbreviations used
in the inscription by the original writer, or editorial
additions of letters omitted in error by the original

[1] Use of brackets in epigraphy and papyrology differs from
that in the text of other manuscripts, where by custom [   ]
indicate that enclosed words are in a manuscript or manuscripts, yet are believed to be not words which the original
author wrote, or meant to write, but words which were added
to his text by another person later.

[2] [   ] in the translation indicate words for which the Latin
is lost and has no place in my Latin text even by guesswork.

[3] In dealing with literary manuscripts, these brackets by
custom mark modern restorations of a text where part is lost ;
not so in epigraphy and papyrology.

writer, but not otherwise 'lost' from the inscription. Where any part of the Latin text is requoted in an English footnote, italic type is used. An arrow pointing left ⟵ indicates that words of the inscription, although in this book printed as written from left to right as is our way, in the inscription itself were written from right to left. Where other words in the same inscription are written from left to right, an arrow pointing right ⟶ is used. Otherwise this arrow is not used, because nearly everything in the surviving inscriptions is in fact written from left to right. Small figures in the left margin of the Latin pages (mostly 5 and its multiples) and (where most helpful) in the right margin of the English pages, mark the line-number of the inscription itself, not of the print on the pages. The critical notes on the Latin text give, where desirable, in thin black type, letters in their proper shape as they stand in the inscription; the fascimiles are, however, only roughly accurate. In the text also the uprights in the sign HS and the figure I = one are, in the inscriptions themselves, plain strokes. The number of each inscription as given over the head of each, both in the Latin text and in the English translation, and at the beginning of some critical notes, is my own number according to the relevant category of the inscriptions as arranged in this book. The black numbers given in the left margin of the Latin pages are the relevant numbers in the *Corpus Inscriptionum Latinarum* for which see below, p. xliii. In the figures employed in any critical note, the larger type indicates the number of the inscription in this collection, the smaller type the relevant line of the inscription.

INTRODUCTION

Political Terms, mainly referring to Rome's organisation of Italy.

The notes here given will help in the full understanding of a number of inscriptions.

cives :·'·' citizens,' are Romans and others to whom were applied all or some of the rights and burdens of citizenship of the city of Rome.

peregrini : 'foreigners,' is the general term for all people—Latins, other Italians, Greeks and others—who, living or present in Italy, did not possess Roman citizenship. Sometimes the Latins are, at least verbally, distinguished from other *peregrini*. After 89 B.C. all Italians of any race became Roman citizens.

nomen Latinum : the official designation of the aggregate of such non-Roman communities as, whether Latins or others, possessed *ius Latinum* or 'Latin rights' with reference to Rome. Such communities had local autonomy, and the inhabitants, though they were *peregrini* (see above), had full rights of commerce (but not, apparently, except in an early period, full rights of intermarriage) with Romans, and they could obtain citizenship of Rome, after holding a local magistracy in their own community; and even if they never held such magistracy, could, if resident in Rome, vote in an allotted tribe of the Roman *comitia tributa*, without however becoming citizens of Rome.

socii : 'allies.' These are normally the Italians; from whom Rome demanded military or naval forces at will. They included the Latins, though in theory these were not *socii*.

civitas foederata : 'state under treaty,' a town in Italy or in a Roman province (outside Italy), recognizing Roman sovereignty, and generally bound by Rome's foreign policy, but otherwise its own mistress, in theory free from Roman garrisons, governors, and taxation, its privileges being confirmed by a treaty (*foedus*). *civitas libera (et immunis)*: 'state free and immune,' similar to a *c. foederata*, but holding its privileges only by a Roman *lex* ('act of parliament'; see below) or by a decree of the Roman senate. *c. stipendiaria* 'state tributary,' paying tribute to Rome, which has, at any rate in practice, received by surrender the ownership of its land and all else, of which Rome grants to the town the usufruct.   Most towns in Roman provinces were of this type, having local constitution, jurisdiction, and taxes.   They and their territory formed the Roman governor's *provincia*.

colonia : ' a tillage,' originally a piece of land cultivated by a *colonus* (tiller, cultivator); but as a Roman political term it is a community sent out by Rome normally to some part, and to an already existing town, of Italy and organised on the pattern of Rome.   If only Romans formed the colony, it was a Roman colony or *c. civium Romanorum* who kept their Roman citizenship ; a *colonia civ. Rom.* could also be so called because all who joined it became Roman citizens if they were not such before ; if Latins shared in the original foundation, it was a *c. Latina*, such non-Latins as belonged to it becoming in status Latins. The Roman colonies (not the Latin), not being themselves *civitates* but parts of Rome, were subject to jurisdiction of the Roman *praetor urbanus* (at Rome) who acted through *praefecti iure dicundo* in the colonies.   The business of conducting the colony to its site was looked after by *III viri (triumviri) coloniae deducendae* ' Board of Three for conducting a colony.'

INTRODUCTION

municipium : a town, not Rome nor created by or from Rome (see *colonia* above), but which, by incorporation into the Roman state, possessed some part of the Roman citizenship—mostly the burdens only (a *municeps* was a person liable to dues and duties imposed by Rome). From the third century some had full Roman citizenship, after 89 B.C. all had, and the term *municipium* came to be used of any kind of Italian town other than Rome. For jurisdiction *municipia* were like colonies dependent on the Roman *praetor urbanus.* Even before that date we find towns called *municipia Latina,* these having *ius Latinum* (not Roman citizenship—see above) given by Rome by incorporation.

forum : ' market '; apart from the *fora* in Rome, *f.* is a rustic commune of citizens established usually on a Roman road, by a Roman magistrate by rightful authority, and dependent probably wholly on Rome for its jurisdiction and census (for the latter being attached to the nearest *municipium*) but possessing a local ' senate ' (see below) and probably local officials (*magistri ?*). After the ' Social ' war, such *fora* tended to become more independent like *municipia* and *coloniae.*

conciliabulum : a country-centre of meeting for Roman citizens for purposes of administration, having otherwise the same status as a *forum* (see above).

vicus : (*a*) a street, ' ward,' or ' quarter ' being any part of Rome or any other town, having local officials ; (also a group of buildings whose owner allowed other owners access through them to their own houses;) (*b*) a rural village commune dependent on a local town (Roman or non-Roman) and having local officials (*magistri* ' foremen,' not magistrates) **or** *aediles*, but no separate communal existence. Some of them were merely market-villages with no local officials.

castellum : ' fortress ' (distinct from a reservoir of an aqueduct, pp. 192–3): similar to the second type of *vicus* (see above), but with special reference to fortification or to original foundation for soldiers of the local community. These *castella* are also called *castra*.

pagus : a fortified hamlet or retreat for rustics, and its surrounding district. It possessed its own officials and organisation civil and religious, but was not as free as a *forum* (see above).

praefectura : a town which possesses local organisation and at least part of Roman citizenship, but depends for its jurisdiction on a *praefectus iure dicundo* sent from Rome. The name could be applied to *fora* and *conciliabula* and to the original part of a town to which the Romans had sent a colony. The word *praefectura* was also used in a narrower sense to describe a type of *municipium* which had no local magistrates but received a praefectus yearly from Rome, like Capua for some time after the second Punic War.

Local organisation in towns in Italy. The local populations, if a full local organisation was allowed, consisted of magistrates, council or senate, and people, all becoming more and more closely modelled on the Roman pattern. (*a*) Magistrates. These were elected as in Rome by popular vote for one year only. Their titles vary owing to preservation of original customs, but the magistrates are mostly collegiate. Some towns had *praetores*, some a *dictator*, some *consules* ; but normally there were two *duoviri iure dicundo*, ' Board of Two for Pronouncing Justice ' at the head of the community, and under them two (*duoviri*) *aediles* or *duoviri aedilicia potestate*.[1] The whole board of four was called *quattuorviri*; the expression *quattuorviri iure dicundo* includes the *duoviri aediles* and *quattuorviri aedilicia potestate* includes the *duoviri iure dicundo*. Likewise the term *quattuorvir* could designate any one member of the whole board. In every fifth year a census was taken, and two or all four of the usual magistrates of that year were given the additional title *quinquennales* ' in a fifth year,' held the census, and arranged public contracts. In some places this business was done apparently (as at Rome) by *censores*. The *aediles* looked after streets, buildings, markets, corn-supply, etc. There were also *quaestores* for local finance, and *praefecti aerarii* in charge of the local treasury. (*b*) Council or Senate. This was the sovran body, usually called in Italy a *senatus* or *curia*, its members being usually *decuriones*,[2] sometimes *conscripti*, sometimes *senatores*, chosen, from those who had a required extent of property, by the *quinquennales* (see above), normally for life. Their number was usually 100, and included the magistrates but not ex-magistrates. Notable benefactors were elected by the local senate to the title of *patroni*. (*c*) People. (*cives*, *coloni*, *municipes* according to the status of their community as indicated above). The inhabitants as a whole were divided into *curiae* or *tribūs* of

---

[1] On pp. 186–7 we have two *praetores* called *duoviri*.

[2] This suggests some original division into tens (*decuriae*). Such a ' squad ' or *classis* was originally, according to Columella, a group of ten farmworkers because ten was a convenient number for working together and to supervise. The word *decuria* ceased to imply a group of actually ten men.

which each *curia* or *tribus* formed a voting unit in election and legislation; otherwise their assembly had little real power. Resident aliens who had house or land within the town's territory were called *incolae* (περίοικοι) 'inhabitants,' other resident aliens who had no such property being *adventores* 'newcomers' (ξένοι); people of neither class nor of the class of cives were called *attributi* 'assigned.'

Some Roman official terms. lex : leges as a term in the broadest sense (cf. *legare* 'to give directions') means any directions or instructions about a course of behaviour, prescribed by a private person or by the state. In the political sense it means official ordinances by the state and its officials to be binding on others, and in inscriptions means generally not only Laws in our sense (which it often of course bears in Latin) but any 'acts of parliament' and 'acts of officials' thus:

(*a*) *lex rogata*, 'law asked for,' is an 'act of parliament' passed by the Roman people after being asked in an assembly, and includes *plebiscita* (passed by the plebeians in their *concilium*) which had the binding force of *leges rogatae*.

(*b*) *lex data*, 'law given,' or charter, is a series of official directions about constitution and rights, delivered to other people by a Roman official having *imperium* or state authority; in most cases such regulations were never submitted to the Roman people in assembly.

(*c*) *lex dicta*, 'law spoken,' is a series of lawful directions by any person or body; in state affairs it is directions declared by a competent Roman official or body as right interpretation of laws in our sense of that word, and in the sense of 'act of parliament'— *lex rogata*. In state affairs such directions have, like *leges datae*, the authority of some *lex rogata* behind them.

senatus consultum or *s. decretum :* decree of the Roman Senate which ought to have had behind it the authority of a *lex rogata* of the whole people, although, in the period of senatorial supremacy at Rome, such decrees were mostly accepted by the whole people without their initiation or authorisation.

provincia : the sphere of activity of any person's official task; then, by extension, the sphere (especially military) of a Roman magistrate acting for Rome in Italy outside Rome; then, the whole sphere of authority of a Roman governor in a province, outside Italy; and, in particular, it means such governed territory (outside Italy) as a geographical unit or province.

triumviri capitales : a ' Board of Three for capital duties,' that is to say, duties affecting any one's *caput*, his person. They assisted the higher magistrates in criminal jurisdiction, conducted the first examination after a criminal charge had been made, had the custody of accused persons before trial, and guarded and carried out the execution of persons condemned to death. They also dealt with ordinary misdemeanours, and were a kind of street police. In certain cases involving slaves and, it seems, foreigners, they could deliver final judgment.

recuperatores : ' receivers.' Originally a mixed board appointed to try cases of violence between Roman citizens and foreigners; but later the name was applied to special judges appointed to try certain cases between citizens alone.

quaestiones perpetuae : ' standing inquisitions ' or criminal courts established to try criminal cases.

The first, ' de repetundis ' ' concerning recovery of money extorted,' was established in 149 B.C., and the number was brought by Sulla up to eight or nine. Each *quaestio* was governed by a fundamental law. The *quaestiones* did not cause the abolition of, nor even an essential change in another method of administering justice, namely the cumbrous trials by the assembly of people, but they were free from *provocatio* ' appeal to the people' and from *intercessio* ' veto ' by a tribune. The president of a *quaestio* was a *praetor* who as such president was called *quaesitor* at least from Sulla onwards. Particular details are added in footnotes to relevant places of the translation.

The Roman Calendar. trinum nundinum : A *nundinum* ' nine days' time ' was a Roman period of eight (not nine) days of which the first day was called *nundinae*. It is not certain whether the expression *trinum nundinum* means *tria nundina* or a period of time containing three *nundinae*, that is to say 17 days at least or 31 days at most. Note that all dating given in the inscriptions of this volume by day of the month follows the system which was used until Caesar's reform of the Calendar in 46 B.C. Thus in the archaic period March, May, July and October had 31 days, February 28, and the other months 29. Further points about dates are given in footnotes to relevant places of the translation. See also the extant pre-Julian calendar given in part on pp. 450 ff.

collegium : (*a*) a board of magistrates all belonging to the same magistracy ; (*b*) a similar board of priests ; (*c*) a company of business-men such as revenue-farmers, for which the normal term was *societas publicanorum*; (*d*) as in a number of these inscriptions, a guild of three or more private persons, not necessarily male, for a common object under a binding agreement. Until Cicero's time these associations were mainly for religious purposes; some (under the empire, many) were mainly industrial, and even these engaged in the activities of some cult besides looking after the interests of their trade. The characteristics of each were a common cult, common meetings, and a common sepulchre, and apparently a common fund, though there is no evidence that this was employed for the relief of members. These *collegia* (also called *corpora*) may be called 'Friendly Societies.' They appointed *magistri* 'masters,' 'foremen,' 'overseers' (quite different from *magistratus* 'magistrates,' and from local officials as of *vici*—see above, p. xxxvii) for various purposes. See p. 100. In the *Lex Acilia*, p. 335, another kind of *collegium* seems to be referred to. *sodalicium* or *sodalitas*, association, was used sometimes for the guilds described above, or for similar societies, but usually it meant an unlawful association for getting votes for candidates at elections.

Bibliography

Corpus Inscriptionum Latinarum

In the list of works given below I confine myself chiefly to such as are pertinent to the study of inscriptions belonging to the archaic period as defined above.

The *Corpus Inscriptionum Latinarum*. The standard collection of Latin inscriptions is the great *Corpus Inscriptionum Latinarum*, Berlin, 1862 *etc.*, (abbreviated *C.I.L.*). In the second part of the second edition of the first volume of this *Corpus* is found the bulk of the inscriptions which I have given in this book. Its full title is *Inscriptiones Latinae Antiquissimae*, 2nd edition, part 2, edited by E. Lommatzsch, 1918, 1931, 1943 (*C.I.L.*, I, part 2, ed. 2), and contains the inscriptions which up to date were known or believed to belong to the era of the Roman Republic. In this book of Remains this volume of the Corpus is denoted by *C.I.L.*, I, 2, that is, first volume, second part; and it is to be understood that the second edition is meant. The black numbers in the left margin of the Latin pages of this book of *Remains* indicate the relevant number in a volume of the whole *Corpus*; and where, over each inscription (Latin text), towards the left, nothing is shown to the contrary, the black numbers in the left margin refer to the number of the inscription as given in *C.I.L.*, I, 2. Where the inscription is quoted from another source, this source is shown. For a record of publications of newly found inscriptions and of the latest modern studies concerning inscriptions already published, consult the supplements entitled 'Revue de publications Épigraphiques' in the annual *Revue Archéologique*. [*Ephemeris Epigraphica*, ed. H. Dessau and others, supplementary to the *Corpus*, continued for 9 vols. only, 1872–1913.]

We now have A. Degrassi. *Inscriptiones Liberae rei publicae*, I, 1957; II, 1963. *Bibl. di Studi sup.* Florence.

Selections.

H. Dessau, *Inscriptiones Latinae Selectae*, Berlin, 1892 *etc.*; C. G. Wilmans, *Exempla Inscriptionum Latinarum*, 2 vols., Berlin, 1873; J. C. Orelli, *Amplissima Collectio*, Zurich I–II, 1828; III, ed. Henzen,

xliv

INTRODUCTION

1856; R. Garrucci, *Sylloge Inscr. Lat.*, Aug. Taur., 1877 (to Caesar's time); J. Wordsworth, *Fragments and Specimens of Early Latin*, Oxford, 1874; F. D. Allen, *Remnants of Early Latin*, Boston (U.S.A.), 1884; W. M. Lindsay, *Handbook of Latin Inscriptions*, Boston (U.S.A.), 1897; A. Ernout, *Recueil de Textes Latins Archaiques*, Paris, 1916; E. Diehl, *Altlateinische Inschriften*, in H. Lietzmanns *Kleine Texte*, 1908 etc., Bonn, nrs. 38–40; *Pompeian. Wandinschr.*, id., nr. 56; F. Richter, *Sacralinschr.*, id., nr. 68. [G. McN. Rushforth's *Latin Historical Inscriptions*, Oxford, 1893, 1930; and R. H. Barrow's *A Selection of Latin Inscriptions*, Oxford, 1934, apply to the imperial period only.] *Metrical Inscriptions :* C. Buecheler, *Carmina Epigraphica*, I, II (Teubner Text), Leipzig, 1895–7; with ' Supplementum,' E. Lommatzsch, 1926. Inscriptions as sources for Roman Law: C. G. Bruns, *Fontes Iuris Romani*, ed. 7, O. Gradenwitz, Tübingen, 1909; P. Girard, *Textes de Droit Romain*, Paris, 6th ed., F. Senn, 1937. E. G. Hardy, *Roman Laws and Charters*, Oxford, 1912 (translations). *Dialect-Inscriptions*: R. S. Conway, *The Italic Dialects*, I, II, Cambridge, 1897. Cf. also *Inscriptiones Italiae ; Academiae Italicae Consociatae ediderunt.* Vol. I, *sqq.* Rome.

Facsimiles.

Priscae Latinitatis Monumenta Epigraphica, ed. Ritschl, Berlin, 1862, five supplements (*Opusc.* IV, 1878). [E. Hübner's *Exempla Scripturae Epigraphicae Latinae*, Berlin, 1885, begins from the death of Caesar.] Cf. also E. Diehl, *Inscriptiones Latinae*, in H. Lietzmanns *Tabulae in usum scholarum*, Bonn, 1912, nr. 4.

INTRODUCTION

The Study of Inscriptions.

Most useful for English-speaking readers are J. E. Sandys, *Latin Epigraphy*, 2nd edition, rev. S. G. Campbell, Cambridge, 1927; J. C. Egbert, *Introduction to the Study of Latin Inscriptions*, New York, 1896, rev. with supplements 1908; cf. also J. E. Sandys in *A Companion to Latin Studies*, ed. 3, 1921 (reprinted 1929), pp. 728 ff.; E. Hübner, ' Roman Inscriptions ' in the *Encyclopaedia Britannica*, London, ed. 9, vol. xiii, abridged and revised by W. M. Lindsay, ed. 11, Cambridge, 1910. H. K. Siegert, *Die Syntax der Tempora und Modi der ältesten lateinischen Inschriften*, Wurzburg, 1939. R. Cagnat's *Cours d'Épigraphie Latine*, Paris, ed. 3, 1898, suppl. 1904, refers chiefly to periods later than the archaic.

Abbreviations of some modern works cited in this book: *H. : Hermes. Notiz. d. Sc. : Notizie degli Scavi di Antichità. R.I.-G.-I. : Rivista Indo-Greco-Italica di filologia, lingua, antichità. B.M. Catal. : Coins of the Roman Republic in the British Museum*, I–III (H. A. Grueber).

Acknowledgement.

The Editors of the Loeb Classical Library thank the Cambridge University Press for permission to reproduce illustrations of three inscriptions in J. E. Sandys' *Latin Epigraphy*, 2nd ed. 1927.

E. H. WARMINGTON,
Birkbeck College,
University of London.

EPITAPH OF LUCIUS SCIPIO, SON OF BARBATUS.

See pp. 4–5. Reproduced from J. E. Sandys, *Latin Epigraphy*, p. 67.

VIAMFECEIABREGIO·AD·CAPVAMET
INEA·VIA·PONTEIS·OMNEISMILIARIOS
TABELARIOSQVE·POSEIVEI·HINCE·SVNT
NOVCERIAM·MEILIA·LI·CAPVAM·XXCIIII
MVRANVM·LXXIIII·COSENTIAM·CXXIII
VALENTIAM·CLXXX
STATVAM·CCXXXII·REGIVM·CCXXXVII
SVMA·AF·CAPVA·REGIVM·MEILIA·CCC
ETEIDEMPRAETOR·IN   XXI
SICILIA·FVGITEIVOS·ITALICORVM
CONQVAEISIVEI·REDIDEIQVE
HOMINES·DCCCCXVII·EIDEMQVE
PRIMVSFECEIVTDEACROPOPLICO
ARATORIBVSCEDERENT·PAASTORES
FORVMAEDISQVEPOPLICASHEICFECEI

MILESTONE OF POPILLIUS.

See pp. 150–1. Reproduced from J. E. Sandys,
Latin Epigraphy, p. 132.

'*FIBULA PRAENESTINA*.'

See pp. 196–7. Reproduced from J. E. Sandys,
Latin Epigraphy, p. 38.

ARCHAIC INSCRIPTIONS

I. TITULI

(i) TITULI SEPULCRALES

Scipionum Elogia

1–2

C. I. L., I, 2.

6   [*L. Corneli*]o Cn. f. Scipio

7   Cornelius Lucius Scipio Barbatus
     Gnaivod patre | prognatus, fortis vir sapiensque,
     quoius forma virtutei parisuma | fuit,
     consol censor aidilis quei fuit apud vos
     [5]Taurasia Cisauna | Samnio cepit,
     subigit omne Loucanam opsidesque abdoucit.

---

[1] The theory of Fay (*Class. Quart.*, XIV, 163 ff.), that the first two elogia which are given here are much later forgeries perpetrated perhaps by Scipio Metellus, an opponent of Caesar, is contradicted by T. Frank in *Class. Quart.*, XV, 169-171. There is at any rate justifiable suspicion that these Scipionic epitaphs are not altogether in their original form; or were not all written until years after the deaths of the persons whom they honour.

[2] Painted in vermilion.

I. INSCRIPTIONS PROPER

(i) EPITAPHS

Epitaphs [1] of the Scipios

On tombs of the Scipios near the Porta Capena.

1–2

Lucius Cornelius Scipio Barbatus, consul in 298, censor in 290. The epitaph [2] on the lid. Saturnians.

Lucius Cornelius Scipio, son of Gnaeus.

The later [3] elogium (after 200 B.C.), on the front.

Lucius Cornelius Scipio Long-beard, Gnaeus' begotten son, a valiant gentleman and wise, whose fine form matched his bravery surpassing well,[4] was aedile, consul and censor among you; he took [5] Taurasia and Cisauna, in fact Samnium; he overcame all the Lucanian land [6] and brought hostages therefrom.

---

[3] Cut in Saturnians; it is later even than the elogium of the second epitaph, given below. Cf. Wöllflin, *Rev. de Phil.*, N.S., XIV, 119.

[4] Or possibly : "whose handsomeness alone matched (came nearest to) his bravery."

[5] In B.C. 298. Cf. Livy, X, 11–12.

[6] *Samnio* is perhaps ablative. It may mean "in Samnium." *Cisauna* is unknown. *Loucanam*, sc. *terram*, that is *Lucaniam*.

TITULI SEPULCRALES

3–4

8   [*L.*] Cornelio L. f. Scipio
[*a*]idiles cosol cesor

9   Honc oino ploirume cosentiont R[*omai*]
duonoro optumo fuise viro
Luciom Scipione. Filios Barbati
consol censor aidilis hic fuet a[*pud vos*];
[5] hec cepit Corsica Aleriaque urbe,
dedet Tempestatebus aide mereto[*d*].

5

10   Quei apice insigne Dial[*is fl*]aminis gesistei, |
mors perfe[*cit*] tua ut essent omnia | brevia,
honos fama virtusque | gloria atque ingenium,
[5] quibus sei | in longa licu[*i*]set tibi utier vita, |
facile facteis superases gloriam | maiorum.
Qua re lubens te in gremiu, | Scipio, recip[*i*]t
Terra, Publi, | prognatum Publio, Corneli.

4 [1] R[*omai*] Ritschl   Romae Sirmond   Romane
Momms.   Romani Grotefend   Romano (*sc.* Romanorum)
Garrucci
    [2] viro [*virorum*] Grotefend   [3] filiom Wölffl in
    [5] urbe [*pugnandod*] Ritschl *non prob.* Wölffl.
    [6] mereto[*d*] Lommatzsch   mereto[*d lubenter*] Grotefend
m. [*votam*] Ritschl

---

[1] Likewise painted in vermilion.
[2] Wölfflin, *op. cit.*, 113, and *Münch. Sitz.-Ber.*, 1892, 191.
[3] In B.C. 259. Aleria was the capital of Corsica—hence
the separate mention of its capture as a further achievement.
[4] *meretod* = *merito*, common in inscriptions, is an ablative
= ' in return for benefits received.' See also pp. 463–4.

4

EPITAPHS

3–4

Lucius Cornelius Scipio, son of Barbatus, consul in 259, censor in 258. The original epitaph [1] on the tomb.

Lucius Cornelius Scipio, son of Lucius, aedile, consul, censor.

The later elogium [2] (about 200 B.C.) cut on a tablet of stone found in the Scipios' sepulchre : Saturnians.

This man Lucius Scipio, as most agree, was the very best of all good men at Rome. A son of Longbeard, he was aedile, consul and censor among you ; he it was who captured Corsica,[3] Aleria too, a city. To the Goddesses of Weather he gave deservedly [4] a temple.

5

Publius Cornelius Scipio, probably a son of Scipio Africanus ; he died about 170 B.C. ? On the front (two pieces) of a sarcophagus : Saturnians.

You who have worn the honoured cap of Jupiter's holy priest : [5]
Death caused all your virtues, your honour, good report and valiance, your glory and your talents to be short-lived. If you had but been allowed long life in which to enjoy them, an easy thing it would have been for you to surpass by great deeds the glory of your ancestors. Wherefore, O Publius Cornelius Scipio, begotten son of Publius, joyfully does Earth take you to her bosom.

[5] This line was added to the rest in smaller letters by a later hand. Cf. Wölfflin, *Münch. Sitz., l.c.,* 196. *apice insigne = apicem insignem.*

6

11   L. Cornelius Cn. f. Cn. n. Scipio
Magna sapientia | multasque virtutes
aetate quom parva | posidet hoc saxsum.
Quoiei vita defecit, non | honos, honore,
⁵ is hic situs, quei nunquam | victus est virtutei,
annos gnatus XX is | l[oc]eis mandatus.
Ne quairatis honore | quei minus sit mandatus.

7

12   L. Corneli. L. f. P. [n.] | Scipio quaist. | tr. mil.
⁵   annos | gnatus XXXIII | mortuos.   Pater |
regem Antioco | subegit.

8

13   [Co]rnelius   L.   f.   L.   n. | [Sci]pio   Asiagenus |
Comatus annoru | gnatus XVI.

9

16   [P]aulla Cornelia Cn. f. Hispalli

6 ⁶ loceis Momms.   Diteist *vel* Deitist Ritschl   diveis
Buecheler   leto est Lachmann   *alii alia*   L. . EIS

---

¹ *i.e.* " in whose case life, not worth, fell short of official
post " (to hold which he did not live long enough); play of
words on *honor* (Wordsworth, 403).   *magna sapientia = mag-
nam sapientiam.*

² The meaning may be : " do not ask what office he held,
because none was entrusted to him." Wordsworth, 403,
renders : " lest you should ask why (*quei* sc. *quo*) he was not
advanced to office." *loceis* is doubtless right; *locus* often
occurs in inscriptions in the sense of a grave.

³ At Magnesia in 190 B.C.

⁴ Unknown. Another sarcophagus, *C.I.L.*, I, 2, 14, has
only :   i|s
           sci]|pionem
           qu]o ad veixei

EPITAPHS

6

Lucius Cornelius Scipio, probably a son of Scipio Hispallus. About 160 B.C. ? Tablet from a sarcophagus : Saturnians. The epitaph.

Lucius Cornelius Scipio, son of Gnaeus, grandson of Gnaeus.

The elogium.

Great virtues and great wisdom holds this stone
With tender age.   Whose life but not his honour
Fell short of honours,[1] he that lieth here
Was ne'er outdone in virtue; twenty years
Of age to burial-places was he entrusted.
This, lest ye ask why honours none to him
        Were e'er entrusted.[2]

7

Lucius Cornelius Scipio, quaestor in 167 B.C., son of Asiaticus. About 160 B.C. ?   On a slab from a sarcophagus.

Lucius Cornelius Scipio, son of Lucius, grandson of Publius, quaestor, tribune of soldiers.   Died at the age of thirty-three years.   His father vanquished[3] King Antiochus.

8

Scipio Comatus.[4]

Cornelius Scipio Asiagenus Nevershorn, son of Lucius, grandson of Lucius, sixteen years of age.

9

Paula, mother of Scipio Hispanus ?

Paula Cornelia, daughter of Gnaeus, wife of Hispallus.[5]

[5] Consul in 176 B.C.   Paula may have been ' daughter of Gnaeus Hispallus.'

10

15   Cn. Cornelius Cn. f. Scipio Hispanus pr. aid. cur.
        q. tr. mil. II Xvir sl. iudik. Xvir sacr. fac.

     Virtutes generis mieis moribus accumulavi,
    5   progeniem genui, facta patris petiei.
     Maiorum optenui laudem, ut sibei me esse creatum
     laetentur; stirpem nobilitavit honor.

11

2660   Cuiq|ue su. | cipo.

———— • ————

12

834   C. Poplicio L. f. Bibulo aed. pl. honoris | virtu-
       tisque caussa senatus | consulto populique
       iussu locus | monumento quo ipse poste-
   5   reique | eius inferrentur publice datus est.

---

10 [5] progenie genui. *edd. vett.*   progenie(m) mi genui
Momms.   progeniem i(n)genui *coni.* Buecheler   progeniem
i(= ei) genui Diels   progeniei ingenui Wilsdorf   **PRO-
GENIEMI GENVI**

---

[1] Both these boards were standing commissions, the former
being annually chosen subordinate judges to whom in the later
Republic cases involving citizenship or freedom were entrusted,
the latter looking after the Sibylline Books.

[2] *sc.* offices held.

[3] Nicorescu, *Ephem. Dacoromana*, I, 52.   *su. cipo = suom
cipom.*

[4] Frank, *Class. Philol.*, XIX, 78. Repeated on the side,
where only the beginnings of the lines are extant.

EPITAPHS

10

Gnaeus Cornelius Scipio Hispanus, probably son of His-pallus, praetor peregrinus in 139 B.C. *About* 135 B.C. ?

On three tablets which formed the front of a sarcophagus. The epitaph.

Gnaeus Cornelius Scipio Hispanus, son of Gnaeus, praetor, curule aedile, quaestor, tribune of soldiers (twice); member of the Board of Ten for Judging Law-suits; member of the Board of Ten for Making Sacrifices.[1]

The elogium, in elegiacs.

By my good conduct I heaped virtues on the virtues of my clan; I begat a family and sought to equal the exploits of my father. I upheld the praise of my ancestors, so that they are glad that I was created of their line. My honours [2] have ennobled my stock.

11

Scratched on tufa near the site of the sarcophagus of Barbatus (pp. 2–3); *first century? B.C. :*

To every man his own gravestone.[3]

———— · ————

12

G. Publicius Bibulus, probably tribune in 209 B.C., *who was perhaps son of Lucius Publicius Bibulus, military tribune in* 216 B.C.

On a tomb found at Rome. Early in the second century B.C. or a later restoration ? [4]

To Gaius Publicius Bibulus, aedile of the plebs, son of Lucius, was granted, at the cost of the State by decree of the Senate and ordinance of the People, to honour him because of his worthiness, a site for a memorial into which himself and his posterity might be conveyed.

13

695   Ser. Sulpicius Ser. f. | Galba cos. | ped. quadr.
XXX

14

1861   Protogenes Cloul[*i*] | suav*is* heicei situst | mimus
plouruma que | fecit populo soueis | gaudia nuges.

15

1202   Hoc est factum monumentum | Maarco Caicilio. |
Hospes, gratum est quom apud | meas restitistei
seedes. |
Bene rem geras et valeas, | dormias sine qura.

16

1299   N. Decumius N. f. | Col. Vaarus scr. | Volusia
C. l. Celsa | C. Volusius C. l. Charit. | In fr.
⁵   p. XIII, in agr. p. XVI.

17

1687   . . . . *h*]oc monumentu | [*sibei et le*]ibreis soueis |
[*fecit*] et leibravit | [*et expo*]livit.

14 ² SVAVEI

---

¹ This gives the area of the burial-plot.
² But cf. Stowasser, *Wien. Stud.*, XXV, 268 (very doubtful
interpretation). *nuges* is *nugeis*. The cutter made a mess of
his work.
³ But it may be much later, the formation of the letters
pointing, some think, even to the Augustan age. Note the
" Accian " double vowels (see *Remains of Old Latin*, II,
xxii and III, 114–15). The epitaph pretends that its reader
is a guest at its house.

EPITAPHS

13

Servius Sulpicius Galba, a consul of 144 *or of* 108 B.C. *On stone. Found at Rome.*

Servius Sulpicius Galba, consul, son of Servius. 30 squ. ft.[1]

14

Protogenes. Found in a wall at Preturo, near Amiternum : c. 165–160 B.C. ?

Here is laid the jolly old clown Protogenes, slave of Clulius, who made many and many a delight for people by his fooling.[2]

15

Marcus Caecilius. On stone. Found at Rome on the Appian Way : c. 140 [3] B.C. : *Saturnians.*

This memorial was made for Marcus Caecilius. Thank you, my dear guest, for stopping at my abode. Good luck and good health to you. Sleep without a care.

16

Numerius Decumius. On stone. Now in the British Museum.

Numerius Decumius Varus, son of Numerius, of the Colline tribe, a clerk ; Volusia Celsa, freedwoman of Gaius ; Gaius Volusius Charito, freedman of Gaius.

Frontage 13 ft., depth 16 ft.

17

Unknown. Tegianum in Lucania.

. . . made, poised, and smoothed this memorial for himself and his children.[4]

[4] *leibreis* = *liberis ; leibravit* = ' balanced in position.

18

1211

Hospes, quod deico paullum est; asta ac pellege.
Heic est sepulcrum hau pulcrum pulcrai feminae.
Nomen parentes nominarunt Claudiam.
Suom mareitom corde deilexit souo.
5 Gnatos duos creavit, horunc alterum
in terra linquit, alium sub terra locat.
Sermone lepido, tum autem incessu commodo.
Domum servavit, lanam fecit. Dixi. Abei.

19–38

1015	(i) L. Aeli. | a. d. III idus | Octob.
1016	(ii) C. Aemili k. Iun.
1019	(iii) A. d. XI k. Apr. | Sex. Aemi.
1024	(iv) Alfenos Luci. | a. d. XII c. Noem.
1028	(v) D. Aponi. | eidus inter. | M. Lucre.
1029	(vi) Pr. k. N. Apronia | IKΛOIVO | cal. int. o.
1038	(vii) L. Kaili. | a. d. III eidus Dekem.

19–38 (vi) Calinico, Garrucci   **CALINTO**

---

¹ There is a pun here on the popular derivation of
sĕpulchrum from sē (sc. sine) and pulchrum.

² These nearly all give the day of the month, but not the
year, of sepulture. Cf. the inscriptions on pillars, pedestals,
and so on at Praeneste (C.I.L., I, 2, 64–357), and those found
on cinerary urns of the Furn and Turpleii at Tusculum (C.I.L.,
I, 2, 50–58). These groups give neither month nor year.
Cf. also those found near Valperga (C.I.L., I, 2, 2140 ff.).
Since the inscriptions were done before 45 B.C., March, May,
July and October have 31 days, February 28, and the rest 29.
An intercalary month had 27 or 28 days. Extant examples
of the epitaphs given are denoted by *.

³ The first two examples are of the normal type.

⁴ Those with the date put first are rare.

⁵ This and the remainder have some peculiar point. Here
the inscription was done by a Greek ill versed in Latin.
c. = Kalendas. Noem. = Novembres.

EPITAPHS

18

Claudia. Tablet or pillar found at Rome, now lost: c. 135–120 B.C.: Senarii.

Stranger, my message is short. Stand by and read it through. Here is the unlovely [1] tomb of a lovely woman. Her parents called her Claudia by name. She loved her husband with her whole heart. She bore two sons; of these she leaves one on earth; under the earth has she placed the other. She was charming in converse, yet proper in bearing. She kept house, she made wool. That's my last word. Go your way.

19–38

On sepulchral urns found in the vineyard of San Cesario on the Via Appia at Rome: c. 150–100 B.C. Most are now lost. A selection [2] from C. I. L. I, 1015–1195 (cp. 1196–1201). The persons were humble folk.

   (i) [3] Lucius Aelius. 15th Octob.

   (ii) Gaius Aemilius. 1st Jun.

   (iii) [4] 22nd Mar. Sextus Aemilius.

* (iv) [5] Alfenus Lucius. 21st Octob.

   (v) Decimus Aponius. The ides of an intercalary [6] month. Marcus Lucretius.

   (vi) 31st Oct.[7] Apronia. . . . 1st of an intercalary month; her bones.

   (vii) Lucius Kailius. 11th Decem.

---

[6] Inserted in every other year after the 23rd of February (a day called *Terminalia*), which in such years ended on that day instead of the 28th. Cf. p. 108.

[7] The signs after Apronia are doubtful. They appear to me to mean *l ka. o. No.* = *pridie kalendas obiit Novembres* 'died on the 31st Oct.' Perhaps Apronia died on the 31st of October, but her bones were not put in their final resting place till four months later, in an intercalary month. *Ob* may be *olla. cal.* = *Kalendis. o.* = *ossa.*

1051   (viii) Σέξστος Κλώδιος | Δεκόμου λιβερτῖνος, | ἀντὶ δῖον τέρτιον νώναις.

1057   (ix) Curiatia obit a. d. eid. Ap.

1058   (x) Exsodium Oᴋ G. Decumi | a. d. id. Iu[n]ias.

1062   (xi) Mai. Fabricia | a. d. IIX eidu. | Sep.

1063   (xii) Farnua | eid. interkal.

1068   (xiii) A. Fulv. A. A. l. | a. d. V k. Mart.

1087   (xiv) Decem. | P. Larci. C. l. | a. d. XIV k. | Hil. p.

1099   (xv) C. Lutat. a. d. IV eid. | inte.

1109   (xvi) Portunalia | Mar[i]a Plotica

1142   (xvii) Protarcus p. k. F. | pub.

1157   (xviii) A. d. IV eid. Dec. | M. Semproni. L. f. Ter. | ossua

1020   (xix) Aemiliai a. d. III non. Fe.

1153   (xx) S. a. d. XII k. Oc. | Salvia Postum.

39

1219   Primae | Pompeiae | ossua heic.|

Fortuna spondet ⟨multa⟩ | multis, praestat nemini ;
[5] vive in dies | et horas, nam proprium est nihil. |

Salvius et Heros dant.

19-38 x IVS IᴧS   xi Mai(o) Garrucci   Man(ia) Momms.
xviii OSSⱯA   xx POSIVV

---

[1] an *exodium* was a comic afterpiece, performed usually after Atellanae, but under the empire after tragedies. Here it means more or less " departure " or " finish." The signs after *exodium* mean perhaps *ob. = obiit* or *o. k. = obiit Kalendis* or *olla*.

[2] *Mai. = Maio = Maior*? Possibly, however, a *praenomen Maia* ; it also occurs as a *cognomen*.

[3] *p. = positus.*   [4] Aug. 17th.   [5] *p. = pridie.*

[6] *s. = sepulta.*

EPITAPHS

* (viii) **Sextus Clodius**, freedman of Decimus, 3rd (*or 5th*) of the month.

* (ix) Curiatia met her death on 12th Ap.

(x) Exit [1] of Gaius Decumius, 12th June.

(xi) Fabricia, elder [2] daughter.   6th Sep.

(xii) Farnua (?); ides of an intercalary month.

(xiii) Aulus Fulvius, freedman of Aulus and Aulus. 25th Feb.

* (xiv) Publius Larcius Hilarus, freedman of Gaius, laid [3] to rest 17th Novem.

(xv) Gaius Lutatius, three days before the ides of an intercalary month.

* (xvi) The Feast of the God of Harbours.[4]   Maria Plotica.

* (xvii) Protarchus, public slave, 29th Jan.[5]

* (xviii) 10th Dec.   Marcus Sempronius, son of Lucius, of the Teretine tribe; his bones.

* (xix) Aemilia's.   3rd Fe.

(xx) Buried [6] 19th Sep.   Salvia Postumia.

39

Pompeia.   At Rome.   Tablet of marble.   End of the second century B.C. ?   *Senarii.*

Here lie the bones of Pompeia, Eldest daughter.

Fortune pledges [7] things to many,
Guarantees them not to any.
Live for each day, live for the hours,[8]
Since nothing is for always yours.

The gift of Salvius and Heros.

[7] omitting *multa* (as does Ritschl), as cut by mistake; or retain *multa*, but read *Fors* for *Fortuna*.

[8] 'for each hour.'   Cf. *in horam vivere*, to live from hand to mouth, to care only for the passing hour.

40

1297   Ultima | suorum | Cupieinnia | L.   f.   Tertulla |
    5   fuveit quius | heic | relliquiae | suprema |
        manent.

41

2138   M. Statius | M. l. Chilo | hic |
     5 Heus tu viator las|se, qu[i] me praete|reis,
        cum diu ambula|reis, tamen hoc | veniundum est
         tibi.
    10 in f. p. X, in ag. p. X.

42

C. I. L., VI.

26192   Hic est illa sita pia frug. casta | pudic. Sem-
        pronia Moschis | cui pro meriteis ab coniuge |
        gratia relatast.

43

C. I. L., I, 2.

708   [. . S]ergius M. f. | Vel. Mena | [. . S]ergius
     5   C. f. Vel. | quom Q. Caepione | proelio est
       occisus. | C. Sergius | C. Sergius

---

[1] The inscriber wrote *Cupieinnia* and tried to correct it. The
meaning of *suprema manent* is not clear. Possibly the sense
is to be completed by understanding *munera.* ' Await the
last honours '?

[2] To your grave, as I came to mine.

EPITAPHS

40

Cupiennia Tertulla.   At Rome.   End of the second century B.C. ?

Cupiennia Tertulla, daughter of Lucius, whose remains here await the very end of time,[1] was the last of her family.

41

Marcus Statius Chilo.   Found near Cremona.   Early in the first century B.C. ?   *Senarii.*

Marcus Statius Chilo, freedman of Marcus, lies here. Ah! Weary wayfarer, you there who are passing by me, though you may walk as long as you like, yet here's the place you must come to.[2]

Frontage 10 ft., depth 10 ft.

42

Sempronia Moschis.   Found at Rome.   First century B.C. *Has hexameter rhythms.*

Here is laid the renowned Sempronia Moschis, dutiful, honourable, chaste, and modest, to whom thanks were rendered herewith by her husband for her merits.

43

Sergius Mena and other Sergii.   Near Rome.   Outside the Porta S. Paolo.   90 B.C.

. . . Sergius Mena son of Marcus, of the Veline tribe ; . . . Sergius son of Gaius, of the Veline tribe, was killed in battle with Quintus [3] Caepio.

Gaius Sergius Gaius Sergius

[3] Ambushed with his army and killed by Pompaedius, Marsian general, in 90 B.C., in the so-called 'Social' War. *vel* means *Velina tribu,* not *veles* 'light-armed soldier '.

17

44

1295   P. Critonius P. f. Polio. | Mater mea mihi |
     5   monumentum | coeravit quae | me desiderat |
           vehementer me | heice   situm   in|mature.
           Vale salve.|

45

1312   Helenai soro|rei meai An|tistianai | ossa heic |
     5   cubant.

46

1610   . . . mullio C. f. Macro | duo vir. quinq. | ex
           testamento | [a]rbitratu   Ofilliai   C.   f. |
     5   [R]ufai uxoris.

47

1638   Q. Cornelius Q. P. l. | Diphilus, Cornelia Q. l. |
           Heraes heic cubant et | hoc liberteis meis et |
     5   libertabus locum concess. | et meis omnibus.

48

1734   P. Marcius P. l. | Philodamus | tector sibi |
     5   sueisque. Hic | Iucunda sepulta | est delicia
           eius.

---

[1] For this, see p. xxxix. This inscription may not be sepulchral.

[2] *Heraes* would hardly be a nominative; it appears to be genitive like other genitives in *-aes* and *-es* that occur in inscriptions and belong almost wholly to proper names of 'humble folk.' Hera would of course be the name of a mortal, with no connexion with the goddess. The case is different with *Dianaes = Dianae* in another inscription given below, pp. 44–5.

EPITAPHS

44

Publius Critonius.   Rome.   Early in the first century B.C. ?

Publius Critonius Pollio, son of Publius.   This memorial to me was superintended by my mother, who deeply longs for me, placed here before my time.   Farewell and good health to you!

45

Helena.   Rome.   Pillar of tufa.

Here lie the bones of Helena Antistiana, my sister.

46

Macer.   At Abella.

To . . . mullius Macer, son of Gaius, member of the Board of Two, in a fifth year,[1] by last will and testament, at the order of the executrix Ofillia Rufa his wife, daughter of Gaius.

47

Cornelius Diphilus and Cornelia.   Pompeii.   Early in the first century B.C. ?

Quintus Cornelius Diphilus freedman of Quintus and of Publius, and Cornelia, daughter of Hera,[2] freedwoman of Quintus, lie here.   I further granted this as a burial place to my freedmen and freedwomen and all who are mine.

48

Marcius   Philodamus.   Beneventum.   Early   in   the   first century B.C. ?

Publius Marcius Philodamus, builder, freedman of Publius, for himself and his.   Here was buried Jucunda his darling.

49

1216

[*C. Caninius C. f.* | *Arn. Labeo pater*
" *Omnes hei mei sunt : filius illum manu*
ille illam mereto missit et vestem dedit.]
⁵ Quoad vixsi, vixsere omnes una inter meos."
" Eundem mi amorem praestat puerilem senexs.
Monumentum indiciost saxso saeptum ac marmori
circum stipatum moerum multeis millibus."

50

1210

Rogat ut resistas, hospes, t[*e*] hic tacitus lapis
dum ostendit quod mandav[*i*]t quoius umbram
te[*git*].
Pudentis hominis frugi c[*u*]m magna fide
praeconis Oli Grani sunt [*o*]ssa heic sita.
⁵ Tantum est. Hoc voluit nescius ne esses. Vale.
A. Granius M. l. Stabilio praeco.

51

1837

Posilla Senenia Quart. f., Quarta Senenia C. l.
Hospes, resiste et pa[*rite*]r scriptum perlig[*e*]:

---

¹ The epitaph is rather obscure. I take it that first a
father speaks, and then his son.
² *vestem dedit* probably means ' *stolam dedit*,' that is, married
her (the *stola* being the normal indoor dress of a free Roman
woman); not, it seems, ' gave her a robe of freedom ' (at a
ceremony in the temple of Feronia where freedmen if they
wished appeared in the dress of a Roman citizen and having a
pilleus (cap) on the head); nor ' gave her a shroud,' that is, a
' best robe ' put on a dead body. Cf. epitaph of Horaea,
pp. 52–3.
³ Cf. an auctioneer Granius in the satires of Lucilius
(*Remains of Old Latin*, III, index; Buecheler, *Rhein. Mus.*,
XXXVII, 521 ff.). This profession seems to have run in this
family.

EPITAPHS

49

*Gaius Caninius Labeo. Found at Rome. Senarii on a
tablet of marble. First century* B.C. *All words down to ' dedit'
are known from a copy only.*

Gaius Caninius Labeo, of the tribe Arnensis, son
of Gaius, the father. " [1] All these here are mine.
Him yonder did my son yonder make a freedman;
her yonder did he make a freedwoman deservedly,
and gave her a robe.[2] As long as I lived, lived all
of them together among my own." " An old man
bestows on me the same tokens—of love, for his boy.
Witness this memorial, beset with stone, and packed
round its wall with marble at the cost of many
thousands."

50

*Aulus Granius. Found at Rome; tablet of marble now at
Rokeby Hall. About* 100 B.C. ?

Stranger, this silent stone asks you to stop, while
it reveals to you what he, whose shade it covers,
entrusted it to show. Here are laid the bones of
Aulus Granius [3] the auctioneer, an honourable man
of high trustworthiness. No more. This he wanted
you to know. Farewell.

Aulus Granius Stabilio, auctioneer, freedman of
Marcus.

51

*Posilla Senenia. Found at Monteleone in the old Sabine
territory; senarii on four pieces of stone.*

Posilla Senenia, daughter of Quartus, and Quarta
Senenia, freedwoman of Gaius.

Stop, stranger, and also read through what is

matrem non licitum ess[*e uni*]ca gnata fruei,
quam nei esset credo nesci[*o qui*] inveidit deus.
⁵ Eam quoniam haud licitum [*est v*]eivam a matre
  ornarie[*r*],
post mortem hoc fecit aeq[*uo*]m extremo tempore;
decoravit eam monumento quam deilexserat.

52

1603 Cn. Taracius Cn. f. | vixit a. XX. Ossa eius hic
        sita sunt. |
Eheu heu Taracei ut acerbo es deditus fato!
Non aevo | exsacto vitai es traditus morti.
⁵ Sed cum te decuit florer*e* aetate | iuenta,
interieisti et liquisti in maeroribus matrem.

53

1221 (*a*) [*L. Au*]relius L. l. | Hermia | [*la*]nius de
        Colle | Viminale
⁵ [*H*]aec quae me faato | praecessit, corpore | casto |
  [*c*]oniunxs una meo | praedita amans | animo |
¹⁰ [*f*]ido fida viro veixsit |; studio pariliqum |
  nulla in amaritie | cessit ab officio.
¹⁵ Aurelia L. l.

52 ⁵ FLORERI
53 ¹² amaritie Schrader, Haupt   AVARITIE

---

¹ *parili* might mean ' equal to mine.'
² not her duty to her patron Lucius ?

written here: A mother was not permitted to enjoy the presence of her only daughter. Some god or other, it's my belief, cast unfriendly eye on her life. Since it was not permitted to her to be arrayed in life by her mother, her mother performed this act after her death, at the limit of her time, as was due; she has provided with a memorial her whom she had loved.

52

Gnaeus Taracius. On a marble tablet found at Capua. Hexameters. c. 85–45 B.C. (Has an 'apex' over one long vowel.)

Gnaeus Taracius, son of Gnaeus, lived twenty years. Here are laid his bones.

Alas alas! Taracius, how bitter the fate to which you were delivered! The years of your life were not all spent when you were given up to death; but at the time when it behoved you to be living in the flower of the age of youth, you passed away and left your mother in grief and sorrow.

53

Lucius Aurelius Hermia and his wife Aurelia. Stone slab now in the British Museum. Found at Rome by the Via Nomentana. Elegiacs. c. 80 B.C. or later. Both persons were Greek freedmen. The wife was dead, but words are represented as spoken by her.

(*a*) Lucius Aurelius Hermia, freedman of Lucius, a butcher of the Viminal Hill.

She who went before me in death, my one and only wife, chaste in body, a loving woman of my heart possessed, lived faithful to her faithful man; in fondness equal to her other virtues,[1] never during bitter times did she shrink from loving duties.[2]

Aurelia, freedwoman of Lucius.

23

(*b*) Aurelia L. l. Philematio.

Viva Philematium sum | Aurelia nominata |
20   casta pudens, volgei | nescia, feida viro. |
Vir conleibertus fuit, | eidem, quo careo | eheu, |
25   ree fuit ee vero plus | superaque parens. |
Septem me naatam | annorum gremio | ipse re-
30   cepit,
     XXXX | annos nata necis potior. |
Ille meo officio | adsiduo florebat ad omnis |
. . .

54

1916   P. Buxurius P. f. | Truentines quie. | coi nomn
     Tracalo | arte tecta.   Salve.

55

1209   Adulescens, tam et si properas, | hic te saxsolus
     rogat ut se | aspicias, deinde ut quod scriptust |
     legas.
5 Hic sunt ossa Maeci Luci sita | Pilotimi vasculari.
  Hoc ego voleba(*m*) | nescius ni esses.   Vale.
  Posteris ius.
  L. Maeci L. l.   Salvi., Manchae Manchae f. |
     Rutilia Rutilae l. Hethaera | Maecia L. f.

54 [3] TRACAⱢ<O *vel sim.*

---

[1] *Philematio = Philematiom*, 'Littlekiss', 'Kissie'.
[2] *potior* is here passive of *potio*, used with the genitive
'to put into the power of'; elsewhere chiefly a Plautine verb.
[3] sc. ἀρχιτέκτης for ἀρχιτέκτων.
[4] *salve* here for *vale*.

EPITAPHS

(b) Aurelia Philematium, freedwoman of Lucius.

In life I was named Aurelia Philematium,[1] a woman chaste and modest, knowing not the crowd, faithful to her man. My man was a fellow-freedman; he was also in very truth over and above a father to me; and alas, I have lost him. Seven years old was I when he, even he, took me in his bosom; forty years old—and I am in the power [2] of violent death. He through my constant loving duties flourished at all seasons. . . .

54

Publius Buxurius. Near Monte Prandone in E. Picenum.

Publius Buxurius of Truentum, son of Publius, lies at rest. His surname was Tracalus. An architect.[3] Good bye.[4]

55

Lucius Maecius Philotimus. Found at Rome. First century B.C. *Senarii (3rd line trochaic octonarius ?).*

Young man, though you are in a hurry, this little stone asks you to look at it, and then to read the message with which it is inscribed. Here lie the bones of Lucius Maecius Philotimus the hardwareman. I wanted you to know this. Farewell.[5]

[*Added by a later hand :—*]

To my posterity full rights.

[*Added later still ? :—*]

Lucius Maecius Salvius, freedman of Lucius; Menahemim, sons of Menahem; Rutilia Hethaera, freedwoman of Rutilia; Maecia, daughter of Lucius.

---

[5] This is like the epitaph on Pacuvius (see *Remains of Old Latin*, II, 322–3). The name Mancha = the Hebrew Menahem, cf. Bormann, *Wien. Stud.*, XXXIV, 360.

56–7

1204 Est hoc monimentum Marcei Vergilei Eurysacis |
pistoris redemptoris.   Apparet.

1206 Fuit Atistia uxor mihei. | Femina optuma veixsit |
quoius corporis reliquiae | quod superant sunt
5 in | hoc panario.

58

1547 [*Heic est situs Q*]ueinctius Gaius Protymus
[*ameiceis su*]mma qum laude probatus
[*quoius ing*]enium declarat pietatis alum.
[*Gaius Queinc*]tius Valgus patronus.

59

1702 [*Hoc nomen, ho*]spe[*s*] sei legis, ne vituperes.
. . . . us L. f. praeco
[*Domicilium fecit viv*]os aeternum hoc sibei,
[*ratus hospitiu*]m esse quod natura trad[*idit*],
5 [*fructusque recte es*]t rebus cu ameiceis sueis
[*sic tu tueis fac*] vivos utarus.   Vale.

59 *suppl.* Buecheler

---

¹ Repeated on another side (*C.I.L.*, I, 2, 1205) and, partly,
on a third side (*C.I.L.*, I, 2, 1203).
² *apparet* is obscure, but is probably a verb, the corresponding noun being *apparitor*, a public servant. The

EPITAPHS

56-7

(a) Marcus Vergilius Eurysaces. On [1] *a very large monument still in situ at Rome. Perhaps as late as 50 B.C.*

This is the memorial of Marcus Vergilius Eurysaces, baker and contractor. He is in public service.[2]

(b) Atistia, his wife. On marble in the form of a bread-basket.

Atistia was my wife. In life she was a dear good woman. All that survives of her bodily remains is in this panary.

58

Gaius Quinctius Protymus. Near Casinum. c. 50 B.C.? Mixed metres.

Here is laid Gaius Quinctius Protymus, approved by his friends in highest praise, whose talents Gaius Quinctus Valgus, patron and fosterling [3] of loyalty, thus proclaims.

59

An unknown auctioneer. Found at Venusia. c. 50 B.C.? Senarii.

Stranger, if you read this name, revile it not . . . auctioneer, son of Lucius. This he made in life an everlasting dwelling-place for himself. He believed that what nature gave him was a guest-chamber,[4] and as was proper he enjoyed his means in company with his friends. See to it that you too use your friends so while you live. Farewell.

inscription was thus written during his lifetime; or perhaps *apparet* means ' you can see this.'
[3] *alum.* = *alumnus.*
[4] not ' the power of giving entertainment ' ?

27

60

1212 Hospes, resiste et ' hoc grumum ad laevam aspice '
ubei
continentur ossa hominis ' boni misericordis
amantis '
pauperis. Rogo te, viator, monumento huic nil
mali feceris.
C. Ateilius Serrani l. Euhodus margaritarius de
Sacra Via in hoc monumento conditus est.
⁵ Viator, vale.
Ex testamento in hoc monumento neminem
inferri neque | condi licet nisei eos lib. quibus
hoc testamento dedi tribuique.

61

C. I. L., VI.

11357 Albia Ɔ. l. Hargula vixit ann. | LVI. Casta, fide
magna; sei | quicquam sapiunt inferi, | ut ossa
eius quae hic sita | sunt bene quiescant.

62

C. I. L., I, 2.

1222 Sei quis havet nostro conferre dolore,
adsiet nec parveis flere quead lachrymis.
Quam coluit dulci gavisus amore puella
[hic locat] infelix, unica quei fuerat,
⁵ [dum contracta sinunt] fatorum tempora Numphe,
[nunc erept]a domu cara sueis tegitur.
[Omne decus volt]us et eo laudata figura
[umbra levis nun]c est parvos et ossa cinis.

62 ¹ (proprium) conferre Momms.

---

¹ The composer apparently introduces literary or stock
metric phrases.
² Partly metrical. Reversed C is Caiae = Gaiae, and, Gaius

28

EPITAPHS

60

Gaius Atilius Euhodus. On the Appian Way. Tablet of marble.

Stranger, stop and " turn [1] your gaze towards this hillock on your left," which holds the bones of a poor man " of righteousness and mercy and love." Wayfarer, I ask you to do no harm to this memorial.

Gaius Atilius Euhodus, freedman of Serranus, a pearl-merchant of Holy Way, is buried in this memorial. Wayfarer, good bye.

By last will and testament: it is not permitted to convey into or bury in this memorial any one other than those freedmen to whom I have given and bestowed this right by last will and testament.

61

Albia Hargula. Rome. Tablet of marble. First century B.C.

Albia Hargula, freedwoman of Albia: lived fifty-six years. Chaste she was and the soul of honour. If the dead below have any sense at all, may her bones which lie here rest in perfect peace.[2]

62

Nymphe (?) Found at Rome. Elegiacs.

If anyone cares to add [his own] grief to ours, here let him be; and with no scanty tears let him deign to weep. Here an unhappy parent has laid to rest his one and only daughter Nymphe [3] whom he cherished in the joy of sweet love while the shortened hours of the Fates allowed it. Now she is torn away from her home—earth covers her, dear to her own; now her fair face, her form too, praised as fair,—all is airy shadow and her bones are a little pinch of ashes.

and Gaia being taken as typical names, especially of married people, means ' of the woman,' here Albia.

[3] or possibly *puella nymphe* a newly wedded bride.

63

1836 Manlia L. f. Sabi[*na*].
Parentem amavi qua mihi fuit parens;
virum parenti proxum[*o colui loco*];
ita casta veitae constitit ra[*tio meae*].
⁵ Valebis, hospes; veive, tibi iam m[*ors venit.*]

64

1355a Vi. | M. Papinius | Q. M. l. Zibax | locum sibei |
⁵ et | sueis liberteis con|leibertis conliber|ta-
busque dat. In fronte | p. XII, in agr. p. XII.

65

1223 ..... lius P. et Clodia[*e*] l. Optatus
vixit annos VI, m. VIII.
[*Hic me*] florentem mei combussere parentes.
[*Vixi d*]um licuit superis acceptior unus,
⁵ [*quoi nemo po*]tuit verbo maledicere acerbo
..... ad superos quos pietas cogi ......
..... modeste nunc vos quon .....
.... tis dicite ' Optate sit [*tibi terra levis.*] '

.... o annorum nondum
¹⁰ ...... [*c*]um ad mortem matris [*de gremio rapior*]
.... manibus carus fui vivos cari[*ssimus illi*]
adverseis quae-me sustulit [*ominibus*],
Desine iam frustra, mea mater, [*desine fletu*]
te miseram totos exagitare die[*s*],
¹⁵ namque dolor talis non nunc tibi [*contingit uni*],
haec eadem et magneis regibus [*acciderunt*].
Clara amaranto ......
av ......

65 ³ ¹² *suppl.* Nohl; ⁵ Bormann; ¹⁰ Henzen; ⁴ ¹¹ ¹³ Buecheler; ¹⁷ *fortasse* Amaranto *cognomen*

EPITAPHS

63

Manlia Sabina.   In the Sabine territory.

Manlia Sabina, daughter of Lucius.

My parent I loved as being my parent, my husband I cherished in the second place after my parent. Thus was my life's account proved right—a spotless one.   I bid you farewell, stranger.   Live your life, death is already on its way for you also.

64

Papinius Zibax.   Rome.   Repeated on another stone.

Still living.   Marcus Papinius Zibax, freedman of Quintus and Marcus, is the giver of this site for himself and his freedmen, fellow-freedmen, and fellow-freed-women.   Frontage 12 ft., depth 12 ft.

65

A child, Optatus.   Found at Rome.   Hexameters, elegiacs.

. . . Optatus, freedman of Publius and Clodia, lived six years and eight months.

Here my parents burnt my dead body in the flower of my age.   So long as was allowed me I lived more acceptable than any other to the gods above, of whom none could speak ill in bitter word . . . to the gods above whom loyalty compels . . . now modestly you . . . say you: ' Optatus, lightly rest the earth on you.' . . . a child who had not yet your share of years . . . when I am torn away from my mother's bosom to death . . . in life I was dear to departed souls, and very dear to the goddess who made away with me under unlucky omens.   Cease now, mother mine, cease to torment yourself in vain sobs of wretchedness each livelong day, for grief such as this has not now befallen you alone; sorrows the same as these have fallen to the lot of mighty kings too.

Bright with never-fade . . .

TITULI SEPULCRALES

66

1572   Alei in venerieis [*rebus vitam conterunt*],
mihei contra r[*ite partam Venerem mors rapit.*]

67

2273   Plotia L. et Fufiae l., Prune haec voc[*i*] | tatast,
         ancilla heic sitast. Haec | qualis fuerit
         contra patronum patro|nam parentem coni-
5   iugem monumen|tum indicat. Salve, salvos
         seis.

68

1259   Q. Brutius | P. f. Quir., v., | mercator bova. | de
5   Campo heic | cubā, frugi | castu amabili |
         ominibus. | Brutia Q. l. Rufa | pia patrono |
10   dum vixsit | placuit.

69

1270   Carfinia M. l. M. . . . | vixit an. XX. | Iucunda
5   sueis | gratissima amiceis | omnibus officiosa |
         fuit.

70

1278   D. Saturius | L. l. Dama | Saturia D. l. | Philo-
5   clea | sibei liberteis | libertabus.

66 *suppl.* Buecheler

---

[1] *v. = vivit.* He set up this memorial before his death.
Cf. 64 above, and note on number 87 below. Campus is the
Campus Martius.

[2] *bova. = bovarius. ominibus* below is a mistake for
omnibus rather than *hominibus.*

[3] or : ' She was a joy to her own people and a dear pleasure
to her friends.' The epitaph has hexameter rhythm.

32

EPITAPHS

66

Unknown person ; at Venafrum.

Others waste life away in Love's *affaires* ;
But my love, rightfully begot, death takes.

67

Plotia, a slave-girl. New Carthage in Spain. First century B.C. ?

The handmaiden Plotia (she was often called Phryne), freedwoman of Lucius and Fufia, was placed here. This memorial shews how she behaved towards her protector and protectress, her father and her husband. Farewell, sir. Be you well.

68

Brutius and Brutia. On a pillar found at Rome.

Quintus Brutius (still living),[1] a cattle-merchant [2] of the Field, son of Publius of the Quirine tribe lies here, an honest man, clean-living, loved by all.

Brutia Rufa freedwoman of Quintus. So long as she lived she loyally pleased her protector.

69

Carfinia. Tablet of marble ; Rome.

Carfinia M. . . ., freedwoman of Marcus, lived twenty years. She was a joy and a dear pleasure to her friends.[3] She was obliging to all.

70

Decimus Saturius and Philoclea. Rome.

Decimus Saturius Dama, freedman of Lucius ; and Saturia Philoclea freedwoman of Decimus. For themselves their freedmen and their freedwomen.

71

1279   A.   Clodius   A.   l. | Apollodorus. | Vettia   Q.   l.
    5   Glucera | A. Cascellius A. l. | Nicepor. monu. |
       fecerunt socei | sibi et sueisque.

72–3

2634   (*a*) A. Salvius A. f.
      (*b*) A. n. Crispinus | anorum LI hic | conditus est. |
    5   Gessit Ferentei | IIIIvir. quater. | Sumo su-
       premo | die cenae . . . . | muro *oc-*
       *c*eisus.
2635   Sex. Salvius A. f. | vix. annos XXCIIX. | IIII vir.
       ter.

74

1296   Critonia Ɔ. l. Nice | locum dat Petilliae | L. l. et |
    5   Alexandro viveis | ob fidelitate et | oficeis
       monume . . . . . | . . . . vix . . .

75

1301   Egnatuleiae | M. l. Hilarae | sibei et leiber. | In
    5   fr. p. XIIX, | in agr. p. XIIX.

73 [8] CENAEIVIC   VTA   [9] MVROCIEISVS   cena[*ns*
est ruin]a mur(i) occeisus Vetter

---

[1] *A. Salvius A. f.* are on the lid; the rest is on the sarcophagus itself.

[2] The last part of the inscription is very uncertain; it seems
that Aulus was killed by the collapse of a wall on top of him
whilst he was at dinner, which was the midday meal of the

34

EPITAPHS

71

Apollodorus, Glycera, and Nicephorus. Rome.

Aulus Clodius Apollodorus freedman of Aulus, Vettia Glycera freedwoman of Quintus, and Aulus Cascellius Nicephorus freedman of Aulus; as partners they made this memorial for themselves and theirs.

72–3

Aulus Salvius and Sextus Salvius. On two sarcophagi of the gens Salvia found at Ferento near Viterbo.

(i) (a), (b) Aulus [1] Salvius Crispinus, son of Aulus, grandson of Aulus, was buried here when 51 years of age. He four times held office on the Board of Four at Ferentum. On [2] the day that was his very last, at luncheon . . . he was killed by a wall.

(ii) Sextus Salvius son of Aulus lived 88 years. He was thrice member of the Board of Four.

74

Grave given to Petillia and Alexander. Rome. c. 106–92 B.C. A. Gordon, in Univ. of Calif. Publ. in Class. Arch. I. 4, 157.

Critonia Nice freedwoman of Critonia presents this burial-place to Petillia, freedwoman of Lucius, and to Alexander, during their lifetime; a memorial for trustworthiness and services . . . lived . . .

75

Egnatuleia. Rome. Early in the first century B.C. ?

Property of Egnatuleia Hilara, freedwoman of Marcus, for herself and her freedmen (*or* children ?); frontage 18 ft., depth 18 ft.

Romans. *Summo supremo die* might mean: ' At the height of his last day,' but it occurs in another inscription (Buecheler, *Carm. Epigr.*, 1045), as the end of an iambic verse.

76

1308   [S]ex. Gegani. Sex. | f. Col. sibei et | suis liberteis. |
   5   In front. pedes | XIIX, in agro | pedes XXVI.

77

1313   L. Herenni. L. f. | Ste. scr. q. ab | aerario III |
   5   dec. et liberteis | eius | q. p. XII.

78

1325   Heic situs sum Lemiso | quem numquam nisi
   mors | feinivit labore.

79

1588   Caeselliae | Ɔ. Q. l. Hymninis | ossa heic sita |
   5   sunt. | Helena l. de | suo fecit.

80

1591   C. Fulmoni | C. l. Metroph|anis Deivitis | ossa
   5   heic si|ta sunt. Leibe|rtei ex testam. |
   curaverunt.

81

1737   ɛ\. f. L. Offellius C. f. C. | vivos sibei sueis | que
   5   maioribus | faciundum | curavit.

77 ⁶ Ο·Ρ·ΧΙΙ

---

¹ *quaquaversum pedes ?* or *quadratos pedes ?* (not *quaestoria
potestate*).   *ab aerario* here is an early example of a designation
rare before post-Augustan times; *a* or *ab* with the ablative
of the word expressing an office (*e.g. a rationibus, ab epistulis*)
designates the official in control of the office; originally it was
servus (or the like) *a* (*ab*) . . .; then *servus* or the like was
dropped and the rest was treated as an indeclinable noun.
For *decuria*, see p. xxxvi, and Sulla's law, p. 304 ff.

² On Ɔ, see p. 28.

³ We expect *postereis*, ' posterity.'

36

EPITAPHS

76

Sextius Geganius.   Rome (repeated on two other stones).

Sextus Geganius son of Sextus, of the Colline tribe, for himself and his freedmen. Frontage 18 feet, depth 26 feet.

77

Lucius Herennius.   Rome.   Tablet of stone.

For Lucius Herennius, son of Lucius, of the Stellatine tribe, clerk-accountant to the treasury of the Three Decuries, and for his freedmen. Twelve ft. each way.[1]

78

Lemiso.   Tablet in a columbarium found at Rome.

Here am I, Lemiso, laid to rest; of my labours nothing but death ever made an end.

79

Caesellia Hymnis.   Capua.

Here are placed the bones of Caesellia Hymnis, freedwoman of Quintus and his wife.[2] Helena a freedwoman made this at her own cost.

80

Gaius Fulmonius Metrophanes.   Capua.

Here are placed the bones of Gaius Fulmonius Metrophanes the Rich, freedman of Gaius. Superintended by his freedmen according to his last will and testament.

81

Offellius.   Beneventum.

. . . Lucius Offellius, son of Gaius, of the Claudian tribe, superintended the making of this memorial during his lifetime for himself and his ancestors.[3]

37

82

1739   C. Petuellius Q. f. Fale|vius monementum
faceiu. | curavit seibi et uxori suae | Epidiae
⁵   P. f. Neriae | eide que probavit.

83

1930   (a) [H]ospes, reseiste et aspice aet[ernam] | domu.
Pro mereitis statuit | coiux coiugei e[t sibei].
(b) . . . . ma ca . . | . . . us coli.

84

2137   L. Lucilius Q. f. | Cn. n. qui fuit | Cla., C. Luci-
⁵   lius | C. l. Statius. Loc. | patet agrei ses- |
cunciam qua|dratus. Arca in | medio est.

85

2161   C. Paguri C. l. Gelotis
Hospes resiste et tumulum hunc excelsum aspic[e],
quo continentur ossa parvae aetatulae.
Sepulta haec sita sum verna quoius aetatula;
⁵ gravitatem officio et lanificio praestitei.

83 (b) [fus]us coli Buecheler
85 ¹ Gelotes cd. Pal. 833   ⁴ heic Grut.

---

¹ faceiu. = faciundum.   ² See p. 144, note 2.
³ or, by consort for consort.
⁴ ca . . . I take to be calathus.
⁵ or 'Lucilius, late son of Quintus.'
⁶ or, 'open to inspection'; but this is less likely to be the
meaning here.

EPITAPHS

82

G. Petuellius.   Beneventum.

Gaius Petuellius Falevius son of Quintus super-intended the making [1] of this memorial for himself and Epidia Neria his wife, daughter of Publius.   He likewise acceptably completed [2] the work.

83

Unknown woman.   Ancona.   Senarii.

(*a*) Stranger, stop and look at an everlasting home. Set up according to deserts by mate for mate [3] and self.

(*b*) *Above this inscription are representations of a woman's bust and of a wool-basket.   Above the latter are letters which may in part mean:*

wool-basket [4] . . . spindle of her distaff.

84

L. Lucilius.   Cremona.

Lucius Lucilius, who was known as son of [5] Quintus, grandson of Gnaeus, of the Claudian tribe; Gaius Lucilius Statius, freedman of Gaius.   This burial-place stretches square over one eighth of a Roman acre of land; the coffin is in [6] the middle.

85

Salvia ?   Ivrea.   Now lost.   Senarii.

Property of Gaius Pagurius Gelos freedman of Gaius.

Stranger, stop and look at this lofty tomb, which contains the bones of a little life of tender age.   Here I lie buried whose tender age was in its spring-time. I brought dignity to attend on my duty, my wool-

39

Queror fortunae cassum tam iniquom et grave.
Nomen [s]i quaeras, exoriatur Salviae.
Valebis hospes.   Opto ut seis felicior.

86

2172   Sei qui minus rem reliquit | liberei sibei quaerant. |
           Tu viator vale. Ad aquas | sunt spissa
5   ♄ ☉☉ | Q. Marcius P. f. Ser. Rex.

87

2261   Vivit. | L. Postumius L. l. Diodor. | vivos sibei
5   fecit | et coniugei | ☉ Pomponiae Pomponi
        [l.] | Calliopae.

88

2280   Οὐᾶλος | Γα[β]άνιος | χαῖρε | Vaalus Gabin[ius] | heic
        situs est.

89

2274   L. Sulpicius Q. f. Q. n. | Col. hic situs est
                             Ille probatus
     iudicieis | multeis cognatis atque | propinqueis.

---

85 [7] ei quaeras *cd.*   exoriatur Buecheler   exaratum
Haupt   est C. Paguri Grut.   exoraturi *cd.*
[8] seis Haupt   sis Grut.   scis *cd.*
89 *suppl.* Henzen

---

[1] The reading is uncertain. Salvia is another name for
Proserpina, but it is simpler to read *exoriatur* and to take
Salvia as the woman's name.
[2] *sc.* of the Styx ? or is it a clue to hidden money ?
[3] ☉ is the 'black theta' of the poets. Originally it was
probably O, then OB, then ☉ = *obiit*, not Θανὼν or Θανοῦσα
'who has died. *Vivit*, 'he lives,' indicates that the person set
up the memorial himself during his lifetime.
[4] χαῖρε is *salve*, and both normally mean 'good day' as a
greeting when persons meet, not when they part; but here
χαῖρε, as often in Greek, is put for *vale*, 'farewell.'

making.   Plaint fills me at Fortune's lot so hard and
unfair.   Should you ask my name, the name of
' Salvia ' would rise up.[1]   I will bid you farewell,
stranger.   I would like you to be happier.

86

Quintus Marcius.   Patavium.

If any man has not bequeathed an estate, let his
children seek for themselves.   As for you, wayfarer,
farewell.   There is a thick mass of 7000 by the
waters.[2]

Quintus Marcius Rex son of Publius, of the Sergian
tribe.

87

Lucius Postumius.   Found in Casus Island.

Still living.   Lucius Postumius Diodorus, freedman of Lucius, made this during his lifetime for
himself and his wife, Pomponia Calliopa, now
deceased,[3] freedwoman of Pomponius.

88

*Valus Gabinius.   Avennio (Avignon).   Early in first cen-
tury* B.C.   *Bilingual.*

Valus Gabinius.   Adieu.[4]   Here lies Valus Gabinius.

89

*Lucius Sulpicius.   New Carthage, Spain.   Early in the first
century* B.C.

Lucius Sulpicius son of Quintus, grandson of
Quintus, of the Colline tribe, is placed here.

" He was approved in many a judgment of his
kinsmen and relatives." [5]

[5] Hexameter verse.

90

C. I. L., II.

1821   Ave! | Herennia Crocine | cara sueis inclusa hoc
⁵   tumulo. | Crocine cara sueis. Vixi ego | et
ante aliae vixere puellae. | Iam satis est.
Lector discedens, | dicat ' Crocine sit tibi
terra | levis.' Valete superi.

91

C. I. L., I, 2.

1378   . . . . o L. l. scurrae homini | [*probi*]ssumo maxu-
mae | [*fidei*] optumo leiberto | [*patronus*] fecit.

92

1328   . . us L. f. Pom. Licinus | . . a Teidia Sex. f. uxsor |
. . . eius L. f. Capito ⟨filius⟩. | [*Sep*]ulcrum
⁵   heredem non | [*se*]quetur.

93

1319   C. Hostius C. 1. Pamphilus | medicus hoc monu-
mentum | emit sibi et Nelpiae M. l. Hymnini |
⁵   et liberteis et libertabus omnibus | poster-
eisque eorum. | Haec est domus aeterna,
hic est | fundus, heis sunt horti, hoc | est
monumentum nostrum. | In fronte p. XIII,
in agrum p. XXIIII.

42

90

Herennia Crocine. Gades, Spain. First century B.C. *Has hexameter rhythms.*

Hail! Herennia Crocine, dear to her own, is shut up in this tomb, Crocine dear to her own. My life is over; other girls too have lived their lives and died before me. Enough now. May the reader say as he departs, " Crocine, lightly rest the earth on you." Farewell to all you above ground.

91

A buffoon. Rome. First century B.C.

for . . . freedman of Lucius, a buffoon by profession, a most respected and excellent freedman of the highest honour, his patron built this monument.

92

Licinus, wife, and son. Rome.

. . . son of Lucius, Pomponius Licinus . . . Teidia his wife, daughter of Sextus, . . . Capito son of Lucius. This sepulchre shall not pass to an heir.[1]

93

Hostius Pamphilus. Rome. Tablet of stone.

Gaius Hostius Pamphilus, a doctor of medicine, freedman of Gaius, bought this memorial for himself and for Nelpia Hymnis, freedwoman of Marcus; and for all their freedmen and freedwomen and their posterity. This for evermore is our home, this is our farm, this our gardens, this our memorial.

Frontage 13 ft., depth 24 ft.

[1] *Sc.* an heir to adjacent or surrounding land.

94

1990   L. Vecilio Vo. f. e[t] | Polae Abelese | lectus I
         datus. | [C.] Vecilio L. f. et Plenese |
     5   lectus I. Amplius nihil | inviteis L. C. Levieis
         L. f. | et quei eos parentaret ; | ne ante
         ponat.

95

1596   P. Octavi A. l. Philom[usi] | ossa heic sita sunt ; |
         deis inferum parentum | sacrum. Ni vio-
     5   lato. | In agro pedes XV, in via | pedes XV |
         Philargurus l. et socius.

96

1597   M. Orfio M. f. Fal. | Rufa Dianaes | l. sibi et
         coiiuci | suuo fecit.

97

2544   L. Mussidio | Romanei l. | Suro, | Vettidia Ɔ. l. |
     5   Leycadium | posieit.

---

[1] This is probable; the name would mean Paula belonging
to a place such as Abella; so also *Plenensis* below. Cf.
Herbig, *Glotta*, II, 191–2. *Lectus* = 'lying-place' in the tomb.

[2] The Latin syntax of this sentence is careless.

[3] that is, his assistant.

[4] *Dianaes*, genitive of *Diana*. Here doubtless the goddess
is meant. Rufa was perhaps a servant of the temple of
Diana in the *pagus* or *vicus Dianae Tifatinae*. *Tifata* is the
mountain-ridge (Monte Maddaloni) north of Capua. See
below, p. 100, and *C.I.L.*, X, i, p. 367.

EPITAPHS

94

Lucius and Gaius Vecilius ; and Pola and Plenese. Falerii.

To Lucius Vecilius, son of Volta, and to Pola Abelensis [1] was granted one funeral couch.

To Gaius Vecilius son of Lucius, and to Plenensis, one funeral couch. Nothing [2] further may be done against the wish of Lucius Levius and Gaius Levius, sons of Lucius, and of him whose duty it is to make sacrifices to their souls. Let no one place a body in front of these dead.

95

Publius Octavius. Naples or possibly Capua.

Here are laid the bones of Publius Octavius Philomusus, freedman of Aulus. Sacred to the gods of dead parents. Damage it not. Depth 15 feet, along the road 15 feet.

Philargyrus, freedman, and his mate. [3]

96

Marcus Orfius. Origin unknown ; probably Campania. Time of Sulla.

To Marcus Orfius, son of Marcus, of the Falernian tribe. Rufa, freedwoman in the service of Diana, [4] made this for herself and her husband.

97

Lucius Mussidius. On a pillar found at Sulmo.

To Lucius Mussidius Syrus, freedman of Romanus ; set up by Vettidia Leucadium, freedwoman of Vettidia. [5]

[5] For Ɔ, see above, pp. 28–9.

98

1347   C. Numitorius | Asclepiades. | Mummia L. l. |
     5   Zosima. | Heis sunt duo | concordes | fama-
         que bona | exsituq. hones. | Felixs.

99

1604   Q. Tiburti Q. 1. | Menolavi | cultrari oss. | heic
         sita sunt.

100

1368   Pontia Prima | heic est sita. | Nolei violare.

101

1224   Conlegei secto[*rum*] serrarium

102

1225   ... anus ad .... | duom vir | conlegi anulari |
         locum sepulchr. m. | in fronte pedes XXV, |
         in agro pedes XXV | de sua pequnia | con-
         legio anulario | dedit.

103

2519   Societatis Cantor. Graecorum quei in | hac
         sunhodo sunt, de pequnia comune[*i*] Maecenas

[1] Partly in Saturnian metre. Buecheler, *Carm. Epig.*, 15.
[2] *sc.* of victims for sacrifice.
[3] This is the only known example of a *duovir* at the head of
a guild, if such he really was—see next note.
[4] *m.* may be *magister* or *monumentum* (-*o*).
[5] *conlegium anularium* can, I think, only be 'ring-making
guild,' 'guild of ring-makers.' But we expect *anulariorum*
or *anulariūm* in both places in this inscription. *Cf.* p. 82, n. 8.

EPITAPHS

98

Numitorius and Mummia. On [1] *a piece of a sarcophagus. Rome. First century* B.C.

Gaius Numitorius Asclepiades, and Mummia Zosima, freedmen of Lucius.

These are two persons of one heart, good report, and honourable passing. Blest.

99

Q. Tiburtius. By a gate at Capua.

Here are laid the bones of Quintus Tiburtius Menolavus, a slaughterer,[2] freedman of Quintus.

100

Pontia Prima (or Pontia, eldest daughter). Rome.

Here is laid Pontia Prima. Do no damage.

101

On a large pillar found at Rome.

The property of the guild of cutters or stone-sawyers.

102

Found at Rome.

. . . member of the Board [3] of Two, of the guild of ringmakers, gave as overseer [4] a burial-place; frontage 25 feet, depth 25 feet, to the guild of ringmakers at his own cost.[5]

103

Association of Greek singers (i.e. players, actors ; or givers of Greek shows). Tablet of stone. Found in a tomb by the Labican Way.

The property of the Fellowship of Greek Singers, and such as are members of this Congregation; built out of their common purse. Approved by Maecenas

D. f. Mal. desi|gnator, patronus sunhodi
probavit. M. Vac[ci]us M. l. Theophilus, |
Q. Vibius Q. l. Simus magistreis sunhodi
5   D[ec]umianorum locu. | sepulchri emendo
aedificando cuuraverunt.

L. Aurelius L. l. Philo, magister septumo synhodi |
societatis cantorum Graecorum quique in
hac | societate sunt, de sua pecunia reficiun-
[d]um coeravit.

104

1600   Pesceniaes | Ɔ. l. Laudicaes | ossa heic sita |
sunt.

105

1578   L. Papius L. f. Ter. Pollio duo vir L. Papio L. f.
Fal. patri | mulsum et crustum colonis Senuis-
anis et Caedicianeis | omnibus, munus gladi-
atorium cenam colonis Senuisanis | et
Papieis. Monumentum HS ⚍ⒸⒸ ex testa-
5   mento | arbitratu L. Novercini L. f. Pup.
Pollionis.

103 ² MAL· *fortasse* MA[E](cia tribu)

---

¹ The stone has MAL. Perhaps it should be MAE, *sc.*
Maecia (*tribu*), of the Maecian tribe.
² Sogliano thinks that the *synhodus* may have been founded
by one Decumus, an adherent of Clodius (Cic., *ad Att.*, IV,
3, 2; *de Domo*, 50).
³ For Ɔ, see pp. 28–9.
⁴ chief magistracy—see pp. xxxviii–ix. ⁵ or ' Falerine.'

48

EPITAPHS

Mal[1] . . ., son of Decimus, master of funeral ceremonies and patron of the Congregation. Marcus
Vaccius Theophilus freedman of Marcus, and Quintus
Vibius Simus freedman of Quintus, chairman of the
Congregation of Decumiani,[2] superintended the
purchase of a site for a tomb and the building of the
same.

Added by a later hand :

Lucius Aurelius Philo, freedman of Lucius, chairman for the seventh time of the Congregation of the
Fellowship of Greek Singers and such as are members
of this Congregation, superintended the restoration
of this work out of his own purse.

104

Pescennia. Capua.

Here are laid the bones of Pescennia Laodica,
freedwoman of Pescennia.[3]

105

Lucius Papius ; public services at Sinuessa and Caedex.
Found at Carinola. c. 60 B.C. ? (has ' apexes.')

Lucius Papius Pollio of the Teretine tribe, son of
Lucius, member of the Board [4] of Two, gave a feast of
mead and pastry in honour of his father Lucius
Papius of the Falernian [5] tribe, son of Lucius, to all
the colonists of Sinuessa and Caedex,[6] and a show of
gladiators and a dinner to the colonists at Sinuessa
and to the Papii. He set up a memorial at the cost of
12,000 sesterces. By last will and testament,[7] and
by approval of Lucius Novercinius Pollio, son of
Lucius, of the Pupinian tribe.

---

[6] a *vicus* near Sinuessa.   [7] *sc.* of his father.

106

2123   Hora[*tius* . . . . . *f.*] | Balb[*us* . . . . | municipibus
5   [*su*]|eis incoleisque [*lo*]|ca sepultura[*e*] s. p.
       dat | extra au[*ct*]orateis et |quei sibei [*la-*]
       queo manu | attulissent et quei | quaestum
10   spurcum | professi essent, singuleis | in fronte
       p. X, in agrum p. X | inter pontem Sapis et
       titu|lum superiorem qui est in | fine fundi
15   Fangoniani. | In quibus loceis nemo huma- |
       tus erit, qui volet, sibei | vivous monumentum
       fa|ciet. In quibus loceis hu|mati erunt,
20   ei d. t., quei | humatus erit, postereis- |
       que eius monumentum | fieri licebit. |

107

1332   (*a*) T. Luscio T. l. Parnaceni | Lusciae T. l.
       Montanae | T. Attius Ɔ. l. Auctus coiugi |
5   T. Luscius Ɔ. l. Corumbus patr|onae pro
       meriteis dant ubei | eorum ossa quiescant. |
       (*b*) C. Laeli Philotae.

---

[1] A river in Umbria.

EPITAPHS

106

Presentation of a graveyard by Horatius Balbus. Found at Sassina. Stone tablet, now missing in part; but the missing portion is partly known from copies.

. . . Horatius Balbus son of . . . is the giver to members of his township and other residents therein, at his own expense, of sites for burial, except such as had bound themselves to serve as gladiators and such as had hanged themselves with their own hand or had followed a filthy profession for profit: to each person a site, 10 ft. in frontage and 10 ft. in depth, between the bridge over the Sapis[1] and the upper monument which is on the boundary of the Fangonian estate. On sites where no one has been buried, anyone who shall so desire shall make a tomb before he dies. On sites where persons have been buried it shall be permitted to build a memorial to him only who shall be buried there, and to his descendants.

107

Graves presented in Rome. Found at Rome.

(*a*) To Titus Luscius Pharnaces, freedman of Titus; and to Luscia Montana, freedwoman of Titus; Titus Attius Auctus, freedman of Attia,[2] to his wife; Titus Luscius Corumbus, freedman of Luscia to his patroness.[3] This they gave, in return for their merits, as a place where their bones may lie at rest.

(*b*) (*on the back*) Of Gaius Laelius Philota.

[2] On Ↄ, see pp. 28–9.
[3] that is, the person who had manumitted him.

108

1570 P. Larcius P. l. Neicia. Saufeia Ɔ. l. Thalea. |
   L. Larcius P. f. Rufus. P. Larcius P. f.
   Brocchus. | Larcia P. Ɔ. l. Horaea.
  Boneis probata inveisa sum a nulla proba.
  Fui parens domineis senibus, huic autem opse-
    quens,
  ⁵ ita leibertate illei me hic me decoraat stola.
  A pupula annos veiginti optinui domum
  omnem. Supremus fecit iudicium dies,
  mors animam eripuit, non veitae ornatum
    apstulit.
  L. Eprius Chilo viat. tr. pl. [E]pria CPI (?)

109

1751 Helviae | Mesi f. | sacerdot. Vener. | filiei de suo.

110

1732 Tu qui secura spatiarus mente viator
   et nostri voltus derigis inferieis,
  Si quaeris quae sim, cinis en et tosta favilla,
   ante obitus tristeis Helvia Prima fui.

---

¹ Freed by P. Larcius Nicia and his wife Saufeia, and
married to their son Brocchus, brother of Rufus.
² Reversed C in inscriptions means *Caiae* = *Gaiae* ' of
Gaia,' this name representing any woman unnamed. Here
it means of a woman of the *gens Saufeia*. But perhaps after
Saufeia not Ɔ but *A* should be read (' freedwoman of Aulus ').
³ See preceding note for Ɔ.
⁴ *stola*, the ordinary indoor garment of a free woman of
Rome; the expression ' arrayed me in a robe ' seems to mean
here ' married me,' not ' gave me a robe of freedom ' nor ' gave
me a shroud ' (that is, buried me). See above, p. 20.
⁵ On this, see Sulla's law about the twenty quaestors,
pp. 304 ff.
⁶ Not *Mesus*?

EPITAPHS

108

Horaea.[1]

Found at Traiectum on the Liris, c. 45 B.C.? *now lost.*

Publius Larcius Nicia, freedman of Publius; Saufeia Thalea, freedwoman of a matron[2]; Lucius Larcius Rufus, son of Publius; Publius Larcius Brocchus, son of Publius; Publia Horaea, freedwoman of Publius and of his wife.[3]

I was a woman respected by the good and hated by no respectable woman. To my old master and mistress I was an obedient servant, but to him yonder my husband I was a dutiful wife; for *they* gave me freedom, and *he* arrayed me in a robe.[4] For twenty years since my girlhood I maintained the whole house. My last day delivered its judgment and death took away my breath, but took not the splendour of my life.

Lucius Eprius Chilo, messenger-attendant[5] on a tribune of the plebs; Epria . . .

109

Helvia's sons. Bovianum.

To Helvia, daughter of Mesius,[6] and priestess of Venus, her sons at their own cost.

110

Helvia Prima (or Helvia, eldest daughter). Found at Beneventum. Elegiacs. c. 45 B.C.?

Wayfarer, you who are walking along with carefree mind and turn your looks to these my funeral gifts, if you ask who I am, being mere ashes, look, and burnt embers, I was Helvia Prima before my

53

[5] Coniuge sum Cadmo fructa Scrateio,
concordesque pari viximus ingenio.
Nunc data sum Diti longum mansura per aevum,
deducta et fatali igne et aqua Stygia.

(ii) TITULI SACRI

1

*An inscription which runs in three lines, without spacing
between words, round the outer edges of three small vases joined
together at the sides into an equilateral triangle. Found at Rome,*

4

 Io. Vei. Sat.[1] deivos qoi med mitat: nei ted
endo cosmis virco sied. | Asted, noisi Ope
Toitesiai pakari [2] vois. | Duenos med feked [3]
en manom einom Duenoi [4] ne med malo [5]
statod.

More than forty attempts have been made to master the
meaning of this inscription, which has been taken as referring
to a domestic gift, as a curse, and as a charm, and so on, and,
as I take it (in view of the article on which the inscription is
written, and the use of the word *mitat*—see below) a dedication
combined with a curse. There are three problems : the
purpose for which the vases and the inscription were made ;
the separation of the whole inscription (which has neither
dividing-points nor spacings) into the right words ; and the
meaning of a number of these. Some of the interpretations
of separate words are quite impossible ; others, like those
maintained by Kent, are so level-headed that one hesitates
to reject any of them. In 1926 E. Goldmann, in *Die Duenos-
Inschrift*, summed up most of the previous work on the
problem ; but his list was made more complete by Kent in

---

[1] IOΛE|SΛT (*littera* I *addita postea inter* E *et* S)
[2] ⊃ΛEΛbI (E = *littera* K *mutata postea in* C)
[3] FEKED (⊃ = *littera* K *mutata postea in* C)

DEDICATORY INSCRIPTIONS

sad departure. The husband I enjoyed was Scrateius Cadmus, and we lived one in heart and twins in disposition. Now, led down by fatal fire and Stygian water, have I been given to Dis to remain with him for long ages.

(ii) DEDICATORY INSCRIPTIONS[1]

1

but probably not Roman work. Fourth century B.C.? *A dedication combined with a curse?*

By the gods Jupiter, Veiovis, and Saturn, he who presents me swears: Let the Maid not be kind to you; may she stand aloof, unless you are willing to make your peace with Lady Bounty Protectress. Goodman made me to be a blessing; so do not let it stand to my account as a bane for Goodman.

his own exposition, in *Language*, II, 4 Dec., 1926, 207 ff.; to which may now be added Hofmann, *Indog. Jahrb.*, XII, 1926, 202; Leumann, *Glotta*, XVIII, 1930, 245; Ribezzo, *R.I.-G.-I.*, XIV, 1930, 90; A. D. Fraser, *A.J.P.*, LIII, 1932, pp. 213–232. Cf. also M. Runes, *Glotta*, XXI, 125 ff.; W. Brandenstein, *Glotta*, XXV, 30; *C.I.L.*, I, 2, 2, Fasc. III, 1943, p. 831. I give here no review of the efforts of previous scholars, but simply what I think is a probable interpretation, relying on what we have rather than on speculation. That the vase and its writing are a forgery is not likely.

The arguments in favour of taking the inscription as a curse, and as addressed to deities dwelling below the earth, and of assuming the whole gift to have some magical intent, are impressive; for the vase is triple, and the inscription is in three lines; when the vase is standing on its base, the

---

[1] on objects dedicated, *i.e.* given to gods, not to men.

---

[4] DNEⱯOI (Ⱶ = *littera* V *addita postea inter* D et E)

[5] WↄⱯⱭO (Ⱶ = Ⅴ = L?)

inscription reads from left to right but is upside down; in
order to read it rightly, the vase must be turned the other way
up, and then the inscription becomes right side up and reads
from right to left. Thus the vase when ' presented ' (cf. *mitat*,
as below) by the ' giver ' was placed upside down, perhaps so
that the underground deities could read it (Kent, 208–211).

Since the three lines are separated by broad gaps, I have
followed the view that the end of each of the lines makes the
end of sense and syntax. The vase speaks (*Duenos med feked*).
deivos is surely acc. pl., not nom. sing. (which would make a
god the speaker). That being accepted, *ioveisat*, if it does not
mean *iurat*, ' swears,' as some believe, will probably mean
Iovem, Veiovem, Saturnum, not *Iovem Saturni* (' Jupiter, son
of Saturn '), nor *Iovem Veiovem Saturni* (' Jupiter and Veiovis,
sons of Saturn '); for this inscription is too early for the
application of Greek mythology to Roman gods. The
accusatives would be due to *iurat* ' swears,' or to an omitted
verb such as *orat* ' prays.' *qoi* is masc. sing.; dat. would not
fit in. There is no doubt that Kent (212–13) was right in
insisting that *mitat* is a present indicative (not subjunctive);
there has been discovered at Tibur a pedestal or altar or block
to which gifts could be attached; of its almost unintelligible
and not wholly Latin inscription, written partly from right to
left, the most certain part reads (from right to left) *edmitat
kapi = med mitat capiat* ? (*C.I.L.*, I, 2, 2658, p. 738) =
' presents me, let him take ' ? Thus *mitat = mittit* ' sends,'
' presents,' probably with the idea of ' dedicates.' *endo* on
our vases is clearly right. *cosmis* must mean *cōmis*, ' kind '
(not ' pretty '). *virco = virgo* I take, as is usual, as a nominative, though it may be vocative. It is usually understood to
mean Proserpina. If it is a vocative, then translate : ' By
the gods . . . may he who presents me not be kind to you,
my girl. . . .' I have toyed with the idea that *virco* means
the dedicated ashes of a girl, placed inside the vases. *asted =
abstet* (so Kent) unless we take *asted* to represent *astet =
adstet* ' be a standby.' With regard to *ope toitesiai*, of various
guesses the simplest appears to me to be that it means the
goddess *Opi Tutesiae* (dative) = *Tuteriae* (not *Titeriae*).
Cf. Tutelina, Tutanus. For *Ops* see pp. 458–459, 461. Or
perhaps *ope* is abl., *Toitesiai* gen. ' with the help of T.' *pakari*
seems simple enough. *noisi . . . vois = nisi . . . vis* (cf.
doivom = divom in Cantovios' dedication, pp. 58–59).

DEDICATORY INSCRIPTIONS

duenos (*due-* = *be-*; cf. *duellum*, *perduellis* = *bellum* **war,
perbellis**; *Duelona* = *Bellona*; *duonoro* = *bonorum* in a Scipionic
epitaph, above, pp. 4–5) may mean 'good,' 'a good
man'; but we expect a proper name here, so I translate
' Goodman.' I cannot see how the name can well represent
Zeno (so Fay), or that it is *Dufnos*; the writing here reads
Duenos, where the *E* is slightly damaged; I accept Thurneysen's
decision that *manom* means 'good,' 'a blessing'; it is known to
have been a very old Latin word with that meaning (Varro
L.L., VI, 2, 4; *al.*). *einom* I hesitate even to guess at, but
it may be *inom* = *enim*. It seems to mean 'therefore' here.
It could hardly mean *unum*? An inscription (dedicatory)
of the Frentani in dialect has *seffi·i·nom suois cnatois* which
may mean *sibi inom suis gnatis* = to himself and his children
too: Wordsworth, 169. Cf. Runes, *R. I.-G.-I.* XX, Fasc. 3-4,
1936, p. 66. Ehrlich interprets *en manom einom* as *in Manium
munus* ' as a present to the Manes' (ghosts of the dead); (' as
a gift to the Deities of Hell' Kent). Cf. Kent, *op. cit.*, 215, 222.
Near the end of the inscription I read *Duenoi . . . malo statod*;
on the vase *Duenoi* seems clear to me. The V, omitted at
first by the writer, was thrust against E when inserted; the
word or name seems here to be dative (hardly genitive, in spite
of *noisi* = *nīsi*, *vois* = *vīs*, above); *malo* (in which the third
letter is wrongly formed, whatever it may be, p. 55, crit. note
5), can be taken as an ablative or as a nominative. The giver
of the set of vases, it seems to me, sets *malo* ' bad ' in deliberate
opposition to *manum* ' good.' He made it to be a good; let it
bring no bad because of the first part of his message. The
syntax of *med* before *malo statod* is not quite clear, but it
would be ablative = *a me*. Lastly, when I first came to know
this inscription, it appeared to me to be written in asclepiad
rhythm; and there has been an attempt (by Florence Bennett,
Trans. and Proc. Amer. Phil. Assoc., XLI, 1911, xxi) to
show that it is written in hexameters. But such Greek
metres from a Latin writer, though Greek influence may exist,
belong to a later date than can possibly be assigned to this
triple vase; and efforts to make consistent metre out of the
inscription break down anyhow. I have indicated that the
number of its lines—three—has probably magical meaning;
and that each probably completes syntax and sense; but
note that *sied* (end of line 1) and *asted* (beginning of line 2)
might well go together ' be kind (*cosmis*) and be a standby.'

2

5   Caso Cantovio|s Aprufclano cei|p

⁵ apurfinem E|salicom enur|bid Casontonia, |

societque doivo|m atolero Actia |

pro l[ecio]nibus Mar|tses.

The inscription appears to me to be dedicatory, but the meaning of some of it is disputed. *Line 1*: *Caso* (genitive presumably *Casonis*), not *Casos* with final *s* dropped. If *casontonia* in 5 is *senat-*, then *Caso* might mean *Senior* = *Maximus*. So I suggest. Anyhow *Cantovios* looks like a gentile name and *Caso* would be a *praenomen*. I would point out that there was an old Latin word *cascus* (Varro, *L.L.*, VII, 28) which Varro traces through the Sabine to an Oscan origin; it was used in the sense of ' old.' However, the resemblance between *Caso* and *Casontonia* may be accidental. *Line 2*: So I suggest. *Aprufclano* I take as *Aprufclanos* (cf. Schulze, *Lat. Eigennamen*, 553 ; we have a C. Aprufenius in another inscription, dedications, n. 43), though it might be a dative : ' a sepulchral pillar to Aprufclanos ', not a god ? Cf. Numasius (man), Numisius (god), Numerius (common name for men, pp. 11, 68–71). I take *ceip* not as *ceipom* but as *ceipos,* boundary stones.' It might be *cepit*. Some suspect that it is an abbreviation of the office held by Cantovios. There is also a proper name *Cipos* (Val. Max., V, 6, 3; Ov., Met., XV, 565). *Line 3*: for *apurfinem*, cf. the frequent joining of preposition to noun or epithet in inscriptions, and *arvorsus* for *advorsus* and *arfuerunt* for *adfuerunt*. *Lines 3–5*: *esalicom enurbid casontonia*. Here there is no doubt that the engraver, who separated his words by points, put a point between *esalico* and *menurbid*. This would make *esalico* = *esalicom* (an unknown word or name; but cf. Aesernia, Aesis, Issa,

---

³⁻⁵ ESA|ICO·MENVRBID
⁶ DOIVO

2

Caso Cantovios and allies.   Bronze plate found in the Fucine Lake.   Dialect-Latin or mixed Marsian and Latin.   Every other line (except 3 and 4) runs from right to left.   Military dedication after a victory, c. 300 B.C.

Caso Cantovios Aprufclanos [set up] pillars at the Esalican boundary in the city Casontonia; and his allies brought a sacred gift to Angitia on behalf of Marsian legions.

Aesuvium); and *menurbid* (abl.) and *casontonia* (abl. or gen.) would not be Latin. Buecheler (*Rh. Mus.*, XXXIII, 490) suggests that *menurbid* would be in Latin *monitu* (cf. *Menerva*, and *promenervat = promonet*)' by the advice ' (= *scitu* ' by decree ') and that *casontonia = casontoniad*, an epithet meaning ' senatorial,' ' of the senate '.   Jordan, *Ind. Lect. Königsb.*, 1883–4, 7, connects it with *casa* (a hut, cabin) in the sense of *curia* or *conventus*.   We have in support of this view *Casuentini* as designating townsmen of Interamna (*C.I.L.*, XI, 4209) and certain Etruscans designated as *Casuntinial* (*C.I.Etr.*, 4203) and *Casntinial* (id., 3688; cf. Schulze, 559). However, the engraver may have put his point or dot in the wrong place—an error which occurs in other inscriptions also; if he had been really careful he would not have written his letters *a* always as Λ, even in reverse from right to left; and to be consistent he should have written line 4 from right to left; I therefore follow those who read *esalicom enurbid casontonia = Esalicum in urbe Casontonia*, though a boundary in a city is strange and Casontonia is unknown elsewhere as a city.   *Line 6*: DOIVOM is correct (it was so read by Dressel and Jordan in careful inspections of the plate; Jordan also took a photograph which he compared with the plate) = *divum*, but the meaning ' sacred ' is doubtful and it may represent *deorum*; not *donum* (DONOM), because all other letters *n* on this plate are consistently N or its reverse И.

Another dedicatory inscription, given below, number 57, has *deivo(m)*. *Line* 7: *atolero* seems right. The upward slanting stroke of the letter *l* (on the plate ꓶ, reading from right to left) corresponds with a crack in the plate,—unless indeed ꓲ = *i* is in fact correct, as it is often taken to be, in which case *atoier* gives us another unknown word. Owing to a gap in the plate, only the top of the second *o* in *atolero* now exists, and it is somewhat pointed in shape. I follow those who interpret the word as *attulerunt*. With regard to *Actia*: only the top of the first letter is preserved. It is probable that this means *Actiae* = *Angitiae* (dative), the name of a Marsian goddess who had a grove near the Fucine Lake in

3

404
    (*a*) L. Mr. Foli. . . . . . |Menerva[*i Lindiai*.
    (*b*) Λεύκιος Μ . . . . . |᾿Αθάναι Λινδίαι.

4

59
    Apolo[*ne* . . .] | Metilio . . . . . | magistere[*i*] | cora-
   ⁵ veron[*t*] | C. Anicio L. st|riando . . .

5

61
    Q. K. Cestio Q. f. | Hercole donu | [*d*]edero.

6

60
    Orcevia Numeri | nationu cratia | Fortuna Diovo
   ⁵ fileia | primogenia | donom dedi.

---

¹ perhaps foremen of a college—see below, pp. 100 ff.
² Jordan, *Ind. Lect. Königsb.*, 1883–4, 10 ff.
³ Cf. K. Meister, *Lateinisch-griechische Eigennamen*, 99 ff. *Cestios* = *Cestius*; here Praenestine differs from Roman Latin, which would have the plural thus: *Q. K. Cestii*.
⁴ Taking *nationu* as *nationu(s)* = *nationi(s)*. But *nationum* may be right—'in thanks for teeming broods' (*nātiones*? sc. of cattle). Orcevia may have been Numerius' daughter.
⁵ *Primogenia* (*Primigenia*), 'first of its kind' when used of Fortuna, is obscure; cf. Pease, ad Cic., *de Div.*, II, 85. For *g* in *primogenia* this inscription has ꓛ

which the plate was found. A dedication to her is given
below, dedications, n. 101. *Aequitia,* ' Equity,' to whom
we have a dedication (see pp. 74–5) is less likely. *Line 8:*
The gap in the plate leaves us only *pro l . . . nibus mar|.*
But all scholars agree with Buecheler's supplement l[ecio]-
nibus. Cf. *Notiz. d. Sc.,* 1877, 328; Jordan, *H.,* XV, 1880, 5,
and *Ind. Lect. Königsb.,* 1883–4, 3; Buecheler, *Rh., Mus.,*
XXXIII, 489; Goidanich, *Stud. Ital.,* X, 23; Conway,
Italic Dialects, I, 294; and other studies given in *C.I.L.,*
I, 2, p. 372. Also v. Grienberger, *Indog. Forsch.,* XXIII,
337; Bacherler, *Bonn. Jahrb.,* CLXXVI, 92; Ehrlich, *Rh.
Mus.,* LXVIII, 607; Ribezzo, *Riv. Indo-Gr.-Ital.,* XIV, 78.

3

*An Oscan merchant (?)   Part of a marble pedestal found at
Lindus in Rhodes;   300–250 B.C.*

(*a*) From Lucius, son of M . . . Folius . . . to
Minerva of Lindus.

(*b*) From Lucius, son of M . . . to Athena of
Lindus.

4

*Pillars or a temple at Praeneste.   On stone found at Praeneste.
3rd century B.C.   Nothing now survives after ' coraveron.'*

To Apollo . . . Metilius and . . ., overseers,[1]
superintended. . . . Gaius Anicius . . . fluting.

5

*Quintus Cestius and Kaeso Cestius.   Pillar found near
Praeneste.*[2]

Quintus Cestius and Kaeso Cestius,[3] sons of
Quintus, bestowed this as a gift on Hercules.

6

Orcevia.   Plate of bronze, Praeneste.   Before 250 B.C.

I, Orcevia, Numerius' wife, gave this for my
people's[4] sake, to Fortune, first-born[5] daughter of
Jupiter.

61

TITULI SACRI

7

62 L. Gemenio L. f. Pelt. | Hercole dono | dat lubs
   ⁵ merto | pro sed sueq.; | ede leigibus | ara
    Salutus.

8

2659 . . . | [H]ercle dedero | [do]no plebe iousi.

9–13

376 (i) Cesula | Atilia | donu | da Diane.
377 (ii) Feronia | Sta. Tetio | dede.
378 (iii) Iunone reç(inai) | matrona | Pisaurese | dono
    dedrot.
379 (iv) Matre | Matuta | dono dedro | matrona. |
    M'. Curia | Pola Livia | deda.
375 (v) Deiv. No[v]esede.; | P. Popaio Pop. f.

14

384 L. Opio C. l. | Apolene | dono ded. | mereto.

---

¹ obscure; a *cognomen*? *lubs merto* = *lubens merito*; for
merto see above on epitaph 4.
² perhaps *plebes iousit* (?).
³ Meister, *Indog. Forsch.*, XXVI, 69.
⁴ on the cult of Feronia, cf. P. Aebischer, in *Rev. Belge de
Philol. et d'Hist.*, XIII, 1934.
⁵ *matrona Pisaurese* is here taken as a clipped plural.
⁶ *deda* may well be a noun, τίτθη, ' a nurse ' (Krahe, *Indog.
Forsch.*, LV, 1937, 121); or *deda* = *dedant* = *dedunt* (cf.
mitat = *mittit*) ' dedicate '. It has been taken as an old 3rd
pers. pl. perf.; cf. (σ)τέσαντι = ἑστᾶσι.
⁷ apparently *deiveis novesedebos*, dative plural.

DEDICATORY INSCRIPTIONS

7

Lucius Geminius. Block of tufa found near Praeneste.
c. 250 B.C.?

Lucius Geminius, son of Lucius, of Peltuinum,[1] on behalf of himself and his loved ones, willingly and deservedly bestows this gift deservedly on Hercules; in the same terms of ritual an altar of Safety.

8

Dedication to Hercules. A pillar found by the Alban Lake.

. . . bestowed it as a gift on Hercules at the command [2] of the commons.

9–13

Five stone pillars found with others at Pisaurum,[3] three of them dedicated by women, and all probably during or before the second Punic War. The Latin is of local dialect, showing unwritten final sounds and phonetic peculiarities.

(i) Caesulla Atilia bestows this as a gift on Diana.

(ii) To Feronia,[4] given by Statius Tettius.

(iii) To Queen Juno a gift, bestowed by matrons [5] of Pisaurum.

(iv) To Mother Morning a gift bestowed by matrons.

Added later?—

Given [6] by Mania Curia and Pola Livia.

(v) To the Newly settled Gods.[7] Publius Poppaeus, son of Publius (?).

14

Lucius Oppius. On stone. Found at Mosciano.

Lucius Oppius, freedman of Gaius, bestowed this as a gift deservedly on Apollo.

15

386   Sa. Burtio V. f. | Iue dono | ded. mereto.

16

387   Sa. Sta. Fl. | Vic. d. d. l. | m.

17

300   . . . . . | A. L. . . . . s L. f. Flaccus | aid. d[e]
stipe Aesculapi | faciundum locavere, | eidem
pr. probavere.

18

389   St. Staiedi. | V. Salviedi. | Pe. Pacio | Foucno |
⁵   aram.

19

390   V. Vetius Sa. f. | Valetudne | d. d. l. m.

20

391   ⁵ Aninus | vecus | Valetudne | donum | dant.

---

¹ On *probare* see n. 2, p. 144.

DEDICATORY INSCRIPTIONS

15

Salvius Burtius.   On stone.   Avezzano.

Salvius Burtius, son of Vibius, bestowed this as a gift deservedly on Jupiter.

16

Salvius Flavius and Statius Flavius.   On stone.   Found near Trasacco.

Salvius Flavius and Statius Flavius gave this as a gift to Victory willingly and deservedly.

17

A dedication in the temple of Aesculapius, Isle of the Tiber.

. . . Aulus L . . . Flaccus son of Lucius as aediles contracted for the making of this work out of Aesculapius' gift-money.   They likewise as praetors acceptably completed it.[1]

18

Staiedius,   Salviedius   and   Pacius.   Pedestal   found   at Trasacco.

Statius Staiedius, Vibius Salviedius, and Petro Pacius, an altar to Fucinus.

19

Vibius Vettius.   On a pillar found near Castelluccio di Lecce.

Vibius Vettius, son of Salvius, bestowed this gift willingly and deservedly on the Goddess of Health.

20

Anian quarter (unknown).   Castelluccio di Lecce.

The Anian quarter bestow this gift on the Goddess of Health.

21

394   ⁵ T.   Vetio | duno | didet | Herclo | Iovio | brat. |
data.

22

2486   Sa. Seio L. p. | Herclei donom | ded. brat. data
⁵   s. | Seio Sa. p. | Herclei | Victurei.

23

392   V. A[t]iediu[s] | Ve[s]une | Erinie et | Erine patre |
⁵   dono me[r]i. | lib[s].

24

399   C. Hinoleio C. l. | Apolone dono ded.

25

18   P. Corn[elios] | L. f. coso[l] | proba[vit] | Mar[te
sacrom].

22 ¹ P *item* ⁴ P (Bendinelli) | ¹ (= F, *sc.* filius) Vetter
(*Glotta*, *XV*, 2) *utroque l.*
25 ² V·F·COSO

---

¹ Surely ablative absolute, *gratia* (*brata*) *data* ' favour
having been granted.'   The word *brat-* occurs in an Oscan law
—cf. Bruns, *Fontes*, 7th ed., p. 49; *C.I.L.*, I, 2, p. 408.   Wordsworth, 169, 411; I. Hofmann, *Stand und Aufgaben der Sprach-
wissenschaft*, p. 390.   See also the next inscription.

DEDICATORY INSCRIPTIONS

21

Titus Vettius.   Found at Navelli (territory of the Vestini).

Titus Vettius bestowed this as a gift on Hercules, Jupiter's son, for favours granted.[1]

22

Salvius Seius.   Pillar found at Superaequum.   Before 220 B.C.

(*a*) Salvius Seius, Lucius' boy bestowed this as a gift on Hercules.   Favours were granted.[2]

(*b*) (*added later :*) Seius Salvius, a boy,[3] to Hercules the Conqueror.

23

Vibius Atiedius.   On stone found at Ortona, now lost ?

From Vibius Atiedius to Vesuna Erinis' daughter, and to Sire Erinis, as a gift willingly and deservedly.

24

Gaius Hinuleius.   On a small casket.   Found near Cales. c. 250 B.C.

Gaius Hinuleius, freedman of Gaius, bestowed this as a gift on Apollo.

25

Publius Cornelius Lentulus, consul in 236 B.C. ?   On the side of an altar.   Rome.   236 B.C. ?

Publius Cornelius, consul, son of Lucius, acceptably completed this as sacred to Mars.

[2] See preceding note.
[3] *p.* = *puer*, that is, slave.   But the reading is not certain.

26

20   [*M. Aim*]ilio M. f., C. An[*io C. f.* | [*prai*]toris
        pro po[*plod* | *vic. par*]ti Diove dede[*re*].

27

26   Aiscolapio dono[*m*] | L. Albanius K. f. dedit.

28

27   C. Bruttius | Aescolapio | dono dedit | meritod.

29

28   Aescolapio | donom dat | lubens merito | M. Pop-
        pulicio M. f.

30

30   M. C. Pomplio No. f. | dedron[*t*] | Hercole.

31

31   M. Bicoleio V. l. Honore | donom dedet mereto.

32

32   . . . onius Q. f. | Numisio Martio | donom dedit |
        meretod.

---

26 [3] *vicesma par*]ti Garrucci   *dec(u)ma par*]ti *coni.* Lommatzsch   [*di*]ti Momms.   *parti = partim = partem*

---

[1] This divinity is not known except in a few inscriptions.
Martius indicates some connexion with Mars, probably ' son
of Mars.'

DEDICATORY INSCRIPTIONS

26

Marcus Aemilius and Gaius Annius. Small brass plate, bought by J. Friedländer at Rome. Third century B.C.

Marcus Aemilius son of Marcus, and Gaius Annius son of Gaius, praetors, on behalf of the people gave a twentieth to Jupiter.

27

Lucius Albanius. Pedestal of stone found in the Tiber. Third century B.C.

To Aesculapius; a gift bestowed by Lucius Albanius son of Kaeso.

28

Gaius Bruttius. Pedestal of stone. Rome.

Gaius Bruttius bestows this as a gift deservedly on Aesculapius.

29

Marcus Populicius. Pedestal of stone found in the Tiber.

To Aesculapius; a gift bestowed willingly and deservedly by Marcus Populicius son of Marcus.

30

Marcus Pompilius and Gaius Pompilius. Pedestal of stone found in the Tiber.

Marcus Pompilius and Gaius Pompilius, sons of Novius, gave this to Hercules.

31

Bicoleius. On stone. Rome.

Marcus (?) Bicoleius, freedman of Vibius, bestowed this gift deservedly on Honour.

32

Unknown. Pedestal of stone found in the Tiber.

. . . son of Quintus bestowed this gift deservedly on Numisius [1] Martius.

33

33   [*Nu*]misio Mar[*tio*] | M. Terebonio C. l. | donum
        dat liben[*s*] | meritod.

34

2135   Mar. Popi. St. f. N. Mart. d. d. me.

35

34   Pl. Specios | Menervai | donom | port.

36

37   M. Mindios L. fi. | P. Condetius Va. fi. | aidiles
        vicesma parti | Apolones dederi.

37

41   Diana | M. Livio M. f. | praitor dedit.

38

45   Diana mereto | noutrix Paperia.

39

47   (*a*) C. Placentios Her. f. | Marte sacrom |
        (*b*) C. Placentius Her. f. | Marte donu dede.

---

[1] not Vatia, which is a *cognomen*.
[2] which was nailed up somewhere, inscribed with inscription
(*a*), and at some time later turned over and inscribed with
inscription (*b*) in a slightly later style.

DEDICATORY INSCRIPTIONS

33
Marcus Trebonius.   Pedestal of stone.

To Numisius Martius; Marcus Trebonius, freedman of Gaius, bestows this gift willingly and deservedly.

34
Marius (?) Popius.   On a bronze urn found in the domain of Capena.

Marius (?) Popius son of Statius bestowed this as a gift deservedly on Numisius Martius.

35
Plautus Specius.   Bronze plate of unknown origin ; now at Florence.

Plautus Specius brings this as a gift for Minerva.

36
Marcus Mindius and Publius Condetius.   Bronze plate of unknown origin.

The aediles Marcus Mindius son of Lucius, and Publius Condetius son of Valesus,[1] gave Apollo's twentieth.

37
Marcus Livius.   On stone, found at Nemi.

Given to Diana by Marcus Livius, praetor, son of Marcus.

38
Papiria, a nurse.   On a bronze spear-point.   Nemi.

To Diana deservedly.   Nurse Papiria.

39
Gaius Placentius.   Bronze plate [2] found near Tibur.

(*a*) Gaius Placentios son of Herius; something sacred for Mars.

(*b*) Gaius Placentius son of Herius bestowed this gift on Mars.

40

46
Spei | Teucus | Mulvio | don. d.

41–2

48
(i) M. Fourio C. f. tribunos
[milita]re de praidad Fortune dedet.

49
(ii) M. Fourio C. f. tribunos
militare de praidad Maurte dedet.

43

383
L. Terentio L. f. | C. Aprufenio C. f. | L. Tur-

5
pilio C. f. | M. Albani. L. f. | T. Munatio T.
f. | quaistores | aire moltaticod | dederont.

44

2442
Q. A. Aidicio Q. f. T. Rebinio Q. f. aidile molta-
tico.

45

388
Vecos Supn. | Victorie seinq. | dono dedet | lubs

5
mereto | queistores | Sa. Magio St. f. | Pac.
Anaiedio St. [f.]

45 ² seign. (*i.e.* signum) Ihm, *Rhein. Mus.*, LVII, 316

---

¹ For all the Furian inscriptions, see *C.I.L.*, I, 50–58.
² *militare* for *militaris*; or else it stands for *militari*; if so, then 'Marcus Furius, tribune, son of Gaius, . . . out of warriors' spoils.' But this is most unlikely.
³ here, local magistrates.
⁴ understand *aire*.
⁵ The meaning of *seinqu.* is unknown. It may be something connected with *Sancus* or *Sanqualis* (= ' of Sancus '). For *vicus* see p. xxxvii.

DEDICATORY INSCRIPTIONS

40

Teucus Mulvius. Pedestal of stone. Genzano.

To Hope; a gift bestowed by Teucus Mulvius.

41–2

Two dedications of Marcus Furius.[1] Small pillars found at Tusculum. c. 225 B.C. or later.

(i) Marcus Furius, military [2] tribune, son of Gaius, gave this to Fortune out of spoils.

(ii) Marcus Furius, military tribune, son of Gaius, gave this to Mavors out of spoils.

43

Lucius Terentius and others. Bronze tablet found near Firmum Picenum.

Lucius Terentius son of Lucius, Gaius Aprufenius son of Gaius, Lucius Turpilius son of Gaius, Marcus Albanius son of Lucius, and Titus Munatius son of Titus, quaestors,[3] gave this out of fines-money.

44

Quintus and Aulus Aedicius and Titus Rebinius. Bronze urceus. Lanuvium.

Quintus Aedicius and Aulus Aedicius, sons of Quintus, and Titus Rebinius, son of Quintus, aediles, out of fines-money.[4]

45

The Supinate village of the Marsians. On stone found at Trasacco.

The Supinate village bestowed this as a gift willingly and deservedly on Victory.[5] . . . Quaestors: Salvius Magius, son of Statius, and Pacuvius Anaiedius, son of Statius.

46

395   A. Cervio A. f. cosol dedicavit.

47

396   Iunonei Quiritei sacra C. Falcilius L. f. consol
dedicavit.

48–57

439-442, (i) Aecetiai pocolom (ii) Aisclapi pococolom (iii)
447, 450-1, Belolai pocolom (iv) Coera pocolo (v) Mener-
444, 452, 455 vai pocolom (vi) Salutes pocolom (vii) Veneres
pocolom (viii) Iunonenes pocolom (ix) Vestai
pocolo (x) ⟵— Ne ven.: deivo

58

460   [*Me*]nerva dono de[*det*].

(iv) **COERAE** *et postea* **COFRΛ** Garrucci   **COFRΛI**
Secchi   **COTRΛ** *vel* **COIRΛ** *ignot. quid.*
(x) **NEVEN : DEIVO** ⟵—

---

[1] a local magistrate, who in some towns had this title.

[2] In spite of the name *poculum*, the **articles** are dishes or
flattish bowls, except (v), (vii) and (ix) which are pitchers.
The name of the deity is in the genitive case.

[3] *pococolom* is a careless dittography of the painter, which
could be imitated in the translation by putting ' didish.'

[4] mistake, or a dialectic form, for Bellona.

[5] cf. note 3. 'Junono's' as it were.

[6] uncertain. Possibly Faliscan, not Latin. Cf. Thulin,
Röm. Mitth., XXII, 308. *ven.* = *vendas* or the like? We
have *doivom* in Cantovios' dedication, above, pp. 58–60.

DEDICATORY INSCRIPTIONS

46

Aulus Cervius, consul [1] of Beneventum. On a fragment of a pillar found at Beneventum. Third century B.C.

Aulus Cervius, consul, son of Aulus, dedicated this.

47

Gaius Falcilius, consul [1] of Beneventum. On an old wall at Beneventum.

Dedicated, as things sacred to Juno Quiris, by Gaius Falcilius, consul, son of Lucius.

48–57

Painted on earthen dishes (paterae) or pitchers (urcei) for temples. Before the second Punic War (cf. C.I.L., I, 439–459).

(i) Equity's dish [2] (*a ' patera ' from Vulci, now in the British Museum*).

(ii) Aesculapius' dish [3] (*a ' patera ' from Clusium*).

(iii) Belola's [4] dish (*a ' patera ' found at Florence*).

(iv) Care's dish (*a ' patera ' found near Horta ; now lost*).

(v) Minerva's dish (*an ' urceus ' found at Tarquinii*).

(vi) Safety's dish (*a ' patera ' found at Horta*).

(vii) Venus' dish (*an ' urceus ' found at Tarquinii*).

(viii) Juno's [5] dish (*a dish found at Vulci*).

(ix) Vesta's dish (*a fragment of an ' urceus ' found at Lanuvium, now in the British Museum*).

(x) Sell you not. For a god [6] (*on a ' patera ' found at Ardea ; the words run from right to left*).

58

On a piece of a dish. Rome.

He bestowed this as a gift on Minerva.

59

607   Hercolei | sacrom | M. Minuci. C. f. | dictator
           vovit.

60

608   M. Claudius M. f. | consol | Hinnad cepit.

61

609   Martei | M. Claudius M. f. | consol dedit.

62

610   C. Aurilius C. f. | praitor | iterum didit | eisdim
   5   consl | probavit.

63

613   [*L. Quinctius L. f. Le*]ucado cepit | [*eidem conso*]l
           dedit.

---

[1] Henzen, *Bull. dell' Instit.*, 1863, 58 ff.

[2] He was really *magister equitum* irregularly given equal power with the dictator or ' pro-dictator ' Fabius Cunctator after a success against Hannibal at Gereonium. On another side of the altar is written Ɩ· Ɩ· XXVƖ, which may have indicated the position (Ɩ = *l* = *locus ?*) of the altar. Some later inscriptions (which do not have Ɩ) confirm this. Possibly *lapis inscriptus ?*

[3] in Sicily. He triumphed in 211, after campaigns 214–212 B.C. Doubled consonant at this date is for Greek Ἔννα.

DEDICATORY INSCRIPTIONS

59

M. Minucius, dictator. On one side of an altar[1] *found at Rome.* 217 B.C.

To Hercules a sacred gift vowed by Marcus Minucius, dictator,[2] son of Gaius.

60

Marcus Claudius Marcellus. On a stone pedestal. Found at Rome. 211 B.C.

Marcus Claudius, consul, son of Marcus, took this as booty from Henna.[3]

61

Another dedication of Claudius Marcellus. On stone. Found at Rome. 211 B.C.

To Mars, given[4] by Marcus Claudius, consul, son of Marcus.

62

C. Aurelius, praetor urbanus in 202[5] *B.C., consul in* 200. *Pedestal of stone. Found in Diana's Grove.* 200 B.C.

Gaius Aurelius, son of Gaius, gave this when he was praetor for the second time; he likewise acceptably completed it when consul.

63

Lucius Quinctius Flamininus. Piece of an architectural abacus. Found at Praeneste. 192 B.C.

Lucius Quinctius, son of Lucius took this as booty from Leucas; he likewise made a gift of it when he was consul.

---

[4] Claudius had originally written *vovit*. But since he paid his vow, the verb was altered.

[5] and again apparently in 201, to judge from the stone.

64

615   M. Folvius M. f. | Ser. n. Nobilior | cos. Ambracia | cepit.

65

616   M. Fulvius M. f. | Ser. n. cos. | Aetolia cepit.

66

622   L. Aimilius L. f. inperator de rege Perse | Macedonibusque cepet.

67

976   Coronicei | T. Terentius L. C. l. donom | mereto dedet.

68

975   Devas | Corniscas | sacrum.

69

40   C. Manlio Aci. | cosol pro | poplo | Arimenesi.

---

[1] He besieged Ambracia (which was defended by Aetolians) in 189, and on the surrender of the place behaved with some moderation, but took away some artistic treasures.

[2] defeated at Pydna, 168 B.C. Cf. *C.I.L.*, I, 2, pp. 725, 739. Guarducci, *Rendic. Pont. Acc.*, XIII, 41 ff.

[3] *Coronicei = Cornici* (*cornix* = crow); see next note.

[4] Not, apparently, dative plural contracted from *-a-is*, but genitive singular (which can certainly be used with *sacrum*), or locative plural (R. Kent, *Forms of Latin*, § 224, n. 1; Linds., *Lat. Langu.*, 463; Ribezzo, *Riv. Indo-Gr.-Ital.*, IV, 77; Hermann, *Nachr. d. Götting. Gesellsch. d. Wissensch.*, 1919, 220). There was a place called *Corniscarum Divarum* ' because these birds were thought to be under the guardianship of Juno ' (Paulus, ex. F., 45, 4); it was somewhere ' across the Tiber.' Thus *Devas Corniscas* may be nom. or acc. pl.

DEDICATORY INSCRIPTIONS

64

M. Fulvius Nobilior.[1] *Pedestal of stone. Found at Rome.* 189 B.C.

Marcus Fulvius Nobilior, consul, son of Marcus, grandson of Servius, took this as booty from Ambracia.

65

Another dedication of Fulvius Nobilior. Pedestal of stone. Found at Tusculum. 189 B.C. *(the inscription recut in the Augustan age ?).*

Marcus Fulvius, consul, son of Marcus, grandson of Servius, took this as booty from Aetolia.

66

Lucius Aemilius Paullus. Tablet of marble. Found at Delphi. 167 B.C.

Lucius Aemilius, son of Lucius, commander-in-chief, took this as booty from King Perseus [2] and the Macedonians.

67

Titus Terentius. A small stone pedestal found at Rome. Not much later than 200 B.C.

To Crow,[3] a gift deservedly made by Titus Terentius, freedman of Lucius and of Gaius.

68

On a stone found near Rome.

Sacred possession of a divine Crow.[4]

69

Gaius Manlius Acidinus, [5] *consul at Ariminum. Small tablet of bronze, dedicated to Diana, Nemi. c.* 190 B.C.

Gaius Manlius Acidinus, consul, on behalf of the people of Ariminum.

[5] Cf. Lucius Manlius Acidinus, consul at Rome, 179 B.C.; *C.I.L.*, I, 2, 621.

70

42   Poublilia Turpilia Cn. uxor | hoce seignum pro
          Cn. filiod | Dianai donum dedit.

71

365   Menerva sacru   ⟵
       La. Cotena La. f. pretod de ⟵
       zenatuo sententiad vootum ⟵
       dedet. Cuando datu, rected ⟵—
       cuncaptum.   ⟵

72

580   Sacro Matre Mursina.

73

1430   Q. Caecilius Cn. A. Q. Flamini leibertus Iunone
          Seispitei | Matri Reginae.

74

359   Iunone Locina | dono pro | C. Rutilio P. f.

75

360   P. Rutilius M. f. | Iunonei Loucina | dedit meri-
          tod | Diovos castud.

---

[1] The inscription runs from right to left and is a mixture of
Faliscan and Latin. Bréal, *Mém. d. l. Soc. de linguistique*,
IV, 237. *pretod* seems to be assimilated to *de*. For Z the
inscription has ⊥. *de zenatuo sententiad = ded senatuos
sententiad* with *ds* written *z* and *ss* reduced by haplography.

[2] Wilson, *Amer. J. Philol.*, XXVIII, 450 ff. *Matre Mursina
= Matri Mursinae.*

[3] The letters are formed out of dots.   [4] See next note.

DEDICATORY INSCRIPTIONS

70

*Publilia Turpilia.   Tablet of bronze, Nemi.   c. 150 or later,
imitating an older style.*

Publilia Turpilia, wife of Gnaeus, on behalf of her
son Gnaeus, bestowed this statue on Diana as a gift.

71

Lars (?) Cotena.[1]   Bronze tablet at Falerii.

The praetor Lars (?) Cotena, son of Lars, by a vote
of the Senate bestowed this as a gift vowed sacred
to Minerva.   When it was bestowed, it was dedicated
duly in set form of words.

72

*A dedication to Mater Mursina.   On the margin of a strainer
found near Cortona.[2]*

Sacred to Mother Mursina.

73

*Quintus Caecilius.   Marble epistyle.   Lanuvium.   Not later
than c. 90–85 B.C.   A. Gordon, Univ. of Calif. Publ. in Class.
Arch., I. 5, 159.*

Quintus Caecilius, freedman of Gnaeus and of
Aulus Caecilius and of Quintus Flaminius, to Juno,
Saviour, Mother and Queen.

74

*Gaius Rutilius ;   someone on his behalf.   Bronze tablet,[3]
ruins of temple of Juno, Norba.   Second century B.C.*

A gift to Juno Lucina on behalf of Gaius Rutilius,
son of Publius.

75

Publius Rutilius.   Bronze tablet.   Norba.   Second cent. B.C.

Publius Rutilius, son of Marcus, gave this deservedly to Juno Lucina in Jupiter's Fasting-time.[4]

TITULI SACRI

76

361   Iunone Loucinai | Diovis castud facitud.

77

1696   (*a*) A. Titinius A. f.   [*Di*]anae | aedicolam votum |
dedit meretod.   (*b*) Αὖλος Τιτίνιος Αὔλω | υὸς
Ἀρτάμιτι εὐχὰν | νάισκον ἀπέδωκε.

78

1531   M. P. Vertuleieis C. f.
Quod re sua d[*if*]eidens asper | afleicta
5 parens timens | heic vovit, voto hoc | solut[*o*]
[*de*]cuma facta | poloucta leibereis lube|tes
donu danunt | Hercolei maxsume | mereto.
10 Semol te | orant se voti crebro | condemnes.

79

2226   Cleon salari. soc. s. Aescolapio Merre donum
dedit lubens | merito merente. Ἀσκληπίῳ
Μήῤῥη ἀνάθεμα βωμὸν ἔστη|σε Κλέων ὁ ἐπὶ τῶν
ἀλῶν κατὰ πρόσταγμα.

---

¹ We have *Diovos castud* in the preceding inscription. But
what is *facitud?* *facto*, thinks Ritschl. *Iovis* (*coniugi*).
caste facito interprets Mommsen. Cf. Pascal, in *H.*, xxx,
548 ff. Ritschl. *Opusc.*, IV, 727; Momms. *C.I.L.*, I, 1, p. 561;
Jordan, *Ind. Lect. Königsb.*, 1882–3, 14. *castud* an adverb?—
Fay, *Class. Philol.*, IV, 307.

² or, 'despairing at his ruined property.'

³ but *merito*, which is usually ablative, may be dative here
'(Hercules) who deserved it.'

⁴ in honour of Hercules, at which the tithe was consumed.
facere decumam is to set aside a tenth, *pollucere d.* is to offer
it up, in this case at the banquet.   ⁵ Hercules.

⁶ by granting their requests, or giving them good luck.

⁷ Cf. Gildemeister, *Rhein. Mus.*, XX, 1 ff.; Ritschl, *Opusc.*,
IV, 657 ff.   *C.I. Semit.*, I, 1, 143, 149.

⁸ In view of the Greek ὁ ἐπὶ τῶν ἀλῶν, *salari.* has been taken
to represent *salarius* 'salt-officer.' But in view of new
inscriptions found at Minturnae (see pp. 112–13) I take
salari. to represent *salariorum.*

DEDICATORY INSCRIPTIONS

76

Unknown.   A broken plate of bronze.   Of Latin origin.

To Juno Lucina, after celebrating [1] Jupiter's Fasting-time.

77

Aulus Titinius.   On a tablet.   Found at Tarentum.   3rd or 2nd cent. B.C.

(*a*) Aulus Titinius, son of Aulus gave a chapel as a vow deservedly to Diana.

(*b*) *Likewise the Greek, where ' meretod ' is implied in* ἀπέδωκε.

78

Marcus Vertuleius and Publius Vertuleius.   On a stone found near Sora.   c. 150 B.C. or later.   Saturnians.

Marcus Vertuleius and Publius Vertuleius, sons of Gaius.   In payment of the vow which their father, disheartened, dishevelled, despairing in his smitten fortunes,[2] vowed here, his children bestow willingly and most deservedly [3] a gift upon Hercules, having set aside a tithe and having offered it at a sacred banquet.[4]   At the same time they pray that you [5] may often doom them [6] to fulfilment of vow.

79

Cleon.   On the bronze base of a column found in Sardinia. Trilingual, c. 150 B.C.[7]

(*a*) Cleon, servant of the Associated Company of Salt-farmers,[8] bestowed this gift willingly and deservedly on Aesculapius Merre the well-deserving.

(*b*) Cleon, foreman of the salt-revenue, set up an altar as a dedication to Asclepius Merre according to Divine command.

[*Punic text follows.*]

80

2225   Himilconi Idnibalis f., | quei hanc aedem ex s. c.
       fac. | coeravit, Himilco f. statuam.

81

990   C. Volcaci. C. f. har. de stipe Iovi Iurario [*dedit ob*
      m]onimentom.

82

626   L. Mummi L. f. cos.

      Duct. | auspicio imperioque | eius Achaia capt.

      ⁵ Corinto | deleto Romam redieit | triumphans.

      Ob hasce | res bene gestas quod | in bello voverat |

      hanc aedem et signu. | Herculis Victoris |

      ¹⁰ imperator dedicat.

81   [*aram cum m*]onimento m(erito) Momms.   *an* dedit
pavimentom ?
82 ⁶ quod [*is*] in Ritschl

---

¹ The inscription is of the 'Honorary' class (see pp. 128 ff.)
but the statue was probably dedicated to the temple's god.

84

DEDICATORY INSCRIPTIONS

80

Himilco. A marble pedestal[1] *found in Sardinia. Not earlier than Sulla's time. Bilingual.*

To Himilco, son of Idnibal, who superintended the building of this temple by decree of the state, Himilco his son set up this statue.

[*Punic text follows.*]

81

C. Volcacius. On a pavement found on the Isle of the Tiber.

Gaius Volcacius, a seer, son of Gaius, gave this, for a memorial,[2] to Jupiter of Oaths; from the offertory.

82

Lucius Mummius, consul 146 B.C., triumphed in 145 B.C.[3] *Tablet of stone found at Rome on the Mons Caelius; dedicated in 142 B.C. Saturnians (except lines 9? and 10). The temple mentioned is otherwise unknown.*

Lucius Mummius, consul, son of Lucius.

Under his leadership his auspices and his command Achaia was taken, and Corinth laid waste. He then returned to Rome in a triumph. In recompense for these exploits prosperously achieved, he the commander is the dedicator of this temple and statue of Hercules the Conqueror; which he had vowed in the war.

[2] How this could be is not clear; but any other suggestion seems unlikely; *munimentum ?* (possibly). *har. = haruspex.*

[3] In 146 he ended Rome's wars in Greece by the destruction of Corinth.

83

630 [*L. Mumm*]ius L. f. imp. | [*ded. Co*]rintho capta |
   [*vico Ital*]icensi.

84

632   Sancte
  De] decuma, Victor, tibei Lucius Munius donum
  mo]ribus antiqueis pro usu[*r*]a hoc dare sese
  visu]m animo suo perfecit tua pace rogans te
 5 *co*]gendei dissolvendei tu ut facilia faxs[*eis*.
  Per]ficias, decumam ut faciat verae ration[*is*,
  pro]que hoc atque alieis doneis des digna mere[*nti*.

85

656 Fortuna[*e*] | sac[*rum*] | T. Quincti[*us*] . . . . . *de*] |
  senati sente[*ntia*].

86

658 C. Fanni M. f. | cos. de | sena. sen. | dedit.

83 *vide Elizabeth Evans, ' The Cults of the Sabine Territory,'*
1939, pp. 70 ff.

---

[1] For other dedications by Mummius, see *C.I.L.*, I, 2,
627–629, 631.

[2] All that remains of this inscription now is . . . *L. f.
imp.* . . . *capta* . . . *nsi.* For *vicus*, see p. xxxvii.

[3] *Sc.* Hercules. Cf. inscription 82.

[4] This is what is on the stone, which hitherto was believed
to record a dedication by L. Mummius. Cf. G. Q. Giglioli,
Athenaeum, N.S. 28, 1950, 267 ff.

[5] possibly : ' He performed his duty as his mind thought
best.'

[6] *moribus antiqueis* might define Munius himself—' a man
of good old-fashioned ways.'

[7] Elizabeth Evans, *The Cults of the Sabine Territory*, 1939,
70 ff. The inscription was wrongly thought to be lost.

DEDICATORY INSCRIPTIONS

83

Another [1] dedication of Lucius Mummius. Found at Italica in Spain. 146 B.C. Dedicated to a god, presented to Italica.

Lucius Mummius, son of Lucius, commander-in-chief, gave this on the capture of Corinth to the country-town of Italica.[2]

84

Dedication by a merchant Lucius Munius. On a carved stone found near Riati, now in the Palazzo Communale there. c. 145–140 B.C. Hexameters. C.I.L., I, 2, 2, Fasc. III, p. 833.

O Hallowed one!

O Conqueror,[3] Lucius Munius [4] fulfilled a vision that he saw in his mind,[5] that by good old custom [6] he should make thee this gift out of tithe in return for interest on money, asking thee by thy grace to make it easy for him to exact and pay debts. Make him afford thee a tithe in true account, and in token of this and other gifts grant worthy blessings to a deserving man.[7]

85

Titus Quinctius, consul in 150 or 123 (or even 198) B.C. On an altar found near Florence.

To Fortune, as a sacred gift from Titus Quinctius, by a vote of the Senate.

86

Gaius Fannius, consul in 122 B.C. On a small stone pedestal found at Rome.

Gaius Fannius, consul, son of Marcus, gave this by a vote of the Senate.

Cf. Lindsay, *Philol.*, LI, 364; Birt, *Rhein. Mus.*, LIV, 213; Stowasser, *Wien. Stud.*, XV, 260 (improbable), Bücheler, *Rhein. Mus.*, XVIII, 776; Ritschl, *Opusc.*, II, 638, 776; IV, 103.

87

693   Q. Minucius Q. f. | Rufus leg. Apollinei | Phutio merito.

88

1513   Q. Pomponius Q. f. | L. Tulius Ser. f. | praitores aere | Martio emerut.

89

801   Sei deo sei deivae sac. | G. Sextius G. f. Calvinus pr. | de senati sententia | restituit.

90

2646   [*L. Cornelius L. f. Su*]lla nomine [*Corneliae s*]ororis suai fecit.

91

1002   T. Quinctius Q. f., L. Tulli[*us . . . . . f. . . . . .*] Caltili.   Calt. l. | mag. de duobus pageis et vicei Sulpicei.

92

1581   Iunone | Loucina | Tuscolana | sacra.

---

[1] Brother of Marcus recorded on an inscription given below. p. 132; for the arbitration of both brothers, see pp. 262 ff.

[2] *i.e.* with money coined from spoils of war; cf. the *Columna Rostrata*, line 15, pp. 130–1.

[3] For these, see pp. xxxvii–viii.

[4] *sacra* sc. *ara.*   *Iunone* etc. are datives.

DEDICATORY INSCRIPTIONS

87

Quintus Minucius Rufus.[1] *On a pedestal found at Delphi.
Between 110 and 106 B.C.*

Quintus Minucius Rufus, the ambassador, son of
Quintus, to Pythian Apollo, deservedly.

88

*Quintus Pomponius and Lucius Tullius. Found at Cora.
Late in the second century B.C. ?*

The praetors Quintus Pomponius son of Qintus,
and Lucius Tullius son of Servius bought this with
Mars' money.[2]

89

*Sextius Calvinus (son of Sextius Calvinus, consul in 124 ?).
On an altar at Rome. c. 90–80 B.C.*

Sacred maybe to god maybe to goddess, this altar
was restored by the praetor Gaius Sextius Calvinus,
son of Gaius, on a vote of the Senate.

90

*Sulla on behalf of his sister. On a fragment of an architrave
found at Verona. Before 78 B.C.*

Lucius Cornelius Sulla, son of Lucius, built this in
the name of his sister Cornelia.

91

*Titus Quinctius and Lucius Tullius. On an altar found at
Rome.*

Titus Quinctius, son of Quintus; and Lucius
Tullius, son of . . . ; and . . . Caltilius, freedman
of Caltilia, presidents from two hamlets and of the
Sulpician quarter.[3]

92

Dedication to Juno Lucina. Capua.

An altar [4] dedicated to Tusculan Juno Lucina.

93

981   Publicia L. f. | Cn. Corneli A. f. uxor | Hercole
      5   aedem | valvasque fecit eademque | expolivit
aramque | sacram Hercole restitu. | Haec
omnia de suo | et virei ⟨fecit⟩ | faciundum
curavit.

94

1512   Paul. Toutia M. f. et | consuplicatrices.

95

1480   Dianai Opifer. | Nemorensei | L. Apuleius L. l.
Antio.

96

2215   . . . . . i L. l. Agato portitor. soc. s. | . . . colum-
nasque mag. fi[*lii sui* | *et su*]o Menervai d.
d. l. m.

97

2216   Abennaeus Catti M. s. maceriem | pinnas et
austia de s[*u*]o fecit Minervae di . . .

93 [8] fecit *a lapidar. erasum*
94 [1] TOVTIA Fabretti   *alii alia*

---

[1] not *portitor* 'ferryman,' 'carrier.' I take it as an
abbreviation for *portitorum* (*sc. sociorum*). See inscriptions
of Minturnae, below, pp. 112–13. Some take it as *Portitor*,
a name. *mag.* = *magisterio?*

[2] in fact a freedman.

[3] *austia = ostia.*

DEDICATORY INSCRIPTIONS

93

Publicia. On a stone tablet found at Rome.

Publicia daughter of Lucius, wife of Gnaeus
Cornelius son of Aulus, built for Hercules a temple
with folding doors. She likewise caused it to be
cleaned, and restored an altar sacred to Hercules.
The performance of all these works she superintended
out of her own and her husband's estate.

94

Paula Tutia. On stone. Now lost.

Paula Tutia, daughter of Marcus, and her fellow-
worshippers.

95

Lucius Apuleius. On an altar found at Tibur. Now lost.

To Diana of the Grove, the Help-bringing Goddess,
from Lucius Apuleius Antiochus (?), freedman of
Lucius.

96

Agatho. On part of an architrave. Found near Trieste.

. . . Agatho, freedman of Lucius and servant of
the associate harbour-masters [1] . . . and these pillars,
under the superintendence of himself and that of
his son, he bestowed as a gift willingly and deservedly
on Minerva.

97

Abennaeus. Found at S. Pelagii.

Abennaeus Cattius, slave [2] of Marcus, made a
wall and its pinnacles and doors [3] at his own cost and
dedicated them to Minerva.

98

1816   Fausta Veidia | votum solvit | l. m. **Iovi.**

99

2440   No. Ofalius No. f. Q. pro | sed et familia soua
Leibero | donum dat meret.

100

1815   Herculei   d.   [d.] | milites   Africa[ni] | Caecili-
⁵   anis ; | mag. curavit | C. Saltorius C. f.

101

1763   P.   Pomponi   N.   f. | Ancitie | donom | dedit |
⁵   lubens | mereto.

102

972   Q. Mucius Q. [l.] | Trupho ser. | vovit leiber solv. |
⁵   l. m. | Bonae Deae | sacr.

103

2541a   Cn. M. Vinucieis Cn. f. | e. h. d. d. me. lu [*bentes.*]

98 ³ ⅃MIONI.
103 ² e(ffigies) h(as), della Corte   e(orum) h(eres) Ribezzo

---

¹ The reading here is not certain.   *Iunoni ?*

² From Castra Caeciliana in Spain ?   *Caecilianis* seems to be
in the nominative case.   It may however be a true ablative,
hardly a locative-ablative.

³ a Marsian deity identified by the Romans with the sister
of Circe and Medea.   For a dedication probably to her by
Cantovios and his allies, see above, pp. 58 ff.

⁴ *effigies has.*   This is doubtful.

DEDICATORY INSCRIPTIONS

98

Fausta Veidia.   A small pillar found near Spurcola.

Paid as a vow to Jupiter [1] willingly and deservedly by Fausta Veidia.

99

Novius Ofalius (Ofellius).   Tablet of marble at Rome.

Novius Ofalius, son of Novius, of the Quirinal tribe, bestows this as a gift deservedly, on behalf of himself and his household, on Liber.

100

African soldiers.   Pedestal found at Avezzano.

To Hercules, bestowed as a gift by African soldiers from The Caecilian Camp.[2]

Gaius Saltorius, son of Gaius, superintended as the overseer.

101

Publius Pomponius.   On a small pillar found at Città d'Antino.

Publius Pomponius, son of Numerius, bestowed this as a gift on Angitia [3] willingly and deservedly.

102

Quintus Mucius.   On an altar found at Rome.

Quintus Mucius Trypho, freedman of Quintus, vowed this when he was a slave, and paid it willingly and deservedly when free.; a gift sacred to the Good Goddess.

103

Cn. Vinucius and M. Vinucius.   On a pillar found at Atina in Lucania.

Gnaeus Vinucius and Marcus Vinucius, sons of Gnaeus, made deservedly a willing gift of these images.[4]

104

1928   Maxima Nasia Cn. f. Apoline dat.

105

1482   Herculei | C. Antestius Cn. f. | cens. | decuma
      5   facta iterum | dat.

106

1617   (*a*) Herculei | sacrum | C. Marci. C. l. Alex. fecit;
          servos | vovit liber solvit. |
      5 (*b*) Herculei | sacrum | C. Marci. C. l. Alex. | dat.

107

1848   T. Corvio At. f. | Feronia | dono meret.

108

2217   Veicae | Noriceiae | A. Poblicius D. l. A. . . |
(*corr.*)   5   P. Postumius P. l. pav. | coir. |
p. **714**)

109

2231   Pamphilus Pescen. | Q. ser. votum quod | pro-
         meisit s. l. M. m. | pro filio.

       107 [1] All   109 [4] PRO—IIIO

---

[1] eldest daughter.

[2] On this see note [4] on p. 82, and pp. 66–7.

[3] So Perdrizet. I suggest however that the writer should
have put *s. l. l. m.*, that is, *solvit laetus lubens merito*. Slave
here means freedman.

94

DEDICATORY INSCRIPTIONS

104

Maxima Nasia.   Round the stone lid of a sacred money-box. Found near Cluentum.

A gift of Maxima [1] Nasia, daughter of Gnaeus, to Apollo.

105

G. Antestius.   A small pedestal found at Tibur, now lost.

To Hercules from Gaius Antestius, censor, son of Gnaeus, a second gift after dedicating a tithe.[2]

106

Gaius Marcius.   Apparently found at Puteoli.   Lost?

(*a*) To Hercules a sacred offering made by Gaius Marcius Alexander, freedman of Gaius.   Slave, he vowed it; free, he paid the vow.

(*b*) To Hercules a sacred gift from Gaius Marcius Alexander, freedman of Gaius.

107

Corvius.   Found at Amiternum.

Titus Corvios, son of Attius (?), to Feronia, as a gift deservedly.

108

Publicius and Postumius.   Near Trieste.

To Vica of Noricum, Aulus Publicius A . . ., freedman of Decimus, Publius Postumius, freedman of Publius, superintended the making of this hard floor.

109

Pamphilus.   On a tablet found at Ienikieui (Amphipolis).

Pamphilus Pescennius, slave of Quintus, willingly and deservedly paid to Mercury [3] on behalf of his son the vow as he promised.

TITULI SACRI

110

2439 C. Saufeio C. f. | C. Orcevio M. f. | Sabini |
⁵ censores | hasce aras | probaveront | Iuno.
Paloscaria.

111

1920 (a) L. Pescennius T. f. | Mircurio dono dedit
mereto. |
(b) Sacra Iovi Stigio.

112

1481 Felicitatei | T. Cauponius T. f. | C. Aufestius C. f.
aed.

113

1805 [*Hoce ut l*]ibet don[*u*] . . . . . | [*d*]edit L. Aufidi. D. |
[*f.* . . . . . *de*]cuma   facta | [*Hercol*]i   mer.
⁵ iterum | . . . . . te orat. Tu es | [*sanctus*] deus
quei tou | . . . . pacem petit | . . . . .
adiouta.

110 ⁷ PALOS†CARIA
113 ¹⁻⁴ *suppl.* Momms. (hoc tibei donum, Garrucci)
⁵ [*simul*] te Momms. ⁶ tou[*tam a te*] Momms.
tou[*am prece*] Buecheler ⁷ [*auxilio*] adiouta Buecheler
[*eum*] adiouta Momms.

DEDICATORY INSCRIPTIONS

110

C. Saufeius and C. Orcevius. On a pillar found at Praeneste.

Gaius Saufeius Sabinus, son of Gaius, and Gaius Orcevius Sabinus, son of Marcus, censors, acceptably completed these altars to Juno of the Fig-Tree.[1]

111

Lucius Pescennius. Bronze tablet found at Firmum. Now lost.

(*a*) Lucius Pescennius, son of Titus, bestowed this as a gift deservedly on Mercury.

(*b*) [2] Sacred to Jupiter of the Styx.

112

Cauponius and Aufestius. Tablet of marble. Tibur.

To Happiness, from the aediles Titus Cauponius, son of Titus, and Gaius Aufestius, son of Gaius.

113

Lucius Aufidius. Found at Barzano (territory of the Vestini).

This has been bestowed with pleasure by Lucius Aufidius, son of Decimus . . . as a further gift deservedly on Hercules, after dedicating a tithe . . . he begs thee. Thou art a holy god who thy . . . seeks thy goodwill. . . . Render help!

---

[1] Cf. Rosenberg, *Rhein. Mus.*, LXXI, 117; Whatmough, *Class. Quart.*, XVI, 190. Paloscaria may well be the same as Caprotina since Caprotina was an epithet of Juno at her yearly feast on the Nonae Caprotinae (17th July) in memory of the warning about the Gauls given by slaves from a wild fig-tree (*caprificus*), and *palusca* was a kind of fig.

[2] (*b*) is possibly Augustan, since it is a phrase in Virgil (*Aen.*, IV, 638); but (*a*) may have been written earlier. *Jupiter Stygius* is Pluto.

TITULI SACRI

114

717
(et. p. 726) (i) [.] Orbius M. f. | mag. | Italiceis.

115

2252 (ii) (a) L. L. Orbieis L. l. mag. | laconicum
Italiceis.

(b) Λεύκιος Ὄρβιος Λευκίου | Λίκινος καὶ Λεύκιος
Ὄρβιος | Λευκίου Δίφιλος Ἑρμαϊσταὶ | γενόμενοι
Ἰταλικοῖς.

116

1624 (i) L. Rantius L. f. Tro. Lumphieis. |

(ii) Λεύκιος Ῥάντιος Λευκίου | υἱὸς Νύμφαις.

*Inscriptions made by organisations in the old Campanian
territory, at Minturnae, and elsewhere.*

Inscriptions have long been known illustrating local activities
in the old ' Ager Campanus ' and other regions; and they
have been increased by further inscriptions found at Minturnae. The documents found in the Campanian **territory**
differ distinctly from those found at Minturnae (I) *Ager
Campanus.*[6] For these inscriptions in general see the discussion by M. W. Frederiksen in *Papers of the British School at
Rome*, xxvii, 80 ff. *C.I.L.*, I, 2, 672–691, 2506.
From 211 onwards to 59 B.C. the Campanian territory was

---

[1] Lucius may have been the Roman commander of Delian
troops who in 87 B.C. defeated the Athenians who had taken
the side of Mithridates.   Athenae., V, 241 f. (Ὀρόβιος).

[2] Probably—*C.I.L.*, I, 2, p. 726.

[3] in business at Delos.

DEDICATORY INSCRIPTIONS

114

Dedications (to Mercury ?) of men named Orbius,[1] and belonging to a guild of Mercuriales, at Delos. Presented to merchants.
(i) *Lucius (?)[2] Orbius. On a pedestal.* 87 B.C.

Lucius Orbius, son of Marcus, foreman for the men [3] from Italy.

115

(ii) *Freedmen of Lucius Orbius. Tablet of marble. Bilingual.*

(*a*) Lucius Orbius and Lucius Orbius, freedmen of Lucius, foremen for the men from Italy ; a Spartan sweating-room.

(*b*) Lucius Orbius Licinus, and Lucius Orbius Diphilus, freedmen of Lucius, having become officers for the worship of Mercury, for the men from Italy.[4]

116

Lucius Rantius. Found on Ischia Island or at Naples. Bilingual.

(*a*) From Lucius Rantius, son of Lucius, of the Tromentine tribe to the Water-Goddesses.[5]

(*b*) From Lucius Rantius, son of Lucius, to the Nymphs.

public state-land of the Roman people, let (after 162 B.C.) to plebeian smallholders and governed, as one whole, not by local magistrates (*duoviri* or the like) and council (*decuriones*) as *municipia* were (see pp. xxxiv ff.), but by a *praefectus Capuam Cumas* sent from Rome. This single whole was (except it seems the city Capua, which was wholly dependent

---

[4] The Greek differs from the Latin. The *Mercuriales*, Ἑρμαῖσταί, were a trade-guild. Other dedications of Orbii : *C.I.L.*, I, 2, 715-716 ; 2242 (to Mercury).

[5] Nymphs ; cf. Walde-Hofmann, *Lat. Etym. Wörterb.*, ed. 2, s.v. *lumpa, limpa* ; Wackernagel, *Archiv f. lat. Lexicogr*, 15, 1908, 218 ff.

[6] see the excursus in *C.I.L.*, X, pp. 365 ff.

on the *praefectus*) organised in *pagi* [1] ' hamlets ' (see p. xxxv) each of which issued decrees, had one or more *magistri* (' foremen,' ' masters ' or ' overseers ') at the head, and was gathered round a shrine of its own which in some cases was at a street corner, in which cases the cult was ' compital.' No cult was a state-cult. Of these *pagi* we know the names of two—the *pagus Dianae* or *p. Tifatinus* round the famous *aedes Dianae Tifatinae* on the western slope of Mons Tifata (Monte Maddaloni north of Capua); and the *pagus Herculaneus* near Capua. The inscriptions *C.I.L.*, I, 2, 674, 677–683, 687–8 seem all to appertain to the *pagus Tifatinus*. These and the other inscriptions indicate that the community and magistri of each *pagus* elected each year, for public purposes connected closely with religion, a *collegium* (' college,' ' guild ') of twelve other *magistri* ' masters ' or ' foremen ' (quite distinct from the *magistri pagi*, and quite distinct from any sort of magistrate), one college for each cult. The members of each college had no official position and were usually all free-born or all freedmen of the male sex, rarely mixed, never slaves.[2] There were also trade guilds of the familiar type, with *magistri* and having duties connected with a cult. The duties of each college were to provide money for the treasury of the *pagus* and to give games unless the pagus decided otherwise. They also made public works such as walls,[3] pillars, porticoes, additions to a theatre, sometimes instead of games, sometimes in addition to these. Dating of the inscriptions, which are on slabs of stone made for public record, is by Roman consuls. After 59 B.C., when the Campanian land with Capua received a Roman colony, conditions of public life were naturally much altered, and some change affecting the status of the colleges or the cults may have taken place because their records cease to survive. Perhaps the organisation by *pagi* became obsolete.
(II) *Minturnae.* J. Johnson, *Excavations at Minturnae; II, Inscriptions; Part I; Republican Magistri.* Rome and Philadelphia, 1933.[4] Minturnae was in the territory north-west from the ' Ager Campanus,' and was an old Auruncan city which was a Roman colony from 295 onwards. Thus

---

[1] and probably also in *vici*, but these do not concern us.

[2] one record indeed (pp. 106–7) has slaves, but they are called *ministri* not *magistri* and were connected with the *Lares.* Here the ministri were either secondary officials

DEDICATORY INSCRIPTIONS

it was a township with full local *res publica*, having magistrates (*duoviri*) and local council (*decuriones*). Here there have been recently discovered oblong rectangular slabs, twenty-nine in number, and fragments of two more. They were *cippi* or *stelae* which apparently served as dedicated altars and were placed upright against a wall. They were involved in a fire which destroyed the *forum* at Minturnae about 50 B.C., and were, after some cutting down, used in the foundations of a temple built early in the first century A.D.; in the excavations of this temple they were discovered. Each of these slabs was dedicated to a deity by a college of 'foremen.' These were, like those recorded from the Ager Campanus, annually elected (single persons being re-eligible), one college for each cult. But the colleges consist mostly of slaves[5], few freedmen and only one free-born member occurring; and several of them are colleges of women only. There are no colleges of both sexes mixed. The college in most cases simply shares in presenting the altar, though one or two additional duties are mentioned. If the cults were compital (cf. Johnson, *op. cit.*, 122) then the members had to share in the duty of keeping the street-corner or roadsmeet (*compitum*) in due order. The basis of election was probably the *vicus* (p. xxxiv); we may assume at any rate that the election was done, as in the ' *Lex Ursonensis* ' = ' *Lex Col. Gen.*,' *C.I.L.*, I, 2, 594, CXXVIII, by the order of the local magistrates and council; and the dating was by the local magistrates (*duoviri*) —in one case by the Roman consuls.

The inscriptions of Minturnae are obviously dedicatory. Those of the Ager Campanus might be classed as inscriptions connected with public works. But even there the records have a religious 'flavour,' some of the works being specifically connected with a deity; and it is convenient to deal with them in conjunction with the inscriptions of Minturnae, for purposes of comparison and contrast. (III) Similar records, of Republican date, exist for other regions in Italy and elsewhere; I give some examples.

---

or primary officials of a cult treated in the *Ager Campanus* as one of lower degree.

[3] The word *fecerunt* sometimes means perhaps not ' made,' but embellished or ' repaired'; cf. *Lex Parieti Faciendo* (pp. 274 ff). [4] *C.I.L.*, I, 2, 2, Fasc. III, 1943, pp. 834–8, 844–5. [5] that at least is what they are called.

117

672 (i) . . . . | . . . nul . . . . | Cn.
5   Minatio | P. Pomponi. M. l. | magistreis |
conlegi | mercatorum | coeraverunt | . . . .
10 | . . . . Calpurnio | cos.

118

674 (ii) . . . . . . G. Maius N. f.; | . . . . V. f.; M. Vibius
M. f. Ru.; | . . . [C]orn[e]li L. f. Cori.; L.
Pomponi. L. f. F.; | . . . . Nerius M. f.; L.
5   Olienus L. f.; | [*he*]isc. mag. Spei Fidei
Fortunae mur[*um*] | faciundu coiravere M.
Minu[*cio*] | S. Postumio cos.

119

675 (iii) N. Pumidius Q. F.; M. Raecius Q. f.; | . . . .
7   (*alii decem* . .) | Heisce magistreis Venerus
Ioviae muru | aedificandum coiraverunt ped.
CCLXX et | loidos fecerunt Ser. Sulpicio M.
Aurelio co[*s.*]

119 [8] COF

---

[1] Cf. *C.I.L.*, I, 2, 673 : in 112 or 111 B.C. a different college
constructs a wall and 4 pillars.
[2] also called Falerine. *F.* might stand for the Fabian tribe,
or for some praenomen.

DEDICATORY INSCRIPTIONS

(I) *Construction and dedication of public works by ' magistri '
of the ' Ager Campanus.'*

117

(i) *Unknown works. Found at Capua.* 112 *or* 111 [1] B.C.

. . . Gnaeus Minatius and Publius Pomponius,
freedmen of Marcus, foremen of the guild of merchants, superintended . . . in the consulship of . . .
Calpurnius. . . .

118

(ii) *A wall to Hope, Faith, and Fortune. Found at Capua.*
110 B.C.

. . . Gaius Maius, son of Numerius; . . . son of
Vibius; Marcus Vibius Rufus, son of Marcus; . . .
Cornelius Cori . . ., son of Lucius; Lucius Pomponius
of the Falernian [2] tribe, son of Lucius; . . . Nerius
son of Marcus; Lucius Olienus, son of Lucius: These
foremen superintended the construction of a wall to
belong to Hope, Faith, and Fortune, in the consulship of Marcus Minucius and Spurius Postumius.

119

(iii) *A wall to Venus.*[3] *Found at Capua.* 108 B.C.

Numerius Pumidius, son of Quintus, Marcus
Raecius, son of Quintus; . . . (*and ten others*).
. . . These foremen superintended the building of a
wall 270 ft. long to belong to Venus, daughter of
Jupiter, and held games, in the consulship of Servius
Sulpicius and Marcus Aurelius.

[3] For another inscription, same people, same year, same
deity, see *C.I.L.*, I, 2, 676.

120

677

    (iv) Ser. Sueti. Ser. l. Bal.; . . . *(alii quattuor . . .)*

7   Cn. Octavi. N. l. Ves., | N. Sexti. N. M. l.,
M. Ocrati. M. l. Pist.; . . . *alii quinque* . . .
Heisce magistreis Cererus murum | et pluteum

10   long. p. LXXX, alt. p. XXI | faciund. coiravere
eidemq. loid. fec. | C. Atilio Q. Servilio cos.

121

678

    (v) T. Iunius N. f.; (. . . *alii ingenui quinque*). . .,
D. Rosci. Q. l. Lintio; . . . *(alii liberti*

7   *quinque)* . . .: Heisce magistrei Castori et |
Polluci murum et pluteum faciundu. | coera-

10   vere eidem loedos | fecere Q. Servilio | C.
Atilio cos.

122

680

    (vi) . . . *(erasa nomina)* . . . M. Antonio . . . A
Postumio cos. | Heisce mag. murum ab grad |

5   u ad calcidic. et calcidicum | et portic. ante
culin. long. p.[. . .] | et signa marmor. Cast.
et Pol. | et loc. privat. de stipe Dian. |
emendum [*et f*]aciendum | coeraver[*e*].

---

121 LINIO

¹ Perhaps simply Balbus. We have Balonius elsewhere,
where, however, it is a gentile name.

² possibly *vestiarius* ' clothes-dealer.'

³ Perhaps Pistoriensis ' of Pistorium '; possibly *pistorius*
' baker.'

⁴ thirteen in all instead of the usual twelve; perhaps one
of the twelve had died and had been succeeded by another.
Another wall to Ceres: *C.I.L.*, I, 2, 679.

⁵ The twelve names were all erased for some reason.
Perhaps their memory had been condemned.

⁶ perhaps a stone platform ($\beta\hat{\eta}\mu a$) is meant.

DEDICATORY INSCRIPTIONS

120

(iv) *A wall to Ceres.   Found at Capua.*   106 B.C.

Servius Suetius Bal.[1] . . ., freedman of Servius;
. . . (*four others*); . . . Gnaeus Octavius Vestinus [2] (?),
freedman of Numerius; Numerius Sextius, freedman
of Numerius and Marcus; Marcus Ocratius Pistorius [3]
(?), freedman of Marcus; . . . (*five others*). . . .
These foremen [4] superintended the construction of a
wall and a parapet 80 ft. long, 21 ft. high, to belong
to Ceres, and likewise held games, in the consulship
of Gaius Atilius and Quintus Servilius.

121

(v) *A wall to Castor and Pollux.   Found at Caserta.*   106 B.C.

Titus Junius, son of Numerius; . . . (*five other free-
born men*) . . .; Decimus Roscius Lintios freedman
of Quintus; . . . (*five other freedmen*). . . . These
foremen superintended the construction of a wall
and a parapet to belong to Castor and Pollux,
and likewise held games, in the consulship of Quintus
Servilius and Gaius Atilius.

122

(vi) *A wall and other works.   Found in an old wall at the
foot of Mons Tifata.*   99 B.C.

. . . [5] In the consulship of Marcus Antonius and
Aulus Postumius these foremen superintended the
construction, out of Diana's offertory, of a wall from
the step [6] to the corner-chamber, and a corner-
chamber and an arcade, in front of the kitchen, —
ft. long, and marble statues of Castor and Pollux;
likewise the purchase of a private [7] place for them.

[7] which now became government property, whether public
or sacred.

123

681   (vii) Hisce ministris Laribus faciendum coe[*rave-*
         runt] | C. Terent. C. l. Pilomus.; . . . (. . .
    servi octo inter quos) Philemo Baloni Baloniae
         s. Flac . . .: | Haec pondera et pavimentum
         faciendum et . . . | Q. Caecilio Q. f. Q. n. T.
         Deidio T. f. co[*s.*]

124

683   (viii) . . . (*nomina libertorum*) . . . [*Heisce*] mag.
     lacum Iovei de stipe et de sua pequn. |
         [*faciu*]nd. coeraver. Cn. Papeirio Carb. iter.
         cos.

125

688   (ix) *In latere: nomina libertorum. In antica:* Iovei
         sacr. *In postica:* Hanc aram ne quis dealbet.

Here may be mentioned *C.I.L.*, I, 2, 687, on a stone (found at Capua) which is only a fragment but records how foremen had something to do with making gardens, won a lawsuit, and also held games (*horto*[*s*] . . . *iudicioque vicere eidem l*[*udos fecerunt*]); did to something something involving eaves (*sucrundam = suggrundam*) of a building, repaired colon-

---

125 **DEALBE**

---

[1] with the freedman Philomusus at their head? or they may in fact have been freedmen likewise. But notice that they are called *ministri*, not *magistri*. They were thus a

DEDICATORY INSCRIPTIONS

123

(vii) Works for Household Gods. Found at Capua. 98 B.C. Known from copies.

The following servants superintended the making of this work to belong to the Household Gods: Gaius Terentius Philomusus, freedman of Gaius . . . (*eight slaves*[1] *including:*) . . . Philemon Flaccus, slave of Balonius and Balonia. . . . These blocks[2] and the making of this floor and . . . in the consulship of Quintus Caecilius son of Quintus, grandson of Quintus, and Titus Didius, son of Titus.

124

(viii) A reservoir to Jupiter. Tablet found at Capua. 84 B.C.

. . . (*names of a college of freedmen*) . . .: These foremen superintended the making of a reservoir, to belong to Jupiter, out of the offertory and out of their own purse, in the second consulship of Gnaeus Papirius Carbo.[3]

125

(ix) An altar to Jupiter ; origin and date unknown.

One one side : names of eleven freedmen.

On the front: Sacred to Jupiter.

On the back: Let no one whitewash this altar.

nades (*porticusque rec* . . .), and also out of their own purse made a dedication to Hercules (*iidemque de sua pecunia Herculei* [. . . .]). The following, though they show no connexion with religious cults, are doubtless to be classed with the preceding dedicatory or quasi-dedicatory inscriptions.

---

secondary college; or else a primary college of a secondary cult—probably the latter; we have another case (59 B.C.) where the Lares are concerned; and again the givers are slaves (*C.I.L.*, I, 2, 753, where *d.d. = donum dant*). Cf. also *C.I.L.*, I, 2, 1446 = n. 144 below.

[2] or official standard weights?

[3] who in the latter part of 84 B.C. was sole consul.

126

2506   (x) Q. Annius Q. l. Fe ...; | P. Bivellius T. l.; |
    5   P. Messius Q. l.; | C. Lusius C. l.; | P. Ovius
              P. l. Plut.; | C. Antonius C. l. | [*tr*]eib. cuniu
              muliere[*bus*] | ludosq. fecerun[*t*] | .... o cos.

127

685   (xi) .... N. f. Faber; .. (*alii*) ... cu[*ne*]os duos in
          teatro faciendos coi[*raver.*]

128

682   (xii) Pagus Herculaneus scivit a. d. X Ter-
          mina[*lia.*] | Conlegium, seive magistrei Iovei
          Compagei [*sunt,*] | utei in porticum paganam
          reficiendam | pequniam consumerent ex lege

128 [1] SCIVIT A O· X·

---

[1] or additions to a theatre, like the next inscription ?

[2] [*tr*]eib = *treibunal* ; *cuniu* = *cunium* (*cuneus* ' wedge ').

[3] The inscription stands on the same stone as the one in *C.I.L.*, I, 2, 686 which records how in 71 B.C. foremen, by the hamlet's decree (*ex pagei scitu*), contributed to the support of a slave in the service of Juno Gaura (*in servom Iunonis Gaurae*).

[4] For *pagus*, see p. xxxviii. This is not the town Herculaneum.

[5] 14th of February. The *Terminalia*, ' Festival of Landmarks ' or ' of the God of Boundaries,' were held on the 23rd of February every year. But in every other year, until Caesar's reform of the calendar, February actually ended on the 23rd, and there followed an intercalary month of 27 or 28 days before March began. In such years therefore, after the Ides (13th) of February dating looked forward either to ' the kalends of an intercalary month,' which was the usual method, or as in this inscription (cf. Cic., *ad Att.*, VI, 1), to the Terminalia. Romans wrongly connected *T*. with the year's end.

[6] These are *magistri collegii*, not of the hamlet; see p. 100.

DEDICATORY INSCRIPTIONS

126

(x) *Additions to accommodation for shows* [1] *at Capua.*
c. 106–92 B.C.?   Not dedicated?

Quintus Annius Fe . . ., freedman of Quintus,
Publius Bivellius, freedman of Titus; Publius
Messius, freedman of Quintus; Gaius Lusius, freedman of Gaius; Publius Ovius Plutus, freedman of
Publius; and Gaius Antonius, freedman of Gaius
built a platform and a block of seats for women,[2] and
held games, in the consulship of . . .

127

(xi) *Additions to a theatre.   Found 'ad S. Prisci.'   Before*
71 B.C.[3] *Not dedicated?*

. . . Faber son of Numerius; . . . (*several others*)
. . . superintended the making of two blocks of
seats in the theatre.

128

(xii) *Statute of the Pagus Herculaneus in the territory of*
Capua.   On a pedestal found apparently near Caserta.   94 B.C.

The inscription records a statute forming a public document
(pp. 242 ff.), *but is reasonably classed among these dedicatory*
inscriptions of the Ager Campanus and Minturnae.

The Hamlet [4] of Hercules resolved, ten [5] days
before the Festival of the God of Boundaries, that the
guild (alternatively the foremen [6]) for Jupiter
Fellow-villager [7] should spend, according to decree [8]
of the hamlet, a sum of money on repairing [9] a
portico of the hamlet at the will and pleasure of the

---

[7] Dative case?   Cf. Livy, XXIV, 44, 8 (*Iuppiter Vicilinus*).
For *vicus* cf. pp. xxxvii–viii.   Inscriptions have *Iovius, -a*, as
epithet for Hercules and Venus; so perhaps here; in which
case *Iovei Compagei* are genitives, ' of Iovius Fellow-villager.'

[8] *lex pagana* probably = *pagi scitum* (cf. line 1).

[9] instead of spending it on games—see below.

⁵ pagana, | arbitratu Cn. Laetori Cn. f. magi-
strei | pagei⟨ei⟩; uteique ei conlegio, seive
magistri | sunt Iovei Compagei, locus in
teatro | esset tamqua sei sei ludos fecissent.

¹⁶ . . . . (*nomina duodecim libertorum*) . . . . | C. Coelio
C. f. Caldo | [*L.*] Domitio Cn. f. Ahenobarb.
cos.

129–132

J. Johnson, *Excavations at Minturnae*; II, *Inscriptions*;
Part I; *Republican Magistri.*

(i) (8 Johnson, p. 25).

2685 . . . . .)
. . . . .) (*desunt*)

duo vir. | Hasc. mag. V. d.d. : | [*T*]ertia D[*o*]matia
⁵ S. f.; | Alfia ꓛ. l. Flora; | Cahia ꓛ. l. Asta-
pium; | Dositea Calidi N. s.; | (. . . *aliae*
. . .).

(ii) (12 Johnson, p. 29).

2689 . . . (*desunt aliquot versus*) Heisc. mag. Spei
d.d. | Antiochus Pulli Q. s.; | Bacchides Pac.
M.s.; | Seleucus Aur. M. C. s.; | . . . (*alii,*
¹¹ *inter quos*) Deiphil. Curt. Titini P. C. s. |
. . . (*alii duo*).

128 ⁶ PAGEIEI   ⁸ LVOOS

---

¹ on *magister pagi* as distinct from *magister collegii*, see
p. 100.

² *tamqua sei sei* is probably right = *tam quasi si.* We often
find *tamquam si* and *quasi si.*

³ See notice given above, pp. 98–101.

⁴ Local magistrates (see pp. xxxviii–ix) added to date the
inscription. As in other cases, the trimming of the stone for
use in the temple (see p. 101) caused the disappearance of
several lines at the beginning. Here only the names of the
magistrates have gone.

DEDICATORY INSCRIPTIONS

overseer of the village [1] Gnaeus Laetorius son of
Gnaeus; and that for the said guild (alternatively the
foremen) for Jupiter Fellow-villager there should
be a place reserved in the theatre as if [2] they had held
games. . . .

(*A list of twelve freedmen follows and then come the Roman
consuls of 94 B.C. :*)

In the consulship of Gaius Coelius Caldus son of
Gaius, and Lucius Domitius Ahenobarbus, son of
Gnaeus.

129–132

(II) *Dedications, on oblong rectangular slabs to serve as
altars, by ‘ magistri ’ and ‘ magistrae ’ of Minturnae. Early
part of the first century B.C. Four of the twenty-nine stones.*[3]

(i) In the year of office of . . ., Members of the
Board of Two.[4] These forewomen [5] present this as a
gift to Venus: Tertia Domatia,[6] daughter of Spurius:
Alfia Flora, freedwoman of a matron [7]; Gaia Asta-
phium, freedwoman of a matron; Dosithea, slave-
woman of Numerius Calidius; (. . . *and others all women*).

(ii) These foremen present this as a gift to Hope:
Antiochus, slave of Quintus Pullius; Bacchides, slave
of Marcus Paccius; Seleucus, slave of Marcus Aurelius
and Gaius Aurelius; (. . . *and others, including :*)
Deiphilus, slave of Publius Curtilius and Gaius
Titinius [8] (*and two others*).

[5] *hasc. mag.* = *hasce magistras ;* here a nominative plural;
compare *-as*, the regular ending of 1st decl. nom. pl. in Oscan.
V. = *Veneri.*

[6] The only free-born member of any of the colleges given
on these stones of Minturnae. [7] For Ɔ see pp. 28–9.

[8] who is mentioned also in Johnson number 22 (cp. also a
freedman of this Titinius in nr. 18.); the democrat Marius
granted him a divorce from his wife Fannia, who later nevertheless gave Marius refuge when he fled from Sulla in 88 B.C.

(iii) (16 Johnson, p. 34).

2693 . . . *(desunt aliquot versus)* Me[n]ander Vargunt. L.[s]; | M. Epidius M. l. Antiocus; | Trupho . . . . ti M. s.; |

⁵ Dama Roci L. s.; | Nicepor. Mescini C. s.; | Philippus Caecil. L. s.; |

Seleucus salinat. soc. s.; | Amphio picarior. soc. s.; | (. . . *alii* . . .).

(iv) (25 Johnson, p. 44).

2702 P. Hirrio M. f. | P. Stahio P. f. | duo vir. | Heisce mag. | Merc. Fel. d.d.: | . . . *(sequuntur nomina; ad extremum:)* Teuphilus Stai. P. s.; |

¹² Antiochus Cae. L. s. mensor; | Leonida Epidi. | M. s.

Of the other inscriptions, Johnson 6 is dated by the Roman consuls of 65 B.C.; 3, 4, 9, 11, 17 have women only as ' foremen '; there are no instances of both sexes on the same list. 10, a late one, records that the foremen (slaves) ' likewise performed stage-plays ' (*isdemque ludos fecer.* [= fecerunt] *scaenicos*); 28 records a *magister ludi* = stage-manager ?; 13 mentions a ' public slave '; 21 ends with ' Sacred to Hope '

---

¹ This Seleucus was an agent of a company of *publicani* who had farmed from the Roman government the revenue of the available salt-pits in Italy; and he worked for that branch of the company which dealt with salt-pits or diggings at or near the famous marshes of Minturnae which must have been salt. *salinat. soc.* = *salinatorum sociorum.* Amphion, the next slave mentioned, was a similar agent of a branch of a company of *publicani* who had farmed the revenue of the available pitch-fields in pine forests which presumably existed

DEDICATORY INSCRIPTIONS

(iii) Menander, slave of Lucius Vargunteius;
Marcus Epidius Antiochus, freedman of Marcus;
Tryphon, slave of Marcus . . .; Dama, slave of
Lucius Rocius; Nicephorus, slave of Gaius Mescinius;
Philippus, slave of Lucius Caecilius; Seleucus, slave
of the Associated Company of Salt-mine farmers [1];
Amphion, slave of the Associated Company of Pitch-
farmers; [2] (. . . *and others* . . .).

(iv) In the year of office of Publius Hirrius son of
Marcus and Publius Stahius son of Publius, Members
of the Board of Two.[3]   These foremen present this as
a gift to Mercury the Blest: (*the names follow, the last
three being :*) Theophilus, slave of Publius Staius;
Antiochus, surveyor,[4] slave of L. Cae . . .; Leonida,
slave of Marcus Epidius.

(*Spei sacr.* = *sacrum*); in 24 the deletion of line six, except
s. = *servus*, is a record of condemnation of a man's memory,
perhaps for sharing in the Social War of 91–88 B.C.; 22 may
give another instance. The oldest of the inscriptions are
apparently 11, 12, 18, 22, 24; indeed, 11 was inscribed perhaps
about 100 B.C., but it gives only a list of names.

---

then in the mountains round the Vescian Plain.—Johnson,
op. cit., pp. 126–7. *picarior.* = *picariorum.* See also next
note.
   [2] See preceding note. Others of these stones mention one
or both of these companies—Johnson, 1, 7, 14, 19 (where the
agent Rahiminanaeus is a Semite), 21, 26.
   [3] On this stone we have the dating undamaged by cutting
down for use in the building of the temple (p. 101). The
usual form of *Stahius* is *Staius* as in line 11 of this inscription.
   [4] Or possibly ' architect.'

133

1618   Merc. retiari . . . . | dan. mag. curarun. | Sex.
Calaasi. Sex. f. (. . . *alii quinque* . . .) . . .

134

1793   L. Statius Cn. f. Chilo | L. Pettius C. f. Pansa |
C. Pettius V. f. Gemellus | L. Tattius T. f.
5   Coxsa | magistri   Laverneis | murum   cae-
menticium | portam porticum | templum Bo-
10   nae Deae | pagi decreto faciundu[*m*] | cura-
runt probaruntq[*ue.*]

135

1794   T. Annius T. f. Rufus | L. Septimius Sa. f. Dentio |
L. Annius T. f. Gritto magistri | ex pagi d.
5   scaina. fac. coir. | T. Annius T. f. Ruf.
L. T. f. Gritto | probaverunt.

135 [5] *scribendum fuit* L. Annius T. f. Gritto

---

[1] apparently *retiari* are here, as usual, gladiators who
tried to throw a net over their opponents' heads. But since
the givers are not slaves, I suggest that *retiari* are net-
merchants, net dealers (cf. *vestiari*); and that *merc.* may mean
not Mercury but *mercatores*.

[2] *dan* looks like an abbreviation of *dandam.*

DEDICATORY INSCRIPTIONS

(III) *Similar dedications from other regions.*

133

Net-fighters of Puteoli.   c. 106–92 B.C.

To Mercury from the net-fighters [1] . . ., the giving [2] hereof was superintended by the overseers Sextus Calasius, son of Sextus . . . [*five others, three being freedmen.*]

134

Works dedicated to the Good Goddess at 'Pagus Lavernus' or Lavernae.   Found at Prezza.

Lucius Statius Chilo son of Gnaeus, Lucius Pettius Pansa son of Gaius, Gaius Pettius Gemellus son of Vibius, and Lucius Tattius Coxsa son of Titus, foremen at Lavernae, superintended, by decree of the hamlet, the construction of a wall of quarry-stone, a gate, a colonnade, and a temple to belong to the Good Goddess; and acceptably completed the same.

135

Theatre.[3]   *Found at Prezza.*

Titus Annius Rufus son of Titus, Lucius Septimius Dentio son of Salvius, and Lucius Annius Gritto, son of Titus, foremen, superintended, by decree of the hamlet, the construction of a theatre.[4]   Acceptably completed by Titus Annius Rufus, son of Titus, and Lucius Annius Gritto, son of Titus.

[3] The inscription may be regarded as Dedicatory, because the work was superintended by *magistri*.   But they may be the secular *magistri* of the pagus.

[4] properly the actors' stage of a theatre; here apparently put for the whole theatre.

136

1000   [*P*]upius A. f. mag. | [*pa*]g. Ianicol. porticu. |
        [*ce*]llam culinam | [*ar*]am de pagi sentent. |
    5   [*fa*]ciundu coiravit.

137

1001   [*Mag.*] pagi Ianic[*olensis*] | GS/ASTOS   et
        mace[*riam* | *de p*]ag. sen. fac. coer. eidemque
        p[*rob.*]

138

1003   M[*ag.*] et flamin. | montan. Montis | Oppi | de
    5   pequnia   mont. | Montis   Oppi | sacellum |
    10 claudend. | et coaequand. | et arbores | se-
        rundas | coeraverunt.

139

1005   L. Rutilius L. l. Artemido. | A. Carvilius L. l.
        Diodorus | P. Sulpicius Q. l. Philocom. | mag.
    5   conl. caprina. galla. | ex d. d. [*f*]ac. coeraver.

---

[1] For *pagus*, ' hamlet ' or district, see p. xxxviii.
[2] *faciundu*, neuter singular; see p. 188.
[3] Reading and meaning uncertain.

DEDICATORY INSCRIPTIONS

136

Public works dedicated at Rome.

(a) On the Ianiculum.   Tablet of stone.

Pupius, son of Aulus, foreman of the Janiculan district,[1] superintended, by a vote of the district, the construction[2] of a colonnade, a store-room, a kitchen, and an altar.

137

On a floor.

Foremen of the Janiculan district superintended, by a vote of the district, the construction of . . .[3] and a wall, and likewise acceptably completed them.

138

(b) On the Mons Oppius.   Tablet of stone.

Foremen[4] and mountain-priests of Mount Oppius superintended, out of the mountain-fund of Mount Oppius, the inclosure and levelling off of a chapel and the planting of trees.

139

On the Tiber-island.

Lucius Rutilius Artemidorus, freedman of Lucius, Aulus Carvilius Diodorus, freedman of Lucius, and Publius Sulpicius Philocomus, freedman of Quintus, chairmen of the guild of Goat's-flesh Gall-wine,[5] superintended the construction of this work by decree of the local Senate.[6]

---

[4] The abbreviated words are *magistri . . . flamines montani . . . (pequnia) montana . . . claudendum . . . coaequandum . . .*

[5] The meaning of this is unknown.   Perhaps the dedicators were a guild of ascetics.

[6] Presumably of Ostia.

140

1443
5
Aed[*itui a*]edis Ca[*st.* | *et*] Pol. ex d.d. | . . . M'.
Avilius ꓛ. l. | Stabilio | . . . Anicius P. l. |
. . . Furius P. l. | . . . Plaetorius D. *l.* |
. . . Volcacius C. l. | . . . mag. fac. coer.

141

2504
13
15
P. Sexteilius L. f. Pilo ; . . . (*alii ingenui quinque*) ;
P. Arelliús Q. l. (. . . *alii liberti quinque* . . .)
. . . magistreis Mirquri Apollini | Neptuni
Hercolei coeraverunt | eisde dedicaverunt
Cn. Papeirio | C. Caecilio cos.

(*additur titulus Graecus.*)

142

2239
L. Oppius L. f., Min. Staius Ov. f., L. Vicirius
[*Ti. f.*] |, A. Plotius M. l., C. Sehius C. l., C.
Claudius C. l. | magistres Mircurio et Maia
donu d.

(*sequitur titulus Graecus.*)

---

[1] If not dedicatory, the inscription records at least a sacred work superintended by a college.
[2] For ꓛ, see pp. 28-9.
[3] The Greek has οἱ Ἑρμαῖσται καὶ Ἀπολλωνιασταὶ καὶ Ποσειδωνιασταί.

DEDICATORY INSCRIPTIONS

140

Dedication [1] at Tusculum. On a stone cippus. c. 106–92 B.C.

The temple-keepers of the temple of Castor and Pollux, by decree of the local senators. . . . Manius Avillius Stabilio, freedman of a matron [2]; . . . Anicius, freedman of Publius; . . . Furius, freedman of Publius; . . . Plaetorius, freedman of Decimus: . . . Volcacius, freedman of Gaius . . . as foremen superintended the construction. . . .

141

Dedication at Delos. Tablet. Bilingual. 113 B.C.

Publius Sextilius Philo, son of Lucius; . . . (*five other freeborn men. . .*); Publius Arellius, freedman of Quintus . . . (*five other freedmen . . .*). . . Foremen [3] of Mercury, of Apollo, and of Neptune superintended this offering [4] to Hercules, and likewise performed the dedication, in the consulship of Gnaeus Papirius and Gaius Caecilius.

The Greek translation does not distinguish the freedmen from the freeborn.

142

Lucius Oppius and others.[5] On a pedestal found at Delos. c. 150 B.C. or earlier. Bilingual.

Lucius Oppius, son of Lucius, Minatus Staius son of Ovius, Lucius Vicirius son of Tiberius, Aulus Plotius, freedman of Marcus, Gaius Sehius freedman of Gaius, Gaius Claudius freedman of Gaius, foremen, bestowed this as a gift on Mercury and Maia.[6]

[Greek text follows.]

[4] ἀνέθηκαν in the Greek. *Apollini*, as the Greek text shows, should be *Apollinis.*
[5] cf. *C.I.L.*, I, 2, 2240–1.   [6] mother of Mercury.

143

(*praecedit titulus Graecus.*)

2235   M. Granius M. l. Her. | Diodotus Seius C. Cn. s. |
5   Apollonius Laelius Q. s. | Prepon Alleius
M. s. | Nicandrus Rasenni M. s. | Iovem
Leiberum statuer.

144

1446   Cisiariei Praenestinei F. P. d. d.; | mag. cur.:
(*et* p. 730)   Tosenianus L. l. Licin. | M. Pompeius
[H]eliod. | Ministrei: Nicephorus C. Tala-
5   barai s. | Nicephorus Mitrei. |

145

1447   Coques Atrienses [*F. P. d. d.*] | Magistres: Rodo
Or[*cevi* . . . . s.] | Artemo Dind. Q. s. Apoli-
[*naris* . . . . *s.*] | Protus Ae[*mili* . . . . . *s.*]

146

1450   Conlegiu. mercator. | pequarioru; mag. coir. |
[*L.*] Muuci. P. f., C. Patroni. C. l. | F. P.
d. d. l. m.

146 [3] *fortasse* Vatronius

---

[1] *i.e.* freedman, as are the three following also.
[2] *statuer.* = *statuerunt.*
[3] On this epithet *Primigenia*, see p. 60, note 5.
[4] Spanish name ? Schulze, 29.
[5] probably part of a temple.

DEDICATORY INSCRIPTIONS

143

Marcus Granius and others.   Tablet of marble, Delos, second century B.C.   *Bilingual.*

[Greek text precedes.]

Marcus Granius Heras, freedman of Marcus, Diodotus Seius slave[1] of Gaius and Gnaeus, Apollonius Laelius slave of Quintus, Prepon Alleius slave of Marcus, and Nicandrus Rasennius slave of Marcus set up[2] this image of Jupiter God of Freedom.

144

Dedications at Praeneste to Fortuna Primigenia.

(a) Gig-makers.   Now lost.

Gig-makers of Praeneste bestowed this as a gift on Fortune, Jupiter's first-born[3]; superintended by the foremen Tosenianus Licinus, freedman of Lucius, and Marcus Pompeius Heliodorus.   Assistants: Nicephorus slave of Gaius Talabaraus,[4] and Nicephorus slave of Mitreus.

145

(b) Cooks.   On a broken pedestal.

Cooks of the Hall[5] bestowed this as a gift on Fortune, Kind to her New-born.   Foremen: Rodos, slave of Orcevius. . .: Artemo, slave of Quintus Dindius; Apollinaris slave of . . .; Protus, slave of Aemilius. . . .

146

(c) Cattle-merchants.   Found at Praeneste, now lost.

The guild of cattle-merchants.   Superintended by the following foremen: Lucius Mucius, son of Publius; Gaius Patronius, freedman of Gaius.   They bestowed this as a gift on Fortune, Kind to her New-born, willingly and deservedly.

147

1445   Fortuna Primig. | L. Dcumius M. f. | don. ded.

148

977   Conlegia aerarior. | Forte Fortunae | donu dant;
        5   mag. | C. Carvilius M. l., | L. Munius L.
            l. . . . . lacus. | Minis. t. Maricarui | . . stimi
            D. Quinctius.

149

978   [F]orte For[*tunai*] | donum dant | conlegiu lanii |
        5   Piscinenses. | Magistreis | coiraverunt | A.
            Cassi. C. l., | T. Corneli. Ɔor. l.

150

980   Forte Fo[*rtunai*
         violaries   —. ΛC—.
         rosaries   co . .
         coronaries.

I suggest that the *violarii* (violet-hangers ?) and *rosarii* (rose-hangers ?) and *coronarii* (garland-hangers ?) formed guilds who supplied flowers and garlands once a year for the *dies violaris* 'day of the violet' (when graves were garlanded with violets)

---

148 [5] L. L////LACUS   [6] MARICARVIⅭ
           149 [3] LANIı

---

[1] Possibly Lacus, Etruscan Laχu; but something has been erased from the stone.

DEDICATORY INSCRIPTIONS

147

(d) Lucius Decumius. On stone. Praeneste.

To Fortune, Jupiter's first-born; bestowed as a gift by Lucius Decumius.

148

Guilds of coppersmiths. On stone. Rome. c. 106–92 B.C.

The guilds of coppersmiths bestow this as a gift on Fors Fortuna. Foremen: Gaius Carvilius freedman of Marcus; Lucius Munius . . . lacus [1] freedman of Lucius. Servants of the temple of Marica [2] (?) . . . Decimus Quinctius.

149

Guild of butchers. A small stone pedestal. Rome.

To Fors Fortuna a gift from a guild: the butchers " near the Fishpond " [3]; superintended by the foremen Aulus Cassius freedman of Gaius, Titus Cornelius, freedman of Cornelia.[4]

150

Guilds of florists. Small stone pedestal. Rome.

To Fors Fortuna from violet-dealers, rose-dealers and garland dealers.[5] Foremen superintended (?).

and the *dies rosalis*, 'day of the rose,' or of '*rosales escae*' (when tombs were garlanded with roses; the ceremony of hanging up being called *rosalia*). The evidence is all epigraphic.

---

[2] cf. goddess Marica at Minturnae (*C.I.L.*, I, 2, 2438) and at Pisaurum (374).

[3] the *piscina publica* at the Porta Capena.

[4] *Ɔor.* = *Corneliae*, whereas *Cor.* would have meant *Cornelii*; for *Ɔ* = ' of a woman,' see pp. 28–9.

[5] The rest of the inscription is incomplete; ΛC = [m]ag-[*istri*] ?; *co* = *collegium* or *collegia* or *coeraverunt* ?

151

364   (a) [*I*]ovei Iunonei Minervai | Falesce quei in
       Sardinia sunt | donum dederunt.   Magi-
       streis | L. Latrius K. f., C. Salv[*e*]na Voltai f. |
5   coiraverunt.

    (b) Gonlegium quod est aciptum aetatei aged[*ai*]
    opiparum a[*d*] veitam quolundam festosque dies,
    quei soueis aastutieis opidque Volgani
    gondecorant sai[*pi*]sume comvivia loidosque,
10   ququei huc dederu[*nt i*]nperatoribus summeis
    utei sesed lubent[*es be*]ne iovent optantis.

152

1510   [*Menti Bo*]nae.   Serveis contul. HS | . . .
    . . . ⅭⅭⅭLV mag. X | . . . dedit HS V |
    . . . us Saleivi. P. s. leiber coeravit | . . .
    Timotheus Poplili. L. M. s.; Anti [*ocus*]
    . . . us pop. s. leiber coeravit. | . . . Petro
    Furi. L. s.; Ra. Furi. L. P. C. s. | . . . Anti-
    ochus Utili. Cn. s. leiber coeravit.

151 [9] *prob.* saisume (= *suavissime*) Marx

---

[1] Sardinia was occupied in 238 B.C. and some date these
inscriptions in about 235 B.C. But it seems rather that they
belong to Gracchan times, but affect an earlier style; (b)
is apparently written in bad Saturnians. The dialect is a
careless mixture of Faliscan with Latin, and there are deliberate
archaisms.

[2] *optantis* may be accusative : ' commanders, in order that
. . . nobly in answer to their desire.' *quolundam* (line 7) =
colendam; ququei (line 10) = *coci, coqui.* The ' commanders '
are the deities Jupiter, Juno, and Minerva mentioned on the
other side of the plate. Cf. *C.I.L.*, I, 2, 2, Fasc. III, p. 831.

[3] In this inscription the slaves are newly made freedmen.
I have taken Saleivi, Poplili, Furi, Utili as nominatives
abbreviated, since the *nomen* of a freedman was regularly

DEDICATORY INSCRIPTIONS

151

Faliscan cooks in Sardinia.   Bronze plate.   Found at Falerii.
c. 125 B.C.[1]

(a) On one side.

To Jupiter Juno and Minerva a gift bestowed by
Faliscans who are in Sardinia; Lucius Latrius, son of
Kaeso, and Gaius Salvena son of Volta were the
foremen who superintended.

(b) On the other side.   Saturnians.

Cooks—a guild that is acceptable for making a
pleasant pastime, and is richly endowed for pursuit of
good living and for making holiday—who time and
again garnish banquets and games with their own
clever tricks by the aid of the Fire-God, bestowed
this on their All-Highest Commanders, desiring [2]
that they may be pleased to help them nobly.

152

Dedications to Good Spirit. (i) *Found at Cora ?   Second
century* B.C.

To Good Spirit.   Slaves [3] contributed . . .
sesterces . . . 3055 given by the ten [4] foremen . . . gave
5 sesterces . . . Saleivius, slave of Publius, superintended when free . . . Timotheus Publilius, slave
of Lucius and Marcus: Antiochus . . . public slave,
superintended when free . . . Petro Furius, slave
of Lucius; Ra . . . Furius, slave of Lucius, Publius,
and Gaius; . . . Antiochus Utilius, slave of Gnaeus,
superintended when free.

that of his patron. Cf. Oxé, *Rh. Mus.*, LIX,115. But the name
may be in the genitive—*e.g.* ' Petro, slave of Lucius Furius.'
This at any rate was a normal way of designating a slave
when the master was mentioned.

[4] as in *C.I.L.*, X, 6513.

153

1817   Nicomacus Saf. L. s. | Paapia Atiedi. L. s. | Dorot.
    5   Tettien. T. s. | Menti Bonae | basim don.
     dant.

154

1439   (*a*) Vediovei Patrei | genteiles Iuliei |
     (*b*) Vedi[*ov*]ei aara |
     (*c*) Leege Albana dicata

155

2269   L. Baebius M. f., L. Cati. M. f., | L. Taurius L. f.,
     Ser. Aefolan . . . . [.*f*]| genio opidi colum-
    5   nam | pompam ludosq. | coiraverunt.

156

Notiz. d. Sc., 1933, 115–6

De doneis | L. Babrinius L. f., K. Vibius K. f.

153 ³ TETTIENI·F·S· Brunn   154 *b* VEDI//LIU

---

[1] *i.e.*, freedman; cp. the preceding inscription.

[2] The gens Iulia had its origin at Alba before the city was destroyed according to tradition, by the Roman king Tullus Hostilius. *Ve(d)iovis* was an important Italian god of which little is known.

DEDICATORY INSCRIPTIONS

153

(ii) *An altar-stone presented by three freedmen. Alba Fucens. Second century* B.C.

Nicomachus Safinius, slave [1] of Lucius; Papia Atiedia, slave-woman of Lucius; Dorotheus Tettienius, slave of Titus bestow this foundation-stone as a gift on Good Spirit.

154

The Julii. On an altar found at Bovillae. Time of Sulla ?

(a) *On the front.* Clansmen of the Julii to Father Vedjovis.

(b) *On one side.* An altar to Vedjovis.

(c) *On the back.* Dedicated in the Alban [2] terms of ritual.

155

Dedication at New Carthage in Spain. Found at Cartagena, now lost ?

Lucius Baebius, son of Marcus; Lucius Catius, son of Marcus; Lucius Taurius, son of Lucius; and Servius Aefolanus, son of . . ., superintended the dedication of a column, a procession, and games in honour of the Guardian God of the town.

156

Dedication of c. 90 B.C., *Aquileia. Stone slab.*

From gifts. Dedicated by Lucius Babrinius, son of Lucius, and Kaeso Vibius, son of Kaeso.

For similar inscriptions of Republican times belonging to places other than Rome, cf. *C.I.L.*, I, 2, 1449, 1451, 1453, 1456 (Praeneste; 1994 (Cosa; mentions *magistrae*); 2108 (Spoletium); 753 (Mantua); 2260 (Samos); 2270 (Carthago Nova); 779 (Tolosa); cf. also 771, 2285, 2286, 2292.

For some inscriptions, concerning Rome and Hellenistic States, and which may all be dedicatory, see pp. 138–143.

TITULI HONORARII

(iii) TITULI HONORARII

1

C. I. L., I. 2.

Columna Rostrata

25   [. . . . . *Secest*]ano[*sque* . . . . op-
  sidione]d exemet; lecione[*sque Cartaciniensis omnis*
  ma]ximosque macistr[*a*]tos l[*uci palam post dies*
  n]ovem castreis exfociont; Mace[*lamque opidom*
5   *p*]ucnandod cepet. Enque eodem mac[*istratud bene*
  r]em navebos marid consol primos c[*eset copiasque*
  c]lasesque navales primos ornavet pa[*ravetque*],
  cumque eis navebos claseis Poenicas omn[*is item ma-*
  x]umas copias Cartaciniensis praesente[*d Hani-*
  baled]
10   dictatored ol[*or*]om inaltod marid pucn[*andod vicet*],
  vique nave[*is cepe*]t cum socieis septer[*esmom I*
  quin-
  queresm]osque triresmosque naveis X[*XX merset*
  XIII.
  Aur]om captom: numei ⊕⊕⊕DC . . . .

---

[1] *suppl*. Momms.
[5] *bene* Momms.   *idem* Wölfflin   [8] NAVEBŌS (*mut.*
ex V *in* O)
[10] pucn[*ad devicet*] Wölfflin

---

[1] The opinion is now generally held that the original
inscription, written under a growing Hellenistic influence, was
renewed early in the imperial period; and in the process of
renewal the restorer, in an attempt to recover the archaic
words, produced linguistic forms of which some were too old
for the date of the original monument, and some were
impossible; and some words he failed to 'archaise' at all.
But some scholars, such as Ritschl and Mommsen, believe
that the inscription was actually first composed in the imperial
period and that it is therefore not archaic at all. Cf. Ritschl,

HONORARY INSCRIPTIONS

(iii) HONORARY INSCRIPTIONS

1

C. Duilius, consul in 260 B.C. In honour of his naval victory over the Carthaginians at Mylae in that year. 'Columna Rostrata.' Marble.[1] *Found at Rome. Now in the Capitoline Museum.*

. . . and the Segestaeans [2] . . . he (Duilius) delivered from blockade; and all the Carthaginian hosts and their most mighty chief [3] after nine days fled [4] in broad daylight from their camp; and he took their town Macela by storm. And in the same command he as consul performed an exploit in ships at sea, the first Roman to do so; the first he was to equip and train crews and fleets of fighting ships; and with these ships he defeated in battle on the high seas the Punic fleets and likewise all the most mighty troops of the Carthaginians in the presence of Hannibal their commander-in-chief. And by main force he captured ships with their crews, to wit: one septireme, 30 quinqueremes and triremes: 13 he sank. Gold taken: 3,600 (*and more*) pieces.

Op., IV, 183 ff.; Wölfflin, *Sitz.-Ber. d. Münch. Akad., Phil.-Hist. Kl.*, I, 293 ff.; Wordsworth, *Fragments and Specimens*, 412–414; Tenney Frank, *Class. Phil.*, XIV, 74; Fay, *id.*, XV, 176; Giglioli *Notiz. d. Sc.*, 1930, 346, t. XV; *C.I.L.*, I, 2, p. 718. M. Niedermann, *Rev. des Ét. Lat.*, XIV, 1936, 276 ff. maintains the view that we have a genuine copy of a lost original. See also *C.I.L.*, I, 2, 2, Fasc. III, 1943, p. 831.

[2] Segesta was besieged by the Carthaginians and relieved by Duilius after the battle at Mylae.

[3] Hamilcar, who with his troops left Segesta without fighting.

[4] Reading *exfociont* (= *effugiunt*) and taking *maximōs macistratŏs* as *maximus magistratus*. Perhaps it should have been *exfodiont :* (Duilius' soldiers) 'rooted out all the Carthaginian hosts and their mightiest chiefs . . .' But this is unlikely. Anyhow *exfociont* and *macistratos* are wrong; the writer assumed that all letters *u* could once be *o*.

Arcen]tom captom, praeda: numei ⊕ . . . . |
15 *Omne*]captom   aes   ⊕⊕⊕⊕⊕⊕⊕⊕ . . . . .
⊕⊕⊕⊕⊕⊕⊕⊕⊕⊕⊕⊕⊕ . . . . Pri-
[*mos qu*]oque navaled praedad poplom [*donavet pri-*
mosque] Cartacinie[*ns*]is [*ince*]nuos d[*uxit in*
triumpod] . . . . . eis . . . . capt . . .
. . . .

2

612   Italicei | L.   Cornelium   Sc[*ip*]i[*one*]m | honoris
caussa.

3

621   L. Manlius L. f. | Acidinus   triuvir | Aquileiae
coloniae | deducundae.

4

623   M. Claudius M. f. Marcelus | consol iterum.

16-17 *triump*]oque navaled *coni.* Buecheler

---

[1] that is, apparently, obtained by sale of the booty, thinks
Mommsen. The numbers which follow in the translation
represent all the signs that have survived in the inscription,
where ⊕ = 100,000.

130

Silver taken, together with that derived from booty[1]: 100,000 . . . pieces. Total sum taken, reduced to Roman money[2] . . . 2,100,000 . . . He also was the first to bestow on the people a gift of booty from a sea-battle, and the first to lead native free-born Carthaginians in triumph. . . .

2

Lucius Cornelius Scipio (later called Asiagenus), praetor in Sicily, 193 B.C. *On a pedestal found in Sicily at Tusa (Halaesa). Now lost.*

' Lucius Cornelius Scipio.'   Statue[3] set up by men of Italy to honour him.

3

Lucius Manlius Acidinus. *On a pedestal of stone at Padua, but made in Aquileia.* 181 B.C. *or later.*

' Lucius Manlius Acidinus, son of Lucius,' member of the Board of Three[4] for conducting the colony of Aquileia.

4

Marcus Claudius Marcellus. *On the plinth of a marble capital found at Luna.* 155 B.C.

Marcus Claudius Marcellus, son of Marcus, consul for the second time.

---

[2] that is, reduced, not to bronze *as*-pieces, but to silver *sestertii*. This final total was of course much larger than that represented by such figures (2,100,000) as survive in the inscription.

[3] a verb *statuerunt* is to be understood. The *Italici* are Italian land-holders in Sicily.

[4] The other two were Scipio Nasica and C. Flaminius.

5

652

. . . .

[*descende*]re et Tauriscos C[*arnosque et Liburnos*
ex montib]us coactos m[*aritumas ad oras*
diebus te]r quineis˙qua[*ter ibei super*]avit
[*castreis*] signeis consi[*lieis prorut*]os Tuditanus.
⁵ [*Ita Roma*]e egit triumpu[*m, aedem heic*] dedit
Timavo,
[*sacra pat*]ria restitu[*it et magist*]reis †radit.

6

692

M. Minucium Q. f. Rufum | imperatorem Galleis |
Scordisteis et Besseis | [*reliqueisque Thraecibus* |
⁵ *devicteis virtutis ergo* | *dedic*]avit populus Del-
phius.

7

2662

Quod neque conatus quisquanst neque [*post
audebit*]
noscite rem, ut famaa facta feramus virei:

5 *suppl.* Buecheler; *alii alia* [*fausteis*] signeis, Tamaro
6 *suppl. ex tit. Graec.* 7¹ *vide* p. 134

---

¹ Livy, Epit., 59. On this inscription, cf. E. Reisch,
Jahreshefte des Öst. Arch. Instit., XI, 276 ff. Buecheler,
Rhein. Mus., LXIII, 321 ff. Cf. 2503, in *C.I.L.*, I, 2, p. 725;
Bruna Tamaro, in *Notiz. d. Sc.*, 1925, 11 ff. where several
restorations of gaps are given.
² a river of Istria. Cf. Tamaro, in *Notiz. d. Sc.*, 1925, pp. 3
(dedication to Temavus), 4; *C.I.L.*, I, 2, 2647, 2503.
³ Reinach, *Bull. de Corr. Hell.*, XXXIV, 305, 327; Bour-
guet, *Bull. de Corr. Hell.*, XXXV, 171. He fought as proconsul against the Thracians (Livy, *Epit.*, 65). For his
triumph over the Scordisci or Scordisti, cf. Vellei. Paterc.,
II, 8. *C.I.L.*, I, 1, p. 53. He was brother of Quintus, *C.I.L.*,
I, 2, 693, given above, p. 88. For their arbitration between
the Genuates and the Veturii, see pp. 262 ff.

HONORARY INSCRIPTIONS

5

*Gaius Sempronius Tuditanus, consul of 129 B.C.; record of a
dedication to the river-god Timavus for victory and triumph
over the Iapydes of Istria.[1] Saturnians.*

*On two fragments of a stone pedestal found near Aquileia.
129 B.C. Saturnians, variously restored by modern scholars.*

. . . and the Taurisci and the Carni and the
Liburni, whom he compelled to come down from the
mountains to the shores of the sea, Tuditanus overcame four times there in thrice five days; overthrown
were their camp and their banners and their counsels.
And so he held a triumph at Rome, and he gave a
temple to Timavus,[2] restored to him his pristine
worship, and entrusted it to overseers.

6

*Marcus Minucius Rufus, consul in 110 B.C.[3] Triumphed
over the Scordisci and Triballi in 109 B.C. On a pedestal found
at Delphi.*

' Marcus Minucius Rufus, commander, son of
Quintus '. Dedicated in statue [4] by the people of
Delphi in token of his valour when he overcame the
Galli and the Scordisti and the Bessi and the rest of
the Thracians.

7

*Exploits of Hirrus in 102 B.C. On stone found at Corinth.
Elegiacs.[5] Suppl. by Lily Taylor, West, Dow, and Fraenkel.*

Learn you of an exploit such as no man has
attempted and no man will hazard hereafter, so that
we may make wide renown of a hero's achievements.

[4] Thus the inscription (Cf. *C.I.L.*, I, 2, 726, 739) is dedicatory as well as honorary; and the dedication was to Apollo,
as is shown by a Greek inscription with the same contents
(on the same stone but referring to another dedication)
and adding Πυθίῳ ’Απόλλωνι—*C.I.L.*, I, 2, p. 522. Cf. an
inscription concerning the Lycians, pp. 140–141.

[5] S. Dow, *Harv. St. in Class. Phil.*, LX, 1951, 81 ff.

Auspicio [*Ant*]oni [*M*]arci pro consule classis
Isthmum traductast missaque per pelagus.
[5] Ipse iter eire profectus Sidam.   Classem Hirrus
Atheneis
pro praetore anni e tempore constituit.
Lucibus haec pauc[*ei*]s parvo perfecta tumultu
magna[*a qu*]om ratione atque salut[*e bona*].
Q[*u*]ei probus est, lauda[*t*], quei contra est
in[*videt illum* ;]
[10]   invid[*ea*]nt, dum q[*uod cond*]ecet id v[*enerent*].

8

825   Q. Folvius Q. f. M. [*n.*] | hance aqua[*m*] | indeixsit
apu[*t*] P. Atilium L. f. | pr. urb.

9

705   C. Iulio C. f. Caesar[*i*] | pro cos. olearei.

10

714   [*L. Licinium L. f.*] Lucullum pro q. | p[*opulus
Athe*]niensis et Italicei et | Graece[*i que*]i in
insula negotiantur.

7 [1] *post audebit* Lommatsch : *alii alia   iam* AV [· ·] *in
fine versus latere putat* S. Dow.   [7] *pauceis* Dow   PAVO̧ S.
[8] *magnaa quom* Fraenkel   *magna ac quom* Taylor, West
salut[e bona] Fraenkel   s. *bonaa mavult* Dow   s. *simul*
Taylor, West   [9] *in[videt actum* Getty   [10] *quod
condecet . . . venerent* Fraenkel   *quos condecet . . . videant*
Taylor, West

---

[1] Undoubtedly Marcus Antonius, who was sent against the
pirates of Cilicia in 102 B.C.   When the memory of Marc Antony
was condemned by Augustus after the Battle of Actium, the
names of his ancestors also were erased, as in this inscription,
from public monuments.   [2] In Pamphylia in Asia Minor.
[3] or, if we supply *illei*, ' has envy against him ' ?
[4] *pr. urb.* = *praetorem urbanum.*   Some legal matter is
alluded to here.   Cf. Mommsen, on *C.I.L.*, X, 8236.

Under the command of Marcus [1] Antonius, proconsul, a fleet was carried over the Isthmus and sent
across the sea. Marcus himself set out upon his
voyage to Sida.[2] Hirrus, as propraetor, stationed his
fleet at Athens because of the season of the year.
All this was accomplished in a few days with little
turmoil; sound strategy and safe deliverance
attended it. He who is upright has praise for him,
and he who is otherwise, looks askance at him.[3] Let
men envy so long as they have reverence for what is
seemly.

8

*Quintus Fulvius. On a stone pedestal. Near Caiazzo. 2nd
century* B.C.

Quintus Fulvius, son of Quintus, grandson of
Marcus, made declaration on these water-works in
the presence of Publius Atilius, praetor of the city,[4]
son of Lucius.

9

Gaius Julius Caesar (father of the dictator). 98–90 B.C.
On a pedestal found at Delos.

To [5] ' Gaius Julius Caesar, proconsul, son of Gaius,'
from the oil-merchants.

10

Lucullus, quaestor in Asia, 88 (?87)–80 B.C. *On two fragments
of a pedestal found at Delos.*

' Lucius Licinius Lucullus proquaestor, son of
Lucius.' Statue [6] set up by the Athenian people, by
men from Italy, and by Greeks, who are in business
in the island.

[5] Statues of this type are presented to a mortal, not to a
god. They are not therefore dedicated.
[6] the word *statuerunt* is to be understood.

11

712   (i) L. Cornelius L. f. Sulla pro cos. | de pequnia quam conlegia | incommune conlatam.

12

720   (ii) L. Cornelio L. [*f.*] | Sullae Feleici | impera- tori | publice.

13

721   (iii) L. Cornelio L. f. | Sullae Felici | dictatori | vicus Laci Fund.

14

722   (iv) L. Cornelio L. f. | Sullae Feleici | dictatori | leiberteini.

15

724   (v) L. Cornelio L. f. Sul[*lae*] | Felici dictato[*ri*] | publice statuta.

16

2510   A. POMPEIO A. F. | CLU. Q. PATRONO | municipi Interamnat. | Nahartis quod eius |
5   opera universum | municipium ex summis |

---

[1] cf. *C.I.L.*, I, 2, 2507, 2508.
[2] the word *dederunt* is to be understood.
[3] *sc.* of Suessa, which had submitted to Sulla at the beginning of the Civil War.
[4] This Lake appears to have been called Lacus Fundani (not Lacus Fundanius or Fundanus), possibly Herculis Fundani. Cf. *C.I.L.*, VI, 9854.
[5] These were the 'Cornelii,' as Sulla called them. They were a picked body of 10,000 slaves freed and enfranchised by him.

11

Lucius Cornelius Sulla.[1]   (i) *On the pedestal of a statue found at Delos.*   87 B.C.

' Lucius Cornelius Sulla, son of Lucius, proconsul.' Out of the money which the companies contributed and presented [2] by general subscription.

12

(ii) *On a pedestal found at Suessa.*   83 B.C.

To ' Lucius Cornelius Sulla, The Blest, son of Lucius, commander-in-chief,' by public gift.[3]

13

(iii) *On a pedestal found at Rome.*   82–79 B.C.

To ' Lucius Cornelius Sulla The Blest, dictator, son of Lucius,' from the quarter of the Reservoir of [4] Fundanius.

14

(iv) *On a large pedestal.*   82–79 B.C.

To ' Lucius Cornelius Sulla the Blest, dictator, son of Lucius,' from his freedmen.[5]

15

(v) *On a pedestal found at Alba.*   82–79 B.C.

To ' Lucius Cornelius Sulla the Blest, dictator, son of Lucius,' a statue set up by public gift.

16

Aulus Pompeius.   Pedestal of marble.   Interamna ? 82 [6] B.C.

To ' Aulus Pompeius, son of Aulus,' of the Clustumine tribe, quaestor, protector of the borough of Interamna-on-Nar, because the whole borough was,

[6] Cichorius, *Röm. Stud.*, 185 ff.

10   pereiculeis et diffi|cultatibus expeditum | et
conservatum est. Ex | testamento L. Licini
T. f. | statua statuta est.

17

Atti della Pont. Acc. Rom. di Arch. Rendiconti, XII, 1936. *G. Marchetti-Longi*, pp. 278–9.

[*Cn.*] Pompeio | Magno | [*i*]mperatori | [*I*]talicei
5   qui | Agrigenti | negot[*iantur*].

18

C. I. L., X.

1797   L. Calpurnio L. f.,   C. Calpurnio L. f.
Capitolino, ...
mercatores qui Alexandr. Asiai Syriai negotian-
tu[*r*].

19

C. I. L., I, 2.

2513   Q. Numerio Q. f. | Rufo q. | stipendiariei | pago-
5   rum Muxsi | Gususi Zeugei.

20

730   (i) [*Rex Metradates Pilopator et Pil*]adelpus regus
Metradati f. | [*populum Romanum amicitiai e*]t
societatis ergo quas iam | [*inter ipsum et
Romanos optin*]et. Legati coiraverunt | [*Ne-
manes Nemanei f. et Ma*]hes Mahei f. |

---

[1] Pompey defeated supporters of Marius in Sicily in 81 B.C.; the inscription supports Cicero's claim (*de imp. Cn. Pomp.*, 21, 61) that Pompey was very moderate in dealing with the Greek cities.

[2] For similar records, cf. *C.I.L.*, I, 2, 831, 845.

[3] not ' tribute-payers ' ?

[4] probably a son or brother of the great Mithridates VI.

[5] Here and in the other inscriptions of this group a verb indicating presentation or rather setting up (*statuere*) is to be understood.

through his services, released and preserved from the greatest dangers and difficulties.

This statue was set up by the last will and testament of Lucius Licinius son of Titus.

17

Pompey the Great.   About 80 B.C. ? [1]

To ' Gnaeus Pompeius the Great, General,' from men of Italy who are in business at Agrigentum.

18

L. Calpurnius and Gaius Calpurnius.   Found at Puteoli.

To ' Lucius Calpurnius Capitolinus, son of Lucius,' and ' Gaius Calpurnius . . . son of Lucius,' from the merchants who are in business at Alexandria and in Asia and Syria.[2]

19

Quintus Numerius.   Found at Utica.

To ' Quintus Numerius Rufus son of Quintus, quaestor,' from the mercenaries [3] of the hamlets Muxum, Gususum, and Zeugeum. (?).

Inscriptions illustrating relations between the Romans and the Hellenistic states during and after the end of the First Mithridatic War of 88–84 B.C.   Mostly bilingual inscriptions set up when ambassadors from the east visited Rome.

20

(a) Mithridates.[4]   On rectangular stone.   Found at Rome. c. 83–80 B.C.   Bilingual.

(i) From King Mithridates Philopator and Philadelphus, son of King Mithridates ; a statue ' The Roman People,' [5] on account of the friendship and alliance which now holds good between himself and the Roman People.   Administered by the ambassadors Naemanes son of Naemanes, and Mahes son of Mahes.

⁵ (ii) [Βασιλεὺς Μιθραδάτης Φιλ]οπάτωρ καὶ Φιλάδελ-
φος | [τοῦ βασιλέως Μιθραδάτ]ου τὸν δῆμον τὸν |
[τῶν Ῥωμαίων φίλον καὶ] σύμμαχον αὐτοῦ |
[εὐνοίας καὶ εὐεργεσίας] ἕνεκεν τῆς εἰς αὐτόν, |
[πρεσβευσάντων Ναιμ]άνους τοῦ Ναιμάνους |
[Μάου τοῦ Μάου]. |

¹⁰ (iii) Ὁ δ[ῆμος] ὁ Ταβηνῶν | φίλ[ος] καὶ σύμμαχος
τοῦ . . . . | Ῥω[μαί]ων·

21

725
(i) [*Ab co*]muni restitutei in maiorum leibert[*atem* |
Lucei] Roma Iovei Capitolino et poplo
Romano v[*irtutis*] | benivolentiae benificique
causa erga Lucios ab comun[*i*]. |

(ii) Λυκίων τὸ κοινὸν κομισάμενον τὴν πάτριον δημο- |
⁵ κρατίαν τὴν Ῥώμην Διὶ Καπετωλίωι καὶ τῶι
δήμωι τῶ[ι] | Ῥωμαίων ἀρετῆς ἕνεκεν καὶ εὐνοίας
καὶ εὐεργεσίας | τῆς εἰς τὸ κοινὸν τὸ Λυκίων.

22

726
[*Populum R*]omanum cognatum amicum sociu[*m*] |
[*honoris causa et benivolent*]iaei beneficique
erga Lucios in comu[*ne*].

---

¹ in Caria.

(ii) From King Mithridates Philopator and Phila-delphus, son of King Mithridates; a statue 'The Roman People' his friend and ally; on account of benevolence and beneficence towards him, the ambassadors being Naemanes son of Naemanes, and Mahes son of Mahes.

(iii) The common people of Tabae.[1]

Friend and ally of the Roman . . .

21

(b) The Lycians.[2]   On rectangular stones.   Found at Rome. The first is now lost.

I. *(Bilingual).* (i) From the Lycian people, as a commune, restored to the freedom of their ancestors, a statue 'Rome' to Jupiter Capitolinus and the Roman people, because of their virtue and benevolence and beneficence towards the commune of the Lycians.

(ii) From the commune of the Lycians, having received back their ancestral democracy, a statue 'Rome' to Zeus of the Capitol and the populace of the Romans because of their virtue and benevolence and beneficence towards the commune of the Lycians.

22

II. The Roman people, their kinsman, friend and ally, for to honour the same, on account of good will and kind services towards the Lycians and their commune.[3]

---

[2] These were granted freedom from taxation by Sulla in 84 for resisting Mithradates. This inscription is really dedicatory, but it comes naturally here. Perhaps the other statues alluded to in these inscriptions are likewise dedicated to a god; but no mention is made of the god.

[3] *in commune* here does not mean 'for a common object.'

23

728   (i) Populus Laodicensis af Lyco | populum Roma-
num quei sibei | salutei fuit, benefici ergo,
quae sibei | benigne fecit.|

(ii) Ὁ δῆμος Λαοδικέων τῶν πρὸς | τῶι Λύκωι τὸν
δῆμον τὸν | Ῥωμαίων γεγονότα ἑ[αυτῶι] | σωτῆρα
καὶ εὐεργέτην | ἀρετῆς ἕνεκεν καὶ εὐνοί[ας] | τῆς
εἰς ἑαυτόν.

24

743   (i) (a) C. Salluio C. f. Nasoni leg. propr. |

(b) Mysei Ab[b]aitae et Epict[ete]s | quod eos
bello Mithrida[ti]s | conservavit, virtutis ergo.

5 (ii) Γ[αί]ῳ Σαλλουίῳ Γαίου υἱῷ Νάσωνι | πρεσβευτῇ
καὶ ἀντιστρατήγῳ Μυσοὶ | Ἀββαειται καὶ
Ἐπικτητεῖς ὅτι αὐτοὺς | ἐν τῷ πολέμῳ τῷ
Μιθριδάτους | διετήρησεν, ἀνδρήας ἕνεκεν.

25

727   Populus Ephesiu[s *populum Romanum*] | salutis
ergo quod o[*ptinuit maiorum*] | souom leiber-
tatem i . . . . . | Legatei Heraclitus Hi . . . . .
5   [*filius,*] | Hermocrates Dem[*etri* . . . . . *filius*].

---

[1] They played a dubious part in the first Mithridatic War,
but were able to obtain good will from the Romans.

[2] Here the Greek gives more than the Latin.

[3] (a) is inscribed on the abacus of the column on which
(b) is inscribed. For these Mysians see Strabo, 625.

HONORARY INSCRIPTIONS

23

(c) The Laodiceans.[1] *Tablet of stone found at Rome.*
Bilingual.

(i) From the people of Laodicea near the river
Lycos; a statue ' The Roman People,' which people
was their salvation, because of the kind deeds which
it did kindly unto them.

(ii)[2] From the populace of Laodicea near the
Lycos; a statue ' The populace of the Romans '
which have become its saviour and benefactor because
of their virtue and good will towards it.

24

(d) Mysians.   Marble pillar found at Nemi.   Bilingual.

(i) (a)[3] To Gaius Salluvius Naso, son of Gaius,
ambassador and propraetor (b) from Abbaitae Mysians
and Mysians of the Epictetos, because he preserved
them in the war with Mithridates.   For valour.

(ii) To Gaius Salluvius Naso, son of Gaius, ambassador and propraetor, from Abbaitae Mysians
and Mysians of the Epictetos, because he watched
over them well in the war with Mithridates.   For
valour.

25

(e) Ephesus.[4] *Tablet of stone.   Found at Rome.*

From the people of Ephesus; a statue ' The people
of Rome ' because of their salvation in that they
maintained the freedom[5] of their ancestors . . .
Ambassadors: Heracleitus, son of . . . Hermo-
crates, son of Demetrius.

[4] Sided with Rome from 86 onwards.
[5] that is, their democratic constitution which under
Mithridates had been in abeyance.

(iv) TITULI OPERUM PUBLICORUM

1

22
<pre>
        XI
   C. Cinci   Q . . . .
   aidile   P. C . . . .
   pleib.   probavero
</pre>

Cf. *C.I.L.*, I, 2, 21 (*c.* 260 B.C.): P. Claudio A[*p.f.*]|C. Fourio [. . .] aidiles Ⅷ (on side of pillar at the top) Ⅹ (near foot of pillar).

2

24
Aid. cur. Ve[*l*]|itern[*u*]s lo[*c*]|avit eisde|m aid. pl. prob.

3

2661
[*P*]e. Remo Pe. f., T. Carpniu. . . . . o, Tit. Titu[*le*]no V. | f. macistres faciedo corave[*ru*]|nt; heice lemena locata p. MC | cos. C. Casio P. Licnio.

4

635
Ser. Folvius Q. f. Flaccus cos. muru. locavit | de manubies.

<pre>
              VE/
2 ¹⁻² ITERNS   Veliternus Buecheler
3 ¹ EREMO   ³ ⊂OCATA. T. ⊓C.
</pre>

---

[1] 'to approve' would be a convenient translation of '*probare*'; but this verb, as often used in inscriptions, takes after it an unexpressed dative case, and means 'to make good to the satisfaction of' some higher authority, by inspection of the work and by rendering accounts.

[2] an unusual title for an *aedilis* in a local Italian town.

INSCRIPTIONS ON PUBLIC WORKS

(iv) INSCRIPTIONS ON AND CONCERNING PUBLIC WORKS

1

Milestone? on the Ostian Road.   Column of stone.   c. 300 B.C.

11 Gaius Cincius, aedile of the plebs.   Acceptably completed [1] by Quintus . . ., and Publius Cornelius.

2

Contract by an aedile.   Origin unknown.   3rd century B.C.

A curule [2] aedile of Velitrae let out by contract and likewise, as aedile of the plebs, acceptably completed the work.

3

Public works at a place unknown, 171 B.C.   Now lost.

Petro Remos, son of Petro, Titus Carpinius . . ., Titus Titulenos son of Vibius, overseers, superintended the construction of this work.   Here were laid thresholds [3] . . . in the consulship of Gaius Cassius and Publius Licinius.

4

Wall built by Servius Fulvius, consul, 135 B.C.   On stone found at S. Angelo in a wall (probably dedicatory).

Servius Fulvius Flaccus, consul, son of Quintus, let out the making of this wall by contract out of spoils- [4] money.

---

[3] The signs which follow are obscure; they may mean *pedes MC*—eleven hundred feet of thresholds and sills; perhaps *locata* means ' were let out by contract,' and what follows might indicate the sum of money involved (cf. pp. 180–183, *opera locata*).   Anyhow what does T after *locata* (see critical note) really represent ?

[4] He subdued the Vardaei in Illyria.

5

694　　[*Ser. Sulpic*]ius Ser. f. Galba cos. pavimentum
　　　　　[*faciundum locavi*]t eisdemque probavit.

6

1529　　L. Betilienus L. f. Vaarus | haec quae infera
　　　　　scripta | sont de senatu sententia | facienda
　　5　　coiravit : semitas | in oppido omnis, porticum
　　　　　qua | in arcem eitur, campum ubei | ludunt,
　　　　　horologium, macelum, | basilicam calecan-
　　　　　dam, seedes, | [*l*]acum balinearium ; lacum
　　10　　ad | [*p*]ortam, aquam in opidum adqu.|
　　　　　arduom pedes CCCXL fornicesq. | fecit, fist-
　　　　　ulas soledas fecit. | Ob hasce res censorem
　　　　　fecere bis, | senatus filio stipendia mereta |
　　15　　ese iousit, populusque statuam | donavit
　　　　　Censorino.

6 10 adque Ritschl　　　　**ADOV**　　　a(d)dou(cendam)
Wagenvoort

---

[1] Note again that *facere* in inscriptions sometimes means not
' to construct ' but to ' repair ' or ' add to,' as it does in the
Lex parieti faciendo, pp. 274 ff.
[2] The inscription is sometimes regarded as honorary
(pp. 128 ff.). On *facere*, see preceding note.
[3] the paths at the sides of the streets.
[4] or, water-clock.
[5] covering with a white stucco. *Basilicae* were halls,
covered but often unwalled, having two rows of columns on
two sides. They were used for legal, business, and other
meetings.
[6] or simply a ' bathing-tank ' as part of the public baths.

INSCRIPTIONS ON PUBLIC WORKS

5

Servius Sulpicius, consul. On a floor of tessellated work,
144 *or* 108 B.C.

Servius Sulpicius Galba, consul, son of Servius, let
out the making [1] of a hard floor by contract and likewise acceptably completed it.

6

Lucius Betilienus Varus and his public gifts. [2] *At Aletrium.*
c. 135–90 B.C.

Lucius Betilienus Varus, son of Lucius, by a vote of
the Senate superintended the construction of the
works which are recorded below: all the street-paths [3]
in the town; the colonnade along which people walk
to the stronghold; a playing-field; a sun-dial; [4] a
meat-market; the liming [5] of the town-hall; seats;
a bathing-pool [6]; he constructed a reservoir by the
gate; an aqueduct about 340 feet long leading into the
city and to the height [7]; also the arches and good
sound water-pipes. In reward for these works the
Senate and people made him censor twice; the
Senate ordered that his son be exempt from military
service [8]; and the people bestowed the gift of a
statue on him over the title of Censorinus. [9]

---

[7] *i.e.* the hill of the citadel or stronghold (*arx*). On the
reading *adou(?)* see A. W. van Buren, *Atti della Pontificia
Acc. Rom. di Arch., Rendiconti*, IX, 1933, 1934.

[8] The phrase means literally 'that fees shall have been
earned,' that is 'that fees earned shall be confirmed.' Here
the sense is 'that services shall be held as performed without
the performance.' *Stipendia merere* is a mere formula with a
special sense of 'perform military service.'

[9] Because he had been censor (twice). *Populus* here and
senatus above are those of Aletrium, not of Rome.

7

1471   M. Saufeius M. f. Rutilus | C. Saufeius C. f.
      Flacus q. | culinam f. d. s. s. c. eisdem |
  5 q. locum emerunt de | L. Tondeio L. f.
      publicum. | Est longu p. CXLVIIIS, | latum
      af muro ad | L. Tondei vorsu p. XVI.

8

1469   C. Saufeius C. f. | M. Saufeius L. f. | Pontanes |
      aid. ex s. c.

9

1903   Q. C. Poppaeei Q. f. patron. | municipi et coloniai |
      municipibus coloneis incoleis | hospitibus ad-
  5 ventoribus | lavationem in perpetuom de |
      sua pecunia dant.

10

617   (i) M. Aemilius M. f. M. n.
        Lepidus cos.

          CCLXIIX   XV

---

[1] of Praeneste; so too the Senate is that of Praeneste.

[2] perhaps for the preparation of sacrificial banquets or feasts; there are other inscriptions in which *culinae* are associated with temples or altars.

[3] But *eisdem | q.* may represent *eisdemque* ' and the same,' not *eisdem quaestores*.

[4] Cf. Henzen, *Bull. dell' Instit.*, 1851, p. 85, 173.

[5] perhaps ' official guests.' See Introduction, p. xl.

[6] Cf. *C.I.L.*, I, 2, 619, 620, two more. Aemilius built the Aemilian Way from Ariminum to Placentia by way of Bononia.

[7] 268 (thousand paces) from Rome, 15 from Bononia, probably at a place whither the stone was removed at a later date, on which the old inscription was recut.

INSCRIPTIONS ON PUBLIC WORKS

7

Public works of Marcus Saufeius and Gaius Saufeius at Praeneste. Found at Praeneste. First century B.C.

Marcus Saufeius Rutilus son of Marcus and Gaius Saufeius Flaccus son of Gaius, quaestors,[1] by a vote of the Senate, superintended the building of a kitchen.[2] The same quaestors[3] bought for public state-property a site from Lucius Tondeius, son of Lucius. It is a structure 148 ft. and ½ long and 16 ft. broad from the wall in the direction of the house of Lucius Tondeius.

8

A work at Praeneste.

Gaius Saufeius Pontanus, son of Gaius, and Marcus Saufeius Pontanus, son of Lucius, aediles, by a decree of the Senate.

9

A bathing-room at Interamna. Two stones[4] with the same inscription.

Quintus Poppaeus and Gaius Poppaeus, sons of Quintus protector of the borough and settlement, give out of their own money a permanent bathing-room to their townsmen, settlers, other residents, strangers,[5] and visitors.

10

Milestones of the Via Aemilia set up in the consulship of Aemilius Lepidus[6] 187 B.C.

(i) *Found at S. Pietro, not far from Bologna.*

Marcus Aemilius Lepidus, consul, son of Marcus, grandson of Marcus.

      (*a*)[7] 268
      (*b*) (*on the side*) 15

618   (ii) M. Aemilius M. f. M. n.
        Lepid. cos.

IIII   XXI
        CCXXCVI

11

638   [*P. Popilius C. f. cos.*] | Viam fecei ab Regio ad
        Capuam et | in ea via ponteis omneis mili-
        arios | tabelariosque poseivei. Hince sunt |
        Nouceriam meilia .LI Capuam XXCIIII |
  5   Muranum .LXXIIII Cosentiam CXXIII |
        Valentiam C.LXXX ad fretum ad | Statuam
        CCXXXI Regium CCXXXVII. Suma af
        Capua Regium meilia CCCXXI. | Et eidem
  10   praetor in | Sicilia fugiteivos Italicorum | con-
        quaeisivei redideique | homines ÐCCCCXVII
        eidemque | primus fecei ut de agro poplico |
  15   aratoribus cederent paastores ; | forum aedis-
        que poplicas heic fecei.

---

¹ 4 from Bononia, 21 from Mutina, and 286 from Rome.
For a milestone for the Via Postumia, 148 B.C., see *C.I.L.*,
I, 2, 624.

² But the missing name may be that of T. Annius Rufus,
acting perhaps as propraetor in 131 B.C.   T. P. Wiseman, in
Papers of the British School at Rome, XIX, 1964, 21 ff.

³ a continuation of the *Via Appia*.

⁴ Hirschfeld (*Kleine Schriften*, 708–9), taking *tabellarii* as an
epithet of *lapides*, suggested that it means a special kind of
milestone, to which was fastened a tablet containing an
inscription.   But I think Cary (*Class. Rev.*, L, 166–7) is right
in taking *tabellarii* as an epithet of *stipites* ' posts ' with wooden
boards or arms fixed to them ; the boards would give the
directions and probably the distances, as do our sign-posts
or ' finger-posts.'   This interpretation is as likely as Hirschfeld's, certainly likelier than the belief that *tabellarii* means
letter-carriers.

INSCRIPTIONS ON PUBLIC WORKS

(ii) *Found near Bologna.*

Marcus Aemilius Lepidus, consul, son of Marcus, grandson of Marcus.

4[1]   21

286

11

Milestone recording the public services probably[2] of Publius Popillius Laenas, consul in 132 B.C. Near Forum Popillii (Polla) in Lucania. 132 B.C.

Publius Popillius, consul, son of Gaius. I made the road[3] from Regium to Capua and on that road placed all the bridges, milestones, and sign-posts.[4] From here there are 51 miles to Nuceria; 84 to Capua[5]; 74 to Muranum; 123 to Consentia; 180 to Valentia; 231 to the strait at the Statue;[6] 237 to Regium. Total from Capua to Regium 321. I also as praetor[7] in Sicily sought out the runaways belonging to men from Italy[8] and gave up 917 persons. Again, I was the first to cause cattle-breeders[9] to retire from public state-land in favour of plowmen. Here I put up a Market[10] and public buildings.

[5] These places lie in one direction, the following in another.

[6] a place called *Columna Regina* whence people usually crossed, as they do now, to Sicily by the narrowest part of the straits of Messina. It was 6 miles north of Regium.

[7] 135 B.C.; he was sent to quell the brigand slaves of rich landowners, and to capture runaways. There was a slave-rising in 135.

[8] I think this means living not in Italy but in Sicily, being Roman equites or possessing *ius Latinum*, cf. inscriptions on pp. 134–5, 138–9.

[9] rich cattle-ranchers in Italy (not Sicily) against whom, among other holders of land beyond the proper limit, Tiberius Gracchus in 133 passed his agrarian law in order to restore the small yeomen to the land.

[10] *Forum Popillii*; *forum*, a place of business—see p.xxxvii.

12

647   (i) M'. Aquillius M'. f. | cos. | CXXXI | [Μάνι]ος
['Α]κύλλ[ι]ος Μανίου | ὕπατος ῾Ρωμαίων | ρλα

13

657   T. Quinctius T. f. | Flamininus | cos. | Pisas

14

661   L. Caecili. Q. f. | Metel. cos. | CXIX | Roma

15

840   M' Sergi. M'.[*f.*]| procos. | XXI

16

402   (i) . . . . (*III versus*) | Q. Ravel[i]o . . . . . |
       P. Cominio P. f. | L. Malio C. f. | quaistores |
    5   senatu d. | consuluere. | Iei . . . censuere |
       aut sacrom | aut poublicom | ese.

16 [6] iei[*d.*] Cimaglia   iei censuere Matth. Aegyptius
lelcensuere *Venusin. cd. Saraceni* 2   et censuere Fabretti
ieis censuere *coni.* Momms.   IEI ⊗ CENSVERE

---

[1] Others of a similar type : *C.I.L.*, I, 2, 647–651.

[2] miles from Ephesus.

[3] Rarely does a Roman milestone give the miles *to* a place.
At one time it was claimed that figures could be read on the
stone after *Pisas*. But fresh examination seems to show that
there were never any figures at all after *Pisas*.

[4] The first three lines are illegible. Cf. also *C.I.L.*, I, 2,
403.

[5] This is uncertain, but something like *senatuom decuriatom*
or *decuriatim* or *decurionom* is probable. The *quaestors* are
here local officials.

152

INSCRIPTIONS ON PUBLIC WORKS

12

Milestone set up by Manius Aquillius.[1] *Found near Dikeli, Pergamum's port.* 129 B.C.

Manius Aquillius, consul, son of Manius   131 [2]

So also the Greek which adds (consul) *of the Romans.*

13

Milestone of Quinctius Flamininus, 123 B.C. (150 B.C.?). *Found near Florence.*

Titus Quinctius Flamininus, consul, son of Titus To [3] Pisae.

14

Milestone of Caecilius Metellus, 117 B.C. *Found in Picenum.*

Lucius Caecilius Metellus, consul, son of Quintus 119 from Rome.

15

Milestone of Sergius in Spain. Found near Barcelona, now lost.

Manius Sergius, proconsul, son of Manius   21

Boundary Stones of various kinds.

16

(i) *Found* [4] *at Venusia, now lost.* c. 225 B.C. *Inscribed with a decree of the local Senate.*

The quaestors Quintus Ravellius, son of . . .; Publius Cominius son of Publius; Lucius Mallius son of Gaius, consulted the local [5] Senate. The Senators resolved that the place should be either sacred or else public state-property.[6]

[6] public meant much the same as sacred, since it meant belonging to the government.

17

366

(ii) Honce loucom | nequs violatod | neque ex-
5   vehito neque | exferto quod louci | siet neque
cedito | nesei quo die res deina | anua fiet;
eod die | quod rei dinai cau(s)a | [*f*]iat, sine
10   dolo cedre [*l*]icetod.   Seiquis | violasit,
Iove bovid | piaclum datod; | seiquis scies |
violasit dolo malo, | Iovei bovid piaclum |
15   datod et a. CCC | moltai suntod; | eius
piacli | moltaique dicator[*ei*] exactio est[*od*].

18

401

(iii) In hoce loucarid stircus | ne [*qu*]is fundatid neve
cadaver | proiecitad neve parentatid. | Sei
5   quis arvorsu hac faxit [*in*] ium | quis volet pro

17 *Item novum exemplar exceptis his*:   ² nequis
violatod   ⁵ caiditod   ⁹ sin [*do*]lo malo cedr[*e*]
[*li*]ceto sequis   ¹⁰ advorsum ead violasit iovei   ¹¹ dato
¹⁶⁻¹⁷ eius piacli e[*xactio dicatori esto*]

---

¹ *dicator*, ' dedicator ' (from *dicare*, ' dedicate '). Thus the
original consecrator was the custodian? And his successors
kept the same title? See *C.I.L.*, I, 2, 2, Fasc. III, 1943, p.
832, for further information about this inscription. There is
no need to read *dictator*, which was in some Italian towns the
title of the regular chief magistrate.

² Cf. a resolution of the senate about a burial-ground,
pp. 252–5.

³ As is indicated by another inscription (*C.I.L.*, I, 2, 1730),
loucarid is ablative of a neuter noun *loucar = lucar = lucus*,
not apparently of the adjective *lucaris* (sc. *ager*). However,
in extant literary authors *lucar* as a noun is always ' forest-
tax.'

INSCRIPTIONS ON PUBLIC WORKS

17

(ii) *Spoletium. Protection of a grove. Found in 1876. A duplicate has recently been found with certain differences : Notiz. d. Sc., XV, 1937, 28–31 (S. Pietrangeli). The inscriptions are probably to be dated not long after 241 B.C., when Spoletium became a Latin colony. Records a ' Lex dicta '.*

Let no one damage this grove. No one must cart or carry away anything that belongs to the grove, or cut wood in it, except on the day when holy worship takes place every year. On that day, person may without offence cut wood as required for the procedure of worship. If any one does damage, he shall make sin-offering to Jupiter with an ox; if any one does damage knowingly and with wrongful intent, he shall make sin-offering to Jupiter with an ox, and moreover let there be a fine of 300 *as*-pieces. The duty of exacting the said sin-offering and fine shall rest with the dedicator.[1]

18

(iii) *Luceria in Apulia. Protection of a grove.*[2] *Now lost. The text depends on a copy. I. B. d'Amelis, ' Storia della città di Lucera,' 1861, ad. fin., n. 80; cf. Mommsen, ' Eph. Epigr.,' II, 1874, 205. Records a ' Lex dicta'.*

In this grove [3] let no one tip dung or cast a dead body or perform sacrifices for dead relations.[4] If anyone shall have acted contrary to this, let there be, as [5] for a judgment rendered, laying of hands upon him,[6]

[4] *fundatid* (for *funditod*), *proiecitad* (for *proiecitod* = *proicito*) and *parentatid* (for *parentatod*) are probably dialectical contaminations unless they are miswritten. Different views : *C.I.L.*, I, 2, p. 720.

[5] as though a claim had been adjudged against him in a law-suit.

[6] that is, on his property rather than his person; cf. p. 254, and *Remains*, III, pp. 425, 432, 437, 506.

    ioudicatod n. [L] | manum iniect[i]o estod.
Seive | mac[i]steratus volet moltare, [li]cetod.

19

400   (iv) R. Vedo . . . . . | V. Autrodiu C. | S. Racectiu
       ⁵   S. | S. Teditiu S. | statuendos | locaverunt.

20

2516   (v) (a) C. Caninius C. f. | pr. urb. | de sen. sent. |
          poplic. ioudic. |

          (b) [P]rivatum | ad Tiberim | usque ad | aquam.

21

C. I. L., XIV.

2772   (vi) Af Specu|lu Diane | usq. f. Cle|mentia- |
       ⁵   no P. Pro|clini pass. | p.m. ∞

18 ⁵ NI | MANVM

---

    ¹ sesterces. The reading is uncertain; N = *nummum*; I should probably be Ⅼ or Ɫ = L = 50.

    ² probably a greater fine = *irrogare multam*; see the *Lex Bantina*, pp. 298–9.

    ³ or possibly Rufus or Rullus, but these were not normally *praenomina*.

    ⁴ *filius* is to be understood ?. See next note.

    ⁵ Perhaps we should translate 'Spurius Racectius, illegitimate.' If not, we have an unusual omission of *filius*.

to an amount of 50 pieces,[1] on the part of any one who shall so desire. Or if a magistrate shall see fit to inflict a fine,[2] he shall be allowed to do so.

19

(iv) *On the right bank of the river Volturnus, in Falernian territory. c. 150–100* B.C. *?*

Retus[3] Vedus . . . Vibius Autrodius, son[4] of Gaius, Spurius Racectius, son of Spurius,[5] and Spurius Teditius, son of Spurius contracted for the setting up of these boundary-stones.

20

(v) *At Ostia ; early[6] in the second century.*

(a) *Repeated on three other sides.*

Gaius Caninius, praetor of the city, son of Gaius, by a vote of the senate adjuged this land to be public state property.

(b) *On a fifth side:*

Private land up to the Tiber as far as the water's edge.

21

(vi) *In Latium. Tablet of marble. Public notice.*

From Diana's Mirror,[7] as far as the Clementian estate, which belongs to Publius Proclinius, 1000 paces more or less.

[6] There was a C. Caninius Rebilus praetor in Sicily in 171 B.C.
[7] Lacus Nemorensis. The inscription may not be archaic.

22

C. I. L., I, 2.

633 (vii) [*L. Caeicili*]us Q. f. pro cos. | terminos finisque
ex | senati consulto statui | iousit inter
Atestinos | et Patavinos.

23

636 (viii) Sex. Atilius M. f. Saranus pro cos. | ex
senati consulto | inter Atestinos et Veice-
tinos | finis terminosque statui iusit.

———— • ————

BOUNDARY-STONES OF THE GRACCHAN PERIOD.

LAND-SURVEYING : ' AGRIMETATIO,' OR ' LIMITATIO,'
OR ' CENTURIATIO.'

When land was distributed by the Roman government to
citizens, it was normally marked off into large blocks (*centuriae*) by a regular survey according to a fixed method called
centuriatio or *limitatio* (' balking,' from *limes* ' balk,' ' rough
road,' ' cross-path,' for which see below, p. 160) or ' *agrimetatio* ' land measuring; wherein straight lines only, and,
with the exception of *subseciva* or ' oddments ' (for which, see
p. 163), right angles only were employed, so that the blocks
were square, less often oblong.[4] Such land was usually called
ager limitatus ' balked land.' This proper survey was quite
different from rough-and-ready fixing or alteration of boun-
dary-lines on areas of land which, not being subject to any
regular survey by the state, was held by owners in irregularly
shaped, unmeasured plots bounded where possible by natural
features such as streams. Such land was called *ager arcifinius* ' bow-bounded land,' ' land with wavy boundaries.'

———————

[1] The inscription is repeated on the same stone and also on
two others—*C.I.L.*, I, 2, 634, 2501.

[2] Now Este.

[3] Now Vicenza.

[4] Something like the same system, with of course different
details and terminology, and on a much smaller scale, was
employed in making a camp. For *centuria*, see below. Note

22

(vii) *Near* [1] *Padua*, 141 *or* 116 B.C.

Lucius Caecilius, proconsul, son of Quintus, by a resolution of the Senate ordered bounds to be established and boundary-marks to be set up between the people of Ateste [2] and the people of Patavium.

23

(viii) *Near Verona*, 135 B.C.

Sextus Atilius Sarranus, proconsul, son of Marcus, by a resolution of the Senate ordered bounds to be established and boundary-marks to be set up between the people of Ateste and the people of Vicetia.[3]

———— • ————

An example of thus fixing boundaries to suit established conditions is to be seen in the arbitration of the Minucii, pp. 262 ff.

In a measured survey or *limitatio* the procedure was something like the following. An *agrimensor* (or *mensor* or *finitor*) ' surveyor,' with assistants, came to the area to be surveyed, bringing a *pertica decempeda* (a ten-foot measuring-rod, pole, or perch), *metae* (guiding-posts for making long straight lines and roads), *termini* (boundary stones and stakes), a chart [5] of the land to be surveyed, and one or more *gromata*. The main element in a *groma* was a figure + (*decussis*, figure ten) fixed on an iron upright for beginning straight lines and making right-angles. The surveyor stood in the centre of the land and set up a *groma* with the bars pointing due north, south, east and west.[6] He then made the east his facing-point for all purposes of recording positions on boundary-

————————————————

that the block is not a man's plot, but an area, containing, when divided, several plots, as will be seen.

[5] called—at least when modified by the surveyor after his surveying was done—' forma,' ' typus,' ' centuriatio '; even ' pertica.'

[6] How due directions could be found is indicated by Hyginus, 188 ff., and Vitruvius, *de Arch.*, I, 6, 6.

stones or stakes when set up, according to his chart. Facing west, not east, had been an old and approved method; facing even north or south was sometimes adopted, but was not approved by the ancient experts in the theory of land-surveying; moreover, the 'orientation' was sometimes made according to the visible sunrise at a place, or the greatest length of the available area, or parallel to the sea-shore if this was adjacent. However, facing east was in historical times the normal method of orientation; and all that follows in this excursus assumes that the surveying obeys this rule. The surveyor proceeded as follows, confirming or altering his chart as he completed each part. He drew a line on the ground running due east and west, and a second line running due north and south and crossing the first line at the centre of the area to be surveyed. Along the line east–west was then made a broad *limes* 'balk,' 'rough road,' 'cross-path,' called the *decumanus* (*sc. limes*) *maximus*, 'main balk of the tenth,' [1] which was, on all relevant boundary-stones, and on the chart (as a line) referred to as DM; and on the line north–south a less broad *limes* called the *kardo maximus*, 'main hinge-[2] balk,' which was referred to as KM. These were later made into public military roads. The region in front of the surveyor as he faced east (his position being taken as fixed) was called *regio antica* 'frontal region' or *r. ultrata* 'region

---

[1] The meaning is disputed, but this seems right. The regular larger unit in dividing land for a colony was the *centuria*, 'hundred' that is to say, a square (usually but not always) of normally but not always 20 *actus* 'drives,' 'ploughing lengths' (240 rods) each way; an *actus*, which was the normal smaller unit, was 120 feet, a square *actus* containing thus 14,400 square feet; a *iugerum*, 'yoke of land,' was an oblong rectangle containing two square *actus* or 28,800 square feet; 2 *iugera* = 4 square *actus* was a square plot in olden times given to each citizen as an *heredium*, 'hereditary plot'; 100 *heredia* = 1 *centuria*; each side of a *centuria* contained the outer side of 10 *heredia*, and thus any balk bounding the centuria was it seems originally called *decumanus* 'adjoining ten heredia'; when later the word *decumanus* was confined to each balk running east-west, the balks north-south being called *kardo*, a *decumanus* would

placed on yonder side' of the kardo maximus; the region behind being called *r. postica* 'hinder region' or *r. citrata*, 'region placed on hither side' of the *kardo maximus*.[3] The region on his right was called *regio dextrata* ('placed on the right' of *decumanus maximus*), that on his left *regio sinistrata* ('placed on the left' of the *decumanus maximus*.) Using, as before, a *groma*, the surveyor, according to the size laid down for the centuries granted, proceeded to mark[4] out on the ground, as already marked as lines on a prepared chart, a number of other [5] balks some parallel to the *decumanus maximus*, others parallel to the *kardo maximus*. All lines on the chart and balks on the ground parallel to the *dec. max.* were often called *prorsi* ('straight forward') *limites*, all parallel to the *kardo max.* were called *transversi* ('cross'), but all these lines or balks were normally called *decumani* or *kardines* respectively as being parallel either to the *dec. max.* or to the *kardo max.* The lines and balks *prorsi* and *transversi* were numbered originally from the starting position of the surveyor, or rather his central *groma*, that is, from the central point of intersection of the *decumanus maximus* and the *kardo maximus*. Thus of lines or balks *prorsi* running east–west, those on the surveyor's right (as he faced east) of the *decumanus maximus* were called *primus* or *secundus* (*sc. limes = decumanus*) or . . . *dextra* ('on right

---

come at every tenth *heredium*, measured along a *kardo*. For *kardines* and *decumani*, see the scheme set out below.

[2] or *cardo*, so-called because *kardo* was originally any balk (of a century) along the line of the meridian, the axis or hinge on which the heavens turned.

[3] This seems clear from Frontinus, 28.3; but some modern scholars take *citrata* as *antica*, *ultrata* as *postica*.

[4] I have no doubt that the regular technical term for this was *degrumare* ' to level off '—though it occurs only in Ennius and Lucilius—see *Remains*, I, 162–3; III, 32–3.

[5] In Italy all *limites* were doubtless balks (or rough cart-tracks called ' *subruncivi* ' ' half-hoed ') and not merely lines of demarcation. At any rate every fifth *limes* (from the *kardo maximus* or the *decumanus maximus*), called *quintarius*, was a fairly broad cart-road, narrower, however, than the *kardo maximus*.

of ') *decumanum* (*maximum*) [1]; lines or balks *prorsi* running east and west and situated on the surveyor's left of the *decumanus maximus* were called . . . *sinistra* ('on left of ') *decumanum* (*maximum*); likewise lines or balks *transversi* running north and south, and placed east (in front of) the *kardo maximus*, were called *primus* or *secundus* (*sc. limes* = *kardo*) or . . . *ultra* ('beyond') *kardinem* (*maximum*), those behind were called . . . *kitra* (*citra*, ' on this side of ') *kardinem* (*maximum*).[2] All such balks were numbered according to their distance from one or other of the main balks—see below. But the system of placing boundary-stones at corners of centuries and plots caused pairs of these expressions to refer not to the *limites* themselves but to inter-sections of the *limites*, so as to mark not a line or a rough cart-road, but a point and an angle; and it seems that carelessness of syntax further caused these expressions to denote something different from their proper meaning. The matter is dealt with below.

By means of these criss-cross balks the surveyor had now marked out the centuries according to the criss-cross lines on the chart. The balks themselves were often, perhaps normally (as in the plan given after p. 487) excluded from the area of a century; but they could be shared between centuries. These were normally square, so that all *limites* as borders to centuries were normally equidistant, *decumani* from *decumani*, *kardines* from *kardines*. Natural objects were included in the centuries, unless they were large, for instance big stretches of water; in such cases they were excepted from *limitatio*. Holy places, drains and so on, and estates of

---

[1] In recording this on chart or boundary-stones or stakes (for which see below) the words *maximus* and *prorsus* were omitted. It has been argued that *primus* was the number of the *decumanus maximus*. This view was recommended by ancient theorists, but not apparently carried out in practice. See below, pp. 164–5.

[2] Any scheme which ignores the dependence of these expressions on the position (regarded as fixed) of the surveyor is wrong. A. Déléage, *Études de Papyrologie*, II, 1934, 151.

[3] But not necessarily; see next note but one.

[4] Thus ; cf. next note.

[5] See plan following page 487. It will be seen that the only

existing proprietors were left unaffected (or, in the case of estates, were modified). Useless ground was likewise included in the centuries but not in allotted plots within the centuries. Any part of a century left over as an oddment after plots were marked out was called *subsecivum* ' under-cut,' ' cut away,' ' spare.'

The surveyor next superintended the marking of each century by boundary-stones (*termini*) on each of which was written signs giving the position of the stone in relation to the whole area surveyed. One stone might [3] be placed at the inner corner of each of the four centuries which lay at the centre of the area; apparently also, at every point where the two borders of a *limes prorsus* met the *kardo maximus*, one stone might be placed (two on the east, two on the west side of the latter), 4 stones in all [4]; at every point where the borders of a *limes transversus* met the *decumanus maximus* one stone might be placed (two on the north, two on the south side of the latter), 4 stones in all; and lastly, one stone certainly was placed at the outer corner of every century—that is to say at the north-eastern corner of every century lying east of the *kardo maximus* and north of the *decumanus maximus*; and at the south-eastern corner of every century lying south of the *decumanus maximus* and east of the *kardo maximus*; at the south-western corner of every century lying west of the *kardo maximus* and south of the *decumanus maximus*; and at the north-western corner of every century north of the *decumanus maximus* and west of the *kardo maximus*. The outer angle of each century as indicated above was called the *angulus clusaris* ' closing angle ' of the century, the stone placed there [5]

---

necessary stones on a surveyed area were a single one placed at every *angulus clusaris*. It was unnecessary to quadruplicate such stones whether the intersections were caused by actual

roads (*e.g.*) or by mere lines of demarcation () or

by intersection of road with line of demarcation (),

though in the case of intersections of any *limites* with the *dec. max.* or *kardo max.* this may actually, though again unnecessarily, have been done by surveyors, or was at least recommended by theorists. It appears that stones at *anguli clusares*, marking centuries, could be placed in the middle of the balk-crossing if the balks were merely lines of demarcation.

giving in brief, as will be shown below, the location of the century looking inwards from the closing angle towards the centre (*i.e.* the intersecting-place of the *decumanus maximus* and the *kardo maximus*) of the whole area surveyed.

As we know from Hyginus, and from boundary-stones which have survived, the expressions used on written records and charts and on boundary-stones relating to an official land-survey were analogous to those stated above as often denoting the various *kardines* and *decumani*[1]; and the following abbreviations were used : D = *decumanus*; also *dextra*; K = *kardo*; also *kitra* (*citra*); M = *maximus*; V = *ultra*; S = *sinistra*. Numbers I, II, III . . . were added when required to denote *prorsi* and *transversi limites* = *kardines* or *decumani*, with special reference, as will be seen, to points of intersection of these *limites* with each other or with the *dec. max.* or the *kardo maximus* from which two latter the numbering of all other *limites* was counted. Thus each of the 4 stones (and the position of them on the chart) that might be placed at the inner corner of each of the four centuries at the centre of the whole area were marked KMDM = *kardo maximus decumanus maximus* because they stood at the point of inter-section of the *kardo maximus* and the *decumanus maximus*.

Next, any stone, for example, placed where the first *limes prorsus* (= *decumanus primus*) north of the *dec. max.* (and therefore in the *regio sinistrata*) met the *kardo maximus* was marked SDIKM, which when spelt out represents, as we know from Hyginus, *sinistra decumanum primum kardo maximus*; and any stone placed where the third *limes transversus* (= *kardo tertius*) west of the *kardo maximus* (and therefore in the *regio citrata*) met the *decumanus maximus* was marked DMKKIII which represents *decumanus maximus kitra kardinem tertium*. And again, any stone in an angle not connected with the *dec. max.* or the *kardo max.*—that is, any stone in an *angulus clusaris* —was similarly marked. Suppose that a stone is marked DDVIIVKIX. We know from Hyginus that the symbols in

---

[1] There was likewise marked on the top of each stone lines crossing at right angles and forming the figure called *decussis* (see above, p. 159); they gave the direction of the relevant balks. They correspond with the crossing bars of the *groma*.

[2] unless indeed we take it, as some do, that it was the *dec. max.* and *k. max.* which were called, in practice as well as in theory, *primus* and assume the expression to mean ' (the next

the latter example spelt out produced *dextra decumanum septimum ultra kardinem nonum*. At first sight this looks as though it must mean ' on the right of the seventh *decumanus*, on yonder side of the ninth *kardo*.' But this tells nothing—there were many *decumani* on the right of the seventh *dec.*, and many *kardines* beyond the ninth *kardo*. It is possible [2] to take the word *dextra* in the latter example as standing alone adverbially to which the word *decumanus* following has been attracted into the accusative *decumanum* as though *dextra* were ' prepositional '; and to take the word *ultra* as a true adverb standing alone, to which the word *kardo* following has been attracted into the accusative *kardinem* as though *ultra* were a preposition. (Similarly with *sinistra* in the example SDIKM above, and any examples having *kitra*.) But in view of the separation of SD from I- and κK from XI- on n. 25 (extant stone), p. 170 below, I see *dextra* and *ultra* (taking the example DDVIIVKIX again) as prepositions, with fusion of two clauses into one which ought to be *dextra decumanum [maximum decumanus] septimus ultra kardinem [maximum kardo] nonus*, whereas *septimus* and *nonus* have been attracted into the accusatives *septimum* and *nonum*. Or again, since the stone stands at a certain place, the full phrase perhaps ought to be *dextra decumanum [maximum ad decumanum] septimum, ultra kardinem [maximum ad kardinem] nonum*, where *ad* would mean ' next to,' ' lying against,' ' at.' We may compare perhaps, though the parallel is not exact, the method of dating by the expression for example *ante diem quintum Kalendas* which really means *die quinto ante Kalendas* ' on the fifth day before the Kalends.' Originally the expression was probably *ante* (preposition) *kalendas quinto die*; then *quinto die* was thrust in parenthetically before *kalendas*, and attracted, because of *ante*, into the accusative case. Anyhow, in land surveying, in this expression DDVIIVKIX the full meaning intended is : intersection of ' seventh [balk-of-the-tenth in the region] on the right of [main] balk-of-the-tenth ' with ' ninth

---

dec.) on right of the 7th *dec.* . . .' This seems, however, forced and unnatural and is not now accepted, though both methods of designation were known to the ancient theorists, and the effect is the same either way on a chart; we know that on charts, and on any stones placed on the *dec. max.*, the *dec. max.* is called simply D, not DI, though it is true that the sign I might be omitted as understood. Cf. Déléage, *Ét. de Pap.*, II, 152.

[hinge-balk in the region] beyond [main] hinge-balk.'[1] Thus, in the above example, the words *dextra* and *ultra*, taken together, give the quarter (quadrant) or region, of the whole surveyed area, in which the stone lies, while the numbered *decumanus* and *kardo* taken together indicate the outer angle and therefore the two outer sides (with reference to the centre-point of the whole area) of a century. I suggest that we cannot resist an inference that, like the expression used in dating, the expression for marking points on surveyed land could be treated as one word—for example *ex* ('from') *dextra decumanum septimum ultra kardinem nonum in* ('as far as') *dextra decumanum octavum ultra kardinem decumum*. Whatever the exact linguistic meaning of such abbreviations may be in Roman surveying, there can be no doubt about what they intended to convey. Except stones or stakes used to mark boundaries of plots inside the centuries, every stone or stake placed on the surveyed area marked the junction of a *kardo* and a *decumanus*; and of these stones or stakes each one placed at an *angulus clusaris* indicated the position of that century which looked inwards from the stone towards the centre of the surveyed area.

Having marked out the centuries the surveyor according to his chart then marked out, within these centuries, each man's plot. We have no inscriptions showing how these plots, which had their own rough roads or balks, were indicated on stones or stakes, so that my plan deals with and shows centuries only. For we know that Augustus laid down that plots should be marked with stakes made of oak while those marking centuries should be of stone; this material was doubtless the rule with the centuries, and it is assumed that extant boundary stones (at least those containing the inscriptions given below from *C.I.L.*, I, 2, 639–40) marked centuries not plots. The final duty of the surveyor was to alter his chart

---

[1] Note that on our surviving stones the symbols indicating the position of the stone are nearly all written on the top; but in the case of centuries very remote from the centre-point, and thus involving big numbers, the relevant stones might have their symbols on the shaft.

[2] most conveniently with each plot 10×6 *actus* square; but four of them could be 12×5 *actus* square, and two 20×3 *actus* square; or five could be 15×4 and one 20×3. Note

INSCRIPTIONS ON PUBLIC WORKS

where he had varied from it, and to add to it a full report in writing.

For Roman surveying, see Fabricius, in Paulys *Real-Encyclopädie*, s.v. 'Limitatio'; A. Déléage, *Études de Papyrologie*, II, 1934, 147 ff., especially bibliographical list, p. 151. Mommsen's work (*Hermes*, XXVII, 90 ff.) fails to satisfy because he reverses the positions of the *regio citrata* and the *regio ultrata*, and takes *dec. max.* and *kardo max.* as *dec.* I and *kardo* I respectively; the article 'Agrimetatio' by H. Roby in Smith's *Dict. of Greek and Roman Antiquities* has the same defect. The original literary sources are the writings of the Roman *agrimensores*, which can be found in *Gromatici Veteres* (*Schriften der röm. Feldmesser*, I, 1848, Blume and Lachmann; II, 1852, Blume, Lachmann, Mommsen and Rudorff), and in the uncompleted *Corpus Agrimensorum Romanorum*, I, 1, 1913, ed. Thulin.

On the lands assigned by Tiberius Gracchus in 133 B.C. such *limites* as were roads were probably the same width as those in the colonies founded by his brother Gaius ten years afterwards. In them the *decumanus max.* was a road 40 feet wide, the *kardo max.* a road 20 feet wide, the other *actuarii* ('drives,' 'cart roads,' in this case the *quintarii*—see above) being 12 feet wide, and the *subruncivi* (see above—probably bounding plots assigned) 8 feet wide. The size of each plot probably varied, though it has been thought (see pp. 382–3) that Tiberius laid down a fixed area of 30 *iugera*; but the size and shape of the century was the normal one of 20 *actus* each side = 200 *iugera*. A whole plot of 30 *iugera* was an oblong rectangle (12 × 5 *actus*, or 20 × 3 *actus*; the *iugerum* itself was an oblong rectangle of 2 square *actus*); and within each century could be placed six such plots [2] with boundaries of century coinciding with boundaries of plots; but there were 20 *iugera* (⅔ of a plot) to spare in each century. However, a plot could

---

that plots of greater length (north-south) than breadth (east-west) were said to be laid down '*per strigas*' (strips); those of greater breadth than length were '*per scamna*' (unbroken grounds?). This form of planning, which deals with plots, not centuries, could be applied within or separate from an area planned in centuries. Plots forming irregular patches seem to have been called *laciniae*, plots with straight but not rectangular boundaries, *praecisurae*.

overrun the boundary of a century, even though a road-balk between 2 centuries then ran through the plot. Probably those men who were chosen to share in an assignment by Tiberius' law were granted their plots by lot. Any man, on arrival at the settlement, could, after reference to a copy of the chart and of other details, and to the stones and stakes set up on the ground, find where his plot stood. The assignments were en-

24–5

(A)

639

(a) C. Sempronius Ti. f. | Ap. Claudius C. f. | P. Licinius P. f.; | III vir. a.i.a. KVII

¹ See *Lib. Col.*, p. 242; Mommsen, *H.*, XXVII, 90 ff.; F. Barnabei, *Notiz. d. Sc.*, 1897, 120 ff.; *etc.* cf. also Schulten, *Abh. d. Götting. Ges. d. W.*, N.S., 1898, 30; Barthel, *Bonn. Jahrb.*, CXX, 97; Carcopino, *Autour des Gracques*, 162, 182–3, 235 ff.; Déléage, *Ét. de Pap.*, II, 152 ff.

² Gaius Gracchus. The first name on any stone is that of the Board's president, the others denoting dormant members.

³ *assignandis.* Possibly *attribuendis* 'attributing.'

⁴ KVII on the shaft shows that the stone stood against a seventh hinge-balk. Absence of any reference on the shaft to a *decumanus* may mean that the stone stood at the intersection of a seventh *kardo* with the *decumanus maximus* = 'main balk-of-the-tenth.' The signs on the top represent (as by the arms of a *groma*) an intersecting K[*ardo*] and D[*ecumanus*], the upright stokes of K and D corresponding with the respective lines. It would be clear to a Roman arriving at this stone and on referring to the other stones on the land, whether this one was in the *regio citrata* or the *regio ultrata*. For the sake of illustration I assume, on the plan following p. 487, that it was in the *ultrata*, and that the normal designation of the stone would be DMVKVII = *decumanus maximus ultra kardinem septimum* 'main balk-

168

trusted by Tiberius to a commission of 3 (of which perhaps only the president functioned, in annual rotation), whose names are recorded on almost every surviving stone connected with their assignment. Of the extant stones only two were certainly placed on *ager limitatus* to indicate position by specified *decumanus* and *kardo*. It is, however, natural to suppose that the other stones also were at least connected with surveyed land.[1]

24–5

(A) *Two pillars, each making the corner of a century on 'ager limitatus.'*

(a) *Found at Atina in Lucania. Now at Naples.* 131 B.C. (Carcopino, *Autour des Gracques*, pp. 237–8).

On the shaft of the pillar:

Gaius [2] Sempronius, son of Tiberius; Appius Claudius, son of Gaius; Publius Licinius, son of Publius; Board of Three for adjudging and assigning [3] lands.　　Seventh hinge-balk.

On the top: a 'decussis' +,
one arm marked: Hinge-balk.
the other: Balk-of-the-tenth.[4]

---

of-the-tenth; beyond hinge-balk: seventh' (for this, see above, p. 165; cf. next inscription). On the plan I have made the stone indicate the century looking inwards towards the centre of the whole area, but if 4 stones were placed at the junction of VKVII and DM (thus ⊥⊢), 2 being north of DM, then it might be any one of these. Some think that the letters on top of this stone are not K and D but V and P = *veteris possessoris* (for which see below, pp. 171–3), which is quite possible. I once thought V might be *ultra* and D *dextra*, or that V̲ might here combine V and K (*ultra kardinem*) and D mean both *dextra* and *decumanum*. If we ought to read C for D, it would not mean *citra*, with V as *ultra*, because they stand on different *limites maximi*. From the position of the letters relative to the four arms of the 'decussis' we can deduce nothing.

169

640

(*b*) C. [*Se*]mpr[*on*]iu[*s Ti. f. Grac.*] | Ap. Claudius
C. f. Polc. | P. Licinius P. f. Cras. ; | III vir.
a.i.a.

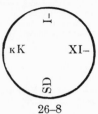

26–8

(B)

643

(*a*) M. Folvius M.f.[*Fl*]ac. | C. Sempronius Ti. f.
Grac. | C. Paperius C. f. Carbo ; | III vire
a.i.a.

---

[1] See pages 164–166. SDIKKXI = *sinistra decumanum
primum kitra kardinem undecimum.* The two short dashes
(grooves) mark the directions of the relevant *kardo* and
decumanus. The groove by SDI indicates the first *decumanus,*
that by KKXI the 11th *kardo.* We know (Frontin., 29, 4)
that in the Ager Campanus, where this stone was found,
the *dec. max.* ran exceptionally north-south ; but since the
plan following p. 487 follows the normal orientation with *dec.
max.* running east-west, I have there shown this stone
accordingly. Two other stones (*C.I.L.*, I, 2, 641–2) have the
same Board of Three inscribed, but there are no symbols. I

INSCRIPTIONS ON PUBLIC WORKS

(b) Found near St. Angelo in Formis. 131 B.C.

On the shaft.	*On the top.*
Gaius Sempronius Gracchus, son of Tiberius; Appius Claudius Pulcher, son of Gaius; Publius Licinius Crassus, son of Publius; Board of Three for adjudging and assigning lands.	On left of balk-of-the-tenth: first. On this side of hinge-balk: eleventh.[1]

26-8

(B) *Three pillars, each marking apparently an angle which bounded the estate of an established occupier, who is to be left in possession, and possibly indicating the boundary of assignable land and public state-land. All were found on the same ' ager.' It is not certain what some of the signs actually are, or what their meaning is. Brunn, Dressel, and Santoli have given different readings.*

(a) *Found at Rocca San Felice (near the old Aeclanum).* 123 B.C. (Carcopino, *Autour des Gracques*, pp. 237–8).

On the shaft.	*On the top.*	
Marcus Fulvius[2] Flaccus, son of Marcus; Gaius Sempronius Gracchus, son of Tiberius; Gaius Papirius Carbo, son of Gaius; Board of Three for adjudging and assigning lands.	Estate allowed to established occupier free of charges.[3]	(?) Limit of (?) Estates.

suggest that they are examples of the *muti lapides* ' mute stones ' that we read of in the gromatic writers, and that if four stones were placed at intersection of, for example, a *decumanus* with the *kardo maximus*, perhaps sometimes only one had the symbols giving the position.

[2] He and Papirius replaced deceased Licinius and Claudius of the preceding inscriptions.

[3] That FVP = *fundus veteris possessoris* is usually accepted. Other signs in this quadrant are uncertain; they seem to be

644   (*b*) M. Folvius M. f. Fla[*c*]. | C. Sempronius Ti. f. G[*rac*]. | C. Paperius C.f. Carb.; | III vire a.i.a.

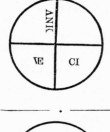

645   (*c*)

All three stones described above under (B) refer at least in part to 'estate of established occupier'; all have lines which at least look like *kardo* and *decumanus*, and it may be that one of

CI. If so, then I suggest that FPVCI means *fundus possessori veteri concessus immunis*, and translate accordingly. Otherwise CI might be *centuria* I or *centum iugera*. In the gromatic writings we read of CVP as representing *concessa veteri possessori*; and *vetus possessor* occurs in the *Lex Agraria*, given below. The other signs on this stone are not at all clear, and have been variously read. Only the letters FF can be distinguished, and I suggest that this means *fundorum fines* 'limit of estates' *sc.* of established occupier's and of those to be assigned under Gracchus' law; land beyond the diameter-line (shown as a blank on the stone) is to be public state-land, or at least outside the assignable area.

172

(b) *Found near the preceding.* 123 B.C.

On the shaft.	*On the top.*	
Marcus Fulvius Flaccus, son of Marcus; Gaius Sempronius Gracchus, son of Tiberius; Gaius Papirius Carbo, son of Gaius; Board of Three for adjudging and assigning lands.	To establish-ed occupier	Allowed free of charges.[1]

(c) *Found near the two preceding.* 123 B.C.

————— . —————

On the top.

Estate of established occupier.[2]

Nothing else has survived on this stone.

the blank spaces on each[3] may show an *angulus clusaris*, which, according to the writers on surveying (the *gromatici*), was usually shown blank on stones in *ager limitatus*. But the marks

---

The signs which were written near the signs FF look rather like ΛNIC which are on the next stone given. But I have not shown them here. See next note.

[1] On this see the preceding note. Comparison with the preceding stone indicates that such letters as can be clearly seen on the top of this stone occur also on the preceding, but the letters F do not occur on this one. Note that two of the letters in the quadrant opposite the one containing CI seem to be IC, which is the same thing. I suggest ANIC = *ager novis incolis concessus.*

[2] Here certainly FPVET means *fundus possessoris veteris.* The blank space of the smaller (inner) angle indicates assignable land?   [3] 28 = (c) has three blank quadrants adjacent.

on the stones do not give the impression that they were on *ager limitatus*. I suggest that, since all were found near each other, and all have reference to 'estate of established occupier,' they were on the outer boundary [1] of an *ager limitatus* or surveyed area, and marked particularly the boundary of the estate of one and the same man, who is to be or has been left in possession on assignment being made of adjacent land to

29

(C)

719   M. Terentius M. f. | Varro Lucullus | pro pr.
  [5]   terminos | restituendos | ex   s.c.   coeravit |
      qua P. Licinius | Ap. Claudius | C. Gracchus
      III vir. | a.d.a.i. statuerunt.

30

1438   (i) In agro | P. Paacili | terminus | totus est | con-
      locā.

31

1385   (ii) C. Sesti C. f. murus | totus proprius est | et
      locus ubei is murus stat.

---

[1] This is particularly suggested by the third stone described above, pp. 172–3.

[2] Frontinus 311—*per proximos possessionum rigores* (*rigor* = straight line on the earth, *linea* a straight line on a chart).

[5] The stone itself is apparently not a boundary-stone. In 82 B.C. Varro Lucullus, who had never held a magistracy, was in command of an army in the 'Ager Gallicus,' where the stone was found; but this is the only record of the title whereby he held the command. Some date the inscription in 75 or 74, because a M. Lucullus was a praetor in 76, consul in 73. But there are objections to this.

citizens; they were on land which was divided or allotted with due respect to the boundaries of neighbouring holders [2] and which may have been land *mensura per extremitatem comprehensus*, surrounded by a measured boundary, but not otherwise measured out. For a Gracchan stone in Africa, see *C.I.L.*, VIII, 12,535; Cichorius, *Röm. Stud.*, 113–116.

29

(C) *Record of re-establishment of Gracchan boundary-stones of 132* B.C. (Carcopino, *Autour des Gracques, pp.* 237–8.) *Small pillar found between Pisaurum and Fanum.* 82 or 81 [3] B.C.

Marcus Terentius Varro Lucullus, as pro-praetor, son of Marcus, by a resolution of the Senate, superintended the re-establishment of boundary-stones where Publius Licinius, Appius Claudius, and Gaius Gracchus, Board [4] of Three for granting assigning and adjudging lands, established them.

OTHER BOUNDARY-STONES.

30

(i) [5] *In Latium, at Marino.* c. 101 B.C.

This boundary-stone has been placed entirely within the land of Publius Pacilius.

31

(ii) *At Rome.*[6]

The whole of this wall, together with the place where the said wall stands, is the property of Gaius Sestius, son of Gaius.

[4] For this Board, see above, pp. 168 ff.
[5] This inscription is repeated on another side of the stone. *conlocā = conlocatus.*
[6] Cf. *C.I.L.*, VI, 29789.

32

1831 (iii) Via inferior | privatast | T. Umbreni C. f.; |
5   precario itur. | Pecus plostru | niquis agat.

33

1606 (iv) Privatum. | Precario | adeitur.

34

839 (v) (*a*) L. Sentius C. f. pr. | de sen. sent. loca |
terminanda coer. | B. f. Neiquis intra | ter-
5   minos propius | urbem ustrinam | fecisse velit
nive | stercus cadaver | iniecise velit.
(*b*) Stercus longe | aufer | ne malum habeas.

35

707 (*a*) Q. Marci[*us*] | Protomacus [*medicus*]. | Facta
L. M. cos. m[*ense*..] |
5 (*b*) Κουίνκτος Μάρκιο[ς Πρωτό] |μαχος Ἡρακλείδο[υ
ἰατρός.] |
[*sequitur titulus Punicus*]

35 ² medicus *suppl. ex tit. Pun.*

---

¹ or *Umbrenus*, which is a cognomen.

² This corresponds to our ' Admission on sufferance only '
and was probably a normal warning that ' trespassers will be
prosecuted.' Umbrenius allows *iter*, that is, use of the road
as a footpath, but not *actus*, use of the road for driving cattle
or carts; cf. a right of way at Amiternum, below, pp. 196–7.

³ The other (*C.I.L.*, I, 2, 838) lacks inscription (*b*). For a
senatus consultum bearing on sacred places on the Esquiline,
see pp. 252–5. For construction of a road, with boundary
stones, see number 67 below.

⁴ b. f. seems to be *bonum factum* used here in the same
way as it was later at the beginning of public announcements,
e.g. Suet. *Div. Iul.*, 80; *Vitell.*, 14. Cf. ἀγαθῇ τύχῃ.

⁵ for cremation of the dead.

INSCRIPTIONS ON PUBLIC WORKS

32

(iii) At Monte Verano.

The lower road is private property of Titus Umbrenius,[1] son of Gaius. Pedestrian traffic, by request only.[2] No person to drive cattle or cart.

33

(iv) At Capua.

Private ground. Entry by request only.

34

(v) One[3] of two stones found on the Esquiline at Rome. Time of Sulla ? A praetor's edict records a decree of the Senate.

(a) Cut on the stone :

The praetor Lucius Sentius son of Gaius, on a vote of the senate, superintended the marking off of this area by boundary-stones.

' In God's name[4] : ' Let none be minded to make a burning-ground[5] or cast dung or carcass within the limits of the boundary-stones on the side nearer to the city.

(b) Painted on the stone :

Carry away dung far off, lest you come to grief.

35

Work of Quintus Marcius. On[6] a stone found at Henchir-Aouin, in North Africa. Trilingual. 91 B.C.

(*a*) Quintus Marcius Protomachus, medical doctor. Made in the consulship of Lucius Marcius, in the month of . . .

(*b*) Quintus Marcius Protomachus, medical doctor, son of Heracleides.

[Punic text follows.]

---

[6] Berger and Cagnat, *Compt. rend. de l'Acad. des Inscr. et B. L.*, 1879, 53.

36

2197   De via Pos[*t*]umia in | forum pequarium . . . . |
        meisit lata p. XXX . . . | de senatuos sen-
        [*tentiad*.]

37

2198   M. Annaus | Q. f. IIII vir i. d. | quinq. porta |
       ⁵   refic. locavit | ex s. c. eidemq. | probavit.

38

809   *Col. I.*   . . . ine . . . | . . . atigu . . . | [*via in lo-*]
          ngitud[*inem in ped*]es | [*singulos* **HS** . . .]
       ⁵   XVIIII. In [*scal*]eis | [. . . *iniei*]s ab cleivo
          [*infi*]mo | [*bustei*]s Galliceis v[*er*]sus | . . . [*ad*
          su]mmum cleivom via | [*in lon*]gitudinem in
       ¹⁰ pedes | [*sing*]ulos **HS** C. Ab scaleis | . . . inieis
          infimeis praeter | . . . Marcias ad viam | . . .
          et pone foros | [*et aedif*]icia C. Numitori |
       ¹⁵ . . . [*i*]nter | . . . porticum | . . . nium
          via | [*in longitudinem in ped*]es sing. | **HS**
          . . . *basi*]licam | . . . eas | . . . [*in pedes
          si*]ng. | **HS** . . .
          Ex. col. II initia solum versuum extant.

39

713   L. Cornelio | Cinna cos. iter. | purgatum | mense
        inr.

---

    39 ⁴ *Ianuario* Momms.   *interkalari* Huebner   INR

---

     ¹ For these, see p. xxxix.
     ² Cf. Huelsen, *Beitr. z. alt. Gesch.*, II, 1902, 259 ff.
     ³ somewhere in the middle of the city. (Livy, XXII, 14.)
     ⁴ near the Forum Boarium? (Livy, XXIX, 37.)
     ⁵ C. Marius had died on 13th Jan. and L. Flaccus had not
yet been made *consul suffectus*. Thus only one consul is
mentioned. As the interval before Flaccus was appointed

INSCRIPTIONS ON PUBLIC WORKS

36

Works at Aquileia (cf. *C.I.L.*, I, 2, 2198). *Aquileia. c.*
100 B.C.?

. . ., by a vote of the Senate, made . . . 30 ft.
wide running from the Postumian Road into the
cattle-market.

37

Gate at Aquileia. c. 100 B.C.?

Marcus Annaus, son of Quintus, member, in a fifth
year, of the Board of Four for Pronouncing Justice,[1] by
decree of the Senate contracted for the restoration of
the gate, and likewise acceptably completed the work.

38

Contract [2] *for repairing roads in Rome.   On five fragments of
stone. c.* 100–85 B.C. *Public document.   Column I.*

. . . the road, along its length . . . 19 sesterces
per foot. On the . . . ian Steps from the bottom
of the slope and the Gallic [3] Graves towards
. . . the top of the slope the road, along its
length, 100 sesterces per foot.   From the bottom of
the . . . ian Steps past the Marcian . . . to the
road . . . and behind the market-places [4] and the
premises of Gaius Numitorius . . . between . . .
the colonnade . . . the road, along its length . . .
sesterces per foot . . . the public hall . . . per foot.

In column II only the beginnings of the lines are preserved.

39

Cleaning of an aqueduct.   Found near Cales. 86 B.C.

Cleansed in the second consulship of Lucius
Cornelius Cinna,[5] in the month of January.

would be short, January, rather than 'intercalary month,'
which would come after Feb. 23rd, is probably right for *inr.*
which seems to be an error in the inscription.

40

1759   M. Caicilius L. f. | L. Atilius L. f. | praef. | pon-
     5   tem peila[*s*] | faciundum | coirave[*re.*]

41

1627   V. Popidius | Ep.   f.   q. | porticus | faciendas |
     5   coeravit.

42

1628   L. Caesius C. f. d. v. i. d. | C. Occius M. f. IIv. |
     5   L. Niraemius A. f. | d. d. s. ex peq. publ. |
           fac. curar. prob. q.

43

808   . . . OPERA LOC . . . | [*IN V*]IA CAECILIA
           DE H[*S . . . MILIBUS NUMMUM.* | *A*]d
           mil. XXXV pontem in fluio, | [*pecuni*]a ad tri-
     5   buta est populo const. | [*HS* . . . .]Q. Pam-
           philo mancupi et ope., | [*cur.*]viar. T. Vibio
           T[*e*]muudino q. urb. ; | [*via gl*]area sternenda

43 *suppl.* Huelsen, Mommsen

---

[1] Schöne, *Quaest. Pomp.*, 1 ff.; Nissen, *Pomp. Stud.*, 128 ff. For the title of the magistrates, see p. xxxix.

[2] Mommsen, *Eph. Epigr.*, II, pp. 199 ff.; Huelsen, *Notiz. d. Scavi*, 1896, p. 88; Persichetti, *Röm. Mitth.*, XIII, 193 ff.

[3] Abbreviations used in this inscription : *mil.* = *miliarium*(-*o*);   *const.* = *constitit*   or   *constat*;   *ope.* = *operīs*; *cur.* = *curator*; *viar.* = *viarum.*

[4] *ope* seems to me to represent *operariis* or *operīs* ' workmen '.

INSCRIPTIONS ON PUBLIC WORKS

40

A bridge and pillars in Samnium. In a wall at Castel di Sangro.

Marcus Caecilius, son of Lucius, and Lucus Atilius, son of Lucius, praefects, superintended the making of a bridge and its piers.

41

Colonnades at Pompeii. Marble tablet. Before 80 B.C.

Vibius Popidius, quaestor, son of Eppius, superintended the making of colonnades.

42

Public works (thermae?) at Pompeii (cf. C.I.L., I, 1627—colonnades). Two stones with same inscription. Found at Pompeii. c. 90–80 B.C.[1]

Lucius Caesius, son of Gaius, member of the Board of Two for Pronouncing Justice; Gaius Occius, son of Marcus, and Lucius Niraemius, son of Aulus, members of the Board of Two, superintended, by a vote of the local senate, the making of this work out of public money, and acceptably completed the same.

43

Works, at public cost, connected with repairs to the unidentified Via Caecilia. Tablet of stone found in an old wall at Rome.[2] *c. 90–80 B.C. Records a public document.*

. . . WORKS LET OUT BY CONTRACT. . . ON THE CAECILIAN ROAD OUT OF. . . THOUSAND SESTERCES IN MONEY.

At the 35th milestone[3] a bridge over the river; sum was assigned: cost to the people: . . . sesterces. . . . . . Quintus Pamphilus contractor and workmen,[4] with Titus Vibius Temudinus, quaestor of the city, as warden of roads; road must be laid down in gravel

af mil. | [*LXXVIII et per A*]p[*e*]nninum
muunien[*da | per m. p.*] XX, pecunia ad tributa
10   [*est | populo c*]ons[*t.*] HS n. [*C*] L [*m.*] ; L.
Rufilio L. L. l. | [. . . .]sti man[*cu*]pi ; cur.
viar. T. Vib.[*q.* ; | *via af*]mil. LXX[*XXV*]III
ad mil. CX . . . . | *sternenda a*]la Interamnium
vo[*rsus | ad mil. C*]XX ; pecunia ad tri[*buta |*
15   *est, popu*]lo const. HS DC(?) m. n. | . . . . . T.
Sepunio T. f. O[. . . | . . . *mancupi* ; *cur.*
via]r. T. Vibio [*T*]em[*uudino q. urb.*] | . . .
arcus dela[*psus . . . . . pecunia adtributa est* ;
populo const. HS . . . | . . . .]mancupi[. . . . |
20   . . . *cur. viar. T. Vibio*] q. urb. . . .

44

737   Q. Lutatius Q. f. Q. [*n.*] Catulus cos. | substruc-
tionem et tabularium | de s. s. faciundum
coeravit [*ei*]demque | pro[*bavit*].

45

1814   P. T. Sex. Herennieis Sex. f. Ser. | Supinates ex
ingenio suo | epointe.

       43 ¹⁰ HSN//////ↃↃLⱮ   ¹¹ *fortasse* [*Ores*]ti
                 ¹⁵ HSOJ CⱮ

from the 78th milestone and paved for a distance
of 20,000 paces through the Apennine range; sum
was assigned: cost to the people 150,000 sesterces
in money. Lucius Rufilius, freedman of two
Lucii . . . contractor, with Titus Vibius, quaestor,
as warden of roads; road must be laid down from
the 98th milestone to the 1 . . . th milestone . . .
side-branch leading towards Interamnium up to the
120th milestone; sum was assigned: cost to the people
600,000 sesterces in money. . . . Titus Sepunius
O . . ., son of Titus . . . contractor, with Titus
Vibius Temudinus, quaestor of the city, as warden
of roads . . . tumbledown arch . . . sum was assigned: cost to the people . . . sesterces . . .
contractor . . . with Titus Vibius, quaestor of the
city, as warden of roads. . . .

44

Additions to a building at Rome.[1] *Lost.   Read by Poggio on
a row of arches now built into modern buildings.*   78 B.C.

Quintus Lutatius Catulus, consul, son of Quintus,
grandson of Quintus, superintended by a vote of
the Senate an undercroft and a record-office; and
likewise acceptably completed the work.

45

Work by Publius Herennius and Titus Herennius.   At Massa.

Publius Herennius, Titus Herennius and Sextus
Herennius, sons of Sextus, of the Sergian tribe and
the Supinate quarter, made [2] this with the help of
their genius.

[1] Jordan, *Annali dell' Inst.*, 1876, 151; 1881, 69; R. Del-
brück, *Hellenist. Baut. in Latium*, I, 23 ff.

[2] obscure. ἐποιοῦντο?   Name of a deity?

TITULI OPERUM PUBLICORUM

46–7

1523 (i) A. Hirtius A. f., M. Lollius C. f. ces. funda-
menta murosque af solo faciunda coeravere,
eidemque probavere. In terram fundamentum est pedes altum XXXIII in terram
5   ad idem exemplum quod supra terra[*m
silici*]. .

1524 (ii) A. Hirtius A. f., M. Lollius C. f. ces. funda-
menta | fornices faciunda coeraver[*e*] eidem-
que | probavere.

48

1527 P. M. Saloniei Ti. f. | aed. | pavimentum | d. s.
p. f. c.

49

1537 A. Aigius C. f. | L. Runtius C. f. Sisipus | M.
5   Fufidius M. f. | [*a*]id. de s. s. | [*ad colligendas* |
aqu]as cae[*lestes*] | clouacas faciun[*d.*] | coer.
eidemque | probarunt.

46 [5] *suppl. ex C.I.L.*, I, 2, 1522

---

[1] and repeated on another wall—*C.I.L.*, I, 2, 1522.
[2] the local censors, not censors of Rome.
[3] *silex* is here the modern *selce*, a lava from extinct volcanoes
in the Alban hills.   When broken up and mixed with lime and
pozzolana (another volcanic product abundant in the ground
under and round Rome, as well as at Pozzuoli), it formed a
very durable concrete. Excavation has shown that the
foundations of the citadel of Ferentinum in fact did not go
down nearly so far as 33 feet; nor would the inclusion, in
fundamentum, of all the lower courses, up to the inscriptions,
make up the difference. Cf. Ashby, *Röm. Mitt.*, XXIV,
1909, 1 ff., especially 34 ff.

INSCRIPTIONS ON PUBLIC WORKS

46–7

Old fortress at Ferentinum, c. 90–80 B.C.

(i) *Written on the outside* [1] *of a wall.*

The censors [2] Aulus Hirtius son of Aulus, and Marcus Lollius son of Gaius, superintended the construction of the foundation and walls, from ground-level, and likewise acceptably completed them. Into the earth the foundation goes 33 feet deep on the same plan into the earth as above the earth, in concrete. [3]

(ii) *Written inside the building.* [4]

The censors Aulus Hirtius son of Aulus, and Marcus Lollius son of Gaius, superintended the construction of foundations and vaults, and likewise acceptably completed them.

48

A pavement at Ferentinum.   Bronze letters on a tablet of stone.

Publius Salonius and Marcus Salonius, sons of Tiberius, aediles, superintended the construction of this hard floor out of their own money.

49

Rain-tanks at Arpinum.   Cicero's time ?

The aediles Aulus Aegius son of Gaius, Lucius Runtius Sisyphus son of Gaius, and Marcus Fufidius son of Marcus, by a vote of the Senate superintended the construction of runs for collecting rainfall, and likewise acceptably completed them.

[4] repeated on the outside above a doorway (*C.I.L.*, I, 2, 1525), where *fornices* is omitted. On *faciunda*, neuter plural, in these inscriptions, see note on 54 below.

50

1694 P. Magius P. f. Iunc. | Q. Minucius L. f. ces. | basilicam fac. | cur. de sen. sent.

51

1511 M. M[*a*]tlius M. f., L. Turpilius L. f. duomvires de senatus | sente[*nt*]ia aedem faciendam coeraverunt eisdemque probavere.

52

1473 Q. Vibuleius L. f. | L. Statius Sal. f. | duo vir. |
    5   balneas reficiund. | aquam per publicum | ducendam d. d. s. | coeravere.

53

1747 L. Mummius L. f., C. Manlius C. f. | pr. duo vir. pro ludeis turris duas | d. d. s. faciundas coerarunt.

51 [1] Manlius, Nibby *al.*   Mallius *vel* Manilius *al.*
Μ/ꟼLIVS

INSCRIPTIONS ON PUBLIC WORKS

50

Public hall at Thurii.

Publius Magius Iuncus, son of Publius, and Quintus Minucius, son of Lucius, censors, by a vote of the Senate superintended the construction of a town hall.

51

Shrine at Cora.

Marcus Matlius, son of Marcus, and Lucius Turpilius, son of Lucius, members of the Board of Two,[1] by a vote of the Senate superintended the construction of a temple and likewise acceptably completed the work.

52

Baths and water-supply at Praeneste. On stone. c. 80 B.C. ?

Quintus Vibuleius son of Lucius, and Lucius Statius son of Salvius, members of the Board of Two, by decree of the local Senate superintended the reconstruction of the baths and the running of a water-supply through public places.

53

Tower at Telesia (cf. C.I.L., IX, 2230).

Lucius Mummius son of Lucius, and Gaius Manlius son of Gaius, praetors, members of the Board of Two, by a vote of the local Senate, superintended the construction of two towers instead of holding games.

---

[1] For these, see p. xxxix. They may here be a special board of *duoviri aedi dedicandae* ' for dedicating a shrine.' I read *Matlius* because in *C.I.L.*, I, 2, 197 we have *Matlia*.

54

1722   C. Quinctius C. f. Valg. patronus munic., | M.
        Magi. Min. f. Surus, A. Patlacius Q. f. | IIII
        vir. d. s. s. portas turreis moiros | turreisque
    5   aequas qum moiro | faciundum coeraverunt.

55

1632   C. Quinctius C. f. Valgus, | M. Porcius M. f. duo
        vir. | quinq. coloniai honoris | caussa spec-
    5   tacula de sua | peq. fac. coer. et coloneis |
        locum in perpetuom deder.

56

1633   C. Quinctius C. f. Valg. | M. Porcius M. f. | duo
    5   vir. dec. decr. | theatrum tectum | fac. locar.
        eidemq. prob.

---

[1] For this man see also other inscriptions given next. He had been elected ' *patronus* ' by Aeclanum for benefactions rendered by him.

[2] Perhaps Minatus Magius who helped Rome in the so-called ' Social' War (Vellei. Paterc., II, 16).

[3] This refers to Magius and Patlacius only. For these magistrates, see p. xxxix.

[4] *faciundum* is not mere carelessness of the inscriber. See 59 given below, also 40, 46–7 above, and dedication number 136, which suggest that composers of such inscriptions were sometimes influenced by a formula such as *faciundum curare* or *faciunda curare* without reference to the gender or the number of work or works actually mentioned. Often the gerundive of *facere* and *reficere* is abbreviated *-und.* in inscriptions.

INSCRIPTIONS ON PUBLIC WORKS

54

Towers and walls at Aeclanum. c. 80 B.C. In the ruins of the eastern gate.

Gaius Quinctius Valgus [1] son of Gaius, and protector of the borough; Marcus Magius Syrus, son of Minatus [2]; and Aulus Patlacius son of Quintus, members [3] of the Board of Four, by a vote of the Senate superintended the construction [4] of gates, towers, and walls, and towers level with a wall.[5]

55

Public services of Gaius Quinctius and Marcus Porcius at Pompeii. Found [7] in the amphitheatre on two pieces of stone. c. 100–80 B.C.

Gaius Quinctius Valgus son of Gaius, and Marcus Porcius son of Marcus, members of the Board [6] of Two in a fifth year,[7] superintended the institution of shows at their own expense for the colony, to honour the same, and gave to the colonists a burial-ground for all time.

56

Smaller theatre at Pompeii. Two stones with the same inscription.

Gaius Quinctius Valgus son of Gaius, and Marcus Porcius, son of Marcus, members of the Board of Two, let out, by decree of the local Senate, the construction by contract of a covered theatre; they likewise acceptably completed the work.

[5] or: 'walls; the towers moreover to be equal in height to their respective walls.'

[6] On these, see p. xxxix; and for Valgus, see the preceding inscription.

[7] See p. xxxix.

57–8

1629   (i) . . . Cuspius T. f. M. Loreiu[s] M. f. | duovir.
[d.] d. s. murum [e]t | plumam fac. coer.
eidemq. pro.

1630   (ii) . . . Cuspius T. f. M. Loreius M. f. | IIII vir.
L. Septumius L. f. | D. Claudius D. f. IIII vir.
⁵   ex | pequnia publica d. d. | s. f. curaverunt.

59

1635   (iii) C. Uulius C. f., P. Aninius C. f. II v. i. d. |
laconicum et destrictarium | faciund. et por-
ticus et palaestr. | reficiunda locarunt ex
⁵   d. d. ex | ea pequnia quod eos e lege | in ludos
aut in monumento | consumere oportuit;
faciun. | coerarunt eidemque probaru.

60

1463   M. Anicius L. f. Baaso M. Mersieius C. f. | aediles
aerarium faciendum dederunt.

---

¹ Of this board they were the two senior magistrates
(*duoviri iure dicundo*), as is shewn by their being recorded as
members of the Board of Two in the preceding inscription.

INSCRIPTIONS ON PUBLIC WORKS

57–8

Works at Pompeii.

(i) . . . Cuspius son of Titus, and Marcus Loreius son of Marcus, members of the Board of Two, superintended, by a vote of the local Senate, the construction of a wall and a battlement; and they likewise acceptably completed the work.

(ii) . . . Cuspius son of Titus and Marcus Loreius son of Marcus, members of the Board of Four [1]; Lucius Septimius son of Lucius, and Decimus Claudius, son of Decimus, members of the Board of Four, superintended the construction of this work out of public money by a vote of the local Senate.

59

(iii) *c.* 90–80 B.C.

Gaius Ulius [2] son of Gaius, and Publius Aninius son of Gaius, Board of Two for pronouncing jurisdiction, by decree of the local Senators contracted for the building of a Spartan sweating-room and a rub-down chamber, and for repairs to porticos and a wrestling school, out of the money which they were required to spend by law towards games or on a memorial. They superintended and acceptably completed the works.

60

Treasury at Praeneste.

Marcus Anicius Baso, son of Lucius, and Marcus Mersieius son of Gaius, aediles, gave means for the construction of this treasury.

[2] Cf. *C.I.L.*, I, 2, 1679, a, b, election-notices of the same man at Pompeii.

61

1576
     M. Herennius M. f. Gallus | Q. Veserius Q. f. duo
       vir. | quinq. | d. d. s. f. c. eidemq. prob. |
   5   Arcitectus Hospes Appiai ser.

62

1853
              . . .]RCATIO

. . . [*ad*] castellum ped. CX; af | . . . [*ad cas-*
tel]lum Ferebra et castellum | . . . [*p.*] ∞ ∞
   5   CCCXX; ab castello ad co|[*llem* . . . . . *cas-*
tel]lum ad vinias Anchariorum ped. | . . . . .
[*af vin*]*ı*//*ı* ieis Ancharum ad castellum qui |
[*est contra vin*]ias Pacianas p. CCCXX; af
vinieis | [*Pacianeis*] ad castellum qui est
contra | [*villam p.*] ÐCCCCL; af villa Paciana
  10 ad castel. | [*qui est s*]ub segete Paciana p.

     62 ³ *ad castel.*, ⁴⁻⁵ co[*llem, supplevi*

---

  ¹ See pp. xxxviii–xxxix.
  ² It is unknown what word formed the headline. Neither
mercatio nor *altercatio* would suit the subject-matter of the
inscription, which refers to repairs, or the like, of an aqueduct.
furcatio or *bifurcatio* are unlikely; *demarcatio* would not be Latin.
It might well refer to preliminary measurements for the laying
down of, or replacement of new pipes or repairs to old ones;
or to cleaning of pipes (*fistulae*). If the C should be G (but
it seems clear that it is C), or is used as an affected archaism
for G, then I suggest *Purgatio*, ' Cleaning.' Another possi-
bility which occurs to me is ' *Arcatio*,' ' Placing of land-marks '
(*arca*, properly a box, chest, coffin, can mean also a quad-
rangular land-mark). It would have relevance here, because,
at any rate in the imperial period, a strip of land 15 feet
wide, marked with boundary-stones at intervals, was left on
either side of aqueducts and no trespassing on it was allowed;
but we need a longer word here, nor does this word *arcatio*
occur anywhere. Note that in Vitruvius, VI, 3, we have
arcatura in the sense of a reservoir or cistern.

61

Building at Caiatia.   Two stones with the same inscription.

Marcus Herennius Gallus son of Marcus, and Quintus Veserius son of Quintus, in a fifth year,[1] as members of the Board of Two, by decree of the local Senate superintended the construction of this work, and likewise acceptably completed it.

Master-builder: Hospes, slave of Appia.

62

Aqueduct at Amiternum.   On stone.   Repairs?

. . . . [2]

. . . to (next) reservoir [3] 110 ft.; from . . . to the reservoir [4] Ferebra and the reservoir . . .; 2,320 [5] ft.; from that reservoir to the hill . . . to the reservoir by the vineyards of the Ancharii [6] . . . ft.; . . . from the vineyards of the Ancharii to the reservoir which is hard by Pacius' vineyards 320 ft.; from Pacius' vineyards to the reservoir which is hard by his country-house 950 ft.; from Pacius' country-house to the reservoir which is beneath

[3] *Castellus* is elsewhere usually a neuter *castellum*. The *castelli = castella* of this inscription designate intermediate reservoirs between the *piscina* (the reservoir built at the source of the aqueduct) and the main *castellum aquarium* built at the walls of a town supplied and forming the ' head of water.' They would hardly be the *castella* built between the ' head ' and the buildings supplied. Perhaps the masculine *castellus* was a normal variant used to designate any intermediate reservoir as distinct from the *castellum aquarium*.

[4] I supply [*ad castel*] and retain *et* after *Ferebra*.

[5] I take it that the number is complete on the inscription. If we supply two more signs, making the number 4,320, the total will exceed the total given on the inscription; and it would probably exceed that figure even if we were to supply one sign only so as to make 3,320.

[6] a Roman family.

CCLXXXV; af | [*castell*]o qui est sub segete
ad castel. ad | [*compitu*]m Traecis p. ∞ CCXC;
a[*b*] angulo | [*Traec.*]? ad cast. qui est ad
compitum Trae|[*cis p . . . . .*]; a[*b*] angul.
15   Traec. ad cast. qui est sub | [*segete*] Gavidi
CCCXLV; ab secete Gavidi ad ca | [*stellu*]m
ped. ÐCCCXXX. S. pe. ⅠↃↃↃↃÐCLXX

63

1898   M. Petrucidi. C. f., L. Pacidi. P. [*f. . . . .*] | aras
crepidine. colu[*mnas . . . . . .*] | magistris de
alec[*torum sententia . . .*]

64

2542 (*et*   . . . Lucilius A. f. Macer T. Annaeus Sex f.
p. 737)   Trhaso [*I*]I virei | [*quin*]q[*ue*]nnales exs s. c.
balneum aedeificandum couravru.

65

1806   T. Sa. Aiopi (?) | C. V. f. magist[*r*]|es de veci
     5 s[*ent.*] | opus faciund[*um*] | couraverunt.

Pacius' cornland 285 ft.; from the reservoir which is under the cornland to the reservoir at the roadsmeet of Traecis (?) 1,290 ft.; from the corner of Traecis (?) to the reservoir which is at the roadsmeet of Traecis (?) . . . ft.; . . . from the corner of Traecis (?) to the reservoir which is beneath Gavidius' cornland 345 ft.; from Gavidius' cornland to the (next) reservoir 830 ft. Total number of feet: 8,670.

63

Building in Picenum. On an old aqueduct between Hadria and Interamnia.

Marcus Petrucidius son of Gaius, and Lucius Pacidius son of Publius, overseers, . . . altars, a socle, columns . . . by a vote of the delegates.[1]

64

A bath at Lacinium. On a mosaic.

Lucilius Macer, son of Aulus, and Titus Annaeus Thraso, son of Sextus, members of the Board of Two, in a fifth year,[2] superintended the construction of a bath by decree of the Senate.

65

A public work among the Vestini. On stone. Precise origin unknown. Second century B.C.

The overseers Titus Aiopius son of Gaius, and Salvius Aiopius son of Vibius superintended the construction of this work by a vote of the village commune.[3]

---

[1] *alectorum = adlectorum.*   [2] for this, see p. xxxix.
[3] For *vicus*, see pp. xxxvii–viii.

66

1847
  Itus actusque est | in hoce delubrum | Feroniai,
    ex hoce loco | in via poplicam | Campanam
   5 qua | proxsimum est | p. ↀCCX . . .

67

1906
  (a) L. Tettaienus L. f. | Barcha |, L. Fistanus L. f. |
     5 iter in Campum ex c. d. | pecunia sociorum |
    Campi faciundum | coeravere eidemq. | pro-
    bavere.

  (b) Extra | maceria | in agrum | praecario.

(v) INSTRUMENTUM

1

Fibula Praenestina.

3
  (i) μανιος μεδ ϝϩε ϝϩακεδ Νυμασιοι. ◄——
  (ii) Manios med fhe fhaked Numasioi.
  (iii) Manius me fecit Numerio.

---

 [1] The whole number has not survived; it was more than 1210 feet.

 [2] The one given here is now lost; the other (*C.I.L.*, I, 2, 1905) is similar; *c.d.* = *conscriptorum decreto; maceria = maceriam; praecario* should be, as on the surviving stones, *precario.*

 [3] *sc.* Numerius. I have given opposite, in 'modernised' letters, the inscription (i) as it stands on the brooch (but from left to right) in Greek characters; (ii) in archaic Praenestine Latin; (iii) in classical Latin. Cf. Buecheler, *Rh. Mus.*, XLII, 317; Darbishire, *Reliquiae Philologicae*, 6 ff.; Lattes, *Le Iscr. Paleolat.*, 71; *C.I.L.*, I, 2, p. 717; Fasc. III, p. 831. Because F is in Greek the digamma, ⊟ = h is put after it to

INSCRIPTIONS ON MOVABLE ARTICLES

66

A right-of-way near Amiternum.

Right-of-way for walking and thoroughfare for driving is permitted to this shrine of Feronia, and from this place to the public road, namely the Campanian, at the nearest point thereof, distance 1, 2 . . . ft.[1]

67

Construction of a road at Interamnia.   On Boundary-stones.[2]

(*a*) Lucius Tettaienus Barcha, son of Lucius, and Lucius Fistanus son of Lucius superintended, by decree of the senators enrolled, the making of a road into the Field at the expense of the associates of the Field, and likewise acceptably completed the work.

(*b*) *On the side :* Entry on ground outside the wall by request only.

For a number of inscriptions recording building of public works, by colleges, and connected with a deity, and so classed among dedicatory inscriptions, see pp. 98 ff.

(v) INSCRIPTIONS ON ALL KINDS OF MOVABLE ARTICLES, MOSTLY FOR PRIVATE USE.

On toilet articles found at Praeneste.

1

A golden brooch made by Manius.   Seventh or sixth century B.C.   *The inscription is in Greek characters (running from right to left) which show the Greek alphabet undergoing a change to fit the needs of Praenestine Latin.*

Manius made me for Numasios.[3]

express the unvoiced nature of the Latin f as compared with the digamma in Greek.   Note also the reduplicated perfect *fefaked.*   See facsimile page xlviii.

2–3

Cistae.

Cista Ficoroniana.

561 (*a*) Dindia Macolnia fileai dedit.

  (*b*) Novios Plautios med Romai fecid.

562 (*c*) Maqolnia (?)

4

(ii) *Another bronze casket, depicting a rustic kitchen-scene; c.* 250–235 B.C. *Two (or more ?) slave-cooks preparing a savoury meal. The inscriptions run partly from right to left as shewn here below. It is usually assumed that half a dozen people are*

560 (*a*) Confice piscim. ⟶

  (*b*) Coeci alia. ⟵

  (*c*) Cofeci. ⟵

  (*d*) Feri porod. ⟵

  [5] (*e*) Made mi recie. ⟶

[4] [b] îⅠ⅃ΛⅠⅠϡΩϽ ⟵ crevi alia *coni.* Diehl coëmi alia Ribezzo coepi alia *vel* coenalia Duvau coena pia *coni.* Lindsay

  [e] MΛDE MIRECIE

---

[1] Both the sentences were inscribed by Novius.

[2] Very uncertain—see Graef, in Benndorf, *Wien. Vorlegeblätter,* 1889, VII, 1 (*a*).

[3] So I translate instead of taking *alia* to mean 'other things'; or 'I have made a garlic paste,' a 'cake' (*coago,* thicken, coagulate) or possibly 'I have collected the garlic-juice' (Cato, *R.R.,* 64, 1; 65, 2; 144, 1).

[4] not A. The figure seems to be that of the same person as has just said *coeci alia.*

198

INSCRIPTIONS ON MOVABLE ARTICLES

2–3

(b) Toilet-caskets.

(i) A bronze toilet-casket made by Novius for Dindia Macolnia. c. 250–235 B.C. On the lid.[1]

(*a*) Dindia Macolnia gave this to her daughter.

(*b*) Novius Plautius made me at Rome.

Under one of the legs.

(*c*) Maqolnia[2]?

4

preparing one dish, but it seems to me there are two people only preparing several dishes for one meal. I have called the two persons A and B and have added what they appear to me to be doing.

A (*who is cutting up a fish*).

(*a*) Prepare the fish!

B (*taking down the lower part of a pig*).

(*b*) I've made the garlic [3] patties thick.

   *   *   *   *   *

B ([4] *with a dish of fish ?-cakes in one hand and a knife in the other*).

(*c*) I've prepared it.

A (*holding out a dish to B*).

(*d*) Beat it up with a leek! [5]

   *   *   *   *   *

B (*Stirring and addressing a large cauldron*).

(*e*) Boil for me royally! [6]

[5] So I suggest. It seems to me to be right. If, however, *poro* is an adverb, then translate : ' Flip further ! ' *or* ' Beat further ' !

[6] Variously read and interpreted; *c* in place of *q* lasted a long while after the introduction of *q*. The best alternative is *made mire, cie* : ' Boil wondrously ! Stir it up ' !

INSTRUMENTUM

(*f*) Misc. sane. ⟵———

(*g*) Asom fero. ———⟶

5

569　　(*a*) ———⟶ Castor. (*b*) Pater poumilionom. ⟵———

6–9

Specula

547　　(i) Opeinod　　　devincam ted.
552 (*et*　(ii) (*a*) Marsuas　　　　　(*b*) Painsscos
p. **714**)　　　　　　(*c*) Vifis Pilipus cailavit.
555　　(iii) (*a*) Taseos　　　　　(*b*) Luqorcos
　　　　　　　(*c*) Pilonicos Taseio filios
559　　(iv) (*a*) Metio　　(*b*) Fasia　　(*c*) Acila
　　　　　　(*d*) Ceisia Loucilia Fata ret. Iunio Setio Atos
　　　　　　　　　ret.

(ii) Vifis, Matthies　　VIƷIS

---

[1] I bring it ' to the fire ' (supine *arsum*) Lindsay; ' to be cooked ' Duvau; ' I'm here ' (*udsum*) Pauline Turnbull. The last may be right. For the whole inscription, cf. Duvau, *Mél. d'archéol. et d'hist.*, X, 303 ff.; Kent, *Language*, V, March, 1929, 18–22; Pauline Turnbull, *id.*, 15–17, and the bibliographical list given by Kent, *id.*

[2] G. Matthies, *Die Prän. Spiegel* (*Zur Kunstgesch. d. Auslandes*, XCV).

[3] *opeinod = ob illud* (?), Kent, *Forms of Latin*, 246, n. 5. Not *opinor* ' I think.'

[4] Painsscos should be Panisscos. *Vifis* should perhaps be *Vibis = Vibius*; of the Vibian *gens* Philippus would be a freedman.

[5] *i.e.* Thasios, eponymous ancestor of the Greeks of Thasos island? The legend is unknown. *Taseio* = Thaseian = son of Thasos? Perhaps Theseus. The reading is doubtful.

INSCRIPTIONS ON MOVABLE ARTICLES

A (*prodding or stirring the food in the cauldron and holding in his left hand a plate of seven cakes*).

(*f*) Well then, mix away!

*　　　*　　　*　　　*　　　*

B (*walking away and perhaps announcing to invisible diners*).

(*g*) The roast in hand I bring.[1]

5

(iii) *Another casket, depicting Castor, Pollux, a dwarf, and companions. Now in the British Museum. Reads partly from right to left.*

(*a*) Castor.　(*b*) Father of dwarfs.

6–9

On mirrors.[2]

(i) *Depicting a boy and a girl playing on a gaming-board.*

Because of that [3], I'll win against you.

(ii) *Depicting Marsyas dancing with Little Pan.*

(*a*) Marsyas.　(*b*) Little Pan.[4]　(*c*) Vifius Philippus engraved this.

(iii) *Depicting Lycurgus, threatening Philonicus and a rescuer.*

(*a*) Thaseus.[5]　(*b*) Lycurgus.　(*c*) Philonicus son of Thaseus.

(iv) *In the Lewis collection, Corpus Christi College, Cambridge. Depicting domestic life. Girl Fasia on Metios' knee. Acila stands near.*

(*a*) Metios.　(*b*) Fasia.　(*c*) Acila (*or* handmaid).
(*d*) [6] Ceisia Lucilia Fata and Iunios Setios Atos. . . .

---

[6] This part is obscure. Jordan, *Krit. Beitr.*, 71; Buecheler, *Rhein. Mus.*, XLII, 320. Should *Fata* be *Ata* or *Atos* be *Fatos*? Ret = names Retus, Reta? We have a freedman's name Retus, below, number 13.

10–11

573   (i) Fove L. Corneliai L. f.

2437   (ii) Med Loucilios feced.

12–16

406   (i) L. Canoleios L. f. fecit Calenos

412   (ii) Retus Gabinio C. s. Calebus fec. te

416   (iii) K. Serponio Caleb. fece veqo. Esqelino C. s.

2489   (iv) L. Canolei off. sum

2487   (v) M. Caleb. verna serv.

12–16 (ii) te *fortasse* testam

---

[1] So 1 take it; the owner meant stroke me softly when I use you. Cf. Buecheler, *Rh. Mus.*, LII, 392; Fay, *Studies in Honour of Gildersleeve*, 194 thinks *fove* = *fui*. Read perhaps *fave*, 'be favourable to Lucia Cornelia,' since the weasel was believed to have magic powers. Or translate '*fove*,' 'cherish,' with the same idea.

INSCRIPTIONS ON MOVABLE ARTICLES

10–11

On scrapers.

(i) *A small weasel, with base and handle. Praeneste.*

Caress [1] me. Property of Lucia Cornelia, daughter of Lucius.

(ii) *Found near Corchiano, Faliscan territory.*

Me Lucilius made.

12–16

On ware made before 220 B.C. at Cales [2] and found in various parts of Italy (see C.I.L., I, 2, 405–417; and id, pp. 720–1, numbers 405a, 406(a), 2487 ff.).

(i) *On a number of paterae.*

Made by Lucius Canuleius of Cales, son of Lucius.

(ii) *On paterae found at Tarquinii.*

I, Retus Gabinius, slave [3] of Gaius, made you at Cales.

(iii) *On a patera bought at Naples.*

Kaeso Serponius made this at Cales, in the Esquiline quarter. A slave of Gaius.

(iv) *On a mould for paterae, found at Capua : now in the British Museum.*

I am from the workshop [4] of Lucius Canuleius.

(v) *On a clay vessel. Rome?*

Marcus? a household slave; at Cales.

---

[2] For the whole series, cf. Pagenstecher, *Die Calenische Reliefkeramik, Arch. Jahrb.*, Ergänz.-heft VIII; and *Arch. Jahrb.*, XXVII, 146 ff.; Koerte, *Götting. Gel. Anz.*, 1913, 253.
[3] Here and in the next inscription slave means freedman.
[4] Or :—'I am the workmanship'; cf. Pliny, XI, 2.

INSTRUMENTUM

17–30

477 (i) Amor med Flaca dede

478 (ii) Rustiae Rustiu iousit caper.

479 (iii) (*a*) Eqo Fulfios   (*b*) maci (?)

480 (iv) Statia catino

488 (v) Pilotimei Lucretei L. s.

498 (vi) Claudio; non sum tua

499 (vii) Ne atigas; non sum tua, M. sum

500 (viii) N(e) atica. me; Cemuci sum

501 (ix) Sotae sum; noli me tanger.

(iii) ΜΛϿ¹   (viii) NATICAME

---

¹ Cf. Dressel, *Ann. dell' Instit.*, 1880, and *C.I.L.*, XV.
6158 ff.

² Fay, *Woch. f. Kl. Philol.*, XXVIII, 989 attributes this to
the reign of Claudius (A.D. 41–54).

³ *capere* or *caperet*, sc. receive it in her grave?

204

17–30

On various articles.[1]   *Before 220 B.C.*

(i) *Ointment-pot.*[2] *Found by the Tiber. Has apex, 'Fláca' (?).*

Love gave me to Flacca.

(ii) *Small pitcher, Esquiline necropolis.*

Rustius asked Rustia to take [3] this.

(iii) *Clay dish.   Rome.*

(*a*) I Fulfios, made it.[4]

(*b*) *On the inside, in another hand :*

Marcus' (?) slave.

(iv) *Pot. Esquiline necropolis.   Under one foot.*

Statia possesses this pot.

(v) *Round the funnel of an ink-well.   Rome.*

The property of Philotimus, slave of Lucius
Lucretius.[5]

(vi) *Lamp. Esquiline necropolis.*

For [6] Claudius.   I am not yours.

(vii) *Lamp.   Esquiline necropolis.*

Do not touch; I am not yours; I am Marcus'.

(viii) *Lamp.   Velitrae.*

Do not touch me.   I am Gemucius'.

25   (ix) *Lamp. Esquiline necropolis.*

I am Sota's.   Touch me not.

---

[4] the verb *feci* is to be understood.   On the inside is written
apparently, so far as I can see, *maci*, which is possibly Marci.
Cf. Lindsay, *Lat. Langu.*, § 109.

[5] or perhaps rather: 'of Philotimus Lucretius, slave'
(freedman) 'of Lucius.'

[6] placed in his grave.

INSTRUMENTUM

504 (x) Statia vilic. nostra

518 (xi) T. Ivilio Ste. S. Hel.

545 (xii) C. Ovio Ouf. fecit

546 (xiii) C. Pomponi Quir. opos

431-2 (xiv) C. Paco. C. f. Q. n.

31
398 Q. Lainio Q. f. praifectos pro trebibos fecit.

32
382 V. Avilio V. f., V. Alfieno Po. f., pagi veheia.

33
462 Eco C. Antonios.

(xi) Ste(ni) s(ervus) H(elenus), Momms.

---

[1] Mommsen, however, suggests Titus Iovilius Helenus, slave of Stenius.

[2] his people, as organised perhaps in voting-units.

[3] Not certain. It might be better perhaps to understand *pagi Veheiani*, 'the Veheian hamlets,' or, 'of the Veheian hamlet' or to take *veheia* to mean in dialect *scitu* or *decreto* 'by decree,' as Jordan does.

INSCRIPTIONS ON MOVABLE ARTICLES

(x) *Lamp. Esquiline.*

Statia, our bailiff's wife.

(xi) *Lamp. Esquiline necropolis.*

Placed by Spurius Helvius for Titus Ivilius of the Stellatine tribe.[1]

(xii) *On the neck of a bronze bust of Medusa. Found at Rome ?*

Made by Gaius Ovius of the Ufentine tribe.

(xiii) *On the cloak of a bronze statue of Jupiter. District of Orvieto.*

The work of Gaius Pomponius, of the Quirine tribe.

(xiv) *On a vessel of Umbrian origin. Found on the Esquiline.*

Gaius Paconius, son of Gaius, grandson of Quintus.

31

On a bronze vessel of Campanian origin. Now in the British Museum.

Quintus Laenius, prefect, son of Quintus, made this in the name of his tribes.[2]

32

On a bronze dish. The letters are formed by punctured dots. From Picenum.

To Vibius Avilius son of Vibius, and Vibius Alfienus son of Publius out of the traffic revenue[3] of the hamlet.

33

On a chalk lid of a well ? Esquiline.

I, Gaius Antonius, made it.

INSTRUMENTUM

Tesserae hospitales

34

611   (i) [*Consc*]riptes cose.   T. Fa [. . . . . *praifecti* | *et*
         p]raifectura tot[*a Fundi hospitium*] |[*f*]ecere
         quom Ti. C[*laudio*]. | [*I*]n eius fidem om[*nes*
      5   *nos tradimus et*] | convenumis; co[*optamus*
         eum patronum] | M. Claudio M. f. [. . . . . *cos.*]

35

1764   (ii) T. Manlius T. f. | hospes | T. Staiodius N. f.

36–40

699–701   (i) Fal. Mas.   (ii) F.   (iii) F. O.
         Q. Lutatio   C. M. Q. L. cos.   M'. Aq. cos.
         C. Mario
         cos.

702   (iv) (*a*) Ar. cer.   (*b*) Cn. Cor. P. Lic.
            C. Domit.   cos.

---

34 [5] *coni.* convenimus co[*optamus e. p.*] *olim* Momms., *Eph.
Epigr.*, II, 147
    36–40 (iii) FO   (iv) (*a*) ᚠR·CER| C·POMIT

---

[1] Usually halved lengthwise, each party keeping one half.
Larger *tabulae patronatus et hospitii*, recording a person's
guestship with a community, were usually hung on a hall-wall
of the person honoured, forming 'Documents' of Class II.
See Introd., pp. xi–xii.   [2] *cose. = consensu.*
   [3] cf. note 1; *C.I.L.*, I, 2, 23; bronze dolphin: I, 2, 828.
   [4] First bottled in 121 B.C.
   [5] So I take it = wax-sealed (*cer. = ceratum*);   or perhaps
ar. is *arvina*, lard, grease.
   [6] Or *Pomitius.*   Name of the owner.

INSCRIPTIONS ON MOVABLE ARTICLES

Portable guest-tokens.[1]

34

(i) *Piece of a fat bronze fish found at Fundi. Between 222 and 153 B.C.*

Unanimously[2] resolved: the Senators on the Roll. Titus Fa . . . the prefects and all the prefecture of Fundi have established a bond of guestship with Tiberius (Claudius)? We entrust all of us to his good faith and in it meet together. We all choose him as a patron. In the consulship of Marcus Claudius son of Marcus and. . . .

35

(ii) *Half of a halved bronze ram's head.*[3] *Trasacco.*

Titus Manlius, son of Titus.
Guest.
Titus Staiodius, son of Numerius.

36–40

On wine-jars or bottles. (i), (ii), (iii) are each on a different jar.
(i) *Esquiline,* 102 B.C.
(ii) *Between Viminal and Esquiline,* 102 B.C.,
(iii) *By the Ostian Way,* 101 B.C.

(i) Falernian-Massic	(ii) Falernian	(ii·) Falernian-Opimian[4]
In the consulship of	In the consulship of	In the consulship of
Quintus Lutatius and Gaius Marius	Gaius Marius and Quintus Lutatius	Manius Aquillius

(iv) *By the Ostian Way,* 97 B.C. *Both* (a) *and* (b) *are on the same jar.*

(*a*) Waxed[5] Arvisian of Gaius Domitius[6]

(*b*) In the consulship of Gnaeus Cornelius and Publius Licinius

209

653   (v) (*a*) Verg.   (*b*) Formianum.
                 pr. G. Sempr.
                 Q. Fabri.

41–48

2323   (i) C. L. Tossieis C. f. | C. Tossius C. l.

2351   (ii) Figl. L. Tetti Balbi ; | Antioc. Tos. Sex.

2371   (iii) Antiocus fixi te.

2374   (iv) L. Q. Au. St. s. fecit.

2375   (v) C. Rufius s. finxit.

2376   (vi) Noli me | tollere. | Helveiti sum.

2391   (vii) A. Septunolena Petr. Maisio dono.

2397   (viii) M. P. Roscieis M. f. Maic.

36–40 (v) (*b*) F͞RMIANVI

---

[1] So I take *pr.*, that is, as *praedium*; or possibly *prelum* ' wine-press.'

[2] There is no record elsewhere of two such names as names of consuls in the same year. But Fabricius may have been elected in 129 B.C. to replace M'. Aquillius, who was consul in that year with C. Sempronius Tuditanus. *Formianum* was added by a later hand.

[3] The same also on a jar—*C.I.L.*, XV, 2501.

[4] *s.* (*servus*) is to be understood; that is, a freedman, as in many of the older inscriptions.

[5] *fixi = finxi*.

[6] This assumes from the nature of the object that *s.* here stands for *sigillator*, *sigillarius*, or *sigillariarius*.

INSCRIPTIONS ON MOVABLE ARTICLES

(v) *Found somewhere in Rome.* 129 B.C.?

(*a*) Vergilian estate [1]   (*b*) Formian
Gaius Sempronius and Quintus Fabricius.[2]

41–48

On various objects, second or first century B.C.

(i) *On [3] a brick. Velitrae.*

Gaius Tossius and Lucius Tossius, sons of Gaius;
Gaius Tossius, freedman of Gaius.

(ii) *On a cask found near Orvieto.*

The pottery of Lucius Tettius Balbus.
Antiochus, slave [4] of Tossius Sextus made it.

(iii) *On a small earthen equipoise. Near Mantua.*

I, Antiochus, modelled [5] you.

(iv) *Clay tile. Cortona ?*

Made by Lucius Quintius Au. (?), slave of Statius.

(v) *On the plinth of a statuette. Origin unknown.*

Modelled by Gaius Rufius, statuette-maker.[6]

(vi) *Under the foot of an ' Arretine ' vessel. Rome.*[7]

Do not filch me. I belong to Helvetius.

(viii) *On a bronze dish. Origin unknown.*

From Aula [8] Septunolena, as a gift to Petro
Maesius.

(viii) *On some pigs [9] of lead found in a mine near Cartagena
in Spain.*

Marcus Roscius and Publius Roscius, sons of
Marcus, of the Maecian tribe.

[7] Cf. pp. 204–5.
[8] or, Aulus Septunolena, a gentile name of Etruscan origin.
[9] Cf. *C.I.L.*, II, 3439, suppl. n. 6247, 4; *Eph. Epig.*, IX, 181.

INSTRUMENTUM

Glandes

49

847   L. Piso L. f. ‖ cos.

50- 57

848   (i) (*a*) Itali.   (*b*) T. Laf. pr.
857   (ii) (*a*) Feri   (*b*) Pomp.

858   (iii) (*a*) Fer ⟵   (*b*) sal.   (*c*) Pom. ⟵   (*d*) fer
860   (iv) Feri Picam.
859   (v) Asclanis[*d*]on.
861   (vi) Fugitivi peristis.
875   (vii) Em tibe malum malo.
877   (viii) (*a*) [*T*]aurum vor[*e*]s   malo.   (*b*) Ta[*m*]en
       evomes omnem.

Tesserae ' consulares ' vel ' nummulariae '

58–63

These are called *tesserae consulares* because each gives
the date by a consulship. They are oblong blocks of bone
or ivory with a handle or hole for attachment, and, when
inscribed in complete form, give a person's name (a slave or
freedman), the name of his master or patron, the word *spectavit*,
or *spect.* or *sp.*, and a day, a month, and a year. Herzog, in
Abh. der Giessener Hochschulgesellschaft, I, 1919, ' Aus der
Geschichte des Bankwesens im Altertum, Tesserae Nummulariae,' argues persuasively that the tickets record the passing
of coins by official test (one ticket—*C.I.L.*, I, 2, 908—had

---

(v) 'ON
(viii) (*a*) ////AVRVM VORſ:S·MALO   *fortasse* voras

---

[1] He is not otherwise known to have besieged Henna,
which was taken by Rupilius in 132 B.C. during a slave-war.
[2] See Zangemeister, *Eph. Epigr.*, I, 1 ff.; VI, 5, ff.; 142.
C.I.L., I, 2, p. 560; Bursian's *Jahresbericht*, LVI, 10 ff.
[3] Pompeius Strabo, sent against Asculum in 91 B.C., was
at first shut up in Firmum (cf. shots marked with *Fir*—*C.I.L.*,
I, 2, 854–5) by the Italian general (*praetor*) Lafrenius (cf. nos.
i–iii below) but later on besieged Asculum.

INSCRIPTIONS ON MOVABLE ARTICLES

On sling-shots found at Castro Giovanni (Henna) in Sicily.
133 B.C.

49

Lucius Piso [1] consul, son of Lucius.

50–57

Sling-shots [2] of lead of the so-called ' Social War.' 90–
89 B.C. (C.I.L., I, 2, 848–884). The first found at Corropoli,
the rest at Asculum.[3] Some of the readings are very uncertain.

(i) (*a*) The Italians. (*b*) Titus Lafrenius, praetor.
(ii) Hit Pompeius! (iii) Bring safety for Pompeius!
(iv) Hit a Pie![4] (v) A gift for the Asculans. (vi)
Runaways, you are done for! (vii) There's hell for
you, damn you! (viii) (*a*) Swallow the bull,[5] and go
to hell! (*b*) Yet you will belch up the lot!

Tickets of bone or ivory.

58–63

apparently *spectat num* which means probably *spectator
nummorum,* ' inspector of coins,' or *spectator numerator*
' inspector and counter.' It was found at Arles, was dated
63 B.C., and is known only from a copy which has NWI); and
I accept this view. Each *tessara* therefore stated that so-and-
so as cashier inspected a batch of coins; and each *tessara* was
attached to a money-basket or *fiscus.* An older view was
that each *tessara* recorded the date on which a gladiator took
his ' ticket of discharge ' and ' became a spectator ' after
release from the arena. Thus the fact that no extant date

---

[4] *Pica* is a magpie. There is a pun on *Picentes.* But since
the bird fancifully connected with Picenum was a *picus*
(woodpecker), perhaps we should read *picum* here and translate it ' pecker.' Indeed, the shot seems to have PICΛ
                                                    OM
[5] cf. *C.I.L.* I, 2, 876. Possibly an allusion to the Samnite
bull stamped on coins struck by the Samnite Papius Mutilus;
taurus also means a kind of beetle—Pliny, XXX, 39. Is there
an allusion to the shape of the shot?

coincides with a regular date for Roman gladiatorial shows was explained. The owner of the slave (or patron of the freedman) was in this view the trainer. Ritschl's view that, on the ticket found at Arles, the words were *spectat*(*us*) *mun*(*ere*), suggests *spectatum satis et donatum iam rude* of *Horace, Ep.*, I, 1, 2. For different views, see Herzog as above,

889   (i) Caputo Memmi. | men. Nove. | Cn. Domit. C. Cas. | spect.

2663 (a)   (ii) Piloxen. soc. fer. | C. Coil. L. Dom. | Spectavit | n. Apr.

890   (iii) Menopil. Abi. L. s. | spectavit | C. Val. M. Her.

891   (iv) Darda. Bab. | non. Febr. | spect. | L. Corn. L. Val.

892   (v) Cocero | Fafini | sp. a. d. III n. Oc. | L. Cin. Cn. Pa.

893   (vi) Bato | Attaleni | sp. a. d. IV n. Mar. | L. Sul. Q. Met.

64

2388   [5] L. d. | ingenuiis | qui ad subfra|gia | descendunt.

---

[1] For many others dating after 80 B.C., see *C.I.L.*, I, 2, 895 ff.; 2663, b–c.

INSCRIPTIONS ON MOVABLE ARTICLES

and Ritschl, *Opusc.*, IV, 572 ff.; Hudson, *Bollett. dell' Istit.*, 1896, 227; Bursian, *Jahresbericht*, LVI, 103 ff.; Wordsworth, *Fragments and Specimens*, 483–5; *C.I.L.*, I, 2, pp. 564–5; Fasc. III, 1943, p. 839; Mommsen, *H.*, XXI, 276 ff.; Henzen, *Annali dell' Istit. d'Arch.*, XX, 273 ff., 357 ff.

(i) *Rome ?* 96 B.C.

Inspected by Capito slave of Memmius, in the month of November, in the consulship of Gnaeus Domitius and Gaius Cassius.

(ii) *Origin unknown.* 94 B.C.

Inspected by Philoxenus, servant of associate ironsmiths, on the 5th of April in the consulship of Gaius Coelius and Lucius Domitius.

(iii) *Near Tarracina.* 93 B.C.

Inspected by Menophilus, slave of Lucius Abius, in the consulship of Gaius Valerius and Marcus Herennius.

(iv) *Near Capua ?* 86 B.C. *Spurious ?*

Inspected by Dardanus, slave of Babius, on the 5th of Feb., in the consulship of Lucius Cornelius and Lucius Valerius.

(v) *Origin unknown. Now in the British Museum.* 85 B.C.

Inspected by Cocero, slave of Fafinius, on the 5th of Oct. in the consulship of Lucius Cinna and Gnaeus Papirius.

(vi) *Rome ?* 80 B.C.[1]

Inspected by Bato, slave of Attalenius, on the 4th of Mar. in the consulship of Lucius Sulla and Quintus Metellus.

64

Private notice of voting-place of a guild. Bronze plate for hanging up. Found at Rome.

Place reserved for the free-born who go down to give their votes.

NUMMI

Inscriptions on coins are generally treated as part of Numismatics, but they are nevertheless a part of Epigraphy also, and their inscriptions are naturally to be classed among the *tituli* on *instrumentum*. Of Roman coins of the Republic which are to be dated before 79 B.C., or show archaisms, I have given below a very few; the inscriptions occurring on these, being in some sense at least translatable, do form a part of Latinity. In the left margin of the Latin pages, I have given references to *C.I.L.*, I, 2, (2,) appendix *nummorum*, pp. 741 ff., and in the right margin of the English pages, I have given references to pages of the *B.M. Catalogue*, that is, *Coins of the Roman Republic* in the British Museum, Vols. I–III (H. A. Grueber, 1910). But it must be remembered not only that much work has been done since that catalogue was issued, but also that recently the establishment of a later date for the first institution of *denarii* by Rome, and other considerations (cf. H. Mattingly and E. S. G. Robinson, ' The date of the Roman denarius and other landmarks in early Roman coinage,' *Proc. Brit. Acad.*, XVIII, 1932, and other work cited below, p. 218) have put much of the results of earlier work out of date in two senses.

Among the very early Latins and Romans the most primitive form of exchange—by barter of anything for anything, especially cattle (*pecus*, whence comes *pecunia*)—was followed first by the use of lumps of impure copper, unshaped or of various shapes, and of undefined or vaguely fixed weights, then by the use of an exchange-unit in the form of a foot-long cast rod or bar (*as* probably = *asser, assula*), at first of copper, then of bronze as an alloy of copper and tin with a little lead. This was at first unmarked (*aes rude* or *infectum*), but was soon, in the casting, stamped, perhaps unofficially, with the figure of an ox, then later with other types. In this system (which modern scholars call *aes signatum* [1]) the foot-length went out of use, the weight alone—usually 4–5 pounds—counting, the shape becoming that of oblong or quadrilateral

---

[1] an unfortunate definition; *aes rude* is all right for the unmarked metal, but any kind of stamped *aes* would be *signatum*—an epithet which could apply to all the real coinage described below. It would be better to give these stamped

COINS

bricks (*lateres*). Bars or bricks thus marked were used well into the third century B.C. Such pieces were not coins, unless the stamping and issue of *aes signatum* was in fact official, and unless the pieces were also really used as money. Institution of a real coinage by Rome came late as compared with other Mediterranean races; but, once it began, the main developments took place within about a century and a quarter. The dates at which modern scholars place the institution and successive changes in real Roman coinage must lack precision, for the early literary tradition about its institution is mythical, and the literary records of the changes are inaccurate; but the following scheme is now winning wide acceptance.

Period (i). *c.* 289 B.C. (or later)—269 B.C. at least. Tradition (Pomponius, in *Dig.*, I, 2, 2, 30) seems to assign the institution of the triumvirate of the mint (see below) at Rome to 289 B.C., and the surviving early coins point to a period going back not earlier than about 290 B.C. These coins (*aes grave*) are a heavy round lenticular cast bronze *as* of rather less than a pound in weight (*as libralis*), and its parts—*semis* ($\frac{1}{2}$), *triens* ($\frac{1}{3}$), *quadrans* ($\frac{1}{4}$), *sextans* ($\frac{1}{6}$), and *uncia* ('ounce,' $\frac{1}{12}$); the values being marked on the coins as I , S, and the following dots :—. . . . (= 4 *unciae* = $\frac{1}{3}$ *as* = *triens*), . . ., . ., and . respectively. Multiples of the *as*—the *dupondius* ' 2 pound piece ' of 2 *asses*, the *tripondius* or *tressis* of 3 *asses*, and probably also the *decussis* of 10 *asses*—were likewise made, by casting, at this period. Bricks of the older kind (see above) were issued till at least 279 B.C. They would be used, as indicated above, not as coins, but, for instance, in the ceremony of formal transfer *per aes et libram*; for which, see *Remains of Old Latin*, III, pp. 428–9. There was as yet no silver or gold coined by Rome, though she already used ingots and foreign coins of these metals.

Period (ii). *c.* 268—*c.* 235 B.C. The bronze described above was still issued but was supplemented by the first issue

---

bricks the name *aes grave signatum*, and to call the later bronze coinage of Periods (i) and (ii), as described below, *aes librale signatum* or something like that.

of a struck silver coinage in the form of a didrachm chiefly, though its tenth (a *litra ?*) also occurs, and by small copper (not bronze) coins chiefly as token-money or small change. This so-called 'Romano-Campanian' [1] silver and copper money is now regarded as minted not only at Capua but at other places also. Though not struck at Rome, it was Roman money, imitated by other Italians. Marks of value were omitted. *c.* 255 appeared 'quadrigate' didrachms, and, for a short time, issues of gold coins in two pieces of 6 and 3 scruples with no value-marks but probably equal to 45 later victoriates (135 *sestertii*), and 22½ vict. (67½ *sest.*) respectively ; for which, see below.

Period (*iii*). *c.* 235–216 B.C. at least. The bronze was still issued but the weight of the *as* was reduced to about half a pound. The silver didrachms continue. Striking of the bronze is introduced.

Period (*iv*). *c.* 216–187 B.C. The same coins were issued, but the *as* was reduced to the weight of about 4 ounces or less, and the silver was supplemented for some time by the issue of new silver coins the *victoriatus* (having no mark of value, but equal to half the quadrigate and to one drachm and to ¾ of the later denarius), and its half and its double, for use outside Rome on a standard already long used in North Italy and in Illyria ; and probably by the first *quinarii* of 5 *asses*—see p. 219.

Period (*v*). Beginning in 187 B.C. The all-important change now assigned [2] by Mattingly and others to about the year 187 was the issue of a new silver coinage of which the highest denomination was destined to dominate the currency of all the civilised west for more than five centuries, and to give its initial letter to an abbreviated designation for our penny. (*a*) This new coin was the (*nummus*) *denarius* or

---

[1] cf. Mattingly, *Journal of the Warburg Inst.*, 1937, 197.

[2] See the revolutionary change of view put forward convincingly by H. Mattingly and E. S. G. Robinson, ' The date of the Roman denarius and other landmarks in early Roman coinage,' *Proc. Brit. Acad.*, XVIII, 1932. Hitherto the date 269 given by Pliny was little questioned. J. G. Milne, *The Development of Roman Coinage*, 1937, puts the first denarii in 217, with less probability ; cf. id., *Class. Rev.*, 1936, 215 ; *J.R. Stud.*, 1938, 70 ; F. Altheim, *T.I.N.C.*, 1936, 137 ; E. Sydenham, *id.*, 262. The new theory, which tends to be

COINS

'tenpiece' of 10 *asses*, with the value-mark X = figure 10. During the Gracchan period (133–122 B.C.)[3] the tariff was raised to 16 *asses* to the denarius. A few denarii exist with XVI on them—they were all issued probably at the time of the tariff change—but the prevailing sign of value becomes ✕, which is not apparently a monogram of XVI (though many a Roman user may have thought so) but letter X deleted to show a value-mark (cp. HS for ||S in the case of the sestertius, dealt with below).[4] The plain sign X was still used, in the end probably only on denarii from other mints than that at Rome, and on coins for the use of provinces. Anyhow, the name of the coin is always denarius, and in the end after 76 B.C. both signs disappear. (*b*) Another denomination of the new coinage was the (*nummus*) *quinarius* of 5 asses, marked V 'five' (very rarely Q—see below, p. 220). (*c*) The lowest denomination of the new silver was the (*nummus*) *sestertius* of 2½ asses (*sestertius* = *semis tertius*, which means either : 'the third piece [*as*-unit] is only half' = 2½; or perhaps : 'the third half-unit,' the first half being ½, the second being 1½), later of 4 asses, and marked ||S (*duo et semis* 'two and a half'). After 187 B.C. the *as* was reduced to two ounces—the 'sextantal' standard; the *dodrans* (¾ *as*) and the *bes* (⅔ *as*) appeared for a short time, perhaps during the Gracchan period; and subdivisions of the *uncia* were introduced. The bronze coinage was more or less dependent on the silver, and tended to be more or less token-money. Lastly, there was a new gold issue : (*a*) pieces with head of Mars, of scruples 3, 2, and 1—60, 40 and 20 *sestertii* (or *asses ?*) and marked accordingly LX, XXXX, XX respectively; (*b*) (at a later date) with head of Janus a piece[5] of 4 scruples and marked XXX (30 victoriates ?). All coins were now struck, not cast.

---

confirmed, upsets all the old expositions including Mattingly's own valuable one in *Roman Coins*, Methuen, 1928, pp. 3 ff.

[3] E. Sydenham, in *Numismatic Chronicle*, 1934, pp. 81–88, argued for the time of Tiberius Gracchus, but H. Mattingly replied (*id.*, pp. 88–91) in favour of the time of Gaius Gracchus.

[4] Though no examples exist Maccianus shows that even *quinarii* (see under *b*) could be marked ✕.

[5] the surviving examples are suspected of being forgeries; but see Mattingly, *Roman Coins*, 15, 24–5.

NUMMI

For all the regular coinage the chief mint was at Rome, except perhaps for quinarii and victoriates; but there were local Roman mints in South Italy, in Spain, and possibly in Sicily.

The gold described above being temporary issues, the *denarius* and its parts and the *as* and its parts remained as the Roman coinage proper, though the victoriate (ousted largely by the quinarius) survived, perhaps merely as a commodity to help trade. Independent Italian currency tends to lapse. The denarius is supreme. For some time fresh issues of *quinarii* and *sestertii* ceased; issues of the former were renewed at intervals under the terms of a *Lex Clodia* of unknown date (c. 113–101 ? perhaps 104 B.C.), with a new tariff of 8 *asses* each, the coins being marked not V as before but Q, and bearing the type and receiving the name of the old victoriati (cf. Pliny, xxxiii, 3, 13); issues of the *sestertii* [1] were renewed for a time under the terms of the *Lex Papiria semunciaria* (or *de asse semunciali* or *de aere publico*) passed in 89 B.C. This law also reduced the *as* to half an ounce—$\frac{1}{24}$ of its original weight,—and suppressed local mints in Italy, especially those which had been created by the rebels during the ' Social ' War (91–88 B.C.). Issues of fresh bronze ceased after 86 B.C. (except outside Rome by generals in the provinces) until 15 B.C.; so also did issues of silver except the denarius. After 88 B.C. Sulla issued in the East on his own authority the first gold *aurei*,[2] but such gold coinage was not official until Julius Caesar after 50 B.C. made a proper gold coinage of aurei and half aurei struck at Rome. However, with this and the important subject of the Roman coinage of the imperial period we are not concerned. Of non-Roman Italian coinage of the Republican period we need say little, important though it was. Not only states having no fixed bonds with Rome could and did make independent coins, but also the Roman ' allies ' of various degrees, including the Latin colonies, of which two examples are mentioned below. After the war (281–275 B.C.) with Pyrrhus, Roman coinage began to predominate, 'and gradually superseded the other coinages in Italy.

---

[1] Note that it was only in the imperial period that the *sestertius* became a brass coin.

[2] not the first actual gold, as we have seen, pp. 218–9.

[3] At the very beginning the coinage may have been supervised by the consuls.

220

COINS

With regard particularly to the coins given below, the following points should be noted. Roman coins of the Republic were never issued by Roman families (as has been popularly believed); nor could individual magistrates issue coins legally on their own authority alone, though some did. The proper coinage was made and issued by the state, and during the republic was controlled by the Roman Senate through Roman officials; but if any change of system (of weight, metal, and even to some extent the types) was undertaken, the whole people passed a law accordingly under which the Senate then made its issues. There is no real certainty about the place or places of minting in Rome. The mint for bronze may well have been at the temple of Saturn, while the mint known to have been at the temple of Juno Moneta (whose name *Moneta*,—meaning according to the Romans ' Adviser,' from *moneo*—was given to this mint and later to all money) was perhaps for silver only. Again there is no certainty as to who were the regular casters or strikers of coins for any regular issues until the first century B.C., but it appears probable that from the beginning or at any rate from an early period [3] of the real coinage of Rome the making and issue was normally directed by administrative officials called *Triumviri* or *Tresviri monetales* ' Board of Three of the Mint,' and, as late inscriptions and coins (not before 72 B.C.) show, *Triumviri* or *Tresviri aere argento auro flando feriundo* ' Board of Three for casting and striking bronze silver and gold.' [4] Tradition seems [5] to put their first creation in 289 B.C. On extant coins they first appear (at first as symbols, then monograms, initials, or abbreviations, then generally full name) on the ' sextantal' bronze, that is, after 188 B.C. (see above), though not on the earliest of this period, the signature guaranteeing the legality of the issue. They do not appear on the earliest gold nor on the earliest *denarii*, *quinarii*, and *sestertii*, but before long they appear on all coins as a rule, though there were some issues without moneyer's names. For a long time perhaps the triumviri were appointed only when issues of money were needed.

---

[4] This full title of course was reached by successive stages marked by the introduction of more than one metal and of striking. *aere* is dative in case.

[5] Pomponius, in *Dig.*, I, 2, 2, 30; cf. Livy, Epit. xi.

NUMMI

Anyhow, round about 100 B.C. the office appears as a minor and doubtless year-long and yearly elective Roman magistracy, held usually before the quaestorship. With a few possible exceptions, the name of only one triumvir appears on any coin; the triumvirs coin not as a Board but individually when called on by the Senate, so that, although these were elected, there was normally nothing for any of them to do, and even when issues were made, two were normally idle. In the latter part of the Republic the *quaestores urbani* also, who controlled the treasury (*aerarium Saturni*), and so in a way had an eye on the coinage, could perhaps take an administrative part in the actual striking and issue of coins. At any rate they had charge of the state's bullion (from which, instead of the market's bullion, coins were sometimes struck) and received the money from the triumvirs so that they could use it for state-purposes. Outside Italy the issues were probably in the hands of the provincial quaestors alone. But when a quaestor's name and magistracy appears on the actual coins, then the issue was for a special purpose (see below). There is probably no exception to this rule. Thus the Board of Three were the normal moneyers of the coinage, whose names might appear on the coins, though sometimes other magistrates were allowed by the senate to coin or to put their names on coins. During the latter part of the Republic, when most of the coins given below were issued, there were really two kinds of coinage, the coinage minted in Rome, and the coinage minted in the provinces. For there were mints at places other than Rome; but all permanent mints, both in Italy and the provinces, were, like the mint at Rome itself, controlled by the Senate. However, there was a good deal of provincial minting (of special issues), some of which was perhaps only nominally within the Senate's control, while some was quite outside it, being the work of powerful Roman generals— proconsuls or *imperatores*—each acting by virtue of his own military authority and usually bearing his name with or without the name of a military moneyer or coin-striker subordinate to him. This tendency is especially clear from Sulla's time onwards, and is one sign of loss of senatorial control in the provinces—a loss fateful for the Republic.

Four further points should be noted with regard to the coins given below :—(i) When a moneyer is mentioned (usually one only is mentioned) on a coin and he is not designated as being any magistrate, he is nearly always *triumvir aere argento auro flando feriundo* and is making a normal issue at the senate's request. Coins issued by administrative persons other than such triumvirs, and not necessarily bearing only one person's name, are a feature of the last century of the Republic; and such coins were issued by decree of the senate acting on its own discretion, in the name or names of more ordinary (that is, not triumviral) magistrates, usually quaestors or curule aediles, for a special purpose other than mere striking, one falling within the ordinary authority of the magistrates. Every moneyer had to be a magistrate, and, whatever the office attributed to the person's name on a coin, that person is in some sense at least a moneyer. It is generally held that no triumvir of the mint could make a special issue. I think that in exceptional cases he could; see note on p. 238. (ii) The special nature of special issues was further indicated, for purposes of commemoration, in various ways on the coins. Thus *s. c. (senatus consulto)* or *e(x) s. c.* and *d. s. s. (de senatus sententia)* means by official order of the senate—the former expression, ' by decree,' implying perhaps an express command, the latter, ' by vote,' perhaps implying a decree involving other matters also. The signs occur only in the last century of the Republic, and refer to special issues by special moneyers for Rome, Italy and the provinces. Again, the expressions *ex. a. p.* or *p. a. (ex argento publico)* ' from silver of the state ' and perhaps [1] at times *d. a. p. (de aere publico)* ' from bronze of the state ' and also *d. t.* (which Mommsen takes to mean *de thesauro* ' from the treasury ') and *p. (publice* ' officially ') give the source, that is, the bullion of the public treasury, from which the particular issue was struck, such issues being in fact for an emergency, for all our examples belong to the period of the Cimbric Wars (113–101 B.C.) and the ' Social ' War (91–88 B.C.). The bullion for ordinary issues was provided from the ordinary market; and the coins of such ordinary issues (as distinct from special issues), though of course coming officially from the state, bear none of the signs mentioned in (ii) above. (iii) The expression *l. P. (lege Papiria* ' by the Papirian law ') indicates a special issue by the senate but fulfilling the requirements of a people's law—in this case the Papirian, for which see pp. 220, 232—ordaining a change in

---

[1] But see below, p. 232.

the monetary system.   (iv) There occur on coins other marks such as fractions, whole numbers, letters, and symbols, which indicate something other than what we have described above. These signs or mint-marks are very common on coins (usually silver) from *c.* 125–66 B.C., and refer to the various workshops, dies and artists, not to values.   Since at present they are a mystery, I omit them in giving the contents of any coin.   For the rest, I include the inscription, ignoring any other part of the ' type ' unless the ' pictures ' or part of them are of

C.I.L., 1,2, app.	
24c	probom Suesano
40	I I Roma
40	S S Roma
41	X X X X Roma

---

[1] The issue was made after the foundation of the Latin colony by Rome at Suessa in 313 B.C.

[2] Or ' sterling.' This meaning has been questioned by Dressel, *Zeits. f. Num.*, XIV, 1887, 161).   The word is Latin rather than Campanian or Oscan; and the letters are Latin. *Suesano* is either *Suesanorum* or *Suesanom* (nom. sing. neut.).

COINS

historical significance or illustrate the inscription; in this book the lettering and punctuation and arrangement of phrases are editorial and do not indicate their position on the coin except as being on the 'obverse' (as it were the 'heads' side) or the reverse (the 'tails' side). The earlier coins have little translatable matter, so that most of the examples given belong to the period from *c.* 125 onwards, when longer inscriptions become commoner. Unless it is stated otherwise, the coins given were made in Rome.

B.M. Catal.

ITALIAN.

Bronze coins of Suessa Aurunca in Campania. Autonomous issue. Early 3rd century B.C.[1] *Struck at Suessa.*

  obv. Good mintage [2]
  rev. Of the Suessani

ROMAN.

As. After 187 B.C.   **I, 29**

  obv. Onepiece
  rev. Onepiece Rome

Half-as ('semis'). After 187 B.C.   **I, 31**

  obv. Halfpiece
  rev. Halfpiece Rome

Gold piece of 40 sesterces (or asses?). c. 187 B.C.   **I, 27**

  obv. Fortypiece
  rev. Rome

There are Roman coins with *Romano* or *Romanom*. On similar Suessan coins, we have *prboum* and *prbom*, while on copper coins of Beneventum *c.* 268 (when it received a Latin colony) we have *Beneventod* (ablative) *propom* or *proprom* or *pompro*. See B. V. Head, *Historia Numorum*, pp. 42, 28; H. Mattingly, *Numismatik*, 1932, 14; *C.I.L.*, I, 2, app. 24 *c*, 28.

40	IIS Roma
40	|.|S Roma
61c	V Roma Crk. **Ag.**
203	Roma ex s. c. ✱ M. Sergi. Silus q.
226	I. S. M. R. L. Thorius Balbus

61c CR Á

---

¹ For the new dating of the first gold pieces and the first denarii, of which the sestertii were subdivisions, see notice above, pp. 218–19.

² The dot in \|.\|, as indicating the sign as a value, becomes the cross-bar in the expression HS or H̄S common in literary texts and inscriptions to express sesterces or sestertia.

³ After the suppression of the Illyrian pirates, Corcyra became in 229 B.C. an ' ally ' of Rome under a Roman official, issuing its own chiefly bronze coinage which like this coin has the names of magistrates or prytaneis and a monogram of the city's name. This coin is of Roman type and denomination, but was struck at Corcyra. The hitherto accepted date (229 B.C.) of this issue can still hold good, because the *quinarius*, though made part of the *denarius* whose first issue

COINS

Sestertius. c. 180 B.C.[1]   **II, 29**

    obv.   Two-and-a-halfpiece
    rev.   Rome

Sestertius. c. 180 B.C.[2]   **I, 16**

    obv.   Two-and-a-halfpiece
    rev.   Rome

Quinarius. c. 229? or c. 187 B.C. *Struck in Corcyra.*[3]   **I, 29**

    obv.   Fivepiece
    rev.   Rome   Corcyra   Agesandros

Denarius. c. 125–120? B.C. *Struck in Spain.*   **II, 269**

    obv.   Rome   By decree of the Senate[4]
            Tenpiece
    rev.   Marcus Sergius Silus
            quaestor

Denarius. c. 110 B.C.   **I, 225**

    obv.   (*head of Juno*) Juno Protectress Mother
            Queen[5]
    rev.   Lucius Thorius Balbus

is now dated 187 B.C., was instituted earlier; see pp. 218–19.
There were issued also *victoriati* with similar monograms;
B.M. catal., II, 197; Hill, *Hist. Roman Coins*, pp. 44 ff.

[4] All issues under this and similar authority were exceptional
issues, though frequent; see notice p. 223. Silus was probably
a quaestor of the province under the governor. For 'tenpiece'
rather than 'sixteenpiece,' and the sign ✷, see above pp.
218–19.

[5] *Iuno Sospes* (or *Sospita; Sispes; Sispita*) *Mater Regina;*
she appears here for the first time on coins. Her oldest cult
was at Lanuvium, Thorius' birth place. She was protectress
of people in danger, in this case danger from the northern
barbarians.

NUMMI

210   d. P. p.

C. Sulpici. C. f.

217   Roma   P. Laeca   X

            provoco

176   ✱   Laeca

      M. Porc.   Roma

174   ✱

      C. Cassi.   Roma

---

[1] cf. *C.I.L.*, I, 2, *app.* 221; *dei Penates publici* (so Mommsen; *praestites* 'protecting,' Borghesi) represented by the Dioscuri. The allusion may be to return of soldiers after a campaign. But some think with Klügmann that the letters mean *de pecunia publica*, that is, from the state's bullion—see above, p. 223. We have *Lares* on another issue—*C.I.L.*, I, 2, app. 222.

[2] *sc.* to the people; written in exergue below a Roman soldier (or general, accompanied by a lictor) holding a hand over the head of a man in a toga. The coin alludes to an ancestor of the moneyer and to this ancestor's share in passing, at a date unknown, of a *Lex Porcia de provocatione*, which gave citizens outside Rome the right to appeal in criminal cases against decisions of magistrates exercising military authority.

[3] who alludes perhaps to the same ancestor and law mentioned in the preceding note; but there were three *leges Porciae*; cf. Hill, *Historical Roman Coins*, pp. 66 ff.

COINS

Denarius. c. 110 B.C.   **I, 225**

    obv. (two heads of the Dioscuri)   Household Gods
        of the State [1]

    rev.   Gaius Sulpicius son of Gaius

Denarius. c. 110 B.C.   *Local Italian mint.*   **II, 301**

    obv.   Rome   Publius Laeca   Tenpiece
    rev.   I appeal [2]

Denarius. c. 110 B.C. *or earlier.*   **I, 151**

    obv.   Tenpiece   Laeca
    rev. (Liberty crowned by Victory)   Marcus Por-
        cius [3]   Rome

Denarius. c. 104 B.C. *(not later.[4]).*   **I, 53**

    obv.   Tenpiece *(voting-urn)*
    rev. (Liberty in chariot)   Gaius   Cassius
        Rome

[4] Cassius is doubtless C. Cassius Longinus, son of L. Cass. Long. Ravilla, who in 137 B.C. as tribune passed a law imposing ballot-voting at trials before the assembly except in cases of treason. Since it was a very popular law, we have the figure of Libertas. The voting-box or urn *(sitella)*, however, refers not to this law but to the action of Ravilla in rehearing the case of the Vestal virgins tried in 113 under a severe pontifex Metellus. On another coin of *c.* 58 *(B.M. catal.,* I, 482) we have, on obv., head of Vesta and inscription *Q. Cassius Vest.*; on rev., temple of Vesta with *AC (absolvo, condemno).* This refers to the *quaestio* about those Vestals. A coin of *c.* 52 of L. Cass. Longinus has on obv. Vesta and letter *A,* on reverse a citizen dropping into a *cista* (box, not *sitella* urn) a tablet with letter *V.* Here *A = antiquo* 'I reject,' *V = uti rogas* 'As you propose' or 'As you put the question,' these being formulas of voting against or for a bill in the assembly. The coin refers to voting under Ravilla's law.

NUMMI

195 Q. C. Egnatulei. C. f.
       Roma   Q

211 p. e. s. c.
     Lent. Mar. f.

212 ex a. p.
     C. Fabi. C. f.

198 Piso Caepio q.
     ad fru. emu. ex s. c.

---

¹ Cf. *C.I.L.*, I, 2, (2,) *app.* 194, 196. Hill, *Hist. Roman Coins*, pp. 72–5. The roughly contemporary quinarii of Cloulius (*C.I.L.*, I, 2, *app.* 194) have *Q* on the reverse only. Here the *Q*. is on both sides. Lenormant held that it means *quaestor*, because the reverse of Egnatuleius' coins, *e.g.*, has Victory writing on a shield attached to a trophy at foot of which is a Gallic military trumpet. He suggested that Egnatuleius was a quaestor of Marius in the war against the Teutones and the Cimbri and that the coin is part of a mintage for the army of 102. We need not doubt that the Victory commemorates Marius' victory over the Teutones at Aquae Sextiae in 102 or over the Cimbri near Vercellae in 101; but the *Q* would seem to mean *quinarius*. The issues of the *quinarius*, in abeyance for some time, were revived by the *Lex Clodia* (? *c.* 104 B.C.), and it is this coin-name, and not *quaestor* that is probably meant by *Q* on these coins. The old sign *V* could no longer hold good strictly, because the quinarius now consisted of 8 not 5 *asses*. Besides, the *Q* on the obverse seems to be separate from the moneyer's name. The coins were struck, it seems, in Rome.

² p. (*publice*) means surely struck from silver bullion of the treasury; see notice above, p. 223, and next coin and note.

COINS

Quinarius.   c. 104 B.C. (*perhaps* 102–1).[1]   **I, 164,**

   obv.   Fivepiece   Gaius   Egnatuleius   **II, 158**
            son of Gaius
   rev.   Rome   Fivepiece

Denarius.   c. 104–89 B.C.;   *perhaps c.* 99 B.C.   **I, 232,**

   obv.   By decree of the senate   From public   **235**
            supply [2]
   rev.   Lentulus son of Marcellus

Denarius.   c. 104–89 B.C.;   *perhaps* 91 *or* 90 B.C.   **I, 222 4**

   obv.   From silver [3] bullion of the State
   rev.   Gaius Fabius son of Gaius

Denarius.   100 B.C.   **I, 170**

   obv. (*Saturn*)   Piso and Caepio [4] quaestors
   rev.   By decree of the Senate [5]   For purchase
          of corn

[3] cf. *C.I.L.*, I, 2, app. 243 : *arg. pub.* ; 266 : *a. pu.* ;
272 : *p. a.* (given below). The *aerarium* ' bronze-store ' or
treasury kept its old name though it now contained silver as
well as bronze bullion. Such issues as this, struck from the
state's and not the market's bullion, were due to the press of
the Cimbric invasions (113–101 B.C.) or the ' Social ' War
(91–88 B.C.), and may be connected with an inventory of
the treasury made at the beginning of the ' Social ' War
(Pliny, *N.H.*, XXXIII, 55). Victory in chariot on the rev.
of this coin may refer to some military success.

[4] L. Calpurnius Piso and Q. Servilius Caepio. The latter,
quaestor (doubtless *q. urbanus*) in 100 B.C., opposed Saturninus' reintroduction of corn-distributions at a moderate
price, but the law was passed with violence (*Ad Herenn.*, I,
12, 21 ; App., *B.C.*, I, 30), and the senate must have made this
issue to help the market. The head of Saturn, harvest-god,
indicates probably that the bullion for it came from the
treasury, which was in Saturn's temple below the Capitol.

[5] This expression authorises the issue of the coin not the
purchase of the corn.

NUMMI

240   Roma   M. Cato

               Victrix st.

249   [. . . .]

     l. P. d. a. p.

268   Numa Pompili.   Ancus Marci.

       Roma   C. Censo.

269   ex s. c.

   L. C. Memies L. f. Gal.

---

¹ *ST.* = *stipendium* ; thus Borghesi. The money would be
used for paying the legions serving in the 'Social' War. But
Cavedoni thinks it may be an epithet (*stata* or *stabilis* ' stead-
fast ') of Victory.

² This expression, which is extant also on the *as*, *semis*,
quadrans and *sestertius* in the shortened form *ELP* (*E* = *ex*)
is taken by Mommsen to mean *Lege Papiria de aere publico*
(*de assis pondere* Gaebler), for which see notice, pp. 220, 223.
The important point here is that the law reduced the *as*
to half an ounce ($\frac{1}{24}$ of its original weight) in 89 B.C. so as to
conform to the half-ounce standard used by many Italian
towns. Papirius had himself just shared in a great law (90
or 89 B.C.) giving franchise to Italians in revolt ('Social'
War). These Italians were now incorporated in the Roman
State and ceased to coin locally. On this coin DAP may

COINS

Denarius. About 90 B.C. **II, 303**

  obv. Rome   Marcus Cato
  rev. (*Victory*) Goddess Victorious **Pay-**
      money [1]

Bronze triens. c. 89–88 B.C. **I, 282**

  obv. Fourpiece
  rev. By the Papirian law about state's
      bronze [2]

As. c. 87 B.C. **I, 301,**

  obv. (*2 heads*) Numa Pompilius Ancus Mar- **305**
      cius
  rev. Rome   Gaius Censorinus [3]

Denarius. c. 87 B.C. **I, 307**

  obv. (*head of Saturn*) By decree of the senate
  rev. Lucius Memmius and Gaius Memmius [4]
      sons of Lucius of the Galerian tribe

represent ' *de aere publico* ' ' struck from the state's bronze
bullion ' (see above), without reference to the Papirian law;
or ' *de assis pondere* '.   The four dots = 4 ounces = triens = $\frac{1}{3}$
of an *as*.

  [3] Doubtless C. Marcius Censorinus, a prominent supporter
of Marius and probably special moneyer for him and Cinna
who in 87 B.C. coined the bullion in the treasury.   The *gens
Marcia* claimed descent from the Roman Kings Marcius and
Pompilius.

  [4] The head of Saturn on the obverse means perhaps that
these Memmii were not triumvirs of the mint (see notice,
p. 221) but, although it is not shown, were urban quaestors
who had charge of the treasury (*aerarium Saturni*—see p. 222)
which provided this issue.

NUMMI

272   aed. pl.

     M. Fan. L. Cr ⊢   p. a.

288   L. Sulla

    imper. iterum

274   C. Cassi   L. Salin. d. s. s.

287   C. Val. Fla. imperat.   ex s. c.   H   P

---

[1] The obverse has head of Ceres goddess of corn, the reverse having figures of the *aediles* on the *subsellium* (seat, bench) behind an ear of corn. Thus the issue was made on the occasion of public distribution conducted by the *aediles*, perhaps when Cinna in 86 B.C. removed war-time restrictions on public distributions of corn. *PA = publico argento*.

[2] Struck by Sulla on his own ' authority ' as an outlaw in his war against Mithridates. This coin was probably among those coined (largely from plundered temple-treasuries of Greece) at Sulla's orders by his quaestor Lucullus in the Peloponnese (Plut., *Lucull.*, 2) after the war; others (see below) were coined in Asia Minor (*id.*, 4) from the 20,000 talents levied on the cities of Asia Minor by Sulla. The trophies refer probably to the battles of Chaeroneia (86 B.C.) and Orchomenos (85 B.C.) over Archelaus, general of Mithridates. Sulla, was hailed ' general ' by his troops first perhaps during the ' Social ' War or after the Cilician campaign of

234

COINS

Denarius.   *c.* 87 B.C., *perhaps* 86 B.C.   **I, 314**

obv.[1]   Aediles of the plebs
rev.   Marcus Fannius and Lucius Critonius
         From silver bullion of the state

Aureus.[2] *c.* 85–82 B.C.   *Struck in Greece and Asia* **II, 459**
Minor.

obv. (*Cupid and Venus*)   Lucius Sulla
rev. (*2 trophies*)   General second time

As.   *c.* 85 B.C.   **I, 321**

rev.   Gaius Cassius and Lucius Salinator[3]
    By vote of the Senate   Onepiece

Denarius.   *c.* 84 B.C.   *Struck in Gaul.*[4]   **II, 388**

obv. (*bust of Victory*)
rev.   Gaius Valerius Flaccus general By
    decree of the Senate (2 *standards and*
    legionary eagle) Lancers Forefighters

92 B.C., and next probably after the battle of Orchomenos.
As regards the obverse of this coin, Sulla thought he was
under the protection of Venus who gave him victory in war
as well as in love. For another *aureus* struck by Sulla's
orders, see below, pp. 236–37.

[3] Perhaps the Julius(?) Salinator who was an officer in
Sertorius' army (Plut., *Sert.*, 7), the other moneyer being
perhaps C. Cassius Longinus Varus, who was later consul in
73 B.C. It looks as though these two moneyers were ordinary
triumvirs of the mint. Yet the issue was a special one.

[4] Flaccus was propraetor in Gaul in 83 B.C. having already
been hailed imperator. In 81 B.C. he triumphed for successes
in Gaul and Spain. *H = hastati ; P = principes* 'fore-
fighters,' though in fact the latter formed the second line, the
hastati the first, the third being *triarii* 'thirdliners.'

282   Hispan.

    A. Post. A. f. S. n. Albin.

286   C. Anni. T. f. T. n. pro cos.   ex s. c.

      L. Fabi. L. f. Hisp. q.

290   A. Manli. [A. f. q.]

    L. Sulla fe[li. dic.]

301   M. Voltei. M. f. s. c. d. t.

307   (i)   g. p. R.

    ex. s. c.   Cn. Len. q.

---

[1] alluding perhaps to the successes of Lucius Postumius Albinus against the Vaccaei and the Lusitani in 180–179 B.C.

[2] Gaius Annius Luscus served against Jugurtha in 107 B.C.; and was in 82 B.C. sent by Sulla against Sertorius in Spain. This issue was made there by the authority of the Senate (doubtless under the dictator Sulla's orders) for the Roman army, in the names of Annius and his quaestors Fabius (as shown on this coin) and (as other coins show) C. Tarquitius.

[3] Compare this coin with the aureus of Sulla given above, pp. 234–35. It was doubtless struck from the 20,000 talents levied on the cities of Asia Minor by Sulla after the first Mithridatic war (Plut., *Lucull.*, 4). Sulla was declared

COINS

I, 351

Denarius. *c.* 82 B.C.

    obv. (*head of Hispania*)   Spain [1]

    rev.   Aulus Postumius Albinus son of Aulus
        grandson of Spurius

Denarius. *c.* 81 B.C.   *Struck in Spain.*   **II, 352**

    obv. By decree of the Senate   Gaius
        Annius [2] proconsul son of Titus
        grandson of Titus

    rev. (*Victory in chariot*)   Lucius Fabius Hispan-
        iensis quaestor son of Lucius

Aureus. *c.* 81 B.C.   *Struck in Asia Minor.*[3]   **II, 463**

    obv. Aulus Manlius quaestor son of Aulus

    rev. (*statue of Sulla on a horse*) Lucius Sulla
        the Blest dictator

Denarius. *c.* 80 B.C.   **I, 388,
392**

    obv. (*head of Apollo*)

    rev. (*tripod*)   Marcus Volteius son of Marcus
        By decree of the Senate   From the
        treasury [4]

(i) *Denarius.* *c.* 75 B.C.   *Struck in Spain ?*   **II, 358**

    obv. (*bust*)   Genius of the Roman people

    rev. By decree of the Senate Gnaeus [5] Len-
        tulus quaestor

dictator in 82 B.C., and at his triumph in 81 took the surname
Felix and was granted a statue of himself by the senate.

[4] So Mommsen (*senatus consulto de thesauro*), though others
have thought *DT* represents *donum tulit* ' brought a gift.'
The ' treasure ' would be the bullion in the treasury (see above),
and, as the types indicate, the coins were issued probably on
the occasion of a celebration of the *Ludi Apollinares*, when
there would be unusual expenses.   [5] Corn. Marcellinus.

NUMMI

(ii)   g. p. R.

    ex. s. c.   Lent. cur. ✳ fl.

330   M. Lepidus Aimilia ref. **s. c.**

332   Floral. primus
    C. Serveil. C. f.

---

[1] cf. *B.M. catal.*, II, 358–9. *CVR ✳ FL = curator denariis flandis.* These coins both belong to special issues ' by decree of the senate.' Any designation of the moneyer by an expression showing that he was a *triumvir* of the mint (see notice above, p. 221) is exceptional, and does not occur until towards the end of the Republic. I suggest that the second coin was struck a little later than the preceding; that he had made an issue as special moneyer when he was quaestor (see preceding coin), and when he became triumvir of the mint, as such made a new special issue, and was allowed to designate himself as mint-manager to distinguish this act from the issue which he made as quaestor. Had his issue as triumvir preceded his issue as quaestor, no designation as *curator* would have appeared on that first issue. If this is correct, the second issue at least was struck in Rome, not in Spain. However, the assumption that here *curator* means *triumvir* may be wrong. Yet any moneyer had to be a magistrate of some sort. If this *curator* was not a triumvir, what magistracy did he hold? There is no reason why triumvirs should have been excluded from making special issues. *flare* ' cast '; but all coins were now struck—see pp. 219, 221.

COINS

(ii) *Denarius.* *c.* 76–72 B.C.[1]   **II, 359**

  obv. (*bust*) Genius of the Roman people
  rev. By decree of the Senate Lentulus
        manager for mint-casting of ten-
        pieces

Denarius. *c.* 65 B.C.   **I, 450**

  obv. (*head of Vestal Virgin Aemilia*)
  rev.[2] By decree of the Senate Marcus
        Lepidus   Restoration of
        Aemilia's Hall

Denarius. *c.* 63 B.C.[3]   **I, 469**

  obv. (*head of Flora*) First to hold Flora's
        festival
  rev. Gaius Servilius son of Gaius

[2] The reverse has a view of the Basilica Aemilia with shields attached to the columns. The coin commemorates the restoration of this basilica by Lepidus' father Marcus Aemilius Lepidus in 78 B.C. This man decorated it with shields or portraits of his ancestors (Pliny, *N.H.*, XXV, 3, 13). On one occasion the Vestal virgin Aemilia rekindled the dead fire by throwing on it one of her loveliest garments (Val. Max., I, 1, 7). *REF* = *refecta.* For *basilica,* see above, p. 146. The archaisms on this and the following coins seem to me to be deliberate as befitting the older events to which they allude, and may show the influence of the spelling used on public records both during and after the 'archaic' period.

[3] This coin commemorates the institution of the *ludi Florales* in 240 or 238 B.C., which became annual (April 28th–May 3rd, five days) in 173 B.C. This Servilius was probably a triumvir of the mint, since his office is not here designated. But he may have been an aedile; at any rate an ancestor of his must, as aedile, have been a manager of games (*curator ludorum*) when they were first instituted. Perhaps this issue of coins was made during the *ludi Florales.* On this coin *FLORAL* = *floralia.*

NUMMI

341   M. Scaur. aed. cur.   ex s. c.   Rex Aretas

     P. Hypsaeus aed. cur.   C. Hypsae. cos.

     Preiver. captu.

354   Quirinus   C. Memmi. c. f.

     Memmius aed.   Cerialia preimus fecit

---

[1] Scaurus, made governor of Syria by Pompey, in 64 B.C.
entered Judaea to settle the dispute of Hyrcanus and Aristo-
bulus. Aretas III, King of the Nabataeans, had been inter-
fering. In the end Scaurus forced him to make peace on good
terms but to pay 300 talents to Pompey. Scaurus on his
return to Rome held, as curule aedile, the most extravagant
games, for whose expenses the Senate gave him and his
colleague P. Plautius Hypsaeus the right to coin in their own
name. On this coin a moneyer celebrates an exploit of his
own. *PREIVER CAPTV = Preivernum captum.* This place
was taken in 329 B.C. by the consul C. Plautius Decianus

COINS

Denarius.   *c.* 58 B.C.   **I, 483-4**

    obv. (*Aretas kneeling with olive-branch*)   By decree   **II, 589**
             of the Senate
    Marcus Scaurus[1] curule aedile
                King Aretas
    rev.   Publius   Hypsaeus   curule   aedile
         Gaius   Hypsaeus   consul
         Capture of Privernum

Denarius.   *c.* 51 B.C.   **I, 496**

    obv. (*head of Quirinus = Romulus*)   Quirinus
         Gaius Memmius son of Gaius
    rev. (*Ceres seated*)   Memmius aedile was first
         to hold Ceres' festival [2]

(called Hypsaeus on this issue), who thus finally quelled the
Volscians. It had been taken also by C. Plautius Venno
Hypsaeus in 341 B.C. Perhaps the two are confused. A
number of these coins exist; on some of these coins *AID*
= *aidilis*) occurs for *AED.*

  [2] This refers to the institution of the first *ludi Cereales*
before 202 B.C. The festival was a plebeian one (April 12th–
19th). The Memmii claimed descent from the Trojan Menes-
theus through Romulus.

241

II. INSTRUMENTA

SIVE

ACTA

1

Sacred law (or laws ?), of about 500 B.C. or earlier, inscribed on the four faces of a four-sided and tapering block of tufa of which the top is broken off. Found between the Forum and the comitium at Rome under a black marble pavement. The lines of the inscription, of which only the lower part is preserved, run vertical to the base, the letters lying on their sides when the pillar is upright. Lines 1, 3, 5, 7, 11, 12, 14 read from right to left, that is, from below upwards on the pillar ; 2, 4, 6, 10, 13, 15, from left to right, that is, from above downwards ; 8, 9, 16 are as

1

  ⟵ 1 Quoi hoɪ . . .
  ⟶ 2 sakros es
  ⟵ 3 ed Sora[no . . .]
  ———————
  ⟶ 4 . . . . ia . . . . ias
  ⟵ 5 recei:ic. . . .
  ⟶ 6 . . . [d]evam
  ⟵ 7 quos:r. . . .
  ———————
  ⟵ 8 . . . m:kalato
  ⟶ 9 rem ha[ruspex . . .] } (*inversa*)
  ⟶ 10 . . . iod: iouxmen
  ⟵ 11 ta: kapia: dotav . . .
  ———————

II. INSCRIPTIONS

DEEDS

or ' Documents,' written on durable material, for public or private information. See Introduction, pp. xii–xiv.

1

it were upside down ; 8 reads from right to left = from above downwards ; 9 and 16 from left to right = from below upwards ; 16, which ends the inscription, is in smaller letters on an edge of the stone between the first and fourth faces.   Some of the words seem to be separated by vertically arranged points, generally three, but the separation is perhaps not accurate and is apparently not complete ; until the 5th line none at all are certain, and there are other punctures not made by the writer.   I give the inscription in full and translate what appears to be intelligible.

1   He who (violates) this . . .
2–3 that he be solemnly forfeited to Soranus.

---

4   — . —
5   to the King
6   goddess (*or* divine)
7   whom (*or* which)

---

8   summoner
9   soothsayer ?
10   draught-cattle
11   let him take

⟵ 12 m i⋮ te ri . . .

⟶ 13 . . . m⋮ quoi ha

⟵ 14 velod : nequ[e] . . .

⟶ 15 . . . od iovestod

⟶ 16 doivo : viod . . . (*inversum*)

From the meagre scraps of writing which remain, it appears that the pillar recorded for public information some laws, or one law protecting a sacred piece of ground or a sacred object or building, and served as a boundary-stone for the same. Separate laws or clauses may be distinguished as follows: Lines 1–4 (no apparent points between words); 6–9 (which a passer-by could read without changing his position— Huelsen, *Beiträge*, II, 231); 10–11?; 12–16? Note the following: *Line* 1: There is doubtless to be read a space between *quoi* and *hoi*, but there is no trace here, or in lines 2 and 3, of separating points. *hok*[e] von Grienberger. *Lines* 2–3: *esed* is probably the later *esset* rather than *sit* or *erit.* I accept Thurneysen's supplement *Sora*[*no*] (Warren, *A.J.P.*, XXVIII, 387), though even the *a* is doubtful; *sorde* von Grienberger. Soranus was a Sabine god connected with the lower world. *Line* 4: [*n*]*oxagias* von Grienberger; which suggests 'damage(s).' *Line* 5: *recei* (*regei* v. Grienberger) is probably dative of *rex*. The person meant would be the *rex sacrorum* (*rex sacrificulus*), or, if the inscription belongs to the monarchic period, the King of Rome. *Line* 8: the *kalator* would be a servant of or attendant on priests. *Line* 9: I conjecture *har*[*uspex*]; *hap*[*ead*] = *habeat* v. Grienberger. *Line* 10: [*q*]*uod* v. Grienberger. *iouxmenta* is certain; cp. *iugum, iungo*. *Line* 11: perhaps the four points ⋮ should have been put after the next letter—*kapiad*⋮. But I believe that, as occurs elsewhere with other consonants, a *d* has been dropped before another *d*, and combine this suggestion with another (Warren, op. cit., 387)—that *dota* is an error of the inscriber for *dato*. Read therefore perhaps *kapiad datov*[*e*] (*dotaq* v. Grienberger). *Line* 12 looks as hopeless as line 4; if this could be read from left to right, and we could assume that ꟼ(= R) and Ⅎ are put wrong-side-forward, then perhaps . . . *ir et im* = . . . *ir et eum* ('and him . . .',

12   — . —
13   whoever this
14   covering neither
15   legitimate (*or* be . . . to Jupiter)

---

16   god . . . (*or* divine . . .)

i.e. the trespasser; cp. *Twelve Tables, Remains*, III, pp. 482, 502 *im* for *eum*) ; but it is clear that the line must be read from right to left. The reader must not be confused here; in the printed Latin text the words are put as though they did read from left to right. So in all cases where ←— is used. The interpunctuation being so vague, I think we might well read *iteris*, old gen. of *iter* ' walk,' ' way,' ' path.' *Lines* 13–14 : *havelod* is probably, however, one word. *Line* 15 : *iovestod* seems to mean *iusto* ' regular,' ' permitted,' ' legitimate.' But perhaps there should be a space : *Iovei estod*. Note Paulus, from Festus, ' iovistae ' compositum a Iove et iustae.' *Line* 16 : If we have the letters right (and this is doubtful), this line reads the same either way, if we ignore the uncertain separating point. But some insist that the letters are *loivquiod*; von Grienberger read *louquiod* and thinks it means ' appertaining to a grove ' (*lucus*). For various studies of this inscription, see Comparetti, *Iscrizione arcaica del Foro Romano* (1900): *C.I.L.*, I, 2, pp. 367, 717; *Rivista di storia antica*, IV, V, VI, VII, VIII. Bursian's *Jahresbericht*, CXXVII, 257–280; CXLIV, 162 ff.; Ribezzo, *R.I.-G.-I.*, XIV, 89; Stroux, *Philologus*, LXXXVI, 460 ff. There is also an interesting study by Warren, in *A.J.P.*, XXVIII, 249 ff., 373 ff. He thinks the inscription protects a sacred grove or tree, and fills in the gaps by conjecture. Von Grienberger, *Indog. Forsch.*, XXX, 210; XXXVII, 122, from a rubbing may have discovered a few more letters. Cf. also V. Pisani, *Rendiconti dell' Acc. dei Lincei, Sc. Morali*, 1932, 735–744; and *C.I.L.*, I, 2, 2, Fasc. III, 1943, page 831, where further studies are referred to. There are casts of the block in the British Museum, the Ashmolean Museum, Oxford, the Mus. of Arch., Cambridge, and at Harvard and Johns Hopkins Universities.

2

2545 Kaia | ..... IV prendere | .... [*rev*]ellere quod
in | [*eam aedem donum da*]tum est seiquis |
⁵ ...... [*h*]ic rerum fecer|is piaclu . . .

3–19

Sortes

2173- *(i) Conrigi vix tandem quod | curvom est fac-
2189 tum [*c*]rede.

(ii) Credis quod deicunt? Non | sunt ita. Ne
fore stultu.

(iii) De incerto certa ne fiant | si sapis caveas.

*(iv) De vero falsa ne fiant | iudice falso.

(v) Est equos perpulcer, sed tu | vehi non potes
istoc.

(vi) Est via [*p*]er [*c*]livom ; qua vi[*s*] | sequi, non
[*datur ista.*]

(vii) Formidat omnes ; quod | metuit id sequi
satiust.

---

2 ¹ KAIΛ = Ka(lendis) Ia(nuariis) ?
² IVPRENDERE
3–19 (i) crede Ritschl
(ii) sunt ita ne Rossi   SIIIT ITA RE Kellermann
sin te ita re Ritschl
(vi) per clivom Buecheler   fertilivom *cd. Vat.* 5248,
n. 15   vis Buecheler   vi *cd.*   datur ista *suppl.* Buecheler

---

¹ The first four letters are undoubtedly *kaia*, though we
expect *kala*[*tor* . . .] The last word *piaclu*(*m*) here may mean
' wicked act ' which would alter the meaning of *feceris* to
' shall have done.' If this inscription records a law, the
prohibition would be in the third person. I suggest therefore *fecer.* (= *fecerit*), *is piaclum* . . . ' shall have committed
. ., he shall make atonement . . .'

LAWS AND OTHER DOCUMENTS

2

Fragment of a temple notice or law. On stone found at S. Vittorino. Second century B.C.?

Jan. 1st . . . 4, to seize . . . or filch anything which has been brought as a gift into the said temple.   Any person who shall have committed . . . of the articles herein, you shall make atonement. . . .[1]

3–19

Oracular replies on bronze of unknown origin [2] *and now mostly lost. Date apparently first century* B.C. *Mostly in single bad hexameters.*

* (i) Believe you that what has once been made crooked can hardly now be made straight.

(ii) Believe you what they say? Affairs are not so. Don't be a fool.[3]

5 (iii) If you are wise, about [4] uncertainty beware lest things become certain.

* (iv) Don't let falsehoods arise from truth by being a false judge.

(v) That horse is a very fine one, but *you* can't ride *him*.

(vi) It's an uphill road; you are not empowered to follow by the road you want to.

(vii) He fears all men; it is better to chase what he is afraid of.

---

[2] possibly from a temple of Fortune near Padua. The temple was connected with the *Fons Aponus,* a place of divination. Cf. Ritschl, *Opusc.,* IV, 397 ff.; Stowasser, *Wien. Stud.,* XXIV, 485 ff. The examples still extant are here marked *. All the seventeen sortes (except no. xi) are given on *cod. Vat.* 5248.

[3] *ne fore stultu* is haplographic for *ne fores stultus*; the reading is not quite clear.

[4] or possibly : beware lest things turn out to be certain from uncertainty; cf. the next utterance and no. (ix).

(viii) [*Mendaces*] homines multi sunt; | credere noli.

(ix) Hostis incertus de certo nisi caveas.

*(x) Iubeo, et is ei sifecerit | gaudebit semper.

*(xi) Laetus lubens petito; quod | dabitur gaudebis semper.

*(xii) Non sum. mendacis quas | dixti; consulis stulte.

*(xiii) . . . nunc me rogitas, nunc | consulis? Tempus abit iam.

(xiv) Permultis prosum; ubei | profui, gratia nemo.

(xv) Postquam ceciderunt s[*p*]es [*o*]m[*nes*], | consulis tun me?

(xvi) Quod fugis, quod iactas, tibei | quod datur spernere nolei.

*(xvii) Qur petis postempus consilium? | Quod rogas non est.

20–22

C. I. L., XI.

1129

(i) [*Quid*] nunc consoltas? Quiescas ac vi[*ta fru*]-ari[*s*].

. . . . . mo[*rt*]em procul apste habe . . .

[*n*]on potest prius m[*o*]rtem adficier quam venerit fa[*tum*]

. . . . ndis valetudo ostenditur [*m*]agn[*a*].

(viii) [*mendaces*] vel [*fallaces*] *Ritschl*

(ix) hostis [*fit*] . . . . . [*non*] certo *Ritschl*   hostis incertus de certo [*fit*] *Ritschl*

(x) Iubeo ut iussei; sei faxsit *Ritschl*   iubeo [o]eti; sei sic fecerit *Momms.*

(xiii) nunc[*ine*] *Ritschl*

(xiv) gratia noenu *coni. Buecheler*

(xv) spes omnes *Ritschl*   sei sunt mala *Momms.*   sei [*odio*] sum *Buecheler*   sei sum *cd. Vat.* 5248, n. 11

(xvi) quor fugis quor *Momms.*   quom datur *Ritschl*

10 (viii) Many men are liars. Don't believe them.

 (ix) An untrustworthy foe will arise from a trustworthy man, unless you take care.[1]

* (x) I command it, and if he does it for him, he will be glad for ever.

* (xi) Seek you joyfully and willingly, and you will be glad for ever, because [2] of what shall be given.

* (xii) We are not the liars [3] you said. You ask advice like a fool.

15* (xiii) Is it now you keep asking me, it is now you seek advice? It is too late by now.[4]

 (xiv) Very many do I help. When I have helped, no one thanks me.

 (xv) After all your hopes have fallen do you really ask my advice?

 (xvi) Spurn not what you flee, what you toss aside, I mean what is granted you.

* (xvii) Why do you seek advice after the occasion? What you ask does not exist.

20–22

Oracular replies found on a bronze tablet at Forum Novum. Written in prose. First century B.C.?

(i) Why do you now seek my advice? Be at rest and enjoy life.

You have death far from you. Death cannot be fastened on you before the doom is come.

A great illness is revealed.

---

[1] that is, your seemingly trustworthy friend will turn out to be a treacherous foe instead.

[2] or : because it will be given.

[3] *quas*, feminine, because the *sortes* (feminine) speak of themselves. Ribezzo takes *sum* to be *sunt*, not *sumus*.

[4] or : 'The right time has gone by now.'

249

(ii) [*frau*]de lucrum quaesivit su[*um*]

    [. . . . . *p*]rotendit turbam [*m*]agnam

    [*fu*]giesque eam semp[*er*].

(iii) [. . *fe*]ret quae ante sterilis fuit.

23

C. I. L., VI, 2104, v. 31ff.; **I, 2.**

Carmen Arvale.

What the words of the song mean is imperfectly known; without giving all the proposals that have been made, I give a conjectural translation of the words more or less as they stand on the stone. The song dates from the earliest days of the brotherhood, and by the time of the empire was neither understood nor correctly recorded; doubtless mistakes or corruptions and confusions and modifications had crept in. For the most part there are no spaces between the words. To judge from the song, the singers divided up into three groups, unless the whole choir sang each phrase, with dance, thrice (cp. *tripudiare*). It looks also as though the song was a processional hymn. For various studies of scholars see *C.I.L.,* I, 2, pp. 369, 712, 739; Fasc. III, 1943, p. 831; Stowasser, in *Wien. St.,* XV, 78; v.

Ibi sacerdotes clusi succincti libellis acceptis carmen descindentes tripodiaverunt in verba haec:

2   Enos Lases iuvate! | [*E*]nos Lases iuvate! Enos Lases iuvate!

      Neve lu[*e*] [1] rue Marma(*r*) sins incurrere in pleores. Neve lue rue Marmar | [*si*]ns incurrere in pleores. Neve lue rue Marmar sers incurrere in pleores. [2]

> 20–22 suppl. Buecheler, Bormann
> 20 (*fin.*) *fortasse: grandis valetudo*
> 2 [1] LVAE
> [2] PLEORIS

LAWS AND OTHER DOCUMENTS

The other two are much mutilated :

(ii) He got his profit by fraud.
. . . it holds out mighty turmoil.
. . . and you shall always escape from it.
(iii) She who was barren will bear a child.

23

Song of the Twelve Arval brothers, perhaps of the sixth century
B.C. *Processional Hymn? It has metrical groups, including
Saturnian rhythms.*

Grienberger, *Indog. Forsch.*, XIX, 140; H. Ehrlich, *Rh. Mus.*,
LXVIII, 603; Cocchia, *Riv. Indo-Grec.-Ital.*, I, 1; Goidanich,
Studi di lat. arc., *Stud. Ital.*, X, 270, etc.; E. Norden, *Aus
altrömischen Priesterbüchern*, Lund, 1939 (cf. Weinstock, *J.R.
Stud.*, xxx, 84 ff.). It should be noted that the song, as
recorded on a tablet of A.D. 218, does not really count as an
archaic inscription; there is nothing to show that the Arval
brothers had in their possession any ancient epigraphic document containing their song. But the song is itself so very
ancient that I have included it in this collection. From one
point of view it may be taken as a 'copy' of an ancient
inscription.

Marble Tablet of A.D. 218 *found at Rome. The records of a
meeting of the brethren in that year say :* Then the priests, the
doors being closed, girt up their robes, took the books, and
dividing up danced and sang a song to the following words :

Oh! Help us, ye Household Gods! Oh! help us, ye
Household Gods! Oh! help us, ye Household Gods!
And let not bane and bale, O Marmar, assail
more folk.[1] And let not bane and bale, O Marmar,
assail more folk. And let not bane and bale, O
Marmar, assail more folk.

[1] Doubtful; it can hardly be *flores* (Lanzi) though Mars
was an agricultural god. In fact *pleores* looks like a genuine
old word (*pleioses*? *pleios*, πλείων). Cf. Kent, *Forms of Latin*,
302. Perhaps : ' the multitude.' Or : ' Don't let us through
bane or bale join the majority.'

Satur fu, [*f*]ere Mars, limen | [*sal*]i! Sta! Ber-
ber! Satur fu, fere Mars, limen sali! Sta!
Berber! Satur fu, fere Mars, limen sa[*l*]i!
S[*t*]a![1] Berber! |

[*Sem*]unis alternei advocapit conctos. Semunis
alternei advocapit conctos. Simunis altern-
[*ei*][2] advocapit | [*conct*]os.

Enos Marmor iuvato! Enos Marmor iuvato!
Enos Ma[*r*]mor iuvato!

Triumpe! Triumpe! Triumpe trium | [*pe tri*]umpe!

Post tripodationem deinde signo dato publici introierunt
et libellos receperunt.

24

C. I. L., I, 2.

Senatus Consultum de Pago Montano.

591 . . . . . eisque curarent tu[*erenturque* | *ar*]bitratu
aedilium pleibeium | [*quei*]comque essent;
neive ustrinae in | eis loceis recionibusve
5 nive foci ustri|nae⟨ve⟩ caussa fierent nive
stercus terra[*m*]|ve intra ea loca fecisse
coniecisseve veli[*t*] | quei haec loca ab paaco
Montano | [*redempta habebit, quod si stercus in
eis loceis fecerit terramve* | *in ea*] loca iecerit,

1 SAIISIA
2 ALTERNIE
24 [8] *redempta habebit et uti, si qui stercus i. e. l. f. t. i. e. l.*
iecerit, in eum HS. Bruns

---

[1] This is a guess (= *verberā !*). It may be merely an
ejaculation. ' Leap the threshold ' points to an old processional
hymn. Preller suggested : ' Enter thy temple (cross the
threshold) and stay thy scourge.'

Be full satisfied, fierce Mars.   Leap the threshold!
Halt!   Beat the ground![1]   Be full satisfied, fierce
Mars.   Leap the threshold!   Halt!   Beat the
ground!   Be full satisfied, fierce Mars.   Leap the
threshold!   Halt!   Beat the ground!

By turns address ye all[2] the Gods of Sowing.   By
turns address ye all the Gods of Sowing.   By turns
address ye all the Gods of Sowing.

Oh!   Help us, Marmor!   Oh!   Help us, Marmor!
Oh!   Help us, Marmor!   Bound, bound, and bound
again, bound and bound again!

After the dance, at a given signal, public slaves came in and
took away the books.

24

Resolution of the Roman Senate for the protection [3] of a burial-place on the Esquiline. On a pillar found at Rome. c. 150–120 B.C.

. . . and that they should take good care and guard
it at the discretion of the aediles of the plebs in office
at any time, and that there should be no burning-
grounds on the said sites and areas and no fire-places
for burning the dead; and that no one who shall
hold these places by rent or [4] purchase from the
Mountain hamlet should be minded to make dung-
heap or cast earth within the said places, and that
if he shall have made dung-heap on the said sites
or shall have cast earth onto the said places, against

[2] Some take *conctos* as nom. sing. = quisque, with *advocapit*
as 3rd pers. sing.   But I take *conctos* as acc. plur. and *advocapit*
as *advocapite* = advocate since all the other sentences are
imperative.   *Semunes* (cp. *Semo Sancus*) might be *semi-
homines*, ' half-men,' half animals; but the meaning ' sowers '
is perhaps more attractive here.

[3] See also protection of groves, pp. 154–7.

[4] *redimere* in both senses combined seems natural here.

in . . . . . [*uti HS* . . . . | *ma*]nus iniectio pig-
norisq. capi[*o siet.*]

25

614   L. Aimilius L. f. inpeirator decreivit | utei quei
Hastensium servei | in turri Lascutana habi-
tarent | leiberei essent; agrum oppidumqu. |
⁵   quod ea tempestate posedisent | item possi-
dere habereque | iousit, dum poplus senat-
usque | Romanus vellet. Act. incastreis |
a. d. XII K. Febr.

26

Epistula Consulum ad Teuranos de Bacchanalibus.

581   [*Q.*] Marcius L. f., S. Postumius L. f. cos.
senatum consoluerunt n. Octob. apud aedem |
Duelonai. Sc. arf. M. Claudi. M. f., L. Valeri. P. f.,

---

¹ that is, summary seizure of his property, not arrest of his
person (cf. pp. 154–5). The whole phrase was a convenient
formula for instituting an *actio*. See *Remains*, Vol. III, 425,
432, 437, 506.

² The inscription itself is, however, in less archaic style
than the *Epistula consulum de Bacchanalibus* of 186 B.C. (next
inscription). Cf. Huebner, *H.*, III, 243 ff.; R. Menéndez Pidal,
Historia de España, II, *Esp. Romana*, Madrid, 1935.

³ This means, perhaps, no more than ' people under
domination.' But some think that the ' slaves ' were runaways who had served the Romans against their masters and
inhabited a *castellum* (outlying dependent community) called
turris Lascutana. inpeirator for inpĕrator is a mistake of the
inscriber, or a false archaism—see pp. xvi–xviii.

⁴ Hasta Regia, not far from Gades.

⁵ (*senatus consultum*) or at least a part of the resolution;
the whole document here given is not, however, in itself a
senatus consultum but an *epistula consulum*, or probably a
copy of the actual letter which the Teurani were commanded
to make and post up (see below). For the origin of this

him there shall be, for a fine of . . . sesterces, laying of hands upon him,[1] and taking of pledge.

25

Decree of Lucius Aemilius Paulus, proconsul of Further Spain in 189 B.C.,[2] freeing a community from the control of their neighbours at Hasta. Plate of bronze found near Gades. Now in the Louvre.

Lucius Aemilius, son of Lucius, commander-in-chief, decreed that the slaves[3] of the people of Hasta[4] dwelling in the tower of Lascuta should be free. The land and the town which they had possessed at that time he ordered that they should possess and hold as heretofore so long as the Roman people and Senate are willing. Done in camp on the nineteenth day of January.

26

Letter of Quintus Marcius and Spurius Postumius, consuls in 186 B.C., to the people of the Ager Teuranus, of the Bruttii, informing them of the Roman Senate's resolution[5] about Bacchanalian orgies. Tablet of brass found at Tiriolo in the land of the Bruttii. Now in Vienna. 186 B.C.

The consuls Quintus Marcius son of Lucius, and Spurius Postumius son of Lucius, consulted the senate on the seventh day of October in the temple of Bellona. Present as witnesses to the record[6]: Marcus Claudius son of Marcus; Lucius Valerius son of Publius; and Quintus Minucius son of Gaius.

decree, cf. Livy XXXIX, 8–18. See also Wordsworth, 416 ff.; Cichorius, *Röm. Stud.*, 21 ff.; *C.I.L.*, I, 2, p. 723; Fasc. III, 1943, p. 832; also W. Krause, in *Hermes*, LXXI, pp. 214–220; Fränkel, in *Hermes*, LXVII, 369 ff.; Keil, in *id.*, LXVIII, 306 ff. S. Accame, *Riv. Fil.*, N.S. xvi, 225.

[6] In normal practice these were a small committee who determined the final form of a *senatus consultum*.

INSTRUMENTA

Q. Minuci. C. f. De Bacanalibus quei foederatei |
esent, ita exdeicendum censuere:

Neiquis eorum [B]acanal habuise velet;
seiques | esent, quei sibei deicerent necesus ese
Bacanal habere, eeis utei ad pr. urbanum |
5 Romam venirent, deque eeis rebus, ubei eorum
v[e]r[b]a audita esent, utei senatus | noster
decerneret, dum ne minus senatorbus C adesent
[quom e]a res cosoleretur. | Bacas vir nequis
adiese velet ceivis Romanus neve nominus Latini
neve socium | quisquam, nisei pr. urbanum
adiesent isque de senatuos sententiad, dum ne |
minus senatoribus C adesent, quom ea res cosole-
retur, iousise⟨n⟩t. Censuere. |
10 Sacerdos nequis vir eset; magister neque vir
neque mulier quisquam eset; | neve pecuniam
quisquam eorum comoine[m h]abuise ve[l]et;
neve magistratum | neve pro magistratu[d]
neque virum [neque mul]ierem quiquam fecise
velet; | neve posthac inter sed conioura[se ne]ve
comvovise neve conspondise | neve conprom-
esise velet neve quisquam fidem inter sed
15 dedise velet. | Sacra in (o)quoltod ne quisquam
fecise velet, neve in poplicod neve in | preivatod
neve exstrad urbem sacra quisquam fecise velet,
nisei | pr. urbanum adieset, isque de senatuos

26 ⁵ VTR A   ¹² MAGISTRATVO
          ¹⁵ DQOLTOD

---

[1] The Italian *socii.* In the first prohibition which follows,
Bacanal habuise may be taken as 'keep a shrine of Bacchus'
as well as 'hold an orgy of B.'
[2] to whom the orgies properly belonged.

LAWS AND OTHER DOCUMENTS

In the matter of the orgies of Bacchus they passed a resolution that the following proclamation should be issued to those [1] who are in league with the Romans by treaties:

'Let none of them be minded to keep a lodge of Bacchus. Should there be some who say that they must needs keep a lodge of Bacchus, they must come to the praetor of the city at Rome, and our Senate, when it has heard what they have to say, shall make decision on those matters, provided that not fewer senators than 100 be present when the matter is deliberated. Let no man, whether Roman citizen or person of the Latin name or one of the allies, be minded to attend a meeting of Bacchant women [2] unless they have first approached the praetor of the city and he have authorised them, by a vote of the Senate, to do so, provided that not fewer Senators than 100 be present when the matter is deliberated.' Passed.

'Let no man be a priest.[3] Let not any man or woman be a master [4] or any likewise be minded to institute a common fund; nor let any person be minded to make either man or woman a master or vice-master or mistress, or be minded henceforth to swear, vow, pledge, or make promise with others, or be minded to plight faith with others. Let no one be minded to hold ceremonies in secret; nor let anyone be minded to hold ceremonies in public capacity or in private or outside the city, unless he have first approached the praetor of the city and he have authorised them, by a vote of the Senate, to do so,

[3] only a woman can hold such priesthood. Livy, XXXIX, 13, 8.

[4] manager of the non-religious business of the organisation.

257

sententiad, dum ne minus | senatoribus C adesent
quom ea res cosoleretur, iousise⟨n⟩t. Censuere. |

Homines plous V oinvorsei virei atque mulieres
20 sacra ne quisquam | fecise velet, neve inter ibei
virei plous duobus, mulieribus plous tribus |
arfuise velent, nisei de pr. urbani senatuosque
sententiad, utei suprad | scriptum est.

Haice utei in conventionid exdeicatis ne minus
trinum | noundinum, senatuosque sententiam
utei scientes esetis, eorum | sententia ita fuit:
sei ques esent, quei arvorsum ead fecisent, quam
25 suprad | scriptum est, eeis rem caputalem facien-
dam censuere; atque utei | hoce in tabolam
ahenam inceideretis, ita senatus aequom censuit, |
uteique eam figier ioubeatis, ubei facilumed
gnoscier potisit; atque | utei ea Bacanalia, sei
qua sunt, exstrad quam sei quid ibei sacri est, |
ita utei suprad scriptum est, in diebus X,
30 quibus vobeis tabelai datai | erunt, faciatis utei
dismota sient.   In agro Teurano.

---

[1] 'in that company,' not, apparently, ' meanwhile.'

[2] *in contione*, at a special or informal meeting called by the magistrate.

[3] at least 17, at most 31 days; there is doubt whether *trinum nundinum* is *tria nundina* or is a length of time in which 3 *nundinae* fall.   See pp. xlii, 453 ff.

[4] an ancient altar or consecrated statue, as Livy shows—

provided that not fewer Senators than 100 be present when that matter is deliberated.' Passed.

' Let no single person in a company beyond five in all, men and women, be minded to hold ceremonies, and let men not more than two, and not more than three women be minded to attend there among,[1] unless it be by the advice of the praetor of the city, and a vote of the Senate as recorded above.'

You shall proclaim these orders at a public[2] meeting for a period[3] covering not less than three market-days; and that you might be aware of the vote of the Senate, they voted as follows : They resolved that ' should there be any persons who act contrary to the purport of the proclamation as recorded above, proceedings for capital offence must be taken against them. ' And the Senate resolved that it be ' right and proper that you engrave this proclamation onto a tablet of bronze and that you order it to be fastened up where it can be most easily read; and that within ten days after the delivery of this State-letter to you, you see to it that those lodges of Bacchus which may exist are dispersed, in the manner recorded above, save if there be concerned anything holy[4] therein.' In[5] the domain of the Teurani.

XXXIX, 18, 7. *Bacanalia* here refers particularly to ' places ' or ' lodges devoted to Bacchus.'

[5] These words, being in larger letters, are perhaps added by a different hand, and so they would not be part of the letter except that they may have been an instruction, on the original letter, to the letter-carrier, added later to this bronze plate for completeness' sake when it was copied from the document as received from the Senate. On lines 23–30 especially, cf. Fränkel, *Hermes*, LXVII, 369 ff., and further discussion by J. Keil in *Hermes*, LXVIII, 306–312.

INSTRUMENTA

27

Epistula Praetoris ad Tiburtes.

L. Cornelius Cn. f. pr. sen. cons. a.d. III Nonas
Maias sub aede Kastorus. |

Scr. adf. A. Manlius A. f., Sex. Iulius . . . . . L.
Postumius S. f. | Quod Teiburtes v. f. quibusque
de rebus vos purgavistis ea senatus | animum
advortit utei aequom fuit; nosque ea ita audi-
⁵ veramus | ut vos deixsistis vobeis nontiata esse.
Ea nos animum nostrum | non indoucebamus ita
facta esse propterea quod scibamus | ea vos
merito nostro facere non potuisse; neque vos
dignos esse | quei ea faceretis neque id vobeis
neque rei poplicae vostrae | oitile esse facere.
Et postquam vostra verba senatus audivit |,
¹⁰ tanto magis animum nostrum indoucimus, ita
utei ante | arbitrabamur, de eieis rebus af vobeis
peccatum non esse. | Quonque de eieis rebus
senatuei purgati estis, credimus vosque | animum
vostrum indoucere oportet, item vos populo |
Romano purgatos fore.

LAWS AND OTHER DOCUMENTS

27

Letter of the praetor Lucius Cornelius to the people of Tibur announcing a decree of the Senate about them. Tablet of bronze found at Tibur, now lost. Late second or early first century B.C.[1]

Lucius Cornelius, praetor, son of Gnaeus, consulted the Senate on the 5th day of May in the Temple of Castor. Present as witnesses[2] to the record: Aulus Manlius son of Aulus; Sextus Julius . . .; Lucius Postumius son of Spurius.

The Senate took due and proper notice, people of Tibur, of the matter whereof you made verbal report and of the matters whereof you set forth a justification of yourselves, and we had heard beforehand the details as you say they were reported to you. We were not able to bring our minds to believe that such acts were performed as you said, for the reason that we knew our merits could not have deserved that you should perform the same, and that it was not worthy of you to perform them, and that it would be of no advantage to you or to your State to perform them. And now that the Senate has heard what you reported verbally, so much the more do we bring our minds to believe, as was our opinion heretofore, that on those matters no wrong has been done by you. And now that you are cleared of the said matters in the minds of the Senate, we believe, and you also may rightfully bring your minds to believe, that you will be cleared in the minds of the Roman people likewise.

---

[1] The praetor Cornelius (see below) may be he who was consul in 156 B.C.

[2] See note 6 on p. 255.

INSTRUMENTA

28

Sententia Minuciorum inter Genuates et Viturios.

Q. M. MINUCIEIS Q. F. RUFEIS DE
CONTROVORSIEIS INTER | Genuateis et Vei-
turios inre praesente cognoverunt, et coram inter
eos controvosias composeiverunt, | et qua lege
agrum possiderent et qua fineis fierent dixserunt.
Eos fineis facere terminosque statui iuserunt; |
ubei ea facta essent, Romam coram venire
iouserunt. Romae coram sententiam ex senati
⁵ consulto dixerunt eidib. | Decemb. L. Caecilio
Q. f., Q. Muucio Q. f. cos.

Qua ager privatus casteli Vituriorum est, quem
agrum eos vendere heredemque | sequi licet, is
ager vectigal. nei siet.

Langatium fineis agri privati. Abrivo infimo,
qui oritur ab fontei in Mannicelo ad flovium |
Edem; ibi terminus stat. Inde ¹ flovio suso

¹ *fortasse scribendum fuit* inde flovio Ede suso

---

¹ who inhabited a *castellum*, that is, an outlying community
dependent on Genua.
² Cf. A. Passerini, *Athenaeum*, XV, 1937, pp. 26 ff. The
language of this inscription attempts inconsistently the style
of an earlier period. For other inscriptions relating to these
two brothers, see pp. 88–9, 132–3.
³ That is, boundary-stones.
⁴ *vectigal* presumably = *vectigalis* abbreviated.
⁵ Langates = Langenses (see below—they are the same
as the Veturii) of the modern Langasco. For topographical
details, cf. Grassi and Desimonis, *Atti della Società ligure di
storia patria*, III, 393 ff.; Poggi, *ibid.*, XXX.
⁶ *Mannicelum* is doubtless the hill still called Maniceno;
the Edus is probably the Sadodela. The various names
which follow are Ligurian.
⁷ It seems best to assume that *inde flovio susu vorsum*, and
the like in other sentences which follow, means 'thence
upstream along the brook' so that the streams were boundaries

LAWS AND OTHER DOCUMENTS

28

Arbitration of Quintus Minucius and Marcus Minucius fixing the territories of the Genuates and the (Langenses) Veturii or Viturii.[1] *Plate of bronze found near Genoa in the Vale of Polcevera.* 117 B.C.[2]

Quintus Minucius Rufus and Marcus Minucius Rufus, sons of Quintus, inquired on the spot into the quarrels between the Genuans and the Veturians and in their hearing settled the quarrels between them and informed them of the conditions on which they were to hold their land and of the conditions on which boundaries were to be fixed. They ordered them to fix the boundaries and to cause boundary-marks[3] to be set up; they ordered them to come to Rome in person when these commands were carried out. In person at Rome the Minucii made a report by a resolution of the Senate on the thirteenth day of December in the consulship of Lucius Caecilius son of Quintus, and Quintus Mucius son of Quintus.

' Wherever there is private land belonging to the fortress of the Veturii, land which they may sell and which can pass to an heir, the said land shall not be put under charges.[4]

The boundaries of the private land of the Langenses[5] are: from the lowest reach of the water-course which rises from the spring on Manicelum, at the stream Edus[6]; there a boundary-mark stands. Thence along the stream uphill[7] to the stream

(ablative of 'road by which,' strengthened by an adverb). It is less likely that *inde flovio susu vorsum* means ' thence from the stream uphill.' . . . The land would in any case be called officially *ager arcifinius* = ' bow-bounded,' ' with wavy boundaries,' not *ager limitatus* with boundaries squared off by a surveyor (for which see pp. 158 ff.).

vorsum in flovium Lemurim. Inde flovio Lemuri
susum usque ad rivom Comberane(am). | Inde
rivo Comberanea susum usque ad comvalem
Caeptiemam; ibi termina duo stant circum
viam Postumiam. Ex eis terminis recta | regione
inrivo Vendupale. Ex rivo Vindupale inflovium
Neviascam. Inde dorsum fluio Neviasca in
10 flovium Procoberam. Inde | flovio Procobera⟨m⟩
deorsum usque ad rivom Vinelascam infumum;
ibei terminus stat. Inde sursum rivo recto
Vinelesca; | ibei terminus stat propter viam
Postumiam. Inde alter trans viam Postumiam
terminus stat. Ex eo termino, quei stat | trans
viam Postumiam, recta regione infontem in
Manicelum. Inde deorsum rivo, quei oritur ab
fonte enManicelo, | ad terminum, quei stat
adflovium Edem.

Agri poplici quod Langenses posident, hisce
finis videntur esse. Ubi confluont | Edus et
Procobera, ibei terminus stat. Inde Ede flovio
sursuorsum in montem Lemurino infumo; ibei
15 terminus | stat. Inde sursumvorsum iugo recto
monte Lemurino; ibei termin[u]s stat. Inde
susum iugo recto Lemurino; ibi terminus | stat
in monte pro cavo. Inde sursum iugo recto
inmontem Lemurinum summum; ibi terminus
stat. Inde sursum iugo | recto incastelum quei
vocitatust Alianus; ibei terminus stat. Inde

---

[1] The Lemne or Lemo?   [2] made in 148 B.C.
[3] belonging to Genua.
[4] *iugum* is here perhaps used simply to express 'hillside,'
'mountain-side,' 'slope.'
[5] Not 'fort'? See p. 193.

Lemuris.[1] Thence along the stream Lemuris uphill
as far as the watercourse Comberanea. Thence along
the watercourse Comberanea uphill as far as the valley
Caeptiema; there two boundary-marks stand on
either side of the Postumian Way.[2] From these
boundary-marks, in a straight line to the watercourse
Vendupale. From the watercourse Vendupale to
the stream Neviasca. Thence downhill along the
stream Neviasca to the stream Procobera. Thence
downhill along the stream Procobera as far as the
lowest reach of the watercourse Vinelasca. There a
boundary-mark stands. Thence straight up the
watercourse Vinelasca. Here a boundary-mark
stands by the Postumian Way. Thence across the
Postumian Way stands a second mark. From that
which stands across the Postumian Way in a straight
line to the spring at Manicelum. Thence downstream
along the watercourse which rises from the spring
on Manicelum to the boundary-mark which stands
by the stream Edus. The boundaries of such public
state-land [3] which is in the possession of the Langenses
appear to be these: at the confluence of the Edus and
the Procobera, there a boundary-mark stands.
Thence along the stream Edus uphill to Mount
Lemurinus, at the foot; there a boundary-mark
stands. Thence uphill on Mount Lemurinus, straight
along up the ridge [4]; there a boundary-mark stands.
Thence up further straight along up the ridge Lemurinus; there a boundary-mark stands on the mountain
in front of a hollow. Thence up straight along up
the ridge to the top of Mount Lemurinus; there a
boundary-mark stands. Thence up straight along up
the ridge to the reservoir [5] often called Alianus; there
a boundary-mark stands. Thence up straight along

265

sursum iugo recto in montem Ioventionem;
ibi terminus | stat. Inde sursum iugo recto in
montem Apeninum quei vocatur Boplo, ibei
terminus stat. Inde Apeninum iugo recto | in
montem Tuledonem; ibei terminus stat. Inde
deorsum iugo recto inflovium Veraglascam in
20 montem Berigiemam | infumo; ibi terminus stat.
Inde sursum iugo recto in montem Prenicum;
ibi terminus stat. Inde dorsum iugo recto in |
flovium Tulelascam; ibi terminus stat. Inde
sursum iugo recto Blustiemelo in montem Claxe-
lum; ibi terminus stat. Inde | deorsum infontem
Lebriemelum; ibi terminus stat. Inde recto
rivo Eniseca infloviom Porcoberam; ibi terminus
stat. | Inde deorsum in floviom Porcoberam,
ubei conflouont flovi Edus et Porcobera; ibi
terminus stat.

Quem agrum poplicum | iudicamus esse, eum
agrum castelanos Langenses Veiturios po[*si*]dere
fruique videtur oportere. Pro eo agro vectigal
25 Langenses | Veituris in poplicum Genuam dent
in anos singulos vic. n. CCCC. Sei Langenses eam
pequniam non dabunt neque satis | facient
arbitratuu Genuatium, quod per Genuenses mo[*r*]a
non fiat, quo setius eam pequniam acipiant: tum

---

[1] The modern Giovo delle Reste, or near it.

[2] The natural order of words would be : *inde iugo recto in
montem Apeninum Tuledonem.*

[3] *infumo = infumum.*

[4] Doubtless modern La Secca, near which this plate was
found.

[5] about 300 denarii, or possibly less by the date of this
inscription. *vic. n. = victoriatos nummos,* of silver, struck

up the ridge to Mount Ioventio [1]; there a boundary-mark stands. Thence up straight along up the ridge to that height of the Apennine Mountains which is called Boplo; there a boundary-mark stands. Thence straight along up the ridge to the Apennine mountain Tuledo [2]; there a boundary-mark stands. Thence downhill straight along down the ridge to the stream Veraglasca at the foot [3] of Mount Berigiema; there a boundary-mark stands. Thence uphill straight along up the ridge to Mount Prenicus; there a boundary-mark stands. Thence downhill straight along down the ridge to the stream Tulelasca; there a boundary-mark stands. Thence uphill straight along up the ridge Blustiemelus to Mount Claxelus; there a boundary-mark stands. Thence downhill to the spring Lebriemelus; there a boundary-mark stands. Thence straight along the watercourse Eniseca [4] to the stream Procobera; there a boundary-mark stands. Thence downhill to the stream Procobera at the point of the confluence of the streams Edus and Procobera; there a boundary-mark stands.

Whatever land we judge to be public state-land, that land we think the fort-holders, namely the Langensian Viturii, ought to hold and enjoy. For the said land the Langensian Veturii shall pay into the public treasury at Genua every year 400 [5] pieces of the " Victory " stamp. If the Langenses fail to pay the said money and do not give satisfaction according to the will and pleasure of the Genuans (on such condition that it is not through the fault of the Genuans that any delay hinders them from receiving the money)—in this case the

by the Romans as equivalents to the *drachmae* of Massilia for use in these regions of the Po and Liguria. See pp. 218, 220.

quod in eo agro | natum erit frumenti partem vicensumam, vini partem sextam Langenses inpoplicum Genuam dare debento | in annos singolos.

Quei intra eos fineis agrum posedet Genuas aut Viturius, quei eorum posedeit K. Sextil. L. Caicilio | Q. Muucio cos., eos ita posidere colereque liceat. E[i]s [1] quei posidebunt vectigal Langen-
30 sibus pro portione dent ita ut ceteri | Langenses, qui eorum in eo agro agrum posidebunt fruenturque. Praeter ea in eo agro ni quis posideto, nisi de maiore parte | Langensium Veituriorum sententia, dum ne alium intro mitat nisi Genuatem aut Veiturium colendi causa. Quei eorum | de maiore parte Langensium Veiturium sententia ita non parebit, is eum agrum nei habeto nive fruimino.

Quei | ager compascuos erit, in eo agro quo minus pecus [p]ascere Genuates Veituriosque liceat ita utei incetero agro | Genuati compascuo niquis prohibeto, nive quis vim facito neive prohibeto quo minus ex eo agro ligna materiamque |
35 sumant utanturque.

Vectigal anni primi K. Ianuaris secundis Veturis Langenses inpoplicum Genuam dare | debento. Quod ante K. Ianuar. primas Langenses fructi sunt eruntque, vectigal invitei dare nei debento. |

[1] EVS

---

[1] The meaning is those who are holders of long standing must pay their share no less than new holders.

[2] here and below *maiore parte* is a harsh attraction for *maioris partis.*

[3] This was not common pasture-land but special pasture-land, belonging to a certain district, on which local farmers could legally graze cattle. Cf. Lex Agraria, pp. 383, 393.

Langenses shall be required to pay into the public treasury at Genua every year one twentieth part of the corn and one sixth part of the wine which shall have been produced on the said land.

Any Genuan or Veturian who has come into possession of land within the said boundaries, if he held possession on the first day of August in the consulship of Lucius Caecilius and Quintus Mucius, may thus remain in possession and till the land. Those who shall [1] possess a holding must pay to the Langenses a charge in the same proportion as the remaining Langenses such of them as shall possess and enjoy any area within the said land. Furthermore within the said land no one must possess a holding unless it be by a majority [2]-vote of the Langensian Veturii, and on condition that he admits no other onto his holding for the purpose of tilling unless he be a Genuan or a Veturian. If any of the said persons shall not appear to obey this condition (by a majority-vote of the Langensian Veturii), he shall not keep the land or enjoy it.

No man shall hinder the Genuans and the Veturii from pasturing cattle, on such of the said land as is associate pasture-land,[3] in the way in which it is allowed on the remaining associate pasture-land of Genua, and no man shall use force or hinder them from taking from the said land firewood and building-timber and using the same.

The Langensian Veturii are required to pay into the public treasury at Genua a first year's rent on the first day of January next but one. For such land as the Langenses have enjoyed and shall enjoy before and up to the first day of January next they are not required to pay against their will.

Prata quae fuerunt proxuma faenisicei L.
Caecilio Q. Muucio cos. in agro poplico quem
Vituries Langenses | posident et quem Odiates et
quem Dectunines et quem Cavaturineis et quem
Mentovines posident, ea prata | invitis Langensibus
et Odiatibus et Dectuninebus et Cavaturines et
40 Mentovines, quem quisque eorum agrum | posi-
debit, inviteis eis niquis sicet nive pascat nive
fruatur. Sei Langueses aut Odiates aut Dectu-
nines aut Cavaturines | aut Mentovines malent
in eo agro alia prata inmittere defendere sicare,
id uti facere liceat, dum ne ampliorem | modum
pratorum habeant, quam proxuma aestate habue-
runt fructique sunt.

Vituries quei controvorsias | Genuensium ob
iniourias iudicati aut damnati sunt, sei quis
invinculeis ob eas res est, eos omneis | solvei
mittei leiber[are]ique [1] Genuenses videtur
oportere ante eidus Sextilis primas.

5 Seiquoi de ea re | iniquom videbitur esse, ad nos
adeant primo quoque die et ab omnibus [2] contro-
versis †et hono publ. li† |

Leg. Moco Meticanio Meticoni f., Plaucus
Peliani. Pelioni f.

[1] LEIBERIOVE
[2] CONTROVERSIS ET·HONO PVBL· LI

---

[1] *proxumā faenisicei,* ' ready for the mower,' as being newly
reclaimed. If we take the words as *proxumā faenisicei,*
ablatives ' at the last hay-mowing,' here is the only example
of *faenisex,* feminine, in the sense of *faenisicia;* elsewhere
faenisex is always a mower, masculine.

[2] These were inhabitants of other *castella* dependant on
Genua.   [3] That is, lay claim to.

[4] *Genuenses* on the bronze must here have been added by
mistake unless we accept the syntax *videtur oportere Genuenses*

LAWS AND OTHER DOCUMENTS

The meadows which were ready for the mower,[1] during the consulship of Lucius Caecilius and Quintus Mucius, within the limits of the public state-land in the possession of the Langensian Veturii, and the public state-land in the possession of the Odiates [2] and the Dectunines, and the public state-land in the possession of the Cavaturini and the Mentovini—the said meadows no one shall mow or use as pasture or enjoy against the will of the Langenses and the Odiates and the Dectunines and the Cavaturini and the Mentovini, in the case of the land which any of the said peoples shall severally possess. If, on the said land, the Langenses or the Odiates or the Dectunines or the Cavaturini or the Mentovini prefer to let grow, fence off,[3] and mow other meadows, they shall be allowed to do so provided that they hold no larger measure of meadow-land than they held and enjoyed last summer.

If any one of the Veturii who have been judged or found guilty in respect of quarrels with the Genuans on account of contumelious wrongs is in prison because of such matters, we think that all of them should be released, discharged, and set free [4] before the thirteenth day of August next. If any shall think that there is unfairness in this matter, they must come to us [5] on the first possible day and [6] be quit of all quarrels. . . .

Commissioners: Mocus [7] Meticanius son of Meticonus; Plaucus Pelianius son of Pelionus.

solvi = 'we think that it behoves the Genuenses that (such prisoners) should be released'—a construction without parallel.

[5] the commissioners named below.

[6] Here the engraver seems to have gone entirely wrong—see opposite.

[7] These are Ligurian names—cf. Schulze, *Zur Gesch. Lat. Eigennamen*, 585.

29

709 (*et*
p. 714.)

(*a*) [*C*]N. POMPEIUS SE[*X. F. IMPERATOR*]
VIRTUTIS CAUSSA

Equites Hispanos ceives [*Romanos fecit in castr*]eis
apud Asculum a. d. XIV. K. Dec. ex lege
Iulia.   In consilio [*fuerunt . . .*]
L. Gellius L. f. Tro., Cn. Octavius Q. f. . . . .
. . . *multi alii* . . .

(*b*) TURMA SALLUITANA

(*col.* 1)	(*col.* 2)
Sanibelser Adingibas f.	Ilerdenses
Illurtibas Bilustibas f.	Ootacilius Suisetarten f.
Estopeles Ordennas f.	Cn. Cornelius Nesille
Tersinno Austinco f.	P. Eabius Enasagin f.
(. . . *alii* . . .)	5 Begenses
	Turtumelis Atanscer f.
	Segienses
	Sosinaden Sosinasae f.
	(. . . *alii* . . .)

29 vide *C.I.L.*, I, 2. 709 et p. 714

---

[1] See *C.I.L.*, I, 2, pp. 528, 714, 726; Cichor., *Röm. Stud.*,
131 ff.; Gatti, *Bull. Commun.*, 1908, 169 ff.; 1910, 273;
Lanciani, *Athenaeum*, 30th Jan., 1909; T. Ashby, *Class. Rev.*,
XXIII, 158; Stara-Tedde, *Una nuova importantiss. iscr. rom.*;
De Sanctis, *Atti della R. Acc. di sc. di Tor.*, XLV, 3 ff.; G. H.
Stevenson, in *Journ. of Rom. Stud.*, IX, 1919, pp. 95 ff., *et al.*
Pompeius besieged and took Asculum in 89 B.C. during the
'Social' War.   For sling-shots of this siege see p. 212, n. 2.
For this decree P. relies on a *Lex rogata*—cf. next note.

[2] Of 90 B.C. which, as we know from other sources, gave
Roman citizenship to all Latin communities and all other
communities not in arms; and, as this inscription shows,
authorised its award for good service in the field.

[3] including apparently Lepidus, consul in 78; Rabirius, defended by Cicero, 63 B.C.; and the famous Pompey the Great.

LAWS AND OTHER DOCUMENTS

29

Decree of Gnaeus Pompeius Strabo, consul in 89 B.C. Fragments of a bronze tablet found at Rome. Selections from the inscription.[1]

(a) GNAEUS POMPEIUS, COMMANDER-IN-CHIEF, SON OF SEXTUS, FOR VALOUR

made Spanish horsemen Roman citizens in camp at Asculum on the 17th day of November, according to the Julian[2] law. Present at the council . . . Lucius Gellius son of Lucius, of the Tromentine tribe, Gnaeus Octavius, son of Quintus . . .

(the inscription gives a number of others.[3] *. . .).*

(b) THE SALLUITAN SQUADRON.

(col. 1)	(col. 2)
Sanibelser, son of Ad-ingibas[4]	*Ilerdans*
	Otacilius, son of Suise-tarten
Illurtibas, son of Bilus-tibas	Cn. Cornelius, son of Nesille
Estopeles, son of Orden-nas	Publius Eabius, son of Enasagin
Tcrsinno, son of Aus-tinco	*Begensians*
(. . . *others* . . .)	Turtumelis, son of Atanscer
	Segiensians
	Sosinaden, son of Sosinasa (?)
	(. . . *others* . . .)

---

[4] These Iberian names seem to be indeclinable; or I at any rate treat them so here. The Salluitans are Spanish (of Salduba, Pliny, III, 24), not the Celtic or Ligurian Salluvii of Narbonensis (Pliny, III, 36, 47). Cichorius, *Röm. Stud.*, 133, conjectures that the name of the squadron may be derived from that of its commander, perhaps Salvitto. Note that some of the Ilerdans mentioned are half 'Romanised.'

INSTRUMENTA

(*col.* 4) Cn. Pompeius Sex. f. imperator
　　　　virtutis caussa turmam
　　　　Salluitanam donavit in
　　　　castreis apud Asculum
　　5 cornuculo et patella torque
　　　　armilla palereis et frumentum
　　　　duplex.

30

Lex Parieti Faciendo.

698　　　Ab colonia deducta anno XC
　　　　N. Fufidio N. f., M. Pullio duo vir. | P. Rutilio,
　　　　Cn. Mallio cos.

Col. I.　　　　　　　Operum Lex II

　　5 Lex parieti faciendo in area quae est ante |
　　　aedem Serapi trans viam. Qui redemerit |
　　　praedes dato praediaque subsignato | duum-
　　　virum arbitratu. | In area trans viam paries qui
　　10 est propter | viam in eo pariete medio ostiei
　　　lumen | aperito; latum p. VI altum p. VII
　　　facito. Ex eo | pariete antas duas ad mare
　　　vorsum proicito | longas p. II crassas p. I∴. In

---

¹ *corniculum,* an ornament for the helmet, awarded for valour.

² This was a military decoration for men, and does not mean the trappings of the horses. So also the double ration of corn is for the men, not the horses.

³ Corresponding, as in many other Italian towns, to the consuls at Rome. See pp. xxxviii–xxxix.

⁴ *Lex* seems to mean ' contract' rather than ' law '. As will be seen, the main business is the construction of a porch in front of a wall. Cf. Wiegand, *Jahrbb. f. Philol.,* Suppl.-Band

(col. 4) Gnaeus Pompeius, commander-in-chief, son of Sextus, in camp at Asculum, for valour presented the Salluitan squadron with the helmet-horn,[1] a plate, a necklace, a bracelet, breast-pieces,[2] and a double ration of corn.

30

Contract, issued perhaps as a municipal decree, of the Roman colony Puteoli relating to building-work in front of the temple of Serapis. Tablet of marble, now at Naples, written in three columns; found at Puteoli. 105 B.C. It was cut or recut in the imperial age, but was copied from an original document.

In the ninetieth year from the foundation of the colony, in the magistracy of Numerius Fufidius, son of Numerius, and Marcus Pullius, as Board of Two,[3] and the consulship of Publius Rutilius and Gnaeus Mallius.

Second Contract relating to Works.

Contract for making a wall [4] in the vacant building-space which lies in front of the temple of Serapis across the road. The contractor shall provide bondsmen and register their estates as securities at the will and pleasure of the members of the Board of Two. In the middle of the party-wall which is near the road and which is in the vacant space across the road, [10] he shall open a gap for a doorway. He shall make it 6 ft. wide, 7 ft. high. From the said wall on the side which faces towards the sea he shall cause to jut out two side-pillars 2 ft. long and 1 ft. and $\frac{1}{4}$ [5]

XX, pp. 661 ff.; *Die Puteolanische Inschrift*, Leipzig, Teubner, 1894; the plans are reproduced in *C.I.L.*, I, 2, pp. 525–6. But undoubtedly the roof of the porch was not flat but triangular, topped with a *margo*. Cf. Wordsworth, 476–478.

   [5] · = 1 inch;   : · (as here) = 3 inches.

super id limen | robustum long. p. VIII latum
¹⁵ p. I : altum p. s : | inponito. Insuper id et antas
mutulos robustos | II crassos s : altos p. I proicito
extra pariete | in utramq. partem p. IV. In-
super simas pictas | ferro offigito. In super
Col. II. mutulos trabiculas | abiegineas II crassas quoque
²⁰ versus s inpon(i)to | ferroque figito. In asserato
asseribus abiegnieis | sectilibus crasseis quoque
versus : : ; disponito ni plus s : | Operculaque
abiegnea inponito ex tigno pedario | facito.
Antepagmenta abiegnea lata s : crassa Ɛ | cumat-
²⁵ iumque imponito ferroque plano figito, | portula-
que tegito tegularum ordinibus seneis | quoque
versus. Tegulas primores omnes in ante|pag-
mento ferro figito marginemque inponito. | Eis-
dem fores clatratas II cum postibus aesculnieis |
facito statuito ocludito picatoque ita utei ad aedem |
³⁰ Honorus facta sunt. Eisdem maceria extrema
paries | qui est eum parietem cum margine altum
facito p. X. | Eisdem ostium intro itu in area quod
nunc est et | fenestras quae in pariete propter
eam aream sunt | pariete⟨m⟩ opstruito ; et parieti
³⁵ quod nunc est propter | viam marginem perpet-

---

30 ¹³ id *fortasse delendum*   ¹⁴ P *ante* S *delendum?*
²⁰ *lege* inasserato   ²⁵ *lege* portulamque
³⁴ PARIETEM (*delendum* M)

---

¹ s. = *semissem* from *semis*, ' one half.'
² not the modern ' mutules.'
³ or : latticed boarding.
⁴ Ɛ = half an inch.

thick.   Above the doorway he shall place a lintel of [15]
hard oakwood, 8 ft. long, 1 ft. and $\frac{1}{4}$ wide, $\frac{3}{4}$ [1] ft.
deep.   On the top of it and the side-pillars he shall
cause to jut out from the wall, on the outside,
4 ft. on both sides, oaken top-beams [2] 2 ft. and $\frac{2}{3}$
thick and 1 ft. wide.   On top he shall fasten up,
with iron, chased ogee-mouldings.   Above the top-
beams he shall place, and along them fasten with [20]
iron, 2 cross-beams made of fir-wood and $\frac{1}{2}$ ft. thick
each way.   He shall rafter them over with rafters
hewn from fir-logs and made $\frac{1}{3}$ ft. thick each way;
he shall arrange them not more than $\frac{3}{4}$ ft. apart.
And he shall place in position wainscot-panelling [3]
of fir-wood; he shall make them out of foot-wide
blocks.   He shall place in position frontal fittings
of fir-wood $\frac{3}{4}$ ft. wide and $\frac{1}{2}$ an inch [4] thick, and a
waved moulding, and shall fasten same with flat
clamps of iron.   He shall also roof the small door [25]
with a roof having six rows of tiles on each side.
He shall fasten all the lowest tiles on either side to
the corresponding frontal fitting with iron, and he
shall place a coping on top.   The same person shall
also make two latticed folding-doors having posts of
winter-oak and shall put up and close and pitch them
in the same way as was done to the doors at Honour's [30]
temple.   In regard to the wall which forms the outer-
most enclosure, he shall further reconstruct the said
wall 10 ft. high including coping.   He shall also
block up the doorway which now forms an entrance
into the vacant building-space and also wall up the
windows which are in the wall along the said
vacant space; and on the wall which is at present
along the road he shall put an uninterrupted coping. [35]
And all those walls and copings which will be found

277

uom inponito eosq. parietes | marginesque omnes,
quae lita non erunt, calce | harenato lita politaque
et calce uda dealbata recte | facito. Quod opus
structile fiet, in te[r]ra calcis | restinctai partem
⁴⁰ quartam indito.   Nive maiorem | caementa[m]
Col. III. struito quam quae caementa arda | pendat p. XV,
nive angolaria altiorem :: Ɛ facito. | Locumque
purum pro eo opere reddito. | Eidem sacella aras
signaque quae in | campo sunt quae demon-
⁴⁵ strata erunt, | ea omnia tollito deferto componito |
statuitoque ubei locus demonstratus | erit duum-
virum arbitratu. | Hoc opus omne facito arbitratu
duo vir. | et duovira[l]ium qui in consilio esse |
⁵⁰ solent Puteoleis, dum ni minus viginti | adsient
cum ea res consuletur. Quod | eorum viginti
iurati probaverint probum | esto;   quod ieis
inprobarint inprobum esto. | Dies operis: K.
⁵⁵ Novembr. primeis. Dies pequn. : | pars dimidia
dabitur ubei praedia satis | subsignata erunt;
altera pars dimidia solvetur | opere effecto pro-
batoque. C. Blossius Q. f. | H̶S̶ oo Ð, idem praes.
Q. Fuficius Q. f. | Cn. Tetteius Q. f. C. Granius
C. f. Ti. Crassicius.

⁴⁹ DVOVIRATIVM

---

¹ this would be volcanic ash.
² this means tiles and copings, apparently.
³ *caementa*, neuter plural, usually quarry stones unhewn;
but here *caementa = caementam*, sc. *tegulam*.
⁴ *sc.* of the bondsmen.
⁵ Cf. Paul., ex Fest., 139, 4 : ' *Manceps* ' is a term applied
to a man who has bought or hired something from the people.
. . . ' idem praes ' 'likewise bondsman' is a term also applied
to him because he is bound ' *praestare*,' to make good what he
has promised to the people just as much as a man who has
been made bondsman for him.
⁶ These are names of sureties or bondsmen for Blossius.

uncoated he shall cause to be well coated with a plaster of lime-mortar mixed with sand[1] and varnished and whitewashed with wet lime.   Material requiring preparation[2] that he will use in this structure he shall make of clay mixed with one fourth part of slaked lime.   And the rough tiles[3] which he shall [46] lay shall not be larger than such rough tile as turns the scale at 15 lbs. weight when dry, nor make the corner-tiles more than $4\frac{1}{2}$ inches high.   And he shall clear the site according to the requirements of the work.   Likewise the chapels, altars, and statues which are on the building-ground and which shall be pointed out to him he shall remove transfer arrange and set up in a place which shall be pointed out to [45] him, at the will and pleasure of the magisterial Board of Two.   He shall complete the whole of this work at the will and pleasure of the members and ex-members of the Board of Two who customarily sit in council at Puteoli, provided that not less than twenty members are present when the proposal shall be [50] under discussion.   Whatever may be approved by twenty of them on oath shall be legally valid; whatever they may not approve shall be legally invalid. **Day for** beginning the work: the first day of November next.   **Day of payment:** one half of the sum shall be [55] handed over when the estates[4] have been registered to satisfaction as securities; the other half shall be paid off when the work is completed and approved.

Gaius Blossius son of Quintus; he contracts for 1500 sesterces; is likewise[5] surety.   Quintus[6] Fuficius son of Quintus; Gnaeus Tettius son of Quintus; Gaius Granius son of Gaius; Tiberius Crassicius.

For a statute of the Pagus Herculaneus in the Ager Campanus, *recorded on a pedestal (of a dedicated altar ?), see pp. 108–111.*

INSTRUMENTA

31–2

Tabellae devotionis (defixionis).

1614   (i) L. Harines Her. Maturi | C. Eburis | Pom-
          5   ponius | M. Caedicius M. f. | N. Andripius
               N. f. | Pus olu solu fancua | recta sint, pus
               flatu | sicu olu sit.

1615   (ii) Nomen delatum | Naeviae L. l. | Secunda
          5   seive | ea alio nomini | est.

33

One of five thin plates or tablets of lead, pierced and crowded
round a nail. Each of them curses in detail one person—
Plotius, Avonia, Maxima Vesonia, Aquilia and an unknown
man (the tablet on which it is written is called Secunda [5] for
convenience) respectively. Since the contents of the curse are
similar in each case, the tablets can be supplemented by each
other. All the tablets were inscribed in the month of February
by the same person, presumably a sorcerer employed by those

2520   (iii) Bona pulchra Proserpina, [P]lut[o]nis uxsor, |
               seive me Salviam deicere oportet, | eripias

31 [6–8] *sc.* ut illorum omnium fancua recta sint, ut flatus
siccus illorum sit

---

[1] Cf. *C.I.L.*, I, 2, 1012, 1013, 2541; X, 8214.
[2] The meaning of *fancua* is unknown; it may or may not be
obscene. Cf. *tabula de fix.*, also of Cumae, *Notiz. d. Sc.*, 1913,
474, l. 3 fankeam. *Pus*: seems to mean *ut* (Oscan *puz, pous*).
olu : *illorum, solu* : *omnium* (cf. Latin *sollo* ' whole '). Cf.
Bréal, *Mém. de la soc. de ling.*, XV, 146–8; Bücheler, *Rhein.
Mus.*, LXII, 554 ff.; *Bonn. Jahrb.*, CXVI, 291 ff.

LAWS AND OTHER DOCUMENTS

31–2

Curses.[1]

(i) *A round tablet of lead found apparently at Cumae. Mixed Latin and Oscan. Interpretation of the names, etc., is not certain.*

Lucius Harines, son of Herius Maturus, Gaius Eburius, Pomponius, Marcus Caedicius son of Marcus, Numerius Andripius, son of Numerius. May the —— [2] of the whole lot of them stand upright! May their breath [3] be dry!

(ii) *A small bronze plate found in a sepulchre at Cumae.*

Summoned to [4] Hell's court: Naevia Secunda, freedwoman of Lucius, or whatever other name she goes by.

33

(iii) *A curse by enchantment. Lead plate. Found at Rome? Now at the Johns Hopkins University. First century B.C., not later than about the year 40.*

who wanted to curse the object of their hatred. The year of writing is probably later than 80 B.C., but I include here one of the curses (that which curses Plotius) as an old example of this kind of document. Cf. W. S. Fox, in *The American Journal of Philology*, XXXIII, 1912, Supplement (after p. 124), 'The Johns Hopkins Tabellae Defixionum.' See also Fox, in *A.J.P.*, XXXIII, 301 ff. on the throwing of curse-tablets into water.

O wife of Pluto, good and beautiful Proserpina (unless I ought to call thee Salvia),[6] pray tear away

---

[3] cf. *C.I.L.*, I, 2, 2541.

[4] sc. *apud inferos*, among the dead below.

[5] The tablet was nearest but one to the nail's head.

[6] Only here do we find this epithet as certainly applicable to Proserpina. It probably represents the Greek Σώτειρα 'Saviour goddess.' The writer has to make sure that he addresses the right deity rightly; involves in the curse all the parts and qualities of the victim; and keeps secret the name of the curser lest the latter suffer magic penalty or the penalties of the law against using *defixiones*.

salutem, c[*orpus, co*]lorem, vires, virtutes |
Ploti. Tradas [*Plutoni*] viro tuo. Ni possit
5   cogitationibus | sueis hoc vita[*re. Tradas*]
illunc | febri quartan[*a*]e, t[*ertian*]ae, cotti-
dia[*n*]ae, | quas [*cum illo l*]uct[*ent, deluctent*;
illunc] | ev[*in*]cant, [*vincant,*] usq[*ue dum ani-
mam* | *eiu*]s eripia[*nt. Quare ha*]nc victimam |
10   tibi trad[*o Prose*]rpi[*na, seiv*]e me, | Proser-
pin[*a, sei*]ve m[*e Ach*]eruosiam dicere |
oportet. M[*e mittas a*]recessitum canem |
tricepitem, qui [*Ploti*] cor eripiat. Pollicia-
15   rus | illi te daturum t[*r*]es victimas, | palma[*s,
ca*]rica[*s*], por[*c*]um nigrum, | hoc sei p[*erfe-*]
cerit [*ante mensem*] | M[*artium. Haec, P*]r[*o-
serpina Salvia, tibi dabo*] | cum compote
fe[*cer*]is. Do tibi cap[*ut*] | Ploti Avon[*iae.
20   Pr*]oserpina S[*alvia*] | do tibi fron[*tem Plo*]ti.
Proserpina Salvia, | do [*ti*]b[*i*] su[*percilia*]
Ploti. Proserpin[*a*] | Salvia, do[*tibi palpe-
tra*]s Plo[*ti.* | Proserpina Sa[*lvia, do tibi
pupillas*] Ploti. | Proser]pina Salvia, do tibi

[7] illo *suppl. coll. tab. de Avonia et tab. de Vesonia* (illa).
deluctent illunc *recte? desunt omn. tabb.*
[11] Acheruo— *lapsu pro* Acherou—
[13] Ploti *suppl. coll.* [Avoniae]s *in tab. de Av.*
[17] Proserpina *recte? deest cett. tabb.*
[19] *fortasse* Avoniaes *ut in tab. de Av.,* 14, 19–23
[22] palpetras *Ves.* palpe . . . s *Av. deest tab.* ' *Secundae* ' *et
tab. de Aquillia*

---

[1] malaria is the fever meant; 'fourth-day' = returning
every *third* day; 'third-day' = returning every *other* day.
[2] or possibly 'fight him down.' *deluctent* is a guess; all
the five tablets have a gap here. *quas* is nominative.
[3] So the tablet cursing Avonia, the only tablet intact at this
point. But probably we should read *Proserpinam*: ' victim

from Plotius health, body, complexion, strength,
faculties. Consign him to Pluto thy husband.
May he be unable to avoid this by devices of his.
Consign that man to the fourth-day, the third-day,
the every-day fever.[1] May they wrestle and wrestle
it out[2] with him, overcome and overwhelm him
unceasingly until they tear away his life. So I
consign him as victim to thee, Proserpina, unless o
Proserpina,[3] unless I ought to call thee Goddess of
the Lower World. Send, I pray,[4] someone to call
up the three-headed dog[5] with request that he may
tear out Plotius' heart. Promise Cerberus that thou
wilt give him three offerings—dates, dried figs, and
a black pig[6]—if he has fulfilled his task before the
month of March. All these, Proserina Salvia, will
I give thee when thou hast made me master of my
wish.[7] I give thee the head of Plotius, slave of
Avonia. O Proserpina Salvia, I give thee Plotius'
forehead. Proserpina Salvia, I give thee Plotius'
eyebrows, Proserpina Salvia, I give thee Plotius'
eyelids.[8] Proserpina Salvia, I give thee Plotius'
eye-pupils. Proserpina Salvia, I give thee Plotius'

---

to thee, Proserpina, whether I ought to call thee Proserpina
or Acherusia.'

[4] *me = mihi*, as attested by Festus.

[5] Cerberus, watch-dog of Acheron or of the house of Pluto
and Proserpina. The victims mentioned in the next sentence
are to be three so as to provide one for each mouth; besides,
three was a magical number.

[6] These offerings are all characteristic of the worship of
underground deities.

[7] *compote = compotem*. The complete sense is *cum me voti
compotem feceris*.

[8] *palpetrae* for *palpebrae* was used also by Varro (*L.L.*, Fr. 23
Kent, *L.C.L*). Some Romans said *palpetrae* means really eyelids, *palpebrae* eyelashes.

25 *nare*]s, | labra, or[*iculas, nasu*]m, lin[*g*]uam, |
dentes P[*loti*] ni dicere possit | Plotius quid
[*sibi dole*]at; collum, umeros, | bracchia,
d[*i*]*git*[*os, ni poss*]it aliquit | se adiutare;
30 [*pe*]c[*tus, io*]cinera, cor, | pulmones, n[*i possit
sentire quit* | sibi doleat, [*intes*]tina, venter,
um[*b*]licu[*s*], | latera, [*n*]i p[*oss*]it dormire;
scapulas, | ni poss[*it*] s[*a*]nus dormire; viscum |
35 sacrum, nei possit urinam facere; | natis,
anum, [*fem*]ina, genua, | [*crura*], tibias, pe[*des,
talos, plantas,* | *digito*]s, ungis, ni po[*ssit s*]tare
[*sua* | *vi*]rt[*u*]te. Seive [*plu*]s, seive parvum |
40 scrip|[*tum fuerit,*] quomodo quicqu[*it*] | legi-
tim[*e scripsit*], mandavit, seic | ego Ploti
ti[*bi tr*]ado, mando, | ut tradas, [*mandes
me*]nse Februari[*o* | *e*]cillunc. Ma[*le perdat,
mal*]e exse(a)t, | [*mal*]e disperd[*at. Mandes,
45 tra*]das, ni possit | [*ampliu*]s ullum [*mensem
aspic*]ere, | [*videre, contempla*]re.

---

²⁹ iocinera *recte?* . . . inera *tab. de Ves.*. . . . nera *tab. de Av.
et tab.* ' *Secunda* '. *deest tab. de Aquillia*
³¹ umblicus *Av.* umb . . . *Ves.* umblicus ' *Sec.*' *deest Aqu.
expectes* umblicum
³⁶ plantas *recte?* . . . la. . . . *Av. deest rell. tabb.*
³⁷⁻⁸ sua virtute *recte* su . . . te *Av.* . . . tute *Ves.* . . . .
tu ' *Sec* '. *deest* Aqu.
³⁹ quicqui *Av.* . . . q . . . t. ' *Sec.*' *deest Ve., Aqu.*
quisqu[e] *vel* quisqu[is] Vetter, *Glotta,* XII, 66
284

nostrils, lips, ears, nose, and his tongue and teeth
so that Plotius may not be able to utter what it is
that gives him pain; his neck, shoulders, arms,
fingers, so that he may not be able to help himself
at all; his chest, liver, heart, lungs, so that he may
not be able to feel what gives him pain; his abdomen,
belly,[1] navel, sides so that he may not be able to
sleep: his shoulder-blades, so that he may not be
able to sleep well [2]; his sacred part, so that he may
not be able to make water; his buttocks, vent,
thighs, knees, legs, shins, feet, ankles, soles, toes,
nails, that he may not be able to stand by his own
aid. Should there so exist any written curse,[3] great
or small—in what manner Plotius has, according to
the laws of magic, composed any curse and entrusted
it to writing,[4] in such manner I consign and hand
him [5] over to thee, so that thou mayest consign and
hand over that fellow, in the month of February.
Blast him! damn him! blast him utterly! Hand
him over, consign him, that he may not be able to
behold, see, and contemplate any month further!

[1] *venter* is here apparently accusative of a colloquial neuter
form; so I suppose is also *umblicus = umbilicus,* which is
properly masculine. *viscum* below is used for *viscus* (neuter),
genitive *visceris.*

[2] or ' sleep a healthy sleep ' (so Fox).

[3] written by Plotius against me. Here begins a counter-
charm. The verb *scribo* here means ' hand over ' or ' give by
written curse '.

[4] So Fox. But possibly : written any curse and entrusted
it (to another person).

[5] *Ploti. = Plotium.*

---

⁴⁴ mandes *recte* . . . nd . . . *Av.* m . . . . ' *Sec* '.   *deest*
tabb. Ves., Aqu.

INSTRUMENTA

34–48

Programmata.

1641(*c*)   (i)   L. Aqutium d. v. v. b. o. v. c.

1644(*a*)   (ii)   N. Barcha II v. v. b. o. v. f., ita vobeis Venus
                     Pomp. sacra [*sancta propitia sit*].

1644(*c*)   (iii) N. Vei Barca tabescas!

1672(*a*)   (iv)   N. Veium I[*I*] v.v.b.o.v. co[*l.*]

1672(*a*)   (v)   Amator. vest. faciat. aed. M. Ma.

1656(*a*)   (vi)   M. Marium aed. faci. oro vos.

1656(*g*)   (vii) M. Mari v. b. o. c.

1645(*a*)   (viii) Q. Caecil. q. v. benefic. o. v.

1645(*b*)   (ix)   Q. Caecil q. v. b. et be[*nef*]icum.

1647   (x)   P. Carpin. II v. v. b. o. v. f.

1652(*a*)   (xi)   P. Fur. II v. v. b. o. v. f.

1658   (xii) L. Nir. II v. b.

1668   (xiii) M. Sept[*umium*] II v. v. b. [*o. v.*] co[*l.*]

(ix) Q·ⅤB·ꞪE BE ICVM bonum ho(minem) *vel* he(rum)
be[nef]icum Momms.

---

[1] cf. Zangemeister, *C.I.L.*, IV, 1 ff.; I, 2, 1640–1679.
*Abbreviations : d.v., duovirum ; IIv., duovir(um) ; v. b., virum
bonum ; o. v., oro vos ; col. or c., coloni ; f. or faci. or faciat.,
faciatis ; aed., aedilem ; q., quaestorem ; benefic., beneficum.*

LAWS AND OTHER DOCUMENTS

34-48

Election notices [1] *painted in red on walls of tufa at Pompeii. Time of Sulla.*

(i) Lucius Aqutius, a fine man; settlers, I appeal to you to elect him member of the Board of Two.

(ii) Numerius Barcha, a fine man; I appeal to you to elect him member of the Bd. of II. So may Venus of Pompeii, holy, hallowed goddess, be kind to you.

(iii) Numerius Veius Barcha, may you rot!

(iv) Numerius Veius, a fine man; settlers, I appeal to you to elect him member of the Bd. of II.

(v) [2] Your best friend—Marcus Marius. Elect him aedile!

(vi) Marcus Marius; I appeal to you to elect him aedile.

40 (vii) Marcus Marius, a fine man: I appeal to you, settlers.

(viii) Quintus Caecilius, a generous man. To be quaestor—I appeal to you.

(ix) Quintus Caecilius, a fair and generous man. To be quaestor.

(x) Publius Carpinius, a fine man. I appeal to you to elect him member of the Bd. of II.

(xi) Publius Furius, a fine man. I appeal to you to elect him member of the Bd. of II.

45 (xii) Lucius Niraemius, a fine man. To be member of the Board of II.

(xiii) Marcus Septumius, a fine man. I appeal to you, settlers—member of the Bd. of II.

---

[2] *amatorem vestrum faciatis.* Though written just under the last, it is a separate notice; cf. nos. (vi) and (vii).

1674   (xiv) M. Ve[.]assid. quod rog.
1665   (xv) Quintio siqui recusat, assidat ad asinum . . .

49

735   C. Pumidius Dipilus heic fuit | a.d. V. Nonas Octo-
       breis M. Lepido Q. Catul. cos. | çųm (?)

50–52

2540a-b (i) (*a*) [' *Quid fi*]t? Vi me oculei posquam deducx-
          stis in ignem,'
        [. . .] vim vestreis largificatis geneis.'
       [' *verum*] non possunt lacrumae restinguere
          flamam ;
       [*hae*]c os incendunt tabificanque animum.'

Tiburtinus epoese

(ii) (*b*) [*Accurrunt*] veicinei, incendia participantur,
      . . . [*in*] flammam tradere utei liceat.

    50 (a) [1] quid fit? vi Buecheler   aeditui Baehrens
          [2] non ad vim Buecheler   lumphae vim B
          [3] verum non Buecheler   vanum; non B

---

[1] I take *rog.* as *rogo* and *assid.* as an abbreviation of *assiduo*
or *assidue* (hardly for *assiduus*, ' man of property ', of old
Roman law), with no connexion with *assidat* of the next
inscription, unless *assidat* means here also ' take a seat ' on the
Board.

[2] or perhaps ' on an ass '. But could *asinus* here be a
translation of the Greek ὄνος in the sense of a mill-stone ?—
' Sit at a mill-stone ', instead of on any council or board
of magistrates. *Quintio* may be not a name, but a word
meaning a pervert; cf. Todd, *Class. Quart.*, xxxvii, 1943, 109,
110.

288

LAWS AND OTHER DOCUMENTS

(xiv) Marcus Veius (?). What I ask again [1] and again. . . .

(xv) Quinctius. Let anyone who votes against him take a seat by an ass.[2]

49

Pumidius at Pompeii. Written on the inside of a wall in the basilica at Pompeii, 78 B.C.

Gaius Pumidius Diphilus was here on the 3rd day of October in the consulship of Marcus Lepidus and Quintus Catulus, with (?). . . .

50–52

Scratched on a wall of the smaller theatre at Pompeii, c. 90–80 B.C. *All by the same hand.*

(i) *A lover's lament. (Quotation from a poet ?)*

(*a*) 'What's up?[3] Now that your eyes have drawn me down by main force into a blaze, . . . you wet bountifully your cheeks.'[4]

' But tears cannot quench the flame; see here, they burn the face and waste the heart away.'

Written near :

Composed by Tiburtinus.

(ii) *Near and perhaps in derision of these lines the same person wrote the following :*

(*b*) Up run the neighbours, and take part in the conflagrations . . . that they may deliver them to the flames.[5]

---

[3] The beginnings of the lines have disappeared and we cannot restore the real words. Two people speak? cf. Wick, *Atti dell' Accad. di Arch., Lettere e Belle Arti di Napoli,* XXVI, 18. epoese = ἐπόησε.

[4] Or ' pour floods of tears from your eyelids.'

[5] The sense is obscure. Perhaps *participantur* is deponent— ' two neighbours share in a conflagration (of tears).'

2540c (iii) Sei quid amor valeat nostei, sei te hominem
       scis,
    commiseresce mei, da veniam ut veniam.
    Flos Veneris mihi de . . .

C. I. L., IV.

4972 (iv) Caesia sei n . . .
    Sei parvom p . . .
    Es bibe lude . . .
    nec semper . . .

4973 (v) Solus amare va[*let qui scit dare multa puellae.*]
    Multa opus sunt s . . .
    quod nesceire dare . . .

53

C. I. L., I, 2.

1680 Urna aenia pereit de taberna. | Seiquis rettulerit,
    dabuntur | H-S JXV.   Sei   furem | dabit
    ⁵   unde [*re*]m | servare po[*ssimus, H-S.*] |
    XXCⁱⁱⁱⁱ

51 ¹ *fortasse* sei n[*ummos*
52 ¹ *suppl.* Buecheler
53 ¹ urna aenia Zangemeister   Urnannia (*nomen ancillae?*) Momms.   urna vinaria *coni.* Wordsworth (*pater*)
   ² seiquis Zangemeister   s.q. eam Momms.   s. e. q. Wordsworth (*pater*)

(iii) *Unfinished love poem addressed to a youth (?) by the same hand :*

If you know how strong love is, if you know yourself for a human being, have pity on me, give me leave to leave [1] here for you.   May Venus' flower be (given to me ?).

(iv) *Epigram on or to Caesia ; ends of lines lost :*

51   Miss Grey-eyes, if . . .
     If a little . . .
     Eat, drink, and be merry . . .
     Nor always . . .

(v) *On love-making :* [2]

52   He only can make love properly who knows how to give a girl plenty of things.
     Plenty—that's what he must have . . .
     For, not to know how to give . . .

53

Reward offered for a theft.   Painted [3] *on a wall at Pompeii. Late in the second or early in the first century* B.C.

Lost from this shop—a bronze water-pot.   65 sesterces REWARD to anyone who brings back the same.   If he produces the thief, from whom we may rescue our property, 84 sesterces.

---

[1] pun on *venia* and *venio*.
[2] Other fragments of the same writer—*C.I.L.*, IV, 4968 ff.
[3] Some of the words are very uncertain.

[4-6]) *sic* Zangemeister   qui abduxerit dabitur duplum a
Vario, Wordsworth (*pater*)

54

C. I. L., X.

7296   (a) ΣΤΗΛΑΙ | ΕΝΘΑΔΕ | τυποῦνται καὶ | χαράσ-
5   σονται | ναοῖς ἱεροῖς | σὺν ἐνεργείαις | δημο-
σίαις.

    (b) TITULI | HEIC | ordinantur et | sculpuntur |
5   aidibus sacreis | cum operum | publicorum.

55

C. I. L., I. 2.

Th. Sauciuc-Saveanu, *Dacia*, III–IV, 1927–32, 456*sqq.*; S.
Lambrino, *Compt. R. de l'Acad.d. Inscr. et B.L.*, 1933, 278*sqq.*;
A. Passerini, *Athenaeum*, XIII, 1935, pp. 57–72.

2676   . . . *Poplus Romanus hostes et inimicos popli Calla-*
tini per suos agros et quibus inperat poplus
Romanus ne sinere transire debeto dolo m]alo
quo po[plo Callatino queive sub imperio eorum
erun]t b[e]llum face[re possint neve hostes neque
armis neque p]equ[n]ia adiova[n]to [publica
5   *voluntate dolo malo. . . . Seiquis po]plo Calla-*
tino bellu[m faxit, poplus Romanus, seive
poplo Rom]ano queive sub inperio[eius erunt,
populus Callatinus, quod e foederibus po]plo
Romano utei et [Callatino licebit, sei quis

---

[1] This gives in English the sort of error made by the Sicilian
stonemason in putting the Greek for 'with' (or 'by') public
labours.' He put 'cum' with the genitive because at the
moment he thought of μετά which in Greek takes the genitive
when it means 'in company with.' Further, the Latin
ordinantur is not the right translation of τυποῦνται. Even
his Greek is weak; ἐνέργεια is not used of public labour, and
he should have put *operis* (abl. of *operae*) *publicis*, 'public
labourers.'

LAWS AND OTHER DOCUMENTS

54

A Sicilian stonemason's advertisement ; bilingual.   Found at Panormus, Sicily ?

(*a*) Here slabs for holy temples are modelled and engraved with letters by public labours through us.

(*b*) Here inscriptions for holy temples are arranged and engraved by public labours through we.[1]

55

Part of a Treaty [2] *of Alliance between Rome and Callatis on the West coast of the Black Sea.   On stone found on the site of the ancient town.   Now at Bucarest in a private collection. Probably late second or early first century* B.C.

. . . It shall not be held right that the people of Rome should allow persons who are foes of or un-friendly to the people of Callatis to pass through territories belonging to the Romans or to Roman subjects with wrongful intent whereby they may be able to make war against the people of Callatis or peoples who shall be their subjects; nor shall the Romans, with wrongful intent, by expression of public will, assist such foes with arms or money. . . . Should any one have made war against the people of Callatis; and likewise should any one have made war against the people of Rome or against those who shall be in subjection to them :—the people of Rome and the people of Callatis shall the one assist the other accordingly at such times as when any one

[2] The inscription is a fragment first published by Th. Sauciuc-Saveanu in *Dacia*, III–IV, 1927–32, 456 ff., and edited by S. Lambrino in *Comptes Rendus des séances de l'Acad. des Inscr. et Belles Lettres*, 1933, 278 ff., and again, in *Athenaeum*, N.S. XIII, 1935, pp. 57–72, by A. Passerini; the latter's tentative but probable restoration, made after comparison with extant Greek texts of other treaties with Rome, I accept here.   Callatis is the modern Collati.

bellum] prior faxit [*p*]oplo [*Callatino seive poplo*
Romano, tum po]plus Romanus popl[*us Calla-*
10   *tinus alter alterum adiovant*]o. Sei quid ad
hance[*legem societatis exve hac lege*(?) *utrisque*
volen]t[*ibu*]s adere exime[*re v*]e[*lint, quod*
voluerint? publico consilio? communi] voluntate licet[*o, quodque addiderint id additum*
quodque e]xe[*meri*]nt id societat[*e exemptum*
sit. . . . *hoc foedus in tabulam ahe*]nam utei
scriberetur ac [*figeretur altera Romae in*
15   *Capitolio loc*]o optumo in faano Concor[*diae*
altera Callati . . .]

56

Lex Reperta Bantiae.

*A Law,[3] containing, it is generally held, part of the concluding
portion or ' sanctions ' of a treaty concerning Bantia on the
borders of Lucania and Apulia. But it may be the Lex Appuleia
of Saturninus, about treason, passed in 103 or 100 B.C. Fragment of a bronze plate ; the following Latin inscription is on one
side, an entirely different Oscan inscription being on the other.
The Oscan law deals with local affairs of Bantia, the Latin (which
is a Roman Law—all the magistrates mentioned are Roman) with
either some relations between Bantia and Rome, or offenders
against the proposed law of treason. The objection to dating this*

---

[1] *lex ;* this may refer to some individual condition (*lex*) in
the treaty ; or to the conditions taken as a whole set of terms ;
or to the whole treaty as a Roman act of parliament (*lex*).

[2] that is, the place where it can be mostly clearly inspected.

[3] *C.I.L.,* I, 2, p. 439; Fasc. III, 1943, p. 832. Kirchhoff,
Stadtr. v. Bantia, 90 ff., thinks the law is judiciary; H. Stuart
Jones, *J.R.S.,* XVI, 171, that it is the *Lex Appuleia de maie-*

shall have first made war against the people of
Callatis or the people of Rome; the people of
Rome and the people of Callatis acting herein as
shall be permissible, according to treaties, to the
people of Rome and the people of Callatis alike.
Should either party desire to add anything to these
conditions [1] of alliance or remove anything from
these conditions by expression of the will of both
parties, such change as they shall have desired by
public formulation of policy and common expression
of will shall be permitted; and anything which they
shall have added to the conditions of alliance shall
have been validly added, and anything which they
shall have removed therefrom shall have been validly
removed. . . . that this treaty be written out on to
a tablet of bronze; and that one such copy be fastened
up at Rome on the Capitol in the best possible place [2]
in the Temple of Concord, and a second at Callatis. . . .

56

*document after 118 B.C. is the mention of the Board of Three for
granting and assigning lands, which existed as a regular commission from 133 to 118 B.C. only. But their mention in lines
15–16 simply includes them in a list of officials who may be
elected hereafter ; their mention by logical guesswork in the gap
in line 7 is likewise admissible. If this is Saturninus' law, their
inclusion in the gap in line 14 can only be right if we assume that
Saturninus had in fact somehow revived the Gracchan land-com-
mission* (H. Stuart Jones, *J.R. Stud.*, XVI, 170–171). *This
document is a copy sent by Rome to Bantia for its information.*

---

state, herein agreeing with Gelzer (*H.*, LXIII, 124, cf. *Gnomon*,
V, 652, Carcopino, *Autour des Gracques* 205 ff.). For the Oscan
and a modern rendering of it into Latin, see Bruns, *Fontes* (ed. 7)
48 ff.; see also Wordsworth, 420 ff.; I. Naber, *Verslagen en
mededeeligen der K. Ak. van Wetenschappen*, X, 1,104. The
'*sanctio*' of a law contained provisions against cases of violating
the law and details of penalties for such violation.

582

    . . . [*n*]eque prov[*inciam*] . | . . in sena[*tu sei*]ve
in poplico ioudicio ne sen[*tentiam rogato tabellamve
nei dato* . . | . *neive is testumon*]ium deicito neive
quis mag. testumonium poplice ei de[*ferri neve
den*]ontiari | [*sinito. Neive ioudicem eum neive
arbitrum neive recupe*]ratorem dato. Neive is in
poplico luuci praetextam neive soleas h[*abet*]o
⁵ neive quis | [*mag. ibei praetextam soleasve habere
eum sini*]to. Mag. queiquomque comitia concil-
iumve habebit eum sufragium ferre nei sinito |
[*neive eum censor in senatum legito neive in senatu*]
relinquito.|

    [*Sei tr. pl., q., III vir cap., III vir a. d. a., ioudex*]
quei ex hace lege plebeive scito factus erit,
senatorve fecerit [*g*¹]esseritve, quo ex hace lege |
[*quae fieri oporteat minus fiant quaeve e*]x h. l.
facere oportuerit oportebitve, non fecerit sciens
d. m.; seive advorsus hance legem fecerit | [*sciens*

¹ C

---

¹ *Publicum iudicium* included the now rare trials before the
whole people, and ordinary trials before *iudices*. The offender
here indicated must not sit in the Senate or be asked his opinion
there, or be given a voting-ticket in a trial.

² as *arbiter* = umpire agreed on by contending parties in
preliminary proceedings before a magistrate when the dispute
was complicated (see *Remains of Old Latin*, III, pp. 424 ff.), or
as *iudex* singly or on one of the regular juries.

³ Here *recuperator* means a member of a board of three or
five, instituted originally for judging cases where foreigners
were involved, but later employed in other kinds of cases.

⁴ not those ordinarily worn by Romans, but a red kind
called *mullei* worn by those who had held curule office.

⁵ *comitia*, a meeting of the whole people, *concilium* of a part
only, usually the *concilium plebis*.

LAWS AND OTHER DOCUMENTS

. . . nor province . . . neither in the Senate nor
at a public trial let person ask him for his opinion
or hand him a voting ticket [1] . . . nor let him give
evidence; and let no magistrate allow him to be
publicly proclaimed or summoned as a witness; nor
let magistrate grant him as an ordinary judge or
umpire [2] or special judge [3] nor let him wear the
broidered gown or the sandals [4] by day in the public
view; nor let any magistrate allow him thus to wear
the broidered gown and sandals. Whosoever as
magistrate shall hold a meeting of the assembly of
the whole people or of parts [5] let him not allow him
to vote; nor let any censor choose him for admission
into the ranks of the Senate or leave him therein.

If a tribune of the plebs or a quaestor or a member
of the Board of Three for capital duties [6] or of the
Board of Three for granting and assigning lands,[7] or
a judge who shall have been made such under [8] this
law or resolution of the plebs,[9] or a senator shall have
done or acted whereby the provisions required under
this law may be set at nought, or shall have knowingly and with wrongful intent failed to do what he
was or shall have been required to do by this law;
or if knowingly and with wrongful intent he shall
have acted contrary to this law, let him be condemned

[6] These superintended prisons and executions and jurisdiction over slaves and freemen of the lowest classes.

[7] Set up by Tiberius Gracchus in 133 B.C., but abolished as
a regular office in 118 B.C.   See pp. 168 ff.

[8] *quei ex hac lege* etc. applies only to *iudex* here.   If this is
Saturninus' law, the *iudex* is to be president of the new
quaestio (criminal court) *de maiestate* (for treason) set up by
the law.

[9] which had the force of law from 287 B.C. onwards; hence
its inclusion in the formula representing ' by this law.'

d. m. HS . . . n. populo dare damnas esto et] eam
pequniam quei volet magistratus exsigito. Sei
¹⁰ postulabit quei petit, p. recuperatores | . . .
[*quos quotque dari opo*]rteat dato iubetoque eum,
sei ita pariat, condumnari popul. facitoque ioudi-
cetur. Sei condemnatus | [*erit, quanti condem-
natus erit, praedes*] ad q. urb. det aut bona eius
poplice possideantur facito. Sei quis mag. mul-
tam irrogare volet, | [*quei volet, dum minoris*]
partus familias taxsat, liceto, eiq. omnium rerum
siremps lexs esto, quasei sei is haace lege | [*pe-
quniam quae s. s. e. exigeret.*] |

[*Cos., pr., aid., tr. pl., q., III vir cap., III vir
a. d. a. qu*]ei nunc est, is in diebus V proxsumeis,
quibus queique eorum sciet h. l. popolum pleb-
¹⁵ emve | [*iousisse, iouranto utei i. s. est. Item*] dic.,
cos., pr. mag. eq., cens., aid., tr. pl., q., III vir
cap., III vir a. d. a., ioudex ex h. l. plebive scito |
[*factus . . . quei quomque eorum p*]ost hac factus

---

¹ that is, a fine of a sum fixed by law, whereas *irrogare
multam* below means demand a greater fine than the fixed
amount.

² see preceding note.

³ *partŭs*, genitive of *pars*; *familias*, genitive of *familia*.

⁴ This could not in fact apply after 118 B.C. to the Board
of Three for granting and assigning lands unless the latter
Board had been revived. See p. 297, n. 7; p. 295.

⁵ in the *comitia* as a law proper.

⁶ in the *concilium plebis* as a *plebiscitum* having the force of
law.

to a fine to the people of . . . sesterces in money; and let any magistrate who shall be so minded exact that sum. If he, who shall demand infliction of fine,[1] shall make request for special judges, let the praetor grant them. . . . Let him grant whosoever and as many as shall be required, and let him order that defendant, if a case is proved, be condemned to pay the fine to the people, and let him cause judgement to be pronounced on him. If he shall have been condemned to pay, he must present bondsmen before a quaestor of the city for the amount in which he shall have been condemned, or in default let the praetor cause his goods to be publicly confiscated. If any magistrate shall be minded to inflict a greater fine,[2] let it be allowed him who shall be so minded, provided only that the same comes to less than a half part [3] of the defendant's estate; and let the law hold good for the said magistrate in all respects just as if he had exacted, under this law, the sum above set forth.

Let any consul or praetor or aedile or tribune of the plebs or quaestor or member of the Board of Three for capital duties or member of the Board of Three for granting and assigning lands, now in office,[4] within the next five days following the day when any one of the said officials shall know that the people [5] or the plebs [6] have ordained this law, take oath as set forth below. Again let any dictator or consul or praetor or master of the horse or censor or aedile or tribune of the plebs or quaestor or member of the Board of Three for capital duties or member of the Board of Three for granting and assigning lands, or judge created hereafter under this law or resolution of the plebs . . . within the next five days

erit, eis in diebus V proxsumeis, quibus quisque
eorum mag. inperiumve inierit, iouranto | [*utei
i. s. est. Eis consistunto pro ae*]de Castorus
palam luci in forum vorsus et eidem in diebus
V apud q. iouranto per Iovem deosque | [*Penateis
sese quae ex h. l. oport*]ebit facturum, neque sese
advorsum h. l. facturum scientem d. m., neque
seese facturum neque intercessurum | [*quo quae
ex h. l. oportebit minus fiant. Qu*]ei ex h. l. non
iouraverit, is magistratum inperiumve nei petito
20 neive gerito neive habeto neive in senatu | [*sen-
tentiam deicito deicereve eum*] ni quis sinito neive
eum censor in senatum legito. Quei ex h. l.
ioudicaverit,[1] is facito apud q. urb. | ⌈*eius quei ita
utei s. s. e. iouravit nomen persc*]riptum siet; quaestorque ea nomina accipito et eos quei ex h. l.
apud sed iourarint facito in taboleis | [*popliceis
perscribantur.*]‖

[*Quei senator est eritve inve senatu sententi*]‖am
deixerit post hanc legem rogatam eis in diebus
X proxsumeis, quibus quisqu[*e eorum sciet* |
hance legem popolum plebemve iousisse, i]‖ouranto
apud quaestorem ad aerarium palam luci per
25 Iovem deosque Penate[*is sese quae ex h. l.* | *oportebit
facturum esse neque se*]se advorsum hance legem

---

[1] iouraverit *scribendum putat* Fuchs

following the day when one or any of the said officials
shall have entered on his magistracy or authority,
take oath as set forth below. Let them within five
days take their stand together in front of the temple
of Castor in the day-time publicly, facing the forum,
and let them each one, in the presence of a quaestor,
take the oath by Jupiter and the Household Gods,
each one as follows: that he will do all that will be
required under this law, and that he will not knowingly and with wrongful intent do anything against
this law, and will not interpose a veto or so act that
the provisions required by this law will be set at
nought. Whoever shall not take oath under this
law, let him not seek or take up or hold office or
authority, nor record an opinion in the Senate; nor
let anyone allow him to speak, nor let any censor
choose him for admission into the ranks of the
Senate. Let him who shall have acted as judge
under this law cause the name of any one who has
taken the oath as above set forth to be written out
in full in the presence of a quaestor of the city; and
let the quaestor receive the said names and cause
full details of those who have taken the oath according to this law in his presence to be written out by
him in full on public records.

Let each of those who are or shall be senators or
shall have expressed an opinion in the Senate after
the passing of this law, within the ten days following
the day on which he shall know that the people or
the plebs have ordained this law take oath in the
presence of the quaestor at the treasury publicly in
the day-time, by Jupiter and the Household Gods as
follows: that he will do all that will be required under
this law and that he will not do anything against

26-32 facturum esse neque seese, quominus sei | . . .
se hoice leegei . . . anodni . . . [*i*]uraverint]
. . . e quis magistratus p . . . [*u*]ti in taboleis
popl[*iceis* . . . *tr*]inum nondin[*um*] . . . is erit
uu . . .

57

Lex Cornelia de XX Quaestoribus.

587   [*L. Cornelius l. f. dictator . . . populum ioure
rogavit populusque ioure scivit in foro . . . a.d.
. . . Tribus . . .*] | principium fuit; pro tribu |
[*. . . preimus scivit.*]

VIII.   . . . *ad*]q. urb., quei aerarium
de xx q. provinciam optinebit, eam | mercedem deferto;
quaestorque qui aerarium provinciam | optinebit,
eam pequniam, ei scribae scribeis que heredive |
eius solvito idque ei sine fraude sua facere liceto,
5 quod | sine malo pequlatuu fiat, olleisque hom-
inibus eam | pequniam capere liceto. |

    Cos. quei nunc sunt iei ante K. Decembreis
primas de eis, quei | cives Romanei sunt, viatorem

---

[1] On this, see p. xlii.
[2] Where the Romans normally kept State records. The
inscription is a good example of the transition from archaic to
classical Latin. The extant portion of the law fixes regulations
for the employment of additional *viatores* and *praecones* by the
quaestors. Cf. Mommsen, *Ges. Schr.*, III, 455 ff.; Keil, *Wien.
Stud.*, XXIV, 548 ff. The law raised the quaestors to twenty.
[3] *Foro* because the mention of voting by tribes indicates
the *comitia tributa*, which was nearly always the assembly
used by Sulla; he would never have used the *concilium
plebis* which likewise voted by tribes. The heading of this law

this law, and that he will not . . . whereby if . . .
that he will to this law . . . they shall have sworn
. . . any magistrate . . . that in the public records
. . . a period covering three market-days[1] . . . he
shall be. . . .

57

*Fragment of Sulla's Law about the twenty quaestors. Tablet
of bronze found in the ruins of the temple of Saturn[2] at Rome,
81 B.C. Now at Naples.*

Lucius Cornelius, son of Lucius, dictator . . .
duly proposed to the people, and the people duly
resolved in the forum[3] . . . on the . . . day of . . .
the . . . tribe voted first; the first to vote on behalf
of his tribe was. . .

VIII[th 4] Concerning the Twenty Quaestors . . .
the amount of said salary the magistrate shall
report to a quaestor of the city who shall have the
treasury as his department, and such quaestor
who shall have the treasury as his department
shall pay the said money to the said clerk (or
clerks) or to an heir and he shall be permitted to do
so without risk of personal penalty, in so far as it is [5]
done without fraudulent embezzlement, and the
aforesaid persons shall be allowed to take the money.

The consuls now in office shall, before the first day
of December next choose, from those who are Roman
citizens, one messenger who shall attend as mes-

is supplied from the Lex Quinctia given by Frontinus *de Aquis
Urbis Romae*, 129. In the case of Sulla's law, which covered
more than eight tablets, the heading ran along the top of all
the tablets, the words *principium fuit pro tribu* running
along the top of this one. After this tablet, there followed
probably a ninth, the last of this law. The words VIII *de xx q.*
are in the margin.
[4] The eighth *tabula* of the law.

unum legunto, quei in | ea decuria viator appareat,
10 quam decuriam viatorum | ex noneis Decem-
bribus primeis quaestoribus ad aerarium | apparere
oportet oportebit. Eidemque cos. ante K.
Decembr. | primas de eis quei cives Romanei
sunt, praeconem unum | legunto, quei in ea
decuria praeco appareat, quam | decuriam prae-
15 conum ex noneis Decembribus primeis | quaestor-
ibus ad aerarium apparere oportet oportebit. |
Deinde eidem consul. ante K. Decembreis primas
viatorem | unum legunto quei in ea decuria
viator appareat quam | decuriam viatorum ex
noneis Decembribus secundeis | quaestoribus ad
20 aerarium apparere oportet oportebit. | Eidemque
cos. ante K. Decembreis primas praeconem |
unum legunto, quei in ea decuria praeco appareat,
quam | decuriam praeconum ex noneis Decem-
bribus secundeis | quaestoribus ad aerarium ap-
parere oportet oportebit. | Deinde eidem cos.
25 ante K. Decembreis primas viatorem | unum
legunto, quei in ea decuria viator appareat, |
quam decuriam viatorum ex noneis Decem-
bribus tertieis | quaestoribus ad aerarium apparere
oportet oportebit. | Eidemque cos. ante K. De-
cembris primas praeconem | unum legunto, quei
30 in ea decuria praeco appareat, quam | decuriam

---

¹ *appareo* is used in the special sense of ' serve as attendant.'
decuria meant a division composed of ten, a tithing or decade,
but used of numbers more than ten. The *decuriae* concerned
in this inscription were the *decuriae viatoriae* (a *viator*, in the
official sense, being a ' travelling messenger ' or ' summoner '
attendant on certain Roman magistrates, in the latter Republic
generally those with *potestas* and not attended by *lictors*), which
we know from other epigraphic evidence, and the *decuriae* of

senger in that department [1] of messengers which is
or shall be required to attend the quaestors at the
treasury on and after the fifth [2] day of December
next. And the same consuls shall, before the first
day of December next, choose, from those who are
Roman citizens, one herald who shall attend as herald
in that detachment of heralds which is or shall be
required to attend the quaestors at the treasury on
and after the fifth day of December next.

Again the same consuls shall, before the first day
of December next, choose one messenger, who shall
attend as messenger in that detachment of messengers which is or shall be required to attend the
quaestors at the treasury on and after the fifth day
of December next but one. And the same consuls
shall, before the first day of December next, choose
one herald who shall attend as herald in that detachment of heralds which is or shall be required to
attend the quaestors at the treasury on and after
the fifth day of December next but one. Again
the same consuls shall, before the first day of December next, choose one messenger who shall attend
as messenger in that detachment of messengers
which is or shall be required to attend the quaestors
at the treasury on and after the fifth day of December
next but two. And the same consuls shall, before
the first day of December next, choose one herald
who shall attend as herald in that detachment of
heralds which is or shall be required to attend the

praecones (' criers '), which *decuriae* were probably called
decuriae praeconiae. The precise meaning of the regulations
laid down by this law for the composition of the *decuriae* is
not certain.

[2] when the quaestors entered on their magistracy.

305

praeconum ex noneis Decembribus tertieis |
quaestoribus ad aerarium apparere oportet
oportebit. | Eosque viatores eosque praecones
omneis, quos eo | ordine dignos arbitrabuntur,
legunto. Quam in quisque | decuriam ita viator
³⁵ lectus erit, is in ea decuria viator | esto item utei
ceterei eius decuriae viatores erunt. | Qamque
in quisque decuriam ita praeco lectus erit, |
is in ea decuria praeco esto ita utei ceterei
decuriae | praecones erunt. Sirempsque eis via-
toribus deque | eis viatoribus q. omnium rerum
⁴⁰ iuus lexque esto, quasei | sei ei viatores in eam
decuriam in tribus viatoribus | antea lectei sub-
lectei essent, quam in quisque decuriam | eorum
ex hac lege viator lectus erit. Sirempsque eis |
praeconibus deque eis praeconibus quaestori
omnium | rerum iuus lexque esto, quasei sei ei
⁴⁵ praecones in eam | decuriam in tribus praecon-
ibus antea lectei sublectei | essent, quam in
quisque decuriam eorum ex hac lege | praeco
lectus erit.

Quos quomque quaestores ex lege plebeive
scito viatores | legere sublegere oportebit, ei
⁵⁰ quaestores eo iure ea lege | viatores IIII legunto
sublegunto, quo iure qua lege q., | quei nunc sunt,

quaestors at the treasury on and after the fifth day
of December next but two.

And they shall choose all the said messengers and
heralds according as they believe them worthy of
the said rank. For whatever detachment each
person shall have been so chosen messenger, he shall
be a messenger in the said detachment on the same [35]
footing as the remaining messengers of the said
detachment shall be. Again, for whatever detachment each shall be so chosen herald, he shall be
a herald in the said detachment on the same footing
as the remaining heralds of the said detachment
shall be. Again, for and in regard to the said
messengers, legal and judicial powers in all matters
concerning them shall belong to the quaestor and
shall hold good for them exactly as if the said mes- [40]
sengers had been formerly chosen for or substituted
in whatever detachment consisting of three messengers, for which detachment, no matter what, each
of the said persons shall have been chosen as
messenger under this law. Again, for and in regard
to the said heralds, legal and judicial powers in all
matters concerning them shall belong to the quaestor
and shall hold good for them exactly as if the said [45]
heralds had been chosen for or substituted in whatever detachment consisting of three heralds, for
which detachment thereof each of the said persons
shall have been chosen as herald under this law.

Whomsoever the quaestors shall be required, by
law or resolution of the plebs, to choose or substitute
as messengers, the said quaestors shall choose or
substitute such messengers, making four in number, [50]
according to the rights and conditions under which
the quaestors now in office chose or substituted three

307

viatores III legerunt sublegerunt. Quosque |
quomque quaestores ex lege plebei ve scito
praecones legere | sublegere oportebit ei quae-
stores eo iure ea lege praecones | IIII legunto
sublegunto, quo iure qua lege quaestores, quei |
⁵⁵ nunc sunt, praecones III legerunt sublegerunt,
dum niquem | in eis viatoribus praeconibus legun-
deis sublegundeis in eius | viatoris praeconis
locum viatorem praeconem legant | sublegant,
quoius in locum per leges plebeive scita viatorem |
praeconem legei sub legi non licebit. Ita que de
⁶⁰ eis quattuor | viatoribus quaestor queiquomque
erit viatores sumito | habeto utei ante hanc legem
rogatam de tribus viatoribus | viatores habere
sumere solitei sunt. Itaque de eis quattuor |
praeconibus quaestor queiquomque erit prae-
cones sumito | habeto, utei ante hanc legem
⁶⁵ rogatam de tribus praeconibus | praecones habere
sumere solitei sunt. Itemque eis viatoribus |
praeconibus, quei ex hac lege lectei erunt, vica-
rium dare | subdere ius esto licetoque, utei
cetereis viatoribus praeconibus, | qua in quisque
decuria est, vicarium dare subdere iuus erit |
licebitque. Iterum quaestor. ab eis vicarios
⁷⁰ accipiunto | utei aacetereis viatoribus praeconibus
vicarios accipei | oportebit. |

Viatores praecones quei ex hac lege lectei

messengers. And whomsoever the quaestors shall
be required, by law or by a resolution of the plebs,
to choose or substitute as heralds, the said quaestors
shall choose or substitute such heralds, making four
in number, according to the rights and conditions [55]
under which the quaestors now in office chose or
substituted three heralds; provided that they do
not, in choosing or substituting the said messengers
or heralds, choose or substitute a messenger or
herald in the place of a messenger or herald in whose
place it shall not be allowed by any laws or resolu-
tions of the plebs to choose or substitute a messenger
or herald. Moreover out of the said four messengers
shall the quaestor, whoever he shall be, take and [60]
employ his messengers in the same way as they
have been used to take and employ messengers,
before the passing of this bill into law, from the
three messengers. Moreover also out of the said
four heralds shall the quaestor, whoever he shall be,
take and employ heralds, in the same way as they
have been used to take and employ heralds, before [65]
the passing of this bill into law, from the three
heralds. Likewise also it shall be rightfully permissible, for one of the said messengers or heralds,
who shall be chosen by this law, to grant or substitute a deputy on the same footing as it shall be
rightfully permissible, for one of the remaining
messengers and heralds, according to whatever
detachment each belongs to, to grant or substitute a
deputy; and likewise the quaestors shall receive
from the said persons deputies on the same footing [70]
as they shall be required to receive deputies from
the remaining messengers and heralds.

A magistrate or a person acting as a magistrate

sublectei erunt, | eis viatoribus praeconibus magi-
stratus pro ve mag. | mercedis item tantundem
75 dato, quantum ei viator. ¡ praeconei darei oporteret, sei is viator de tribus viatoribus isque
praeco de tribus praeconibus esset, | quei ante
hanc legem rogatam utei legerentur | institutei
sunt. |

Quas in decurias viatorum praeconum consul
80 ex hac | lege viatores praecones legerit, quorum
viatorum | praeconum nomina in eis decurieis ad
aedem Saturni | in pariete contra cau[*l*]as proxume
ante hanc legem | [*scripta erunt, eorum viatorum*
praeconum ad quaestorum | *urbanum, quei aerarium*
provinciam optinebit, | *eam mercedem deferto . . .*]

58

Fragmentum Florentinum.   Pars postica.

On one side, which is called *pars antica* or ' front side '
because the lettering is larger and better than that on the
other side, are preserved (*C.I.L.*, I, 2, 595) parts of sentences
from a law which is usually taken to refer to a *quaestio perpetua*,
but it is impossible to come even to any tentative conclusion in
this matter.   On the other side, the *pars postica* or ' back side,'
are preserved (*C.I.L.*, I, 2, 596) parts of another law which
certainly do refer to a *quaestio perpetua*.   I suggest that this
law regulated in such *quaestiones*, and in individual cases in
each, some provisions of the *Lex Cassia tabellaria* of 137 B.C.;
this imposed secret voting in all cases except at trials for
treason before the assembly of people, where secrecy was

---

82 caulas Lachmann   CAVIAS

---

[1] *institutei sunt* is put by attraction for *institutum est*:
' who, it was appointed, should be chosen (regularly) '.

shall pay, to the messengers and heralds who shall
be chosen or substituted by this law, just so much
by way of salary as would be required to be paid to
a messenger or a herald if such messenger or herald [75]
were chosen from the detachment of three messengers
or three heralds respectively who were appointed [1]
to be chosen before the passing of this bill into law.

According to the detachments of messengers and
heralds for which the consul shall have by this law [80]
chosen messengers and heralds (messengers and
heralds whose names in the said detachments shall
be posted up in writing, directly preceding this law,
on a wall facing the passages [2] by the temple of
Saturn)—he shall make over the salary of the said
messengers and heralds to the quaestor of the city
who shall have the treasury as his department. . . .

58

*Fragments of a law of the Gracchan period or later, written
on one side of a piece of bronze plate (C.I.L., I, 2, 595–6) which
is now at Florence.*

imposed by the *Lex Caelia tabellaria* on 107 B.C. One of the
two laws was perhaps annulled before use of the plate for the
other; I give here all that is found on the *pars postica*, because
it deals with allotment of jurymen in setting up a court, and
it is of some interest to compare it with certain parts of the
Lex Acilia Repetundarum given below, pp. 316 ff.; cf. A.
Rudorff, *ad Leg. Acil. de pec. repet.* (1862), 485–7. C. Klenze,
Fragm. Leg. Serv. (1825), prol., IV. The clauses indicated
below describe the action to be taken in regard to *pilae*.
These were small ' balls ' or ballots which in this law are
applied to the selection of jurymen before a trial. The word
aequare means here to make the number of *pilae* provided equal

---

[2] possibly however these were the walls or railings of the
enclosure of the temple or of the treasury.

to the number of jurymen on some list of eligible persons, to have them all of the same material, each inscribed with a separate name, and all shuffled together; compare *aequare sortes*, for which see Plaut., *Casina*, II, 6, 35; Cicero, *fr. Or. Corn.*, I, 449 O.; cf. Asconius, *in Milon.*, 34 K—S, where he shows that a *Lex Pompeia* of 52 B.C. (to which Klenze refers this fragment) ordained that the balls on which the names of the jurymen had been written should be made completely coincident (*aequarentur*) in the presence of plaintiff and defendant; then should take place next day the allotment of jurymen so that there should remain a list of 81 persons.

596   . . . [*pr. iudic*]is omnis iur[*are iubeto* . . .

     . . . esi easque pilas om[*nes* . . .

     . . . *numere*]ntur aequenturqu[*e* . . .

     pr. facito ubei pilae o[*mnes aequatae erunt* . . .]

   5   . . . sorticolis singolis sinc[*illatim eductis* . . .

     . . . *quoius iudicis nomen ibe*]i scriptum erit, eius nom[*en pronontiato* . . .

     . . . *quoius nomen ex h.*]l. pronontiatum erit eu[*m* . . .

     [1] iud *an* iur *incertum*
     [3] *scriba*]ntur Mommsen
     [4] o[*mnes scriptae aequataeque erunt*] Momms.

---

   [1] So I supply.
   [2] It is not certain whether the plate has *iud* or *iur*.
   [3] I supply *numere*]ntur. Mommsen supplies *scriba*]ntur.
   [4] *sc.* a drawing of ballots to provide a jury for a case.
   [5] I take it that these *sorticulae* are the *pilae* = name ballots after they have been drawn by lot, and that they are not the *sorticulae* = jurors' voting tickets mentioned in the *Lex Acilia*, pp. 348 ff. Cf. p. 314. Read perhaps *pilis velut*] *sorticolis*.

LAWS AND OTHER DOCUMENTS

Before any voting took place, plaintiff and defendant should each reject 15 persons so that the jury which voted should be 51 in number. Thus Asconius on Milo's trial in particular. Note that, to cover all possible cases, the *praetor urbanus* had to provide every year a list of men eligible to serve on juries; from this general list was drawn a smaller list for any *quaestio*, and from this smaller list a still smaller one (subject to various conditions by laws from time to time) was chosen to try any separate case; and from this again jurymen could be rejected by the parties concerned. See below, *Lex Acilia*, pp. 324 ff. I reconstruct this fragment as follows.

The praetor shall see that the ballots, giving the names of jurymen, are completely coincident with the official list for this particular kind of quaestio, etc., and shuffled:

[The praetor] [1] must order all jurymen to swear [2] . . . and all the said name-ballots . . . [he shall cause to be] counted [3] and to be found completely congruent. . . .

He shall then conduct a drawing of ballots, as of lots, to provide a jury ('consilium') for a particular case:

. . . The praetor shall, when all the name-ballots shall have been made completely congruent, cause [4] . . . when the allotted ballots [5] have been drawn out, one for each man one by one. . . .

He shall read out the name written on every name-ballot drawn out, and those whose names are so read out shall form the jury for the case:

. . . of juryman whose name shall have been there written, of that juryman he shall proclaim the name . . . he must cause that person whose name shall have been under this law pronounced. . . .

313

INSTRUMENTA

. . . *tabol*]amque, quae ineo tribun[*ali* . . .
. . .] aliter ea nei deleto neiv[*e* . . .
10 . . . *pr. iud*]ices omnis item sortiri iu[*beto* . . .
sentent]iam tolerint, quom omni[*s iudices ad-*
fuerint . . .
. . . mat ineam tabolam qu[*ae ineo tribunali* . . .
. . . *inquibus pileis li*]terae duae aut nulla au[*t*
una . . .
. . . e[*r*]unt, inquibus pileis li[*terae* . . .
15 . . . *iu*]dicis siet h. l., eas pilas om[*nis* . . .]
. . . oportebit tum . . .

58 ¹² [*expri*]mat *vix* [*inpri*]mat ?

---

[1] the praetor's platform or judgment-seat.

[2] maybe the clause forbids any complete deletion unless
any name shall be seriously or wholly wrong. Cf. lines 13–14.
It is not known of what material the *pilae* were made or how
the names were written on them.

[3] Sc. on some ' *exceptio* ' or other special matter arising out
of the name-ballots ? Not for the decision on the case being
tried, when all the jury voted with voting tickets and there
were then no lots concerned; the law is still dealing with
name-ballots—see next note.

[4] So it seems. It has occurred to me that the words ' two
letters or none or one only ' refer not to name-ballots but to
voting-tickets issued to the jurymen for the voting on the case
itself. By the *Lex Acilia* each juryman received one ticket
only, which had inscribed in wax, on one side letter A =
absolvo I acquit, on the other side letter C = *condemno* ' I
condemn ', the juryman in voting to leave on his ticket only
that letter which recorded his opinion or to leave nothing if
he wished (see *Lex Acilia*, pp. 348 ff.). In Cicero's time each
juryman received usually 3 tickets, one inscribed with A, one
with C, and one with NL = *non liquet*, ' not proven '. But we
have *pilae* mentioned again in lines 14 and 15; which would
mean either that clauses about the final voting on the case
were inserted in this law amongst clauses about *pilae*, or that in
lines 13 onwards the meaning of the name *pila* has changed
from name-ballot to *tabella* = voting-ticket (called *sorticula*

LAWS AND OTHER DOCUMENTS

The list of the jury shall be displayed in court :

. . . a tablet which [shall be displayed] on the said platform. . . .[1]

Except for special reasons, no names to be deleted from name-ballots : [2]

. . . must not otherwise delete the said names, or. . . .

Taking and recording [3] *votes on some procedure :*

. . . The praetor must order all the jurymen likewise to draw lots . . . shall have recorded their vote at a time when all the jurymen shall have been present. . .

Rectification of errors, small deletions, and omissions on the name-ballots : [4]

. . . on to the said tablet which [shall have been displayed] on the said platform. . . .
. . . on which name-ballots two letters or none or one only . . .[5]
. . . shall be, on which name-ballots . . . letters (?) [6] . . . [shall be]. . . .
. . . shall appertain to a juryman under this law, all the said name-ballots. . . .
. . . he shall be required then. . . .

in the *Lex Acilia*, pp. 348 ff.), which is possible but unlikely. If these clauses do refer to voting tickets, they deal with accidental deletions or errors discovered on them before the voting, or with the condition of the tickets when inspected after the voting.
[5] I supply *au*[*t una* . . .]
[6] The plate seems to have EI, though some read LI = *literae*. Klenze took LI to mean 51, but this number at this period would probably be .LI or the like.

INSTRUMENTA

59

Lex Acilia de Repetundis.

*A Law concerning the Standing Criminal Court (first
established by the Lex Calpurnia of 149 B.C.) for trying cases of
extortion, passed by Gaius Gracchus during his second tribunate,
122 B.C., through the agency and inspiration of Acilius* [1] *one of*

583 [1] [*M'. Acilius ? . . . tr. pl. plebem ioure rogaverunt
plebesque ioure scivit, in foro . . . a.d. . . .
Tribus . . . principium fuit; pro tribu . . . preimus
scivit. . . .*]

Quoi socium no]minisve Latini exterarumve
nationum, quoive in arbitratu dicione potestate
[2] amicitiav[e populi Romani . | . . ab eo quei dic.,
cos., pr., mag. eq., cens., aid., tr. pl., q., IIIvir cap.,
IIIvir a. d. a., tr. mi]l. l. IIII primis aliqua earum
fuerit, queive filius eorum quoius erit, [queive ipse

---

[1] See J. P. V. D. Balsdon, in *Papers of the British School at
Rome*, XIV (N.S.I.), 1938, 98 ff. Cf. E. Hardy, *Six Roman
Laws*, 1 ff. and in *Journ. Phil.*, XXXII, 96; Bruns, *Fontes* (ed.
VII), I, 55 ff.; Wordsworth, 424 ff.; Mommsen, *Gesamm. Schr.*
I, 1–64; Hesky, *Wien. St.*, XXV, 272 ff.; Brassloff, ib., XXVI,
106 ff.; Berger, in Pauly, *Real-Encycl.*, XII, 2319; *C.I.L.*, I,
2, p. 739. The law was superseded probably in 106 B.C.; but
this plate, possibly because the copy of this law on it was
faulty (see p. 370, note 1), had, before that date, had a copy
of the *Lex Agraria* (see pp. 370 ff.) inscribed on the other side.

[2] The repetitive character of large portions of this law and
of the Agrarian law on the other side of the plate and the
relative positions of the surviving pieces to each other when
placed, like a jigsaw puzzle in the making, in their right
positions as parts of the whole tablet as originally made,
have enabled restorations to be effected in both laws up to a
certain point and with some degree of probability. The method
was first applied by C. Klenze, *Fragm. Legis Serviliae* (which
this law was often thought to be), Berlin 1925 to this law,
and by A. Rudorff to the *Lex Agraria* on the other side of
the plate; the later work of Mommsen is now usually accepted.

59

The Acilian Law on Extortion.

his colleagues. Eleven pieces of a bronze plate or tablet about 6 ft. broad.[2] *Of these pieces two are at Vienna, seven at Naples, and two are now lost again but are known from manuscript copies. The lines run along the whole length of the plate.*

Manius Acilius (Glabrio) . . . tribunes of the plebs duly proposed a bill to the plebs, and the plebs duly resolved in the [3] forum . . . on the . . . day of . . . ; the . . . tribe voted first; the first to vote on behalf of his tribe was . . .

Any person [4] who is one of the allies or the Latin name or any foreign people, or any person living under the sovereignty, rule, authority, or friendship of the Roman people . . . from any [2] person who has been dictator, consul, praetor, master of the horse, censor, aedile, tribune of the commons, quaestor, member of the Board of Three for capital duties or of the Board of Three for granting and assigning lands, or military tribune in any one of the first [5] four legions; or any son of any of the

Nevertheless there is much that is irrecoverable. Other attempts have been recently made, *e.g.* M. A. Levi, *Riv. d. Fil.*, LVII. 383. Carcopino, *Autour des Gracques*, 228 ff. holds that this ' Acilian ' Law is Glaucia's *Lex de Rep.*, to be dated 108 B.C.; but see Balsdon, *op. cit.*; cf. also Gelzer, *Gnomon*, V, 653; Judeich, *Hist. Zeitschr.*, 3[te] Folge, XV, 1913, 491; v. Stern, *H.*, LVI, 281 ff.

[3] The *concilium plebis* met in the *forum*. This heading to the law, wholly missing from the surviving pieces, is restored in part from Frontinus; cf. heading to the Agrarian law, pp. 372–3.

[4] These may be accusers under the law; persons of the Latin name are those who, whether Latins or not, have *ius Latinum*.

[5] The regular force, of which the tribunes were elected by the people and so counted as magistrates. For the two Boards of Three, see pp. 297, 168 ff. All these officials can be accused under the law.

vel] quoius pater senator siet, in annos singolos
3 pequniae quod siet amp[*lius HS . . . n. .* | . .
pro inperio prove potestate ipsei regive populove ipsius
parentive ipsius queive in potestate manu mancipio
suo parentisve sui siet fuerit quo]ive ipse parensve
suos filiusve suos heres siet, ablatum captum
coactum conciliatum aversumve siet: de ea re
eius petitio nominisque delatio esto, [*pr. quaestio*
esto, ioudicium ioudicatio leitisque aestumatio, quei-
quomque ioudicium ex h. l. erunt, eorum hace lege
4 *esto. .* | . . *Sei quis deicet, praetorem nomen ex h. l.*
ita non recepisse, utei delatum esset, neque ioudicium
ex h. l. ita datu]m esse utei peteret: de ea re eius
petit*i*o nominisque delatio esto, pr. quaestio esto,
ioudicium ioudicatio leitisque aestumatio, quei
quomque ioudic[*ium ex h. l. erunt, eorum hace lege*
5 *esto . . .* | *. . .*]s iu[*. . . De quo ex h. l. ioudicatum*
erit, sei contra h. l. fecisse deicetur, postquam ea res
ioud]icata erit, aut quoius nomen praevaricationis
caussa delatum erit, aut quoium nomen ex h. l. ex

59 ³ IPSEI · PARENTE.^{VE}SVOS

---

¹ Note that by this law only the official ('senatorial') class
can be accused.
² *i.e.* as head of a family, or husband, or as owner.
³ *sc.* a second time, before a praetor of the next year.
⁴ that is (as throughout this law)— the whole trial of a case of
extortion. The praetor who presides is the *quaesitor* (not
quaestor).
⁵ *praevaricatio* 'walking crookedly' is collusion between
prosecutor and defendant; improper abandonment of a
prosecution was called *tergiversatio* 'turning of back.'

said persons; or any person who or whose father is a senator,[1] for a sum of more than . . . sesterces in [3] money for any particular year . . . such sum having been, in the exercise of official rule or rightful authority, carried off, seized, exacted, embezzled, or misappropriated from the person himself or his king or his people or his parent, or from whoever may be or shall be bound to him or his parent in authority, possession, or formal ownership,[2] or from any person to whom he or his parent or son stands as heir—in such a case the said person shall have the rightful power to sue or summon; the inquiry shall be undertaken by a praetor; and the trial, judgment and assessment of damages shall by this law be undertaken by those persons whosoever by this law shall [4] form the court. . . .

If anyone shall declare that the praetor has not, in obedience to this law, accepted the name of the accused in accordance with the summons; and that a court has not, in obedience to this law, been granted in accordance with his petition—in such a case the said person shall have the power to sue and summon [3]; the inquiry [4] shall be undertaken by a praetor; and the trial, judgment, and assessment of damages shall by this law be undertaken by those persons whosoever by this law shall form the court. . . .

In the case of any person on whom under this law [5] a judgment has been delivered, if he shall be declared to have acted in violation of this law, after judgment shall have been delivered on his case, or against whom a summons shall have been issued by way of collusion,[5] or whose name in accordance with this law shall have been removed from the list of defendants; if any person shall have summoned him a second time

reis exemptum erit: seiquis eius nomen a[*d prae-*
torem denuo detolerit, . . . *quaestio eius pr. esto* ;
6 *ioudicium ioudicatio leitisque | aestumatio quei quomque*
ioudicium ex h. l. erunt, eorum h. l. esto. Sei quis
ali]eno nomin[*e . . . ex h.l. petere nomenve deferre*
volet, de ea re eius petitio nominisque delatio esto],
quaestio eius pr. esto, ioudicium⟨*ve*⟩ ioudicatio litis-
sque aestumatio, quei quomque ioudicium ex h. l
erunt, eorum h. l. esto. Is eum unde petet in
ious ed[*ucito ad pr., quoius ex h. l. in eum annum*
quaestio erit et ante k. Sept. quae eo anno erunt,
7 *nomen deferto . . | .*] deque eo homine de[*. . . ita*
uti i. s. est, res agitor. Post k. Sept. sei quod nomen
deferetur, sei is quei petet volet, is praetor de ea re
recuperatores dato. Qu]oius eorum ita nomen ex
h. l. post k. Sept., quae eo anno fuerint, delatum
erit, quei eorum eo ioudicio condemnatus erit,
quanti eius rei slis ae[*stumata erit, tantam pe-*
8 *quniam quei eum condemnaverit dato . . | . eaque*
pequnia quei petiveri]t eius esto. Praetor, quei
ex h. l. q[*uaeret, facito, quidquid ita . . . ioudi-*
catu]m erit, id utei privato solvatur, quei [*eoru*]m
petet.

---

[1] *sc.* of *recuperatores* (for which, see p. 296). Such a suit
would be a private one; hence the payment (see below) of the
damages direct to a successful accuser.

before the praetor—[in such a case the said person shall have the power to sue or summon;] the inquiry shall be undertaken by the said praetor; and the trial, judgment, and assessment of damages shall by **6** this law be undertaken by those persons whosoever by this law shall form the court. If any person shall be minded under this law . . . to sue or summon in the name of another, in such a case the said person shall have the power to sue or summon, the enquiry shall be undertaken by the said praetor; and the trial judgment and assessment of damages shall by this law be undertaken by those persons whosoever by this law shall form the court.

Such person shall bring the person whom he shall sue to court before the praetor to whom by this law the inquiry shall belong for that year, and he shall make his summons before the first of September of that year . . ., and the case concerning the said **7** person . . . shall be conducted according to the procedure recorded below.

If any summons shall be made after the first of September, the said praetor shall, if the person suing be so minded, grant special judges. Any of such persons who shall have been summoned as above by this law after the first of September in that year and shall likewise have been convicted by the said court,[1] shall pay, to the person who has brought about his conviction, the amount of money at which the damages in such a matter shall have been assessed . . . and the said money shall belong to the person **8** who has sued him. The praetor, who shall under this law conduct the inquiry, shall cause whatever sum . . . shall have been adjudged as above to be paid to the private person who shall lodge the suit.

De heisce, dum mag. aut inperium habebunt,
ioudicium non fiet. Dic., cos., pr., mag. eq.,
[*cens., aid., tr. pl., q., IIIvir cap., IIIvir a. d. a.,
tr. mil. leg. IIII primis aliqua earum, dum mag. aut*
[9] *inperium habebit, nei in ious educitor . . |* . *Quei
eorum e*]x eo mag. inperiove abierit, quo min[*us
in ious educatur, e. h. l. n. r. . . . .*

De patroneis dandeis. Quei ex h.*] l. pequniam
petet nomenque detuler*it*, quoius eorum ex h. l.
ante k. Sept. petitio erit, sei eis volet sibei
patronos in eam rem darei, pr., ad quem [*nomen*
[10] *detulerit . . |* . *patronos civeis Romanos ingenuos
ei dato, dum*] nei quem eorum det sciens d. m.,
quoiei is, q[*uoius nomen delatum erit, . . . gener
socer vitricus privignusve siet, queive eiei sobrinus
siet pro*]piusve eum ea cognatione attigat, queive
eiei sodalis siet, queive in eodem conlegio siet,
quoiave in fide is erit maioresve in maiorum fide
fueri⟨*n*⟩t [*queive in fide eius erit, maioresve in*
[11] *maiorum fide fuerint . . |* . *queive*] quaestione⟨m⟩
ioudicioque puplico condemnatu[*s siet, quod circa*

[10] ATIIGAT   [11] IOVDICIOOVE

---

[1] For these, see p. 297.

[2] that is, shall not be accused while in office.

[3] *e. h. l. n. r. = eius hac lege nihilum rogatur* or *rogato*(?*r*).

[4] note that a *patronus* was the actual speaker on behalf of
another, and was distinguished from the *advocatus* who
simply advised on certain points; later on the functions of
the two persons were combined in one.

[5] The ensuing clause means that no *patronus* or ancestors
of his shall have been client or patron to the defendant or
his ancestors; and the reverse.

322

LAWS AND OTHER DOCUMENTS

There Shall Be No Trial of The Following So Long as They Hold Magistracy or State Authority

A dictator, consul, praetor, master of the horse, censor, aedile, tribune of the plebs, quaestor, member of the Board of Three for capital duties [1] or of the Board of Three for granting and assigning lands, or military tribune of any of the first four legions, so long as he holds a magistracy or state authority, shall not be brought into court. [2] It is not intended by this law, [3] that any one of the said officials who has laid down his magistracy or state authority shall be exempt from being brought into court . . .

On The Granting of Pleaders [4]

If any person shall sue and summon for recovery of money, and shall bring his suit before the first of September under this law, and shall desire that pleaders be granted him for the said purpose, the praetor before whom he shall have made the summons . . . shall grant him pleaders, the same to be free-born Roman citizens, provided that he do not knowingly and with wrongful intent include among the said pleaders someone to whom he, who shall have been summoned, is related as son-in-law, father-in-law, stepfather, step-son, or who is a cousin or nearer relation than that kinship, or who is his fellow in the same club or guild; or [5] in whose bondship the defendant shall lie or in whose ancestors' bondship the defendant's ancestors have lain; or who shall lie in the bondship of the defendant or whose ancestors have lain in the bondship of the defendant's ancestors . . . or who has been convicted in a criminal inquiry or public court wherefore it is not

eum in senatum legei non liceat, . . . *neive eum que*]i
ex h. l. ioudex in eam rem erit, neive eum que*i*
ex h. l. patronus datus erit.

De patrono repudiando.   Quei ex h. l. patronus
datus erit, sei is mori[*bus suspectus erit, is, quoi ex*
12 *h. l. datus erit, eum reicito* . . | . *Tum quos ex*
h. l. patronos dare licet eor]um pr., quei ex h. l.
quaeret, alium patronum eiei quei s[*ibei darei petet*
dato . . .

De CDL vireis in hunc an]num legundis.   Pr.,
quei inter peregrinos ious deicet, is in diebus X
proxum., quibus h. l. populus plebesve iouserit,
facito utei CDL viros legat, quei in hac ceivit[*ate*
13 *equom publicum habebit habuerit* . . | . *dum nei*
quem eorum legat, quei tr. pl., q., IIIvir cap., tr. mil. l.
IIII primis aliqua earum, IIIvi]rum a. d. a. siet
fueritve, queive in senatu siet fueri*tve*, queiv[*e*

12 LECAT
13 FVERINT·EIE·QVEI   queiv[*e mercaturam vel argentariam exercet exercueritve lege Rubria*, Carcopino (vel *Rubria
Acilia*), ' *Autour des Gracques* ', 223 (cf. *C.I.G.*, 2845 = *I.G.*,
XII, 3, 173

---

[1] To cover all criminal and civil procedure, every year the
praetor urbanus (not the *p. peregrinus*, mentioned below)
provided one general list (*album*) of men eligible to serve as
jurymen (*selecti iudices*) ; from this large list was to be drawn a
smaller list as here (for this *quaestio de repetundis*, the choice being limited—see below—to a certain class).   Perhaps these 450
(to be chosen this year by the *p. peregrinus*) were to be chosen
independently of the general list ; and from this smaller list
another was drawn to form the jury (*consilium*) to try any
separate case belonging to the relevant *quaestio*.
[2] It is uncertain whether we should supply some such phrase
as this, or some phrase describing the property qualification
(400,000 sesterces) of the equestrian status, such as *quei in hac
civitate sestertium quadringentorum milium nummum plurisve*

324

permissible to elect him into the senate . . . nor shall the praetor grant any person who by this law shall have been made a juryman for the matter in dispute, nor any person who by this law shall have been granted as a pleader for the said matter.

ON THE REPUDIATION OF A PLEADER

If any person, who shall have been by this law granted as pleader, shall be a suspected character, the person to whom he shall have been granted by this law may reject him. . . . Then the praetor who [12] shall by this law conduct the inquiry, shall, from the list of those pleaders whom he may by this law grant, grant another pleader to him who shall ask for such to be given him . . .

ON THE ELECTION OF 450 PERSONS [1] FOR THE PRESENT YEAR

The praetor whose jurisdiction shall include resident aliens shall, within the next ten days following the ratification of this law by people or plebs, see to it that he elects a panel of 450 persons all of whom have or shall have had the public horse [2] within this State . . . provided that none of those whom he [13] elects is or shall have been tribune of the commons, quaestor, member of the Board of Three for capital duties, military tribune in any of the first four legions, or member of the Board of Three for granting and assigning lands; who is or shall have been in the

census siet (Cf. Last, in *Camb. Anc. Hist.*, IX, 896). The chosen men are to be non-senators (see below), but there is no proof that they were, in this law, called *equites*. The restriction of choice applied to all juries at this time.

mercede   conductus   depugnavit   depugnaverit . . .
queive quaestione ioudicioque puplico conde]mnatus
siet quod circa eum in senatum legei non liceat,
queive minor anneis XXX maiorve annos LX
gnatus siet, queive in urbem Romam propiusve
u[*rbem Romam p. M domicilium non habeat, queive*
14 *eius mag., quei s. s. e., pater | frater filiusve siet,*
queive eius, quei in senatu siet fueritve, pater frater
filiusve siet, queive trans mar]e erit.

Quos legerit, eos patrem tribum [1] cognomenque
indicet.   Q[*uei ex h. l. in hunc annum quaeret* . . .
is die . . . *ex quo legerit, eorum, quei ex*] h. l. CDL
vireis in eum annum lectei erunt, ea nomina omnia
in tabula, in albo, atramento scriptos, patrem
tribum   cognomenque   tributimque   discriptos
hab[*eto, eosque propositos suo magistratu servato*
. . . *Sei quis describere volet, is pr. permittito*
15 *potestatemque scribendi, quei | volet, facito.   Pr., quei*
legerit, quos e]x h. l. CDL viros legerit, facito reci-
tentur in contione iuratoque sese[*eos ex h. l. legise,*
de quibus sibei consultum siet . . . *optumos eos ioudices*
futuros esse, quosque oetiles io]udices exaestumaverit esse; eosque CDL viros, quos ex h. l. legerit,

[1] TRIBVNVM . . .   IOVDICET . . .
SCRIPTES . . .   COCNOMEN . . .
DESCRIPTOS

---

[1] Except a short period from 106 to 104 or 101 B.C., Senators
were as a result of this law entirely excluded from juries until
81 B.C.   [2] This area counted as part of the city.
[3] the *praetor peregrinus?* (see p. 325); in future, a special
praetor—see pp. 328–9.

Senate,[1] or has or shall have fought as a gladiator
hired for pay . . . or shall have been convicted in a
criminal inquiry or public court, wherefore it is not
permissible to elect him into the Senate, or is less
than 30 or more than 60 years old, or has no domicile
in the city of Rome or within one mile [2] of the city of
Rome . . . or is father brother or son of any of the [14]
said magistrates recorded above, or is father brother
or son of any person who is or shall have been in the
Senate, or shall be beyond the sea.

OF THOSE WHOM THE PRAETOR SHALL ELECT HE SHALL INDICATE THE FATHER'S NAME, THE TRIBE, AND THE SURNAME

He [3] who shall by this law conduct the inquiry for
the present year . . . the same shall on the . . . day
after his election of the said persons, cause the names
of all the 450 persons who shall have been elected by
this law for the present year to be written out in black
on a tablet having a white surface, and arranged
tribe by tribe, together with the father's name, the
tribe and the surname, and he shall keep the list
posted up on view during his magistracy. . . . If
any person shall be minded to make a copy, the said
praetor shall permit the same, and shall cause the
person who shall be so minded to have facilities for [15]
copying. The praetor who shall have elected the
450 persons by this law shall cause their names to be
read out at an informal gathering and shall swear an
oath that he has elected by this law such persons as,
in his well considered opinion . . . will be the best
jurors and such as he has deemed to be suitable jurors,
and all of the said 450 persons whom the said praetor

is pr. omnis in taboleis puplicis scriptos in per-
petuo habeto. |

De CDL vireis quot annis [*legundis. Praetor,*
[16] *quei post h. l. rogatam ex h. l. ioudex factus erit . .* | .
is in diebus X proxumeis, quibus quis]que eorum eum
mag. coiperit, facito utei CDL viros ita legat,
quei ha[*ce civitate equom publicum habebit habuerit
. . . d*]um ne quem eorum legat, quei tr. pl., q.,
III vir cap., tr. mil. l. IIII primis aliqua earum,
triumvir a. d. a. siet fueritve, queive in senatu siet
fueritve, queive merc[*ede conductus depugnavit
depugnaverit . . . queive quaestione ioudicioque
puplico condemnatus siet quod circa eum in senatum*
[17] *legei non liceat,* | *queive minor anneis XXX maiorve
a*]nnos LX gnatus siet, queive in urbe Romae
propiusve urbem Roma[*m p. M domicilium non
habeat queive eius mag., quei s. s. e., pater frater
filiusve siet,*] queive eius quei in senatu siet
fueritve pater frater filiusve siet queive trans mare
erit.

Quos legerit, eos patrem tribum cognomenque
indicet. Quei ex h. l. in eu[*m annum quaeret, is
die . . . ex quo legerit, quei ex h. l. CDL vireis in*
[18] *eum annum lectei erunt* | *in tabula, in albo, atramento*

---

[16] quieve merc[*aturam vel argentariam exercet exercueritve
lege Rubria,* Carcopino (vel *Rubria Acilia*)
[17] IOVDICES (*pro* indicet)

---

[1] apparently a special *praetor de repetundis.*
[2] that is, a *quaesitor* (not *quaestor*) or president of a court
or trial, not 'juryman.'

shall have elected by this law he shall cause to be permanently entered in the public records.

On The Election of 450 Persons Every Year

Any praetor [1] who after the passing of this law shall by this law have been made judge [2] . . . shall, [16] within the next ten days following that on which he began his magistracy, see that he so elect a panel of 450 persons that all of them shall have or shall have had the public horse within this State . . . provided that none of those whom he elects is or shall have been tribune of the plebs, quaestor, member of the Board of Three for capital duties, military tribune in any of the first four legions, or member of the Board of Three for granting and assigning lands; or who is or shall have been in the Senate, or has or shall have fought as a gladiator hired for pay . . . or shall have been convicted in a criminal inquiry or public court, wherefore it is not permissible to elect him into the Senate, or is less than 30 or more than 60 years old, or [17] has no domicile within the city of Rome, or within one mile of the city of Rome, or is father brother or son of any magistrate recorded above, or of a person who is or shall have been in the Senate or is beyond the sea.

Of Those Whom The Praetor Shall Elect He Shall Indicate The Father's Name, The Tribe and The Surname

He who shall by this law conduct the inquiry for the said year the same shall on the . . . day after his election of the said persons, cause the names of all the 450 persons who shall have been elected by this law for the said year to be written out in black [18]

scriptos, patr]em tribu[*m*] cognomenque tributimque discriptos habeto, eosque propositos suo
ma[*gistratu servato. . . . Sei quis describere volet,
is pr. permittito, potestatem*]que scribundi, quei
volet, facito. Pr. quei legerit, is eos quos ex h. l.
C[D*Lv*]iros legeri⟨*n*⟩t, facito in contione recite[*n*]-
tur, iouratoque sese eos ex h. l. legise, de quibus
sibei consu[*ltum siet optumos eos ioudices futuros
esse quosque oetiles ioudices exaestumaverit esse ;
eosque CDL viros, quos ex h. l. legerit, is pr.*
¹⁹ *omnis* | *in taboleis pupliceis scriptos in perpetuo
habeto.*]

    De nomine deferundo iudicibusque legundeis.
Quei ex h. l. pequniam ab a[*rvorsario petet, . . .
is eum, unde petet, postquam CDL virei ex h. l. in
e*]um annum lectei erunt, ad iudicem, in eum
annum quei ex h. l. [*factus*] erit, in ious educito
nomenque eius deferto. Sei deiuraverit calum-
niae causa non po[*stulare, is praetor nomen recipito*
²⁰ *facitoque, . .* | *. utei die . . . ex eo die, quo*
quoiusque quisque nomen detolerit, is quoius nomen
delatum e]rit de CDL vireis, quei in eum annum
ex h. l. lectei erunt, arvorsario edat eos om[*nes,
. . . quoi is queive ei, quoius nomen delatum erit,
gener socer vitricus pri*]vignusve siet, queive ei

---

¹⁸ LEGERINT   CONÇTIONE   RECITETVR

---

¹ for any particular case in this *quaestio*. It will be seen
that out of the list of 450, the plaintiff shall choose 100 not
related to himself or to the defendant; the defendant shall
then choose 50 from the 100. The 50 form the final jury. If
defendant refuse to choose the 50, plaintiff may choose them.
See pp. 332 ff., 337.

² sc. the *praetor de repetundis.*

on a tablet having a white surface, and arranged tribe by tribe, together with the father's name, the tribe, and the surname, and he shall keep the list posted up on view during his magistracy. . . . If any person shall be minded to make a copy, the said praetor shall permit the same, and shall cause the person who shall be so minded to have facilities for copying. The praetor who shall have elected the 450 persons by this law shall cause their names to be read out at an informal gathering and shall swear an oath that he has elected by this law such persons as, in his well considered opinion, will be the best jurors and such as he has deemed to be suitable jurors; and all of the said 450 persons whom the said praetor shall have elected by this law he shall cause to be permanently [19] entered in the public records.

On Summoning a Defendant and Electing Jurors[1]

Any person who by this law shall sue an opposing party for a sum of money . . . such claimant shall, after the 450 persons shall have been by this law elected for that year, bring the person against whom he lodges his suit into court before the judge[2] appointed by this law for that year, and shall register the summons. If he shall swear that his demand is not made by way of a false charge, the said praetor shall accept the summons and, on the . . . day after [20] that on which any person has summoned another, cause the person who shall have been summoned to make to the other party a declaration, out of the 450 persons who shall be elected by this law for that year, of all those persons . . . to whom he, who has been summoned, is related or who are related to him as son-in-law, father-in-law, stepfather, step-son or as

sobrinus siet propiusve eum ea cognat[*ione*]
attingat, queive ei sodalis siet, queive in eodem
conlegio siet; facitoque coram arv[*orsario is quei*
ita ediderit iouret : in CDL vireis, quei in eum
21 *annum ex h. l. lectei erunt, non reliquisse se | nisei*
quei se earum aliqua necesitudine quae supra scripta
sient] non attigeret, scientem d. m.; itaque is
edito iouratoque. Ubei is ita ediderit, tum in
ea[*m quaestionem quei quoiusque ita nomen detolerit,*
is praetor, quoius ex h. l. quaestio e]rit, facito utei
is die vicensumo ex eo die, quo quoiusque quisque
n[*omen*] detolerit, C viros ex eis, quei ex h. l.
CDL vire[*i*] in eum annum lectei erunt, quei
22 vivat, legat, e[*datque . . | . dum nei quis ioud*]ex
siet, quoi is, queive ei, quei petet, gener socer
vitricus privignusve siet, queive ei sobrinus [*siet*
propiusve eum ea cognatione attingat, . . . queive
in eodem conlegio siet, queive e]i sodalis siet, queive
tr. pl., q., III vir cap., III vir a. d. a., tribunus
mil. l. IIII prim[*is aliqu*]a earum siet fueritve,
queive ⟨queive⟩ in senatu siet fueritve, queive l.
23 Rubr[*ia III vir col. ded. creatus siet fueritve . . | .*
queive ab urbe Roma plus . . . passuum] aberit,
queive trans mare erit; neive amplius de una
familia unum, neive eum [*legat edatve, quei*

20 COGNAT   M ATTINGAT
21 COVRATOQVE
          EI
22 QVEIVE QVEI SOBRINVS   ]AE·EARVM

---

[1] not to be the final jury (for any particular trial), which
is to consist of 50—see below, line 26 (p. 337). On absence of
mention of *pilae*, see pp. 348, 310 ff. *vivat* should be *vivent*.

[2] Passed by Gaius Gracchus late in 123 B.C. or early in 122
with the object of founding a colony on the site of Carthage.
It was repealed in 121 B.C.

cousin or nearer relation than that; or are fellows in
the same club or guild; and he shall cause the person
who shall have made such declaration to swear an
oath in the presence of the other party: that among
the 450 persons who have been elected by this law for
that year he has not, knowingly and with wrongful
intent, left anyone other than persons who are not [21]
related to him by any of the said ties of kinship
recorded above; and thus shall the said party declare
and swear an oath. When the said party shall have
thus made declaration, then, for purposes of the inquiry, with regard to the person who shall have thus
summoned anyone, the said praetor, to whom by this
law the inquiry shall belong, shall cause the said
plaintiff, on the 20th day after that on which any such
plaintiff shall have summoned anyone, to choose 100
persons, not deceased,[1] out of the 450 persons who shall
have been elected for that year, and to declare . . . [22]
provided that there be no juror, to whom the said
person who brings the suit is related, or who is related
to him, as son-in-law, father-in-law step-father,
step-son, or as cousin or nearer relation than that . . .
or is his fellow in the same guild or club, or is or shall
have been tribune of the plebs, quaestor, member
of the Board of Three for capital duties, or of the
Board of Three for granting and assigning lands, or
military tribune in any of the first four legions, or is or
shall have been in the Senate, or has been or shall
have been, by the Rubrian [2] law, made a member of
the Board of Three for conducting a colony, . . . or [23]
shall be more than . . . miles away from Rome or
shall be beyond the sea. Nor shall he choose
more than one person from any one household, nor
shall he choose or declare any person who has or shall

*pecuniae captae condemnatus est erit, aut quod cum
eo lege Calpu*]rnia aut lege Iunia sacramento
actum siet, aut quod h. l. nomen [*delatum sie*]t.
Quos is C viros ex h. l. ediderit, d́e eis ita facito
iouret palam apud se coram a[*rvorsario nullum se
edidise scientem d. m., quem ob earum causarum*
24 *aliquam, quae supra scripta sient* . . | . *inter C viros
edere non liceat, queive se earum aliqua*] necesitudine
atingat, quae supra scripta sient.   Is unde
petitum erit, quomi[*nus. . . . Sei is quei petet,
ita C*] viros ediderit iuraritque, tum eis pr. facito,
utei is unde petetur die L[*X postquam*] eius nomen
delatum erit, quos C is quei petet ex h. l. ediderit,
25 de eis iudices qu[*os volet L legat* . . | . *Quei ex
h. l. nomen detolerit, sei is quoius nom*]en ex h. l.
delatum erit, L iudices ex h. l. non legerit edide-
ritve, seive [*ex CDL vireis, quei in eum annum ex
h. l. lectei erunt, quei se adfinitate cognation*]e sodali-
tate atingat, queive in eodem conlegio siet, ex

²⁴ Is, Mommsen   Q

---

¹ An old form of civil action where either party deposited
money; the money of the loser went to the treasury for
sacred purposes.   See *Remains of Old Latin*, vol. III, p. 432.
Thus action under the Calpurnian Law of extortion and the
revision thereof by this Acilian Law was really a civil action for
return of property wrongfully taken.   However, it was not
long before actions for *repetundae* took on the character of
criminal actions.

² Establishing the *quaestio de repetundis*; passed by Calpurnius Piso in 149 B.C.

³ The date and purport of this law are not known.

⁴ that is, among the 100 persons who, the plaintiff declares,
have been chosen by him.

have been convicted for misappropriation of moneys, or by virtue of an action [1] under solemn deposit brought against him in accordance with the Calpurnian [2] law or the Junian [3] law, or by virtue of a summons brought against him in accordance with the present law. The praetor shall so cause the said plaintiff to swear an oath, publicly in his court and in the presence of the other party, that, among the 100 persons whom the plaintiff shall have declared [4] by this law, he has declared knowingly and with wrongful intent none whom for any of the said reasons recorded above . . . it is not permissible to declare [24] among the 100 persons, or who is related to him by any of the said ties of kinship recorded above . . . Person who shall have been sued, to prevent . . . When the person who brings the suit shall have thus declared the 100 persons and has sworn the oath, then the said praetor shall cause the person who shall be sued, on the sixtieth day after the registration of his summons, to choose out of the 100 persons who shall have been declared under this law by the person who shall bring the suit, any 50 jurors whom he shall wish . . .

Should the person who shall have been summoned [25] under this law fail to choose or declare under this law 50 jurors, or, from among the 450 persons who shall have been elected by this law for that year, fail to declare, under this law, anyone who is connected with him by relationship or by blood-kinship, or by club-fellowship, or belongs to the same guild [5]—then

---

[5] Since however the persons here concerned were of higher degree than members of the established guilds, *conlegium* perhaps means here a non-magisterial college (non-magisterial because no magistrate could be accused when he was in office).

h. l. non e[*diderit, tum ei pe*]r eum pr. advor-
sariumve mora non eri[*t quo*]minus legat edatv[*e*
26 *quos volet L de eis C, quos ex h. l. ediderit* . . | . *dum
nei eorum, quos ex h. l. legere non licet, quem sciens
dolo malo ioudic*]em legat.   Quei ita lectei erunt,
eis in eam rem ioudices sunto eorumque eiu[*s rei
ex h. l. ioudicatio slitisque aestumatio esto.*

Iudicum patronorumque nomina] utei scripta in
taboleis habeantur.   Pr., quei ex h. l. quaeret,
fac[*ito eos L viros qu*]os is quei petet et unde
petetur ex h. l. legerint ed[*iderint, e*]osque
27 pat[*ronos, quos quei petet ex h. l. acceperit* . . | . *in
taboleis popliceis scriptos habeat.   Ea nomina q*]uei
petiverit et unde petitum erit, quei eorum volet,
ex taboleis popli[*ceis describundi is pr. potestatem
facito* . . .]

Eisdem ioudices unius rei in perpetuom sient.
Quei iudices e[*x h. l. lectei erunt,*] quam in rem eis
iudices lectei er[*unt, eius rei iudices in perpetuom
28 sunto* . . | . *q*]uei pequniam ex [*h. l.*] capiet, eum
ob eam rem, quod pequniam ex h. l. ceper[*it, nei*

25 MORM · NON   26 *vide C.I.L.*

---

[1] apparently an *eques* and probably an informer.

the person who shall have made the summons under this law shall suffer no hindrance, through any action of the said praetor or of the other party, from choosing or declaring, out of the said 100 persons whom he has declared under this law, any 50 whom he shall wish [26] . . . provided that he does not, knowingly and with wrongful intent, choose as a juror any person whom it is not permissible to choose under this law. Those who shall have been so chosen shall be the jurors for the matter in question, and to them shall belong under this law the adjudication and assessment of damages in the matter in question.

THE NAMES OF JURORS AND PLEADERS ARE TO BE PRESERVED IN WRITING IN THE REGISTERS

The praetor who shall under this law conduct this inquiry shall cause the names of the 50 persons who shall have been chosen and declared under this law by the plaintiff and the defendant, and the names of the pleaders whom the plaintiff has received under this [27] law to be preserved in the public registers. The said praetor shall grant to the plaintiff and the defendant, to either of them who shall be so minded, facilities for copying the said names from the public registers. . . .

THE SAME JURORS SHALL REMAIN IN ANY ONE CASE THROUGH ITS WHOLE COURSE

All jurors who shall have been elected by this law, for whatever case they shall have been elected as jurors, shall remain the jurors in the said case throughout its course. . . . In the event of any [28] person [1] taking money under this law, a censor shall not, on account of such act in taking money under

. . . *neive tribu mo*]veto, neive equom adimito, neive quid *ei ob* eam rem fraudei esto.

29   . . . [*sc*]ripta sient.   Praetor quei ex h. l. . . . | .
[*De iudicio in eum, quei mortuos e*]rit aut in exilium abierit.   Quoium nomen ex h. l. delatum eri[*t, sei is ante mortuos erit . . . aut in exiliu*]m abierit, quam ea res iudicata erit, pr., ad quem eius nomen d[*elatum erit, eam*] rem ab eis item quaerito, [*quei ioudicium ex hace lege erunt, quasei sei is quoius nomen ex h. l. delatum erit, viveret*
30 *inve ceivitate esset* . . | .

De inquisitione faciunda.   Praetor de eo, quo]iu[*s*] nomen ex h. l. ad se delatum erit, facito, utei ioudicium p[*rimo quoque die . . . fiat eique quei ex h. l. nomen detolerit, dies quot sibi videbitur det, utei q*]uod recte factum esse volet, dum neiquid adversus h. l. fiat, [*ad inquisitionem fac*]iundam;
31 neive post h. [*l. rogatam* . . | . *iubetoque*] conquaeri in terra Italia in oppedeis foreis conciliab[*oleis, ubei ioure deicundo praeesse solent, aut extra Italiam*

EI
²⁸ QVID · EIVS · EAM   ²⁹ NDICATA

---

¹ the *equus publicus* of an *eques*.
² These and the *conciliabula* were small places where the civil organisation was not complete.   See p. xxxvii.
³ These prefects were nominated by a Roman praetor (who was not allowed to be away from Rome for more than 10 days, and not all cases could be tried at Rome) as standing magistrates, or sometimes mere circuit-judges, through Roman towns, both those *sine suffragio* and those which had full Roman citizenship.   Their duties lay in civil cases, but, where there were no local magistrates available, they had duties of government also.

this law . . . or remove him from his tribe, or take away his horse,[1] nor shall any disadvantage occur to him on account of such act.

. . . SHALL BE PUT IN WRITING

The praetor who under this law . . .   29

ON INSTITUTING A TRIAL AGAINST A PERSON WHO SHALL BE DECEASED OR SHALL HAVE GONE INTO EXILE

In the case of any person who shall have been summoned under this law, if he shall be deceased . . . or shall have gone into exile before the said case shall have been adjudicated, the praetor, before whom he shall have been summoned, shall conduct the inquiry into the said case through those persons who under this law shall form the court, in the same manner as if the person who shall have been summoned under this law were alive or present in this [30] State. . . .

ON THE HOLDING OF AN INVESTIGATION FOR EVIDENCE

The praetor shall cause the court concerning a person who shall be summoned under this law to be formed on the earliest possible day . . . , and to the person who shall have made the summons under this law he shall grant as many days as he shall think fit, to the best of his ability, for the holding of an investigation for evidence, provided that nothing be done contrary to this law; nor, after the passing of this law, . . . and he shall give orders for evidence to be [31] collected within Italy, in the country-towns and market-towns[2] and meeting-places, where men are customarily sent as prefects for jurisdiction,[3] or outside Italy in country-towns and market-towns and

339

in oppedeis foreis con]ciliaboleis, ubei ioure dei-
cundo praesse solent.   In quibus di[*ebus eum quei
petet prae*]tor quei ex h. l. quaere[*t, conquaerere*
³² *iouserit . .* | .

*Testibus ut denuntietur.   Pr. ioudiciumque post-
quam*] audierit, quod eius rei quaerundai censeant
refere, et c[*ausam probaverit, quibus is quei petet
denuntiaverit, eos homines dumtaxat IIL testimonium
deic*]ere iubeto et quom e*a* res agetur quam in
rem quisque testis er[*it, in eam rem facito eis*]omnes
adsient testimo[*niumque deicant, dum nei quem
³³ testimonium deicere iubeat, quei . .* | . *quoiave in fide
is unde petetur siet maioresve in maior*]um eius
fide [*fuerint*], queive in fide eius siet maioresv[*e
in maiorum eius fide fuerint, queive eius, quoius ex
h. l. nomen delatum erit, c*]ausam deicet dum taxat
unum, queive eius parentisve eius l[*eibertus
leiberta*]ve siet.
³⁴   De inro[*ganda multa. . .* | .

    . . .

    *De testibus tabulisque custodiendis.   Is quei petet,
sei quos ad testimonium deicundum evocari*]t secumve
duxerit dum taxat homines IIL earum re[*rum*

³² QVOM · EI · RES
³³ QVAERAT *pro* fuerit

---

¹ see note 5 on p. 322.   ² *sc.* as his *patronus.*

340

meeting-places where men are customarily sent as prefects for jurisdiction. During the days in which the praetor who shall conduct the inquiry under this law shall have given orders to the person making the summons to collect evidence . . . 32

Notice Must be Given to Witnesses

After the praetor with his court shall have heard all that they deem to be relevant to the matter of inquiry, and shall have approved a true bill, he shall order those persons, not exceeding 48, to whom the person who shall bring the summons shall have given notice of suit, to give evidence, and when that point shall be considered on which each separate person is a witness, he shall cause all such witnesses to be present for the said matter, and to give evidence, provided that he orders no person to give evidence who . . . or in whose bondship the defendant shall 33 lie or in whose ancestors' bondship the defendant's ancestors have lain; or [1] who shall lie in the bondship of the defendant or whose ancestors have lain in the bondship of the defendant's ancestors, or any, with the exception of one person only, who shall plead [2] the cause of the person who shall have been summoned under this law, or who is a freedman or a freedwoman of the said defendant or of his parent.

On the Infliction of a Fine 34

. . . .

On the Safe Custody of Witnesses and Registers

When the party who shall bring a summons has called up or brought with him persons not exceeding 48 in order to give evidence on those matters on which

causa, de quibus id ioudicium fiet . . . e]a, quai ita
35 conquaesiverit et sei qua tabulas | libros leiterasve
pop[*licas preivatasve produ*]cere proferrequ[*e volet*
35 . . | . quaer*]ive de ea re volet apud pr. is praetor
ei moram ne faci[*to, quominus . . . quaer*]at.

Praetor utei interroget. Pr. quei ex h. l.
36 q[*uaeret . . | .*

*Ioudices utei iourent ante quam considant. Pr.
quei ex h. l. quaeret, quei in ea*]m rem ioudices
erunt, ante quam primum caussa d[*icetur . . .
apud se iourent facit*]o. Iudices, quei in eam rem
erunt, omnes pro rostreis in forum [*vorsus*
37 *iouranto . . | . facturumque se, utei quod recte factum
esse vol*]et, utei testium, quei *in* eam rem erunt,
verba audiat, [*. . . neque se facturum quo*] eam
rem minus ioudicet, nisei sei quae causa erit,
quae eie[*i ex h. l. quo eam rem minus ioudicet*
38 *permittet . . | . Quei ita apud se iourarint eorum
nomina is praetor facito in contione r*]ecitentur,
proscripta propositaque palam apud for[*um
habeto . . . neve nisei ita iourarit de ea re considere
sinito quemquam eorum quei ex e*]is C ioudices L
lectei erunt.

---

[1] obviously the production by the plaintiff of records and
letters and the holding of an inquiry rightfully requested by
him.
[2] this clause is missing, and the nature of the examination is
not known.
[3] This means, before the first pleadings which precede the
testimony of the witnesses.

the said trial shall be held, . . . those points on
which he has so collected evidence as above, and if he
shall in any way desire to produce and bring forward [35]
registers books or letters public or private . . . or
shall desire inquiry to be made on such matter before
the praetor, the said praetor shall cause him no
hindrance to prevent [1] . . .

The Praetor Must Hold an Interrogation [2]

The praetor who shall conduct the inquiry under
this law . . .

The Jurors Must Swear an Oath Before They [36] Take Their Seats in Court

The praetor who shall hold the inquiry under this
law shall cause the jurors who shall be elected for the
matter in question to swear an oath in his presence
before the case is first [3] considered. . . . The
jurors who shall be elected for the matter in question
shall one and all, in front of the Rostra towards the
Forum swear an oath . . . and that he will, to the [37]
best of his ability, listen to the words of the witnesses
who shall be called for the said case . . . and will do
nothing to prevent his serving as a juror on the said
case, unless there shall be some cause which shall
under this law excuse him from serving as juror on
the said case. . . . The said praetor shall cause the [38]
names of all those who have so sworn oath in his
presence to be read out at an informal meeting and
shall have them published in writing and posted up in
full view in the Forum . . . nor shall he allow any
one of the 50 who shall have been chosen from the
said 100 persons to take his seat in court concerning
the said matter unless he shall have so sworn oath.

39   Ioudex neiquis disputet. . . | .

[. . . *Sei . . . causam sibi esse deicet, quominus ad id*] iudicium adesse possit, de ea re praetori, quei ex hac[*e lege quaeret cognoscere . . . ius esto.*

De iudicio proferendo vel refere]ndo. Quam rem pr. ex h. l. egerit, sei eam rem proferet, quoi
40 [. . | . *sei refer*]re poterit facito quoius deicet nomen referre . . . it utei is ad sese veniat aut
41 adferatur coram eo, quei postulaver[*it . . | . vol*]et, quoius ex h. l. nominis delatio erit, ei eius rei pe[*titio esto . . . de*]que ea re hace lege iudicium litisque aestumatio essto, quasei sei
42 eius [. . | .

. . . *Sei ioudex q*]uei eam rem quaeret, ex h. l. causam non nover[*it . . . is praetor c*]oram [*iudicib*]us in contione pro rostris sententia ita pro-
43 nontiato: ' fec[*isse videri*' . . | . *Sei de ea re*]iudicium fieri oportebit, ter[*tio die facito iudicium fiat . . . Sei ioudex, quei eam r*]em quaeret, ex h. l.
44 causam non noverit, pr. quei ex h. l. q[*uaeret . . | .

     40 VTEIVS   **41** HOMINIS

---

[1] or ' consult with another juror ' during the hearing—cf. Aristotle, *Pol.*, II, 5, 8.

[2] This at any rate is the purport of the part preserved.

[3] This is uncertain but based on what remains of the clause. The clause probably provided for a subsidiary trial which could hold up the trial proper, thus:—In the event of some gross irregularity in court, the matter was first referred for investigation and then investigated by a committee put under one of the jurors (see lines 42–3, 45), and the praetor then ordered or refused to order a subsidiary trial of the offender. Cf. Hardy, *Six Roman Laws*, 22.

[4] On this doubtful sentence, cf. Hardy, *op. cit.*, 22. Read perhaps nomen referre [*debere*] ' whose name he shall say he must refer . . .'

[5] the case proper, as distinct from subsidiary trial.

344

LAWS AND OTHER DOCUMENTS

No Juror Shall Interrupt [1]

. . . . .

[On [2] Failure to Attend the Court]

... If ... any person shall state a cause of inability to attend the said court, the praetor who shall hold the inquiry under this law, shall have the legal right to investigate the said matter. . . .

On [3] Postponing or Referring a Trial

With regard to action which shall have been taken under this law by the praetor, to wit, should he postpone the case, . . . if he shall be rightfully able [40] to refer it, he shall cause the person whose name he shall state to be pertinent [4] . . . to come before him or be brought before him in the presence of the person who shall have made the demand . . . if he [41] who shall be summoned under this law shall be so minded, he shall have the right to sue in the said matter . . . and on the said matter there shall be under this law a trial and an assessment of damages in the same manner as if . . . [42]

If the juror who shall hold the inquiry into the said matter shall not under this law have acknowledged the excuse as valid . . . the said praetor shall, in the presence of the jurors, at an informal gathering in front of the Rostra, pronounce his decision to this [43] effect, that the person is ' Guilty ' . . . If it be required that a trial take place on the said matter, he shall cause a trial to take place on the third day. . . . If the juror who shall hold the inquiry into the said matter, under this law shall not have acknowledged the excuse as valid, the praetor who shall under this law hold the standing [5] inquiry. . . . [44]

INSTRUMENTA

Ioudices utei iourent, ante quam in consilium eant.
Pr. quei ex h. l. quaeret, ioudices quei ex h. l. in
eam rem erunt, in consilium an]te quam ibunt,
facit[*o*] iurent: sese [*. . . neque facturum q*]uo
quis suae alterius sententiae certior siet, quod
45 p[*er dolum malum fiat . . | .*]aturum esse.

Iudices multam supremam de*bea*[*nt. . . . Sei*
ioudex, quei eam rem qu]aeret, causam non
46 noverit, quei eorum ioudex [*. . | . excu*]satione,
primo quoque die deferatur, isque quaesto[*r . . .*

Iudices in co]nsilium quomodo eant. Praetor,
quei ex h. l. i u[*dicium exercebit . . . Iudex quei*
47 *ad id delectus erit, sei rem, de qua . . | . agitur,*
plus tertiae parti iudicum, quei aderunt, quom ea res
aget]ur, [*non liquere*] deixerit, praetor, *quei* ex
h. l. quaeret, ita pronon[*tiato et ad rem denuo*
agendam alium diem dato . . . eoque die eorum
iudicu]m, quei quomque aderunt, iudicare [*iubeto.*

45 SVPREMA · DEI?
47 pronon[*tiato 'amplius' et ad rem denuo agendam,* Carcopino, 216–217

---

[1] This seems to be the natural meaning. Cf. Hardy, *op. cit.*,
23. There can be little doubt that this clause refers not to the
subsidiary trial but to the trial proper, and also that it should
come after the next.

[2] *sc.* to the *tabularium,* or records-office, suggests Hardy,
op. cit., 23–4; but the point is obscure.

[3] on the case or trial proper, not on the subsidiary trial.

[4] *sc.* of reporting to the praetor whether two thirds of the
jury, as required for a legal decision, were able to give a verdict.

[5] Note that this opinion of 'not proven' is not, in this
clause, the opinion of 'not proven' which, in Cicero's time
at least, could be given in the final voting at a trial (see
below); but comes before the final voting on the matter
takes place; any juryman giving that opinion signifies that
he wants the matter to be considered further before voting.

[6] *i.e.* he shall say '*amplius,*' whereupon the case is to be

346

LAWS AND OTHER DOCUMENTS

The Jurors Must Swear an Oath Before They Retire to Deliberate [1]

The praetor who shall hold the inquiry under this law shall cause the jurors who shall be elected under this law for the matter in question, to swear an oath, before they retire to deliberate, one and all that he will not . . . with wrongful intent cause anyone to become aware of his own or another juryman's vote, [45] and that he will . . .

The Jurors Must be Liable to the Maximum Fine

If the juror, who shall hold the inquiry into the said matter, shall not have acknowledged the excuse as valid, any of the said jurors . . . by such excuse, it [46] shall be handed in [2] on the first possible day, and the said quaestor . . .

On the Procedure of Jurors Retiring to Deliberate [3]

The praetor who shall conduct the trial under this law . . . If the juror, who shall have been chosen for the said [4] object, shall have announced that the matter . . . under deliberation appears ' Not [47] Proven ' [5] to more than one third part of the jurors who shall be present when the said matter shall be deliberated, the praetor who shall hold the inquiry under this law shall pronounce accordingly [6] and shall grant another day for a fresh consideration of the said matter . . . and on that day he shall order all the jurors whoever shall be then present to give a verdict.

postponed by ' ampliatio.' After a second ampliatio, refusers in subsequent ones were fined (line 48). The Lex Servilia of 104 (101 ?) B.C. enforced division of a case into two parts.

⁴⁸ . . |. *Ad quem praetorem ita relatum erit iudicum plus tertiam partem negare iu*]dicare, is HS. n. ⓢ, quotiens quomque amplius bis in uno iu[*dicio iudicare negarint . . . singulis quei iudicare negarint multam dicito. Tu*]m quam ob rem et quantum ⁴⁹ pequ[*niae dixerit, publice proscribito . .* |.

De] reis quomodo iudicetur. Ubei duae partes iudicum, quei ader[*unt, causam sibi liquere deixe-* ⁵⁰ *rint . . . pr. quei de ea re quaeret, utei eis iudice*]s, quei iudicare negarint, semovant[*ur facito . .* |.] rem agito. Tum praetor quom soveis viatoribus apparitoribusque nei de i[*udicio iudex discedat curato . . . sitellamque latam digitos . . . altam digitos*] XX, quo ioudices sorticolas conieciant ⁵¹ [*adponi facito . .* |. *quoius*]que iudicis is praetor sorticolam unam buxeam longam digitos IIII, la[*tam digitos . . . ab utraque parte ceratam . . . in qua sorticola ex altera parti leitera A perscripta siet, ex alte*]ra parti C, inmanu palam dato, al[*teramque utram velit leiteram eum iudicem in-* ⁵² *ducere iubeto . .* |. *Iudex ita inducito*] eamque sortem ex hace lege apertam bracioque aperto literam digiteis opertam pala[*m ad eam sitellam*

⁴⁸ iu[*dicio pronuntiari iusserint iudicareve*, Carcopino, 216–217
⁵² LITIERAM . . . SINCILATIM

---

¹ *i.e.* that they are ready to vote on a verdict.
² the *sitella* at a trial was generally an urn.
³ 16 finger's breadths made 1 foot.
⁴ The normal word was *tabella.*
⁵ *A*, cut in the wax, for *absolvo, C* for *condemno* (see below). Note that this law does not mention ballot-halls used in selecting jurymen. It is quite likely that regulations about such name-ballots were made later than this law, perhaps by the law of which fragments are given above, pp. 310 ff.

. . . The praetor to whom it shall be reported that [48] more than one third part of the jurors refuse to give a verdict, the said praetor shall inflict a fine of 10,000 sesterces in money on each separate juror who shall have refused to give a verdict as often as they so refuse more than twice in one trial. Then he shall cause a written public notice to be made giving the reason and the amount of the fine he has announced. [49]

ON THE PROCEDURE IN GIVING A VERDICT ON DEFENDANTS

When two thirds of the jurors who are present shall have announced that [1] the case is ' Proven ' in their own minds . . . the praetor who shall hold the [50] inquiry into the matter in question shall cause to be removed those jurors who say they will be unable to give a verdict . . . shall proceed with the case. Then the praetor with the assistance of his messengers and attendants shall take care that no juror leave the court . . . and shall cause to be placed at hand a box [2] . . . finger's breadths [3] wide and twenty finger's breadths deep into which the jurors may cast their voting-tickets . . . and the said praetor shall [51] in full view of the court place in the hand of each separate juror one voting-ticket [4] of box-wood, four finger's breadths long, . . . finger's breadths wide and waxed on either side . . . , on which voting-ticket the letter A has been written [5] down on the one side, the letter C on the other, and shall order the said juror to rub out the one or the other according to his wish. . . . The juryman shall likewise rub out the [52] same and in accordance with this law publicly bring forward the said ticket open to view, keeping his arm open to view and the letter covered by his fingers,

deferto eamque sortem in populum . . . i]temque
in eos ceteros singilatim iu[*dices vorsus ostendito,*
53 *itaque in eam sitellam coniecito . .* | .

*Sententiae quomodo pronontientur. Quei iudex
pronontiationis fac*]iundai causa ad sitellam sorti
veniet, is in eam sitellam manum demittito, et
eam devexam popul[*o ostendito . . . i*]udiciu[*m
. . . quamque in eum r*]eum sententia[*m ea sors*
54 *hab*]uerit, is ei [. . | . *palam pronontiato, ubei A
leitera scripta erit ' apsolvo,' ubei C leitera scripta
erit ' con*]demno' ubei nihil scriptum erit, ' seine
sufragio.' Ex qua sorti pronontiarit, eam sortem
proxsumo iudi[*ci . . . in manum*] transdito.
55 De n[*umerandis sententiis. . .* | .

De] reo ap[*solvendo. Nisei eae sententiae ibei
plurumae erunt ' condemno,' pr., quei ex h. l. quaeret,
eum reum pronontiato ' non fecisse videri.'*

*De quo reo pr. ita pronontiaverit, quod postea
non fecerit aut qu*]od praevaricationis causa factum
non erit, is ex hace lege eius rei absolutus esto.

---

[1] Not apparently, ' show to the public the box tilted.'
Note that secret voting for all jurisdiction before the assembly,
except cases of treason, was introduced in 137 B.C. by the Lex
Cassia Tabellaria, and was extended to *quaestiones* later.

[2] See above. In Cicero's time each juryman usually
received 3 tickets, one with A on it, one with C on it, and one
with N L (*non liquet*) on it. See p. 346, n. 5.

[3] *sc.* with his accuser; for *praevaricatio*, see above, p. 318 n.

towards the said box, and shall display the said ticket towards the public . . . and likewise towards the remainder of the said jurors one by one, and in such manner shall cast it into the said box. . . . 53

On the Procedure in Announcing the Votes

The juror who shall by lot come forward to the box for the purpose of making the announcement of the voting shall put his hand into the said box and shall display his hand to the public when moved downwards[1] . . . the court . . . and he shall . . . pub- 54 licly announce to the same the verdict which the said ticket shall hold on the said defendant, saying ' I Acquit ' when the letter A[2] shall have been found there written, ' I Condemn ' when the letter C shall have been found there written, ' No Vote ' when nothing shall have been found there written. He shall pass on into the hand of the next juror each ticket from which he has made the announcement.

On Counting the Votes 55

· · · · · ·

On Acquitting the Defendant

Unless the said votes there given shall by a majority declare ' I Condemn ', the praetor who shall hold the inquiry under this law shall pronounce the said defendant ' Not Guilty '.

A defendant on whom the praetor shall have so pronounced, shall under this law be acquitted of the said charge save he shall hereafter have committed similar act, or an act of collusion[3] shall have been committed.

INSTRUMENTA

De reo condemnan[*do. Sei eae sententia*]e ibei
plurumae erunt ' condemno,' pr., qu[*ei ex h. l.*
56 *quaeret eum reum pronontiato ' fecisse videri '* . . | .

De· eadem re ne bis agatur.   Quei ex h. l. condem-
natus] aut apsolutus erit, quom eo *h.* l. nisei quod
post ea fecerit, aut nisei quod praevaricationis
caussa factum erit, au[*t nisei de litibus*] aestuman-
dis, aut nisei de sanctioni hoiusce legis, actio nei
57 es[*to* . . | .

De praedibus dandis bonisve possidendis.   Iudex,
quei eam rem quaesierit, earum rer]um, quei ex h. l.
condemnatus erit, q. praedes facito det de consili
maioris partis sententia, quantei eis censuer[*int ;*
sei ita p]raedes datei non erunt, bona eius facito
puplice possideantur conq[*uaerantur veneant.
Quantae pequniae ea bona venierint, tantam pequniam iudex, quei eam rem quaesierit, ab emptore*
58 *exigito* . . | . *quaestorique eam pequniam et quanta
fuerit*] scriptum transdito; quaestor accipito et
in taboleis pobliceis scriptum habeto.

---

[1] The *sanctio* of a law contained provisions against cases of
violating the law and details of penalties for such violation;
cf. the Law found at Bantia, p. 294.

[2] The praetor, president of the court.

[3] in charge of the treasury.

LAWS AND OTHER DOCUMENTS

On Convicting the Defendant

If the said votes there given shall by a majority declare ' I Condemn ', the praetor who shall hold the inquiry under this law shall pronounce the said defendant ' Guilty ' . . .   56

There Shall be No Second Procedure on The Same Case

There shall be no further proceedings against a person who shall have been convicted or acquitted under this law save he shall hereafter have committed similar act, or an act of collusion shall have been committed, or unless the proceedings concern the assessment of damages or the penal clauses [1] of this law.   57

On Giving Sureties or Taking Possession of Goods.

The judge[2] who shall have held the said inquiry shall, in regard to such matters, cause the person who shall have been convicted under this law to give a quaestor[3] sureties according to the vote of the majority of the jury and of the amount which shall have been assessed by them. Should sureties not have been so given he shall cause the goods of the said person to be taken into possession by the State, procured, and sold. As regards the amount of money at which the said goods shall have been sold the judge who shall have held the said inquiry shall exact the amount from the buyer . . . and shall hand over the [58] said money, with a statement of the amount in writing, to the quaestor; the quaestor shall receive it and preserve the written statement among the public records.

353

⁵⁹ De leitibus aestumandeis. [*Quei ex*] hac[*e*]
lege condemnatus erit, ab eo quod quisque petet,
quoius ex hace lege peti[*tio erit, id praetor, quei eam*
rem quaesierit, eos iudices, quei eam rem iudicaverint,
aestumare iubeto . . | . *quod ante h. l. rogatam con-*
silio probabitur captum coactum ab]latum avorsum
conciliatumve esse, ea*s* res omnis simpli, ceteras
res omnis, quo*d* post hance legem rogatam co[*n-*
silio probabit]ur captum coactum ablatum avorsum
conciliatumve esse, dupli; idque ad qua[*estorem,*
quantum siet quoiusque nomine ea lis aestumata siet,
facito deferatur.

    De pequnia ex aerario solvenda. Quei iudici,
quei eam rem quaesierit, consilioque eius maiorei
⁶⁰ *parti* . . | . *satisfecerit, nomine su*]o parentisve suei,
quoive ipse parensve suos heres siet, leitem
aestumatam esse; queive eiei iudicei consilioque
eius maiorei pa[*rti eorum sa*]tis fecerit, regis
populeive ceivisve suei nomine litem aestumatam
esse sibei: q[*uanta ea pequnia erit, is iudex facito*
⁶¹ . . | . *sei de ea re praedes dati erunt seive quantae*
pequniae eae lites aestumatae erunt, tanta pequnia

LAWS AND OTHER DOCUMENTS

In the event of a person being convicted under this law, in regard to the sum which shall be claimed from him by each who has a right to claim under this law, the praetor who shall have held the said inquiry shall order the jurors who shall have given verdict on the said matter to make an assessment . . . in regard to effects which shall be proved to the jury to have been seized, exacted, carried off, misappropriated or embezzled before the passing of this bill into law, in all such matters the assessment to be simple, in regard to effects which shall have been proved to the jury to have been seized, exacted, carried off, misappropriated or embezzled after the passing of this bill into law, in all such other matters the assessment to be for double the amount; which, in the name of each person in regard to whom such damages are assessed, must be handed in to a quaestor.

ON THE PAYMENT OF THE MONEY OUT OF THE TREASURY

When any person shall have satisfied the judge who shall have held the inquiry into the matter in question and his jury the majority thereof, that the damages assessed are to be in his own or his father's [60] name or in the name of a person to whom he himself or his father is heir; or when any person shall have satisfied the said judge and his jury the majority thereof that the damages assessed for him are to be in the name of his king or people or a fellow citizen, the said judge shall cause the money to that amount . . . If sureties shall have been given in regard to [61] the matter in question or if under this law money to an amount equal to the said damages assessed shall

ex] hace lege in aerario posita erit ob eam rem quod eo nomine lis aestumata erit, in triduo proxsumo, quo ita satis[*factum erit*] ex hace lege solvatur; neive quis iudex neive quaestor facito sciens dolo m[*alo, quo minus ita satis fiat, itaque*
62 *solvatur* . . | .

De tributo indicendo. Quanti iudex, quei eam rem quaesierit, leites aestumaverit, sei is iud]ex ex hace lege pequniam omnem ad quaestorem redigere non potuerit, tum in diebus X proxsumeis, quibus [*quae potuer*]rit redacta erit, iudex quei eam rem quaesierit, queive iudex hace lege fac[*tus erit, tum cum pequnia illa redacta erit, tributum indicito*
63 . . | . *diemque edito, quo is quoius parentisve quoius eiusve quoi ipse parensve suos heres siet, ita lites*] aestumatae erunt [*aut*] quoius regis populeive nomine lis aestumata erit, legati adessint, dum nei longius C dies edat.

[*De trib*]uto servando. Ubei ea dies venerit, quo die iusei erunt adesse, iudex, quei e[*um tributum indixerit, quanta pequnia de eius, quei ex h. l. condemnatus est, bonis redacta erit, tantam*

---

[1] Usually of money to be paid or received, when it is divided among several persons; but here it is payment of a portion only (to one or more persons) when the whole is not forthcoming.

have been deposited in the treasury in regard to the said matter for which the damages under the said category shall have been assessed, let the money be paid under this law within the next three days after such satisfaction shall have been given; and no judge or quaestor shall knowingly and with wrongful intent so act as to hinder such satisfaction from being given and such money from being paid. . . . 62

On Enjoining an Apportionment [1]

If the judge, who shall have held the inquiry into the matter in question, shall not be able under this law to make full payment to the quaestor of the whole amount of money at which he shall have assessed the damages, then within the next 10 days after so much as shall have been possible has been paid in, the judge who shall have held the inquiry into the said matter, or a judge who shall have been appointed under this law, shall enjoin an apportionment when the aforesaid money shall have been paid in . . . and shall declare a day on which shall appear 63 the person for whom, or for whose parent any damages shall have been so assessed, or for the person to whom he himself or his parent is heir, or the ambassadors of a king or people in whose name damages shall have been so assessed, provided that the time declared by the judge be not longer than 100 days.

On Observing the Apportionment

When the day shall have come on which the parties shall be ordered to appear, the judge who shall have ordered the said apportionment shall assign in due proportion, towards payment of the said several

pequniam in eas lites, quae aestumatae erant, pro
[64] *portioni tribuito . . | . Queique ei iudici consilioque
eius maiori parti eam litem aestumatam esse sibei
satis]* fecerit, ei primo quoque die quaestorem
solvere iubeto, quaestorque eam pequniam eis
sed frude sua solvito.

[*Reliquom*] in aerario siet.   Quod eorum nomine,
quei non aderit, tributus factus [*erit, quaestor in*
[65] *aerario servato . . | .*

De tributo proscribendo.   Quei] praetor ex hace
lege tribuendei causa prodeixerit, is, utei quod
recte factum esse volet facito, quomodo pro-
de[*ixerit, ea omnia m*]aiore parte diei ad eam diem,
donec solutum erit, apud forum palam, ubei de
plano r[*ecte legi possitur, proscripta propositaque*
[66] *habeat . . . praetor, quei eum tributum*] | fecerit
die[*s . . . prox*]umos, ex ea die, qua tributus
factus erit, apud forum palam, ubei de plano recte
legi possitur, proscri[*bito.*

[64] ADFRIT   [66] LECI *?*

---

[1] *sc.* the judge.

damages which had been assessed, money to the full amount realised from the goods of the person who was convicted under this law. . . . And to any [64] person who shall have satisfied the said judge and his jury the majority thereof that the said assessment has been duly made to him, he [1] shall on the first available day order the quaestor to make the payment, and the quaestor shall pay the said money to the said persons without personal liability.

THE RESIDUE SHALL REMAIN IN THE TREASURY

In the event of any apportionment being made in the name of a person or of persons who do not appear, the quaestor shall keep the money in the treasury . . . . [65]

ON PUBLISHING THE APPORTIONMENT IN WRITING

The praetor who shall have given previous notice in the matter of apportionment under this law shall, to the best of his ability, see to it that he have all the said details, consistent with his previous notice, written out and posted up in the Forum publicly where they can be accurately read from the level ground [2] for the greater part of the day until the day when payment shall have been made . . . the praetor who shall have made the said apportionment shall, [66] throughout the next . . . days after the day on which the apportionment shall have been made, keep it written out in the Forum publicly where it can be accurately read from the level ground.

[2] *e plano* or *de plano* also means ' out of court,' ' not on the bench '; not however in this passage.

359

Pequnia] post quinquenium populei fiet. Quae pequnia ex hace lege in aerarium posita erit, quod in anneis qu[*inque proxumeis ex ea die, qua tributus factus erit, eius pequniae quaestor ex h. l. non solverit, populei esto.*

De pequnia a praedibus exigenda. Quaestor, quoi aerarium provincia obvenerit, quoi quaestori ex
67 *h. l. praedes datei erunt, queive quaestor deinceps*] | eandem provin[*ci*]am habebit, eis faciunto, utei quod recte factum esse volet, quod eius is reus non solverit, ab eis pr[*aedibus primo quo*]que die pequnia exigatur.

Pequnia in fiscis opsignetur. Quae quomque pequnia ex hace lege ad q[*uaestorem redacta erit, is quaestor ea pequnia facito in fiscis siet fiscique signo suo opsignentur,* . . . *singulisque fiscis in-*
68 *scribatur*] | quis praetor litis aestumaverit et unde ea pequnia redacta siet quantumque in eo fisco siet. Quaestor, quei quom[*que erit, utei quod*] recte factum esse volet, facito in diebus V proxumeis, quibus quomque eiei aerarium provincia obvenerit, [*fisci resignentur, et sei ea pequnia, quam in eo fisco esse inscriptum erit, ibei inventa erit, denuo*
69 *opsignentur* . . | .

LAWS AND OTHER DOCUMENTS

After Five Years the Money shall Belong to the People

Of the money which under this law shall have been deposited in the treasury, all that a quaestor shall not have paid under this law within the next five years after the day on which the apportionment shall have been made, shall belong to the people.

On Exacting Money from the Sureties

The quaestor to whom the treasury shall have fallen as his department, and to whom sureties shall have been given under this law, and every quaestor who shall have the said department in the future, [67] the same shall to the best of their ability cause such part of the money as the defendant shall not have paid to be exacted from the said sureties on the first available day.

The Money shall be Sealed up in Baskets

Whatever money shall have been paid in to the quaestor under this law, the said quaestor shall cause the said money to be kept in baskets and the baskets to be sealed up with his seal . . . and on each [68] separate basket a written notice shall be put stating the name of the praetor who assessed the several damages, the name of the person from whom the said money was paid in, the amount lying in any said basket. Whatever quaestor shall then be in office shall to the best of his ability cause the baskets to be unsealed within the next five days after the treasury shall have fallen to him as his department, and if the said money, which, according to the statement of the written notice is in such basket, shall have been found therein, to be sealed up anew. [69]

INSTRUMENTA

Quaestor utei solvat.   Quoi] pequniam ex hace
lege, quod sine malo pequlatu fiat, pr., quei ex
hace lege quaeret, darei solvi iuserit, id quaestor
[*quei aerarium pro*]vinciam optinebit, sed fraude
sua extra ordinem dato solvitoque.

Quaestor moram nei facito.   Q[*uaestor . . .*

70 *Iudicium nei quis inpediat.   Quod]* | ex hace lege
iudicium fieri oportebit, quom ex hace lege fieri
oportebit, nei quis magistratus prove magistratu
prove [*quo inperio potestateve e*]rit [*facito qu*]ominus
setiusve fiat iudiceturve; neive quis eum, quei
ex hace lege iudicium exercebit, neive eum, que[*i
ex h. l. iudicabit, neive eum, quei ex h. l. petet
neive eum unde petetur, . . . ab eo iudicio avocato*
71 *neive]* | avocarier iubeto, neive abducito, neive
abducier iubeto, neive facito quo quis eorum
minus ad id iudicium adesse poss[*it, quove quoi
eorum minus in eo iudici*]o verba audeire in consilium eire iudicare liceat; neive iudicium dimi-
tere iubeto, nisei quom senatu[*s ioure vocabitur . . .
aut nisei quom centuriae aut*] tribus intro voca-
buntur, extra quam sei quid in saturam feretur. |

69 PEQVLATVM *?*   70 NDICVM *pro* iudicium

---

[1] particularly a tribune by virtue of his *tribunicia potestas*
together with his *ius intercessionis.*

[2] on which all trials broke up.

[3] *i.e.* except when the *comitia centuriata* or the *comitia
tributa* be called together.

[4] *i.e.* a bill which contains more than one integral proposal.
Introduction of such multiple bills to be passed as one law was
illegal.

LAWS AND OTHER DOCUMENTS

The Quaestor shall make Payments

To any person to whom the praetor, who shall hold the inquiry under this law, shall have ordered any money to be given and paid, provided it be without wrongful embezzlement in so doing, the quaestor who shall hold the treasury as his department shall give and pay the said sum without personal liability and out of the ordinary course.

The Quaestor shall not Cause Hindrance

The quaestor . . .

No Person shall Hinder a Trial

If the holding of any trial shall be required under [70] this law, no magistrate or promagistrate or person [1] acting with state authority or rightful power shall, when holding of such trial shall be required under this law, so act as to prevent the holding of a trial or the giving of a verdict; nor shall any person call away or order to be called away from said trial, or [71] bring away or order to be brought away, . . . the person who shall conduct the trial under this law, or a person who shall serve as a juryman, or the person who shall sue under this law or the person who shall be sued, or so act as to prevent any of the persons from attending the said trial or from hearing without hindrance the speeches at the said trial or from retiring to deliberate on a verdict or from delivering the same; nor shall he give orders to dismiss the court, except when the Senate shall lawfully be called [2] . . . or except [3] when the centuries or the tribes shall be called within the city for proceedings other than a bill brought in by tacking. [4]

INSTRUMENTA

72 [79]   Iudex deinceps faciat pr[*incipe cessante, item*
quaestor]. Sei is praetor quei ex hace lege
quaeret se[*ive is quaestor quoi aerarium vel urbana*
provinc]ia obvenerit *eo magistratu* ioudiciove inperiove abierit abdicaverit mortuosve erit ante
quam ea omnia ioudica[*ta soluta factave erunt,*
quae eum praetorem eumve quaestorem ex h. l.
iudicari iubere solvere facere oportet : quei quomque
deinceps praetor ex h. l. quaeret, queive quaestor
aerarium vel urbanam . . . provinciam habebit, is,
73   *utei quod recte factum*] | esse volet, facito, utei ea
omnia, quod ex hace lege factum non erit,
faciant, fiantque quae ex hace lege fieri oporteret,
s[*ei . . . apud eum ea res acta esset ; deque ea re*
eiei] praetori quaestorique omnium rerum, quod
ex hace lege factum non erit, siremps lex esto,
qua[*sei sei apud eum ea res acta esset . . .*

   De rebus ex lege Calpurnia Iuniave iudicatis.
74   *Quibusquom ioudicium*] | fuit fueritve ex lege quam
L. Calpurnius L. f. tr. pl. rogavit, exve lege, quam
M. Iunius D. f. tr. pl. rogavit, quei eorum eo

72–78   vide *C.I.L.*, Bruns

---

[1] *deinceps,* accus. *deincipem,* is an old adjective.   Lines 72–
78 are repeated in 79–85.   I have conflated 72 and 79, and
given 73 *sqq.* supplemented partly from 80 *sqq.* See p. 370, n. 1.
[2] see notes 2 and 3 on p. 334.

LAWS AND OTHER DOCUMENTS

On Default of the Original Judge, his Successor[1] shall Act. Likewise the Quaestor

If the said praetor who shall hold the inquiry
under this law or the said quaestor to whom the
treasury or the city shall have fallen as his department shall have retired or resigned from the said
magistracy or jurisdiction or state authority or
shall be deceased before all the said matters shall
have been adjudged or paid or completed which the
said praetor or the said quaestor is required under
this law to adjudge or order or pay or complete,
whoever in succession shall as praetor hold inquiry
under this law, or as quaestor shall have the treasury
or the city as his department . . ., the same shall,
to the best of his ability, see to it that he complete [73]
all matters so far as they are not completed under
this law, and that all matters be completed that are
required under this law, if . . . [as though] the said
matter had been wholly carried out in the presence
of the said person; and in reference to the said
matter the law shall hold good for the said praetor
and quaestor in all points so far as they are not
completed under this law, in like manner as though
the said matter had been wholly carried out in the
presence of the said persons. . . .

On Matters adjudged under the Calpurnian Law or the Junian Law [2]

In regard to persons on whom trial has been or [74]
shall have been held under the law introduced by
Lucius Calpurnius, tribune of the commons, son of
Lucius, or the law introduced by Marcus Junius,
tribune of the commons, son of Decimus, in regard
to any of the said persons who has been or shall have

[*ioudicio . . . apsolutus vel condemnatus est eritve, quo*] magis de ea re eius nomen hace lege deferatur quove magis de ea re quom [*eo ex h. l. agatur, eius h. l. nihilum rogato. Queique contra h. l. fecise dicentur, . . . nisei lex rogata erit ante quam ea* 75 *res facta*] | erit, quom eis hace lege actio nei esto.

De praevaricatione. Praetor, quei ex hace lege quaeret, qua de re ei prae[*tori eisque iudicibus, quei ex h. l. ad eam rem io*]udicandam adfuerint, quei vivent, eorum maiorei parti satis factum erit, nomen, quod ex [*h. l. quis detolerit, praevaricationis causa eum detulisse . . .*] |

76 De ceivitate danda. Sei quis eorum, quei ceivis Romanus non erit, ex hace lege alteri nomen [. . . *ad praetor*]em, quoius ex hace lege quaestio erit, detolerit, et is eo iudicio hace lege condemnatus erit, t[*um eis quei eius nomen detolerit, quoius eorum opera maxime unius eum condemnatum esse constiterit, . . . sei volet ipse filieique, quei eiei* 77 *gnatei erunt, quom*] | ceivis Romanus ex hace lege

---

[1] See above, p. 318.

been acquitted or convicted . . . in such trial, it is not intended by this law that such person be further summoned under this law in respect of the said matter or that proceedings be further introduced against him under this law in respect of the said matter. Against any persons who shall have been declared to have acted contrary to this law . . . no proceedings shall be taken against the same by [75] this law unless the law shall have been introduced before the said act was committed.

On Collusion [1]

In the event of the praetor who shall hold the inquiry on any matter under this law and the jurors who were present under this law for the purpose of giving a verdict on a matter and shall not be deceased, or the majority thereof, being satisfied that any person who shall have summoned another under this law summoned the same by act of collusion, the praetor shall, concerning the said matter. . . .

On Granting Citizenship [76]

If any person who shall not belong to those who are Roman citizens shall have summoned under this law another party . . . to the court of the praetor to whom the inquiry shall belong under this law, and the said other party shall have been convicted by the said court under this law, then the person who shall have made the summons against him, and by whose means above all other non-citizens it shall have been proved that the said other party was convicted . . . shall, if he be so minded, and the sons who shall be born to him when he shall be made a Roman citizen under this law, and the grandsons [77]

fiet, nepotesque [*t*]um eiei filio gnateis ceiveis
Romanei iustei sunto [*et in quam tribum, quoius
is nomen ex h. l. detolerit, sufragium tulerit, in eam
tribum sufragiu*]m ferunto inque eam tribum
censento, militiaeque eis vocatio esto, aera
stipendiaque o[*mnia eis merita sunto. Neiqui
magistratus prove magistratu . . . eius h. l.*] | nihi-
lum rogato.

De provocation[*e vocation*]eque danda. Sei
quis eorum, quei [*nominis Latini sunt . . . quei
eorum in sua quisque civitate dicta*]tor praetor
aedilisve non fuerint, ad praetorem, quoius ex
hace lege quaestio erit, [*ex h. l. alterei nomen
detolerit, et is eo iudicio h. l. condemnatus erit, tum
quei eius nomen detolerit, quoius eorum opera
maxime unius eum condemnatum esse constiterit sei
ceivis Romanus ex h. l. fierei nolet, ei postea ad p.
R. provocare liceto tamquam sei ceivis Romanus
esset. Item ipsei filieisque nepotibusque ex filio*] |
⁷⁹ eius militiae munerisque poplici in su[*a quoiusque*

----

¹ *censento = censentor*; cf. *rogato*, p. 322.
² So I translate what is apparently a formula expressing
exemption (see above, pp. 146–7), not 'fees earned by the
same shall be confirmed as valid.'
³ *vocatio* should perhaps be *vacatio*. Yet we have *vocatio*
in the same sense in the so-called *Lex Iulia Municipalis*, 93,
and there may be a legitimate change of vowel. There is
for example evidence that *vacuus* was sometimes spelt *vocuus*.
⁴ i.e. possessed of *ius Latinum*, whether Latins or others.

then born to such son, be full Roman citizens; and in whatever tribe the party whom he shall have summoned under this law shall have voted, in that tribe shall the said persons vote and in that tribe shall they be rated [1] by the 'censors; and the said persons shall have exemption from military service, and all moneys and pay earnable by the same therein shall be regarded as earned.[2] It is not [78] intended by this law that any magistrate or pro-magistrate shall not . . .

On Granting the Right of Appeal and Exemption [3] from Military Service

If any person of those who belong to the Latin name [4] . . . such person not having been dictator [5] praetor or aedile in his particular State, shall have summoned under this law another party to the court of the praetor to whom the inquiry shall belong under this law, and the said other party shall have been convicted by the said court under this law, then the person who shall have made the summons against him, and by whose means above all other non-citizens it shall have been proved that the said other party was convicted, if he shall not be minded to become a Roman citizen under this law, he shall be permitted henceforth to have the right of appeal to the Roman people in like manner as though he were a Roman citizen. Likewise exemption and [79] immunity from military service and public burdens

[5] The local magistrates in towns other than Rome could claim Roman citizenship by virtue of having been appointed to their magistracies.

ceiv]itate [vocatio immunitasque esto . . .]i petetur,
86 de ea re eius [optio est]o, utrum velit vel in sua
87 ceivitat[e . . | . ha]bere liceto. |
88 [Sei quis cei]vis Romanus ex hace lege alte[rei
nomen detolerit . . .
89 . . . Quoi ex h[ace lege provo]catio erit esseve
oporte[bit . . . praetor, quei inter pe]regrinos ious
90 [deicet . . | .]atei q[. . .

60

Lex Agraria.

Agrarian Law. A law passed apparently in 111 B.C., the third of the laws referred to by Appian, B.C., I, 27, embodying and sanctioning the various laws passed concerning lands in

The law deals with public state-land of the Roman government, and its purport is as follows. I. *Land in Italy.* Established ' occupations ' recognised by Tiberius Gracchus' land-commissioners (Board of Three) since 134 B.C. (*lines* 1–2), the commissioners' allocations to colonists (3), to persons in compensation (4), to ordinaries (5):—all such categories (6–7), save land which was specially excepted (*see recurring clause in lines* 1–6) shall be private and entered in the census (8-9).

---

[1] There follows a repetition of 72 *Sei is praetor* . . . —79 *ceiv*]itate . . ., doubtless the result of carelessness on the part of the cutter, since the repetition is entirely needless. The inscriber, when he came to 72, omitted the heading *Iudex deinceps* . . ., discovered his error later, and then re-wrote 72–78 with the proper heading. Cf. Bruns, *Fontes*, pp. 70, *n.* 2, *n.* 3; 73, *n.* 1.

[2] For extortion, some think. But there is no proof that under this law Roman citizens could accuse anyone of extortion.

[3] Cf. E. Hardy, *Six Roman Laws*, pp. 35 ff.; Mommsen, *Gesamm. Schr.*, I, 65 ff. (*C.I.L.*, I, pp. 75 ff.); Bruns, *Fontes*,

shall be granted to himself, his sons, and grandsons begotten from a son, to each in his particular State.[1]

. . . shall be demanded, he shall have in regard to the said matter the right to choose whether he be minded in his own State . . . he shall be permitted to possess. . . .

If any Roman citizen shall have summoned[2] under this law another party. . . .

Whatever person under this law shall have or shall be entitled to the right of appeal. . . .

. . . the praetor who shall have jurisdiction involving resident aliens. . . .

60

Italy since 133 B.C., and finally settling the various kinds of public and private lands.

Engraved on the other side of the bronze tablet on which the Lex Acilia (pp. 316 ff.) was engraved.[3]

Land granted to *viasii vicani* to be regarded as public state land (11–13). Any ordinary occupation since 133 B.C., not over 30 *iugera*, to remain private (13–14). Limited grazing on *ager compascuus* to be free (14–15). Holdings granted in a colony since 133 (*as in line* 3) to be confirmed, if need be, before 15th of March 110 B.C. (15–16); the same for land granted otherwise (16–17). Persons evicted from same to be restored (18). For land made private under this law, no

---

(ed. 7) I, 73 ff.; Wordsworth, 440 ff. Cf. also *C.I.L.*, I, 2, pp. 723, 739. L. Zancan, *Ager Publicus. Ricerche di storia e di diritto rom.* 1935. Against C. Saumagne, *Rev. de Phil.*, Sér. III, 1, 1927, 50 ff., see M. A. Levi, *Riv. d. Fil.*, LVII, 231 ff. See also remarks on the Lex Acilia, above, pp. 316–17. The method of restoration applied by C. Klenze to the Lex Acilia was applied by A. Rudorff (*Das Ackergesetz des Sp. Thorius*, Berlin, 1839; included in *Zeitschrift f. geschichtliche Rechtswissenschaft* X, 1842, 1) to this law. Others, especially Huschke and Mommsen (the latter's results are usually accepted) also have done good work on these laws.

person is to pay rent or pasture-tax (19–20). Land given in compensation for land taken away from possessors by the commissioners, for a colony, to be private, with exceptions (20–23). Confirmation of title or restitution of such land to be made before 15th March 110 B.C. (23–4). Public state-land not let or put to public uses to be free grazing land (24–5; penalty 25) for limited number of beasts (26). Free grazing on public roads and paths (26). Change of land from public to private, and the reverse (27). *Ager patritus* (27–8). Roads to be kept clear (28). All persons may lawfully act on public land after 112–1 B.C. as they lawfully did then (29). Jurisdiction on Latins and *peregrini* as on Roman citizens (29–30). Land of *municipia*, *coloniae*, and state mortgagees to remain public (31–2). Disputes about land made private between 133 and 111 B.C. or by this law to be settled by consul or praetor before 15th March 110 B.C. (33–4), subsequent cases by these or censors (35–6). Judgements about money owed to *publicani*; *recuperatores*; executing sentence (36–39). No risk of penalty for refusing to swear to laws contrary to this law (40), or to obey them (41–2). Colony at Sipontum ? (43). II. *Land in Africa.* Public state-land, with exceptions, to be sold by Roman magistrates. Recovery of purchase-money. Tenure of land sold (44–50; rights of colonists confirmed; *lines 48–50 fragmentary*). Colonists to make claims about land to a *duovir* (50–58, *fragmentary*), who if satisfied shall declare each one's land private unless it exceeds 200 *iugera* or the number of colonists exceeds that laid down by the Lex Rubria (59–61). Confirmation after *professio* of land bought in Rome (62–65). Compensation (a) to loser where same land was sold to two persons (65–6); (b) to colonist whose land has already been sold in Rome (66–7); (c) to purchaser from colonist (67–8); (d) to purchaser from the Roman people when his plot has been granted to a colonist already in possession (68–9). Imposts-farmer (*publicanus*) of purchasers' liabilities to pay into

585   [1]   [. . . *tr. pl. plebem ioure rogarunt plebesque ioure*

scivit in foro . . . a.d. . . . Tribus . . . princi]pium

fuit, pro tribu Q. Fabius Q. f. primus scivit.

LAWS AND OTHER DOCUMENTS

treasury from the 15th March 109 B.C.; meanwhile neither *publicanus* nor purchaser is to pay in; if latter does, he is still liable to pay the *publicanus* (70–2). Purchaser may pay direct to people within a certain date. Sureties and securities required in default of payment within 120 days after sale (73); otherwise purchaser's land to be re-sold by *praetor urbanus* for ready money (74). Compensation (*a*) to seven loyal free towns (*see line* 79) and to free settlements of deserters from Carthage for land sold to Roman citizen (75–77); and (*b*) to *stipendiarii* (77–8). Except land given (as private) to a colonist, confirmed to seven free loyal towns (79–80), given to deserters, sold to Roman citizens publicly in Rome, assigned (as public) to *stipendiarii*, confirmed (as public held in usufruct) to Massinissa's sons (80); except also land (public) where Carthage once stood, and land (public held in usufruct) assigned to Utica (and other places? 81)—all land in Africa shall be allowed as before to *possessores*, subject to rents, tithes, and pasture-tax, except tenants freed by a law of G. Gracchus (82), *peregrini* and citizens paying equal dues (83). [*Misplaced in this law*: Purchasers defaulting in payment to *publicani* treble their debt and must give further securities (83–4).] Charges to conform to *locatio* of 115 B.C. (85–86), but *publicanus* may have to pay more to Rome (87); and must have no greater privileges than those granted by the *locatio* of 115 B.C. or its supplement of 113 B.C. (87–9). Public roads to remain unchanged (89–90). Claimant contrary to this law forfeits land to informer (90–91). Compensation to approved claimant if his land has been sold (91–92). Uncompensated possessor not liable to charges (92–93). Storage of crops and fruits paid as tithe? (94–95). III. *Corinthian land* (*the text is fragmentary*). To be measured out (97); and sold, with securities and sureties for the money (99–100). Judgement by praetor or propraetor (102).

. . . , tribunes of the plebs brought a bill duly before the plebs and the plebs duly voted in the forum on the . . . day of . . . ; the . . . tribe voted first; the first to vote in the name of his tribe was Quintus Fabius son of Quintus.

373

INSTRUMENTA

Quei ager poplicus populi Romanei in terram
Italiam P. Muucio L. Calpur[*nio cos. fuit, extra
eum agrum, quei ager ex lege pleibeive sc., quod C.
Sempronius T. f. tribunus plebei rogavit, exceptum*
² *cavitumve est nei divideretur . .* | . *quem quisque de
eo agro loco ex lege plebeive sc. vetus possesor
sibei a*]grum locum sumpsit reliquitve, quod non
modus maior siet, quam quantum unum hominem
ex lege plebeive sc. sibei sumer[*e relinquereve
licuit*;

    *quei ager puplicus populi Romanei in terra Italia
P. Muucio L. Calpurnio cos. fuit, extra eum agrum,
quei ager ex lege plebeieve sc., quod C. Sempronius
Ti. f. tr. pl. rogavit, exceptum cavitumve est nei*
³ *divideretur . .* | . *quem agrum locum*] quoieique de
eo agro loco ex lege plebeive sc. IIIvir sortito
ceivi Romano dedit adsignavit, quod non in eo
⁴ agro loco est, quod ultr[*a . .* | . ;

---

¹ This was government land, not land open to the public.
In the rest of this translation the word ' state ' is usually
omitted.   The accusative *terram* after *in*, without the idea
of motion towards, is doubtless an echo of a period when
distinction in the use of cases with *in* was not decided.

² in 133 B.C., the year of Tiberius Gracchus' tribunate.

³ consisting mostly of such *ager Campanus* as Gaius had
not allotted to one of his colonies.   He did plan to found a
colony on the *ager Campanus*, but it was not carried out.
Thus most of this *ager*, probably, was excepted.

⁴ Gracchus in 123 B.C. in re-enaction of his brother Tiberius'
law of 133 B.C.   ' Law or plebiscite ' is a mere formula since
both had equal force.

⁵ father of the two law-makers, Tiberius and Gaius Gracchus.

⁶ of public land before 133 B.C.   See above, pp. 171 ff.   Such
were liable to pay charges, often not exacted.

⁷ *sc.* 500 *iugera*, with 250 *iugera* more for each of two sons
(1000 *iugera* thus to be the maximum) allowed by the law of

LAWS AND OTHER DOCUMENTS

In regard to the public state-land [1] in the country [1] of Italy belonging to the Roman people in the consulship [2] of Publius Mucius and Lucius Calpurnius, not including the land [3] which, by a saving clause under the law or plebiscite introduced by Gaius Sempronius,[4] tribune of the plebs, son of Tiberius,[5] was excepted from division, . . . what- [2] ever land or ground any established occupier [6] took or kept for himself out of the said land or ground by law or plebiscite, provided that the measure be not greater than the amount [7] which one man was permitted to take or retain for himself by law or plebiscite [8];—

In regard to the public land in the country of Italy belonging to the Roman people in the consulship of Publius Mucius and Lucius Calpurnius, not including the land which, by a saving clause under the law or plebiscite introduced by Gaius Sempronius tribune of the plebs, son of Tiberius, was excepted from division, . . . whatever land or [3] ground a member of the Board of Three [9] has granted and assigned out of the said land or ground by law or plebiscite to any Roman citizen under allotment [10] provided that that it is not included in the said land or ground beyond . . .;— [4]

Tib. Gracchus in 133 B.C. *reliquit* ('kept,' 'retained'): the full force is 'left fallow' but still his own.

[8] The main clause of this long legal sentence begins below in line 7 of the law, with the words *ager . . . omnis quei supra scriptus est* . . . ' All land . . . which is recorded above . . .' pp. 378–9.

[9] that is a *triumvir agris iudicandis (dandis) assignandis* appointed under Tiberius Gracchus' law in 133 B.C.: cf. pp. 168 ff.   Carcopino, *Autour des Gracques,* 125 ff., 159 ff.

[10] *sc.* of the citizen to be a member of a colony in Italy; Gaius Gracchus in 123 and 122 planned several of these.

INSTRUMENTA

quei ager publicus populi Romanei in terra Italia P. Muucio L. Calpurnio cos. fuit, extra eum agrum, quei ager ex lege | plebeive scito, quod C. Sempronius Ti. f. tr. pl. rogavit, exceptum cavitumve est nei divideretur, de eo agro loco quei ager locus ei, quei agrum privatum in publicum commutavit, pro eo agro loco a IIIviro datus commutatus r]edditus est ;

quei ager publicus populi Romanei in terra Italia P. Muucio L. Calpurnio cos. fuit, ex[*t*]ra eum agrum, quei ager ex lege [*plebeive sc., quod C. Sempronius Ti. f. tr. pl. rogavit, exceptum cavi-*
5 *tumve est nei divideretur . . | . quod eius quis*]que agri locei publicei in terra Italia, quod eius extra urbem Roma*m* est, quod eius in urbe⟨*m*⟩ oppido vico est, quod eius IIIvir dedit adsignavit, quod
6 [*. . | . tum cum haec lex rogabitur habebit possidebitve*] ; . . .

quei ager publicus populi Romanei in terra Italia P. Muucio L. Calpurnio cos. fuit, extra eum agrum, quei ager ex] lege plebive scito, quod C. Sempronius Ti. f. tr. pl. rog., exceptum cavitumve est nei divideretur, quod quoieique de eo agro loco agri
7 locei aedific[*iei . . | . q*]uibu[*s . . . i*]n terra Italia IIIvir dedit adsignavit reliquit inve formas tabulasve retulit referive iusit :—

4 MNVCIO   5 ROMA   VRBEM

---

[1] *reddo* and *restituo* in this law are used constantly in the sense of ' confirming ' or ' leaving in possession ' property of which the title had been disputed.

[2] *sc.* through the said action of the triumvir.

376

LAWS AND OTHER DOCUMENTS

In regard to the public land in the country of Italy belonging to the Roman people in the consulship of Publius Mucius and Lucius Calpurnius, not including the land which, by a saving clause under the law or plebiscite introduced by Gaius Sempronius, tribune of the plebs, son of Tiberius, was excepted from division, . . . whatever land was granted given in exchange, or confirmed [1] by a member of the Board of Three out of the said land or ground to any person who[2] exchanged private land for public ;—

In regard to the public land in the country of Italy belonging to the Roman people in the consulship of Publius Mucius and Lucius Calpurnius, not including the land which, by a saving clause under [5] the law or plebiscite introduced by Gaius Sempronius, tribune of the plebs, son of Tiberius, was excepted from division, . . . whatever portion of the said public land or ground in the country of Italy which is outside the city of Rome or in a city town or village, and has been granted and assigned by a member of the Board of Three, and . . . shall be held and possessed by any person at the time when [6] this law shall be introduced . . .;—

In regard to the public land in the country of Italy belonging to the Roman people in the consulship of Publius Mucius and Lucius Calpurnius, not including the land which, by a saving clause under the law or plebiscite introduced by Gaius Sempronius, tribune of the plebs, son of Tiberius, was excepted from division, . . . whatever part of the said land ground or building . . . in the country of Italy a [7] member of the Board of Three has granted, assigned or left to any person or has entered or ordered to be entered in the plans and registers :—

ager locus aedificium omnis quei supra scriptu[*s est . . . extra eum agrum locum de quo supra*
8 *except*]um cavitu[*mve est, privatus esto . . | . eiusque locei agri aedificii emptio venditi*]o ita, utei ceterorum locorum agrorum aedificiorum privatorum est, esto; censorque queiquomque erit fa[*c*]ito, utei is ager locus aedificium, quei e[*x hace lege privatus factus est, ita, utei ceteri agri loca aedificia privati, in censum referatur . . . deque eo agro loco aed*]ificio eum, quoium [*is ager locus aedificium erit, eam profiterei iubeto, quae de cetereis*
9 *agreis | loceis aedificieis quoium eorum quisque est profiterei iusserit . . .*] est; neive quis facito, quo, quoius eum agrum locum aedificium possesionem ex lege plebeieve scit[*o ess*]e oportet oportebitve, eum agrum l[*ocum aedificium possesionem minus oetatur fruatur habeat possideatque . . . n*]eive
10 quis de ea re ad sen[*atum referto . . | . neive pro magistratu inper*]iove sententia[*m*] deicito neive ferto, quo quis eorum, quoium eum agrum locum aedificium posse[*sio*]nem ex lege plebeive scito esse oport[*et oportebitve . . . eum agrum locum aedificium possesionem minus oetatur fruatur habeat possid*]eatque quove possesio invito, mor[*iuove eo heredibus eius inviteis auferatur.*

10 SENTENTIA

---

[1] that is, shall *remain*, as before, private property, except the first class of land mentioned by this law, p. 374, namely ' occupied ' estates up to 500 *iugera*, now first made private.

[2] more literally ' in regard to the said matter.'

LAWS AND OTHER DOCUMENTS

All land ground or building which is recorded above . . . not including such land excepted by a saving clause as mentioned above, shall be [1] private . . ., and there shall be allowed right of purchase [8] and sale of the said ground land or building in the same way as for all other private grounds lands or buildings; and a censor in office at any time shall cause the said land ground or building, which has been made private, under this law, to be entered in the censor's assessment-lists in the same way as all other lands grounds or buildings . . . and in regard to the said land ground or building he shall order the person to whom the said land ground or building shall belong to make declaration of the same details as he shall have ordered, in regard to all other lands grounds or buildings, the several such persons who own the same to declare . . . and [9] no one shall so act as to prevent any person, to whom the said land ground building or property rightfully belongs or shall rightfully belong by law or plebiscite, from using enjoying holding and possessing the said land ground building or property . . . nor shall any person bring a motion before the Senate to that effect [2] . . . nor shall any person by virtue of a [10] magistracy or state authority express or bring forward a motion whereby any person of those to whom any said land ground building or holding rightfully belongs or shall rightfully belong by law or plebiscite . . . shall be prevented from using enjoying holding and possessing the said land ground building or holding; or whereby possession of the same shall be taken away against his will, if he be living, or, if he be deceased, against the will of his heirs.

379

Quei ager publicus populi Romanei in terram
11 *Italiam P. Muucio L. Calpurnio cos. fuit . . | . quod*
eius IIIvirei a. d. a. viasiei]s vicaneis, quei in terra
Italia sunt, dederunt adsignaverunt reliquerunt:
neiquis facito quo minus ei oetantur fruantur
habeant po[*ssideantque, quod eius possesor . . .*
agrum locum aedifici]um non abalienaverit, extra
12 eum[1] a[*grum . . | . extra*]que eum agrum, quem
ex h. l. venire dari reddive oportebit.

Quei ager locus aedificium ei, quem in [*vi*]asieis
vicanisve ex s. c. esse oportet oportebitve, [*ita*
datus adsignatus relictusve est eritve . . . quo magis
is ag]er locus aedificium privatus siet, quove
mag[*is censor, quei quomque erit, eum agrum locum*
13 *in censum referat . . | . quove magis is ager locus*
aliter, atque u]tei est, siet, ex h. l. n. r.

Quei ager locus publicus populi Romanei in
terra Italia P. Muucio L. Calpurnio cos. fuit,
extra eum agrum, quei ager ex lege plebive
[*scito, quod C. Sempronius Ti. f. trib. pl. rogavit,*
exceptum cavitumve est nei divideretur . . . e]x-
traque eum agrum, quem vetus possesor ex lege
plebeive [*scito sibei sumpsit reliquitve, quod non*
modus maior siet, quam quantum unum hominem

[1] EVM · EVM

---

[1] The *viasii* or *viarii* are otherwise unknown. Doubtless
their land had a frontage on some road which they probably
undertook to repair instead of paying rent.

In regard to the public land in the country of Italy belonging to the Roman people in the consulship of Publius Mucius and Lucius Calpurnius, that part **11** of the same which a member of the Board of Three for granting and assigning lands has granted assigned or left to village roadside-tenants [1] in the country of Italy, no one shall so act as to prevent the said persons from using enjoying holding and possessing the same, so far as the possessor of the same shall not have alienated the same, . . . to wit, land ground or building, not including that land . . . or that land which may rightfully be **12** sold given or confirmed under this law.

In regard to land ground or building which shall have been so given assigned or left to any person who rightfully belongs or shall rightfully belong by decree of the Senate to the category of village roadside-tenants . . . it is not intended by this law that such land ground or building be private land or that a censor in office at any time enter the said land or ground in the assessment-lists . . . or that **13** the status of the said land or ground be other than it is at present.

In regard to the public land in the country of Italy belonging to the Roman people in the consulship of Publius Mucius and Lucius Calpurnius, not including the land which, by a saving clause under the law or plebiscite introduced by Gaius Sempronius Gracchus, tribune of the plebs, son of Tiberius, was excepted from division, . . . and not including the land which an established occupier took or retained for himself by law or plebiscite, provided that the measure be not greater than the amount which any one man was permitted to take or

sibei sumere relinquereve licuit, sei quis tum cum
14 *haec lex rogabitur | agri colendi cau*]sa in eum agrum
agri iugra non amplius XXX possidebit habebitve :
[*i*]s ager privatus esto.

Quei in agrum compascuom pequdes maiores
non plux X pascet, quae[*que ex eis minus annum*
gnatae erunt postea quam gnatae erunt . . . queique
ibei pequdes minores non plus . . .] pascet, quaeque
ex eis minus annum gnatae erunt post ea qua[*m*
15 *gnatae erunt : is pro iis pequdibus .* | *. . . populo aut*
publicano vectigal scripturamque nei debeto neive
de ea re sati]s dato neive solvito.

Ager publicus populi Romanei, que in Italia P.
Mucio L. Calpurnio cos. fuit, eius agri IIIvir
a. d. a. ex lege plebeive scito sortito quoi ceivi
Roma[*no agrum dedit adsignavit . . . quod eius*
agri neque is abalie]navit abalienaveritve, neque
heres eius abalienavit abalienav[*eritve quoive ab*
eo hereditate testamento deditioneve obvenit queive
16 *ab eorum quo emit,* | *quei eorum de ea re ante eidus*
Martias primas in ious adierit ad eum, quem ex h. l.
de eo agro ius deicere oportebit, is de ea re ita ius

---

[1] *sc.* since 133 when Tiberius Gracchus' law divided
reclaimed land into allotments of not more than 30 *iugera*
(about 20 acres) each. This sentence of the present law
recognises occupation of public land by *possessores* since 133,
but limits the area to not more than 30 *iugera* and enforces
cultivation.

[2] See the decision of the Minucii, p. 268, note 3.

[3] or: ' make any due return.'

[4] *sc.* of the said Roman citizen to be a member of a new
colony.

[5] the first day of a new financial year.

[6] for the competent magistrates see below.

retain for himself, if any person, at any time when this law shall be introduced, shall have entered on [1] the said land for the purpose of tillage and shall [14] possess or hold not more than 30 Roman acres of the same, such holding shall be private land.

Any person who shall send to pasture on associated pasture land [2] not more than 10 head of larger cattle and any of their young which shall be less than one year old from birth . . . or who shall send to pasture thereon not more than . . . head of smaller cattle and any of their young which shall be less than one year old from birth, the said person shall not be [15] bound to pay to people or tax-farmer impost or pasture-tax for the said cattle, nor shall he be required to give satisfaction [3] or make payment in regard to the said matter.

In regard to the public land in the country of Italy belonging to the Roman people in the consulship of Publius Mucius and Lucius Calpurnius, any Roman citizen to whom has been assigned by a member of the Board of Three for granting and assigning lands, under allotment [4] by law or plebiscite, any part of the said land . . . provided that the said person has not or shall not have alienated the said land, and that neither his heir has or shall have alienated the same nor anyone to whom the same has fallen by intestate inheritance or will and testament or surrender from him, nor anyone who has purchased same from any of the said persons, should any such person, before the fifteenth [5] day [16] of March next, have come to court in regard to the said matter, before him [6] who by this law shall be rightfully empowered to have jurisdiction concerning the said land, the said official shall so deliver

deicito d]ecernitoque, utei possesionem secund*um*
eum heredemve eius det, quoi sorti is ager datus
adsignatusve fuerit, quod eius agri non abaliena-
tum erit ita utei s. s. est.

[*Ager publicus populi Romanei quei in Italia P.
Mucio L. Calpurnio cos. fuit, quod eius agri IIIvir
a. d. a. veteri possesori prove ve*]tere possesionem
dedit adsignavit reddidit, quodque eius agri
III[*vir a. d. a. in urbe oppido vico dedit adsignavit*
17 *reddidit,* | *quod eius agri neque is abalienavit abaliena-
veritve neque heres eius, quoive ab eo hereditate
testamento deditioneve obveni*]t, queive ab eorum quo
emit: quei eorum de ea re ante eidus Martias
primas in ious adierit ad eum, quem ex h. l. de
eo agro ius deicere oportebit, is de ea re ita ius
deicito d[*ecernitoque, utei possesionem secundum
eum heredemve eius det . . .*] quoi is ager vetere
prove vetere possesore datus adsignatusve *redditusve fuerit,* queive a[*grum in urbe oppido vico*
18 *acceperit . .* | .

16]ECRRNITO   SECVNDO
17 QVEI *pro* quo

1 see n. 10, p. 375 above.

jurisdiction on the said matter and shall so decree that he grant legal possession in favour of the claimant, or his heir, to whom the said land shall have been given or assigned by lot,[1] provided that the said land shall not have been alienated as recorded above.

In regard to the public land in the country of Italy belonging to the Roman people in the consulship of Publius Mucius and Lucius Calpurnius, should any established occupier, or person recognised as such, to whom a member of the Board of Three for granting and assigning lands has granted assigned or restored legal possession of any part of the said land, or a member of the Board of Three for granting and assigning lands has granted assigned or restored any part of the said land in the city or in a town or a village, provided that the said person has [17] not or shall not have alienated the said land, and that neither his heir has or shall have alienated the same nor anyone to whom same has fallen by intestate inheritance or will and testament or surrender from him, nor anyone who has purchased same from any of said persons—should any such person, before the fifteenth day of March next, have come to court, in regard to the said matter, before him who by this law shall be rightfully empowered to have jurisdiction concerning the said land, the said official shall so deliver jurisdiction on the said matter and shall so decree that he grant legal possession in favour of the claimant, or his heir . . . to whom, as original possessor or person recognised as such, the said land shall have been given and assigned or confirmed, or a person who shall have received such land in the city or in a town or a village. . . . [18]

*Sei quis eorum, quorum age]*r s. s. est, ex possesione vi eiectus est, quod eius is quei eiectus est possederit, quod neque vi neque clam neque precario possederit ab eo, quei eum ea possesione vi eiec[*erit : quem ex h. l. de ea re ious deicere oportebit, sei is quei ita eiectus est, ad eum de ea re in ious adierit ante eidus Mar*]tias, quae post h. l. rog. primae erunt, facito, utei is, quei ita vi eiectus e[*st in eam possesionem unde vi eiectus est, restituatur.* |

19 *Quei ager locus aedificium publicus populi Romani in terra Italia P. Muucio L. Calpurnio cos. fuit, quod eius ex lege plebeive sci*]to exve h. l. privatum factum est eritve, pro eo agro loco aedificio proque scriptura pecoris, quod in eo agro pascitur, post quam vectigalia constituerint, quae post h. l. [*rogatam primum constiterint : nei quis mag. prove mag. . . . facito, quo quis populo aut p*]ublicano pequnia[*m*] scripturam vectigalve det dareve **20** debeat, neive quis [*facito . . | .*] quove quid ob eam rem populo aut publicano detur exsigaturve, neive quis quid postea quam [*vect*]igalia consistent, quae post h. l. rog. primum constiterint,

---

¹ The proper place for this clause is in the first part of the law where the kinds of land made private were dealt with. Yet its postponement does not look like an oversight, at least of the inscriber, since the clause did not begin, it seems, in quite the same way as the opening sections of the law.

In the event of any person, of those to whom land as recorded above belongs, being forcibly ejected from possession, provided that the person who is ejected shall be in possession of such land, and that he shall not have taken possession of the same by force or stealth or on sufferance from the person who shall have forcibly ejected him from such possession,—in the event of such a person who has been so ejected coming to court, in regard to the said matter, before the fifteenth day of March next after this law shall be introduced, before him who by this law shall be rightfully empowered to have jurisdiction on the said matter, the said official shall cause the person who has been thus forcibly ejected to be restored to that possession from which he was forcibly ejected.

In [1] regard to the public land ground or building [19] in the country of Italy belonging to the Roman people in the consulship of Publius Mucius and Lucius Calpurnius, with respect to any part of it which has or will have been made private by law or plebiscite or under this law, no magistrate or pro-magistrate shall, from the time when imposts shall have fallen due which shall have first fallen due after the introduction of this law . . . ., cause any person to give or be bound to give to people or tax-farmer any money or impost for the said land or ground or building, or pasture-tax in regard to cattle which are pastured on the said land, nor shall anyone cause . . . any sum to be exacted or given for that reason [20] to people or tax-farmer, nor shall any person, from the time when imposts shall fall due which shall have first fallen due after the introduction of this law be bound to give anything as payment on behalf

ob eos ag[*ros locos aedificia populo aut publicano
dare debeat neive scripturam pecoris, quod in eis
ag*]reis pascetur, populo aut publicano dare
debeat.

Ager locus publicus popul[*i Romanei, quei in*
21 *terra Italia P. Muucio, L. Calpurnio cos. fuit, .* | . .
*extra eum agrum, quem agrum L. Caecilius Cn.
Domitius cens.*] a. d. XI k. Octobris oina quom
agro, quei trans Curione est, locaverunt, quei in
eo agro loc[*o civis*] Romanus sociumve nominisve
Latini, quibus ex formula togatorum [*milites in
terra Italia inperare solent, . . . agrum lo*]cum
publicum populi Romanei de sua possesione vetus
possesor prove vetere possesor[*e dedit, quo in agro
loco oppidum coloniave ex lege plebeive scito con-
22 stitueretur deduceretur conlocaretur, . .* | . *quo in agro
loco IIIvir i*]d oppidum coloniamve ex lege
plebeive sc. constituit deduxitve conlocavitve:
quem agrum [*locum*]ve pro eo agro locove de eo
agro loco, quei publicus populi Roman[*ei in terram
Italiam P. Muucio L. Calpurnio cos. fuit . . . extra
eum a*]grum locum, quei ager locus ex lege
plebeive sc., quod C. Semproni. Ti. f. tr. pl. rog.
23 exscep[*tum cavitumve est nei divideretur, . .* | .
IIIvir dedit reddidit adsignavit, eius quoi is ager

21 XE · K   22 PRO · EO · AGRO · LOCVMVE

---

1 in 115 B.C.
2 What this land was is unknown. *Curione = Curionem ?*
3 This seems to mean military register or census of all non-Roman subjects in Italy.

of the said lands grounds or buildings to people or
tax-farmer, nor be bound to pay to people or tax-
farmer any pasture-tax in regard to cattle which shall
be pastured on the said lands.

In regard to the public land in the country of
Italy belonging to the Roman people in the consulship of Publius Mucius and Lucius Calpurnius
. . . not including the land which the censors [1] [21]
Lucius Caecilius and Gnaeus Domitius let on lease
on the 20th of September together with the land
beyond Curio,[2] with respect to any Roman citizen
on the said land or ground, or member of the allies
or of the Latin name, from whom the government
is accustomed to requisition soldiers in the country
of Italy according to the Roll of Gowned Men,[3]
. . . . . . who as an established occupier, or person
recognised as such, has given up out of his
possession public land or ground belonging to the
Roman people, in order that on the said land or
ground a town or colony might by law or plebiscite
be established conducted and placed, . . . and in [22]
which land or ground a member of a Board of
Three has by law or plebiscite established, conducted, or placed such town or colony ; and in regard
to any land or ground which, in place of the said
land or ground, a member of a Board of Three
has granted restored or assigned out of the said
land or ground in the country of Italy belonging
to the Roman people in the consulship of Publius
Mucius and Lucius Calpurnius, . . . not including
that land or ground, which, by a saving clause under
the law or plebiscite introduced by Gaius Sempronius, tribune of the plebs, son of Tiberius, was
excepted from division,—the said land shall be the [23]

datus redditus adsignatus erit] quoive ab eo heredive eius is ager locus testamento hereditati deditionive obvenit obveneritv[*e queive ab eo emit e*]meritve, queive ab emptore eius emit emeritve, is ager privatus esto.

Que[*i ager publicus populi Romani fuit, quem IIIvir de eo agro loco pro eo agro loco, qu*]o coloniam deduxsit ita utei s. s. est, agrum locum aedificium dedit reddidit adsignavit, quei [*pr. consolve de eo*

24 *agro ex h. l. ious deicet,* | *quo de eo agro ante eidus Martias primas in ious aditum erit, is de ea re ita ious deicito decernitoque, utei possesionem secundum eum h*]eredemve eius det, quoi IIIvir eum agrum locum pro eo agro loco, quo coloniam deduxit, dedit [*reddidi*]t adsignavitve; facitoque is pr. consolve, quo de ea re in ious aditu*m* er[*it, utei . . .*

Ager locus quei sup]ra screiptus est, quod eius agrei locei post *h.* l. rog. publicum populei Romanei erit, extra eum ag[*rum locum, quei publico usui destinatus est vel publice locatus est, in eo*

private property of the person to whom the said land shall have been given restored or assigned, or of the person to whom such land or ground has or shall have fallen by will and testament, by intestate inheritance, or by surrender by the aforesaid or by his heir, or of the person who has or shall have bought the same from him, or of the person who has or shall have bought the same from the buyer thereof.

In regard to the public land belonging to the Roman people, to wit such land ground or building which a member of the Board of Three has granted confirmed or assigned out of the said land or ground in exchange for any land or ground to which he has conducted a colony as above recorded, the praetor or consul who shall have jurisdiction concerning such land under this law, before whom there shall [24] have been an appeal to court concerning the said land before the fifteenth of March next, the same shall so deliver jurisdiction on the said matter and shall so decree that he grant legal possession in favour of the person, or his heir, to whom a member of the Board of Three has granted confirmed or assigned the said land or ground in exchange for any land or ground to which he has conducted a colony; and the said praetor or consul before whom there shall have been an appeal to court on the said matter, shall cause . . .

In regard to land or ground as above recorded, to wit any part of the said land or ground which shall be public land belonging to the Roman people after the introduction of this law, not including that land or ground which has been reserved for public use or has been leased out by public sanction, anyone who shall be so minded may pasture cattle

²⁵ *agro quei volet pascito . | . .]* neive is ager com-
pascuos esto, neive quis in eo agro agrum oqupa-
tum habeto neive defendito, quo mi[*nus quei
v*]elit compascere liceat. Sei quis faxsit, quotiens
faxit, in agri iugra singula L[*HS n. . . . dar*]e
debeto ei, quei quomque id publicum fruendum
redemptum comductumve habebit.

²⁶   Boves, equ[*os, mulos, asinos . . | . in eo agro loco,
quei post h. l. rog. publicus populi Romanei erit,
pascere ad eum numerum pecudum, que*]i numerus
pecudum in h. l. scriptus est, liceto, neive quid
quoi ob eam rem vectigal neive sc[*ripturam dare
de*]beto.

Quod quisque pecudes in calleis viasve publicas
itineris causa indu[*xerit ibeique paverit . . . pro
eo pecore, quod eius in calli*]bus vieisve publiceis
pastum inpulsum itineris causa erit, neiquid populo
²⁷ [*n*]eive publicano d[*are debeto . | . .*

Quei ager publicus populi Rom. in terra Italia P.
Muucio L. Calpurnio cos. fuit, de eo agro loco quem
agrum locum populus ex publico in privatum c*]ommu-
tavit, quo pro agro loco ex privato in publicum
tantum modum agri locei commutav[*it : is ager
locus do*]mneis privatus ita, utei quoi optuma lege
privatus est, esto.

²⁵ OOVPATVM
²⁶ VIEILꟼE (*pro* vieisve) . . . POPVLO ΛEIVE

---

¹ See note 3 on p. 268. *defendere* below means 'lay claim to.'
² *compascere* is here used of grazing cattle on common
pasture-land, not of grazing cattle on *ager compascuus*; cf.
line 14 of this law and note 3 on p. 268.
³ that is, public state-land.

on the said land, . . . nor shall the said land be [25]
associated [1] pasture-land, nor shall any person
occupy hold or fence off land within the said land
so as to prevent any person who shall be so minded
to enjoy common [2] pasture as legally permitted
thereon. Should anyone so act, he shall be bound
to pay, as often as he shall have so acted, 50 sesterces in money *per* Roman acre of land concerned
to whatever person shall hold the usufruct of the
said public property or the rights of purchasing
or renting of imposts on the same.

It shall be legally permitted, on that land or [26]
ground which shall be public land belonging to the
Roman people after the introduction of this law,
to pasture oxen, horses, mules, or asses . . . up to
that number of beasts which is prescribed in this
law, nor shall any person be bound to pay any rent
or pasture-tax to anyone for the said purpose.

Any person who shall have driven beasts on to
public footpaths or roads on purposes of travel
and shall have pastured them there, shall not be
bound to pay anything to people or tax-farmer for
any such flock or herd which shall have been let loose
or pastured on public paths or roads on travel. . . . [27]

In regard to the public land in the country of Italy
belonging to the Roman people in the consulship
of Publius Mucius and Lucius Calpurnius, any land
or ground, out of such land or ground, which the
people shall have made private by exchange from
public,[3] and has for the said land or ground received
an equal measure of land in exchange from private
to public, such land or ground shall be private land
of the owners according to the fullest legal title to
private land belonging to any owner.

393

Quei ager ex priva[*to in publicum commutatus est, quo pro agro tantus modus agri publici ex p*]ublico imprivatum commutatus est: de eo agro siremps lex esto, quansei is ager P. Mucio L. C[*alpurnio cos. publicus fuisset.*

Quei ager patritus ex privato in publicum commutatus est, . | . . pr. consolve quanti agri patriti [28] *publicani publicum L. Caecilio Cn. Dom*]itio cens. redemptum habe[*n*]t, censoribus, quei quomque post hac facteis erunt, ei faciu[*nto id publicum, sei*] volent, tantidem pro patrito redemptum habeant p. p. supsignent.

IIvirum, qu[*ei . . . quae viae publicae p*]er terram Italiam P. Mucio L. Calpurnio cos. fuerint, eas faciunto pateant vacuaeque [29] sien[*t . | . .*

Quod quoieique ex h. l. i]ta utei s. s. est, in agreis, qu[*ei in Ita*]lia sunt, quei P. Mucio L. Calpurnio cos. publiceis populi Ro[*manei fuerunt, ceivi*] Romano facere licebit, item Latino peregrinoque,

[28] EVERINT EACIVNTO

---

[1] by purchase by the State.

[2] It is not certain how this clause began (*Quei ager patritus ex privato in publicum* . . . Hardy, whom I follow) but it refers to safeguarding the government in cases of exchange of land by the government with an owner whose land was *ager patritus,* that is to say land inherited from a father.

LAWS AND OTHER DOCUMENTS

In regard to land which has been made public
state-land by exchange [1] from private, and for which
said land an equal measure of land has been given in
exchange from public to private, the law shall hold
good with respect to the said land exactly as if the
said land had been public in the consulship of Publius
Mucius and Lucius Calpurnius.

In [2] regard to paternal land which has been made
public by exchange from private . . . a praetor or [28]
consul shall see to it that the tax-farmers, according
to the amount for which they hold a contract for
state rent-charge with respect to such paternal land
made in the censorship of Lucius Caecilius and Gnaeus
Domitius, hold the contract for rent-charge with
respect to such paternal land for the same amount
if they shall be so minded under any censors who shall
be in office hereafter, and that they register [3] the
said land under the category of paternal land.

A member of the Board of Two,[4] who . . . roads
which shall have been public throughout Italy in the
consulship of Publius Mucius and Lucius Calpurnius,
the same they shall cause to lie open and clear. . . . [29]

In regard to any act which shall be rightfully
permitted, under this law as above recorded, to a
Roman citizen to perform on lands which, within
the country of Italy, were public lands belonging to
the Roman people in the consulship of Publius
Mucius and Lucius Calpurnius, and likewise to a
Latin or other non-citizen to whom such act was

[3] *sc.* in the *aerarium* or treasury. *p. p.* = *pro patrito*
(*pro praede* Huschke).

[4] for keeping clear roads outside the city of Rome or the
district within 1000 paces from the walls, which counted as
part of the city :—*vieis extra propiusve urbem Romam passus m.
purgandeis*—*Lex. Iul. Mun.*, 50.

quibus M. Livio L. Calpurnio [*cos. in eis agris id
facere . . . ex lege pleb*]eive sc. exve foedere
licuit, sed fraude sua facere liceto.

Quod ex h. l. ita, utei s. s. est, in agreis, que[*i
s. s. sunt, Latinum peregrinumque facere vel non
30 facere oportebit . | . . . sei eorum*] quis qu[*od eum
ex h. l. f*]acere oportuerit, non fecerit, quodve
quis eorum [*h. l. prohibitus erit, fecerit : mag.*]
prove mag., quo de ea re in ious aditum erit,
quod ex h. l. petetur, item iudicium iudi[*cem
recuperatoresve ei, quei ex h. l. petet, et in eum facito
ita det utei ei*] et in eum iudicium iudicem recuperatoresve ex h. l. dare oporteret, sei quis de ea re
iudiciu[*m petisset, quod civem Romanum contra h. l.
31 fecisse diceret. . | . .*]

Sei quei colonieis seive moi]nicipieis seive quae
pro moinicipieis colo[*nieisve sunt civium Rom.*]
nominisve Latini poplice deve senati sententia
ager fruendus datus [*est, seive quei in trientabuleis
est : quei colonei moinicipesve prove moinicipieis . . .*

29 EOEDERE . . . ERAVDE . . . EACERE

---

[1] in 112 B.C. The wording of this law separated *Latini*
from *peregrini ;* but *Latini,* being non-citizens, were part of
the *peregrini.* We do not know what rights these got in 112.

[2] For these, see p. 296.

[3] The distinction is not clear, but possibly *pro colonieis*
means the old Latin colonies and *pro moenicipieis* all other
towns with Latin rights; cf. Hardy, *op. cit.,* 65–6. See also
pp. xxxvi–xxxvii.

[4] This land had been given to the heirs or descendants of
persons who had lent money to Rome during the second Punic
War (218–201 B.C.); it paid a nominal rent to the state.
Trientabulum (in translating which I coin the word ' tierce-
ment ') was land given to such lenders, in lieu of a third part

rightfully permitted on the said lands in the consul-ship [1] of Marcus Livius and Lucius Calpurnius . . . by law or plebiscite or by treaty, such person may rightfully perform such act without liability to personal penalty.

In regard to any act which, under this law as above recorded, a Latin or other non-citizen shall or shall [30] not rightfully perform on the said lands which are recorded above . . . if any of the said persons shall not have performed an act which he should rightfully have performed under this law, or shall have per-formed an act from which he shall have been prohibited by this law, the magistrate or pro-magistrate, before whom an approach shall have been made to court on the said matter in a summons made under this law, shall see to it that he grant, to the person who shall bring such summons under this law, a trial and a judge or special adjudicators,[2] and against the said offender in the same manner as he would be required under this law to grant to such plaintiff and against such offender a trial and a judge or special adjudicators if any person had demanded a trial in regard to the said matter, on the ground that, as alleged by him, a Roman citizen had acted against this law. . . .

In regard to land which has been given for usufruct, [31] by public will or by a decree of the Senate, to colonies or boroughs or [3] places recognised as colonies or boroughs, inhabited by Roman citizens or by members of the Latin name, or land which lies mortgaged among the tiercements [4]; and in regard to colonists or inhabitants of boroughs or places recognised as

of the state debt to them, when money was wanting with which to pay the second instalment. Livy, xxxi, 13, 9.

fruentur, queiv]e pro colonia moincipiove prove
moinicipieis fruentur quei*ve* in trientabule[*is*
³² *fruentur . | . . quod eius agri colonei moinicipesve*
prove moinicipieis habebunt queive a colonia moinici-
piove prove moinicipieis habebunt quodve eius agri
eis in trientabuleis testamento hereditate deditione
ob]venit obveneritve, quibus ante h. [*l. rog. eum*
agrum locum con]ductum habere frui possidere
defendere licuit, extra eum agrum locu[*m, quem*
ex h. l. . . . venire dari reddi]ve oportebit, id,
utei quicquid quoieique ante h. l. r. licuit, ita ei
habere o[*eti frui possidere defendere post h. l.*
³³ *rog. liceto . | . .*]

Quei ager locus publicus p[*opuli Romanei in*
te]rra Italia P. Mucio L. Calpurnio cos. fuit, quod
eius agri loci ex l[*eg*]e [*plebeive scito exve h. l.*
privatum factum est, ante eidus Martias primas sei
qu]id de eo agro loco ambigetur, cos. pr. quei
quomque erit, de ea re iuris[*dictio, iudici iudicis*
³⁴ *recuperatorum datio esto . | . . neive mag. prove*
magistratu de eo agro loco ious deicito neive de eo
agro dec]ernito neive iudicium n[*eive iudicem neive*

---

[1] that is, lay claim to.

boroughs who shall hold usufruct . . . or who shall hold such usufruct on behalf of a colony or borough or place recognised as a borough, or among tierce-ments . . .;—any such land that colonists or members of boroughs, or of places recognised as boroughs [32] shall hold, or persons deriving their holding from a colony or borough or places recognised as boroughs, and any such land that has or shall have fallen to the said persons among the tiercements or by will and testament or by intestate inheritance or by surrender, the same being such persons as have been legally permitted to hold on lease enjoy, possess or fence off[1] the said land or ground before the introduction of this law, not including such land or ground as shall rightly be sold, given or restored under this law . . .: it shall be permitted to any of the said persons to hold use enjoy possess or fence off any such land after the introduction of this law on the same terms as was permitted to any such person before the introduction of this law. . . . [33]

In regard to the public land or ground in the country of Italy belonging to the Roman people in the consulship of Publius Mucius and Lucius Calpurnius, to wit any part of the said land or ground which has been made private by law or plebiscite or by this law, if there shall be any dispute about such land or site before the fifteenth day of March next, the duty of jurisdiction on the said matter and the granting of a court and a judge or special adjudicators shall rest with a consul or praetor whoever shall then be in office, . . . and no magis- [34] trate or pro-magistrate except a consul or a praetor shall deliver jurisdiction on the said land or ground or issue a decree on the said land or grant a court

399

r]ecuperatores dato, nisei cos. pr.ve. Quod
vadimonium eius rei c[*ausa promissum erit, mag.
adpellati quo minus eius r*]ei causa decernant, eius
h. l. n. r.   Quod iudicium iudex recuperator[*es
dati erunt sei magistratus adpellati erunt, quoi
eorum e re publica non esse videbitur, quo minus id
impediat vel intercedat, eius h. l. n. r.* |

35   *Quei ager locus post h. l. rog. publicus p. R. in
terra Italia erit, sei quid de eo agro loco ambigetur,*]
cos. pr. cens. quei quom[*que tum erit, de ea re iu*]ris
dictio, iudici iudicis recuperatorum datio esto
i. u. e. e r. p. f. s. [*v. e.* . . . *neive mag. prove mag.
nisei cos. pr. cens. de e*]o agro loco ious deicito
neive de [*eo agro de*]cernito neive iudicium [*neive
iudicem neive recuperatores dato.   Quod vadimonium
eius rei causa promissum erit, mag. adpellati, quo*
36 *minus eius rei causa decernant, e. h. l. n. r.* | *Quod
iudicium iudex recuperatores dati erunt, sei mag.*

---

[1] that is, magistrates who have been appealed to against
bail demanded by a consul or praetor. *Appellatio* means
appeal to a magistrate, *provocatio* means appeal from a
magistrate to the people.

[2] These magistrates (and, in Italian districts, pro-consuls
and pro-praetors) had *imperium.*

or a judge or special adjudicators. In regard to any bail which shall have been promised on account of the said matter, it is not intended under this law that magistrates [1] who have been appealed to should be prevented from issuing a decree on account of the said matter. Whatever court or judge or special adjudicators shall have been granted, in cases where magistrates shall have been appealed to it is not intended under this law to prevent any of the said magistrates from hindering or obstructing the matter by veto if the same shall not appear to him to be advantageous to the commonwealth.

In regard to the public land or ground in the [35] country of Italy which shall belong to the Roman people after the introduction of this law, if there shall be any dispute about such land or ground, the duty of jurisdiction on the said matter and the granting of a court or a judge or special adjudicators shall rest with a consul praetor or censor [2] whoever shall be then in office, according as shall appear to him to be consistent with the commonwealth's advantage and their own good faith . . . and no magistrate or pro-magistrate except a consul praetor or censor shall deliver jurisdiction concerning the said land or ground or issue a decree concerning the said land or grant a court or a judge or special adjudicators. In regard to any bail which shall have been promised on behalf of the said matter, it is not intended under this law that magistrates who have been appealed to should be prevented from issuing a decree on behalf of the said matter. Whatever court or judge or special [36] adjudicators shall have been granted, in cases where magistrates shall have been appealed to it is not

adpellati erunt, quoi eorum id e r. p.] non esse videbitur, quo [*minus impediat ve*]l intercedat, e. h.
l. n. r.

Quoi publicano e h. l. pequnia debebitu[*r,
nei quis mag. . . . quid ob eam re*]m facito, quo
quis pro agro minus aliterve scripturam v[*ecti-*
37 *galve det, atque utei ex h. l. dare debet debebitve. .* | *. .
Sei quid publicanus eius rei causa sibi deberi*] darive
oportere de[*icat, de ea re cos. prove co*]s. pr. prove
pr., quo in ious adierint, in diebus X proxsumeis,
qu[*ibus de ea re in ious aditum erit, . . . recuperatores ex ci*]vibus L, quei classis primae sient,
XI dato; inde alternos du[*m taxat quaternos is
quei petet et is unde petetur, quos volent reiciant*
38 *facito .* | *. . quei supererunt tres pluresve, eos primo
quoque die de ea re iudicare iubeto,*] quae res soluta
n[*on siet inve iudici*]o non siet iudicatave non siet,
quod eius praevaricationus [*causa . . . vel per
dolum malum petitorum patronorum*]ve factum non
siet. Sei maior pars eorum recuperatoru[*m . . .*]m |
39 id sententia [*pronontiato, quod eius*] rei ioudicandae
maxsume verum esse comperrit, facitoqu[*e . . .*

³⁹ COMMPERRIT

---

[1] whose income equalled or exceeded 100,000 *asses*.
[2] For this, see above, p. 318.   ' Wrongful intent ' by plaintiff
may allude to *tergiversatio*, improper abandonment of prosecution.

intended under this law to prevent any of the said
magistrates from hindering or obstructing the matter
by veto if the same shall not appear to him to be
advantageous to the commonwealth.

In regard to money which shall be owed under
this law to a tax-farmer, no magistrate . . . shall
so act on account of the said matter that any person
shall pay a less sum by way of pasture-tax or other
impost on land or pay the same otherwise than he is
or shall be bound to pay under this law. . . . Should [37]
a tax-farmer allege that any sum is owed or due to
be paid to him on behalf of such matter, the consul
or pro-consul or praetor or pro-praetor, before whom
appeal shall have been made to court, shall, within
the 10 days next after the appeal to court on the
said matter shall have been made. . . . grant in
regard to the said matter 11 special adjudicators,
from a list of 50 citizens who belong to the first
class [1]; from these he shall cause the person who
shall be the plaintiff and the person who shall be the
defendant, each in turn, to reject whomever they
wish, not exceeding four judges each. . . . those [38]
who shall remain, three or more, he shall order to
give a decision on the earliest possible day in
regard to such matter, when the matter has not been
settled by payment or is not still before a court or
has not yet been decided by verdict, provided that
such action has not been taken by way of collusion [2]
or through wrongful intent on the part of the plaintiff
or his pleaders. If a majority of the said special
adjudicators . . . he shall in his sentence make such [39]
pronouncement as he has found most consistent with
the truth in the matter under adjudication, and in
regard to the matter which shall have been so

quod ita ioudicatum e]rit se dolo malo utei is, quei
40 iudicatus erit dare opor[*tere, solvat . .* | .

*Quas in leges pl.ve sc. de ea re, quod, quei agrum
publicum p. R. ita habebit possidebit fruetur, utei ex
h. l. licebit, eum earum q*]uae ag[*rum, quem ita habebit, h*]abere possidere frui vetet ; quasve in leges
pl.ve sc. de ea r[*e quod earum quae ei, quei agrum
publicum p. R. aliter habebit*] possidebit fruetur,
quam ex h. l. licebit, eum agrum, quem [*ita
habebit, habere possidere frui permittat, is, quei
earum legum pl.ve sc. quo iurare iubetur iubebitur, non
41 iuraverit : ei poena multa remissa esto .* | *. . neive
ei ob eam rem mag. q*]uem minus petere capere
gerere habereque liceto, neive q[*uid ei ea res fraudi
esto . . .*]

Si quae lex plebeve sc. est, quae mag., quem ex
h. l. [*de aliqua re decernere oportet, de ea re decernere vetet, is magistratus de ea re nihilo minus decer-
42 nito .* | *. . quaeque eis legibus plebive scitis facere quis
prohibetur, quod quem eorum haec lex facere iubebit,
ea omnia ei sed f*]raude sua facere liceto, inque eas
leges pl.ve sc. de ea re, quod ex[*h. l. . . . non*

adjudged shall cause the person who shall have been condemned to pay, to do so without wrongful intent. . . .

In regard to any laws or plebiscites containing any [40] provision which, in the case of any persons who shall hold possess and enjoy, on the terms which shall be permitted by this law, public land belonging to the Roman people, shall forbid such persons to hold, possess and enjoy such land as he shall hold on the said terms;—or any laws or plebiscites containing any provision which shall permit any person to hold possess and enjoy such land of the Roman people, as he shall hold on the said terms, otherwise than shall be allowed by this law: if the person who, when he is or shall be ordered to swear any oath to the said laws or plebiscites, shall have refused to swear, in his case the penalty or fine shall be deemed to be remitted . . . nor shall he be forbidden on [41] account of such act to seek, take, exercise and hold any magistracy, nor shall such act cause him to be liable to personal penalty.

If there is any law or plebiscite which forbids any magistrate, whose duty it shall be under this law to issue a decree on some matter, to issue a decree on the said matter, the said magistrate shall none the less issue such decree on the said matter . . . and [42] whatever acts any person is prohibited from performing by the said laws or plebiscites, the same being acts which this law shall order any person to perform, it shall be legally permitted to him to perform all the said acts without liability to personal penalty, and to the said laws or plebiscites he may, without personal penalty, refuse to swear an oath on any point in regard to which, under this law, . . . it

decernere aliterve] decernere oportebit, sed fraude
sua nei iurato, neive [*ei ea res fraudi multae poe-*
43 *naeve esto .* | . .

. . .]tus est, dedit adsignavitve, quemve agrum
locum de eo agro lo[*co . . . ex lege*] pl.ve sc.,
quod M. Baebius tr. pl. IIIvir coloni*ae* dedu-
44 cend[*ae rogavit .* | . . *datu*]m adsignatum esse
fuiseve ioudicaverit, utei in h. l. sc. est, quei l. . . .
extra eum agrum locum, quei ager locus in ea
45 cen[*turia supsicivove .* | . . *extraque*] eum agrum
locum, quem ex h. l. colonei eive quei in colonei
numero [*scriptei sunt obtinebunt . . . oportet*] oportebitve, quod eius agri locei quoieique emptum
46 est, [.| . . *neive magis m*]anceps praevides prae-
diaque soluti sunto : eaque nomina mancup[*um*
. . . *quaestor,*] quei aerarium provinciam optine-
47 bit in tableis [*publiceis scripta habeto .* | . . *nei
qui d*]e mag. Romano emit, is pro eo agro loco
pequnia*m* neive praevides nei[*ve praedia populo
dato . . . neive de ea re quis ob eam*] rem, quod

47 PEQVNIA

---

[1] It is uncertain whether this very imperfect clause should
be classed with the section on Africa (see below) or not.
Mommsen believed that it referred to the colony at Sipontum,
founded in 194 B.C. by M. Baebius Tamphilus who was one of
the *triumviri coloniae deducendae*, and possibly repeopled by
Gaius Gracchus. In this case the clause would not belong
to the section on Africa. Carcopino (*Autour des Gracques*,
248 ff., 258 ff.), who offers his own supplements in line 43,
holds that the *lex Baebia* here mentioned by this agrarian
law was a plebiscite of 119 B.C. whereby the agrarian
commission gave place to *triumviri coloniae deducendae*.

[2] *centuria*, a block of plots; *subsicivum*, a patch of less than
a century left over after a distribution; an oddment. See
above, pp. 160, 163.

shall be right not to issue a decree or right to issue a
decree of different purport, nor shall such act render
him liable to personal risk fine or penalty. . . .   43

In [1] regard to land which . . . has granted or
assigned, or any land or ground, out of the said land
or ground, which . . . under the law or plebiscite
introduced by Marcus Baebius, tribune of the plebs
and member of a Board of Three for sending out a
colony . . . shall have adjudged to be or to have [44]
been given and assigned, as prescribed in this law,
. . . not including the land or ground which lies in
the said hundred [2] or surplus-plot. . . . and not [45]
including the land or ground which colonists or
persons who have been registered [3] in the roll of
colonists shall hold under this law . . . is or shall be
required, any part of such land or ground which has
been bought by any person, . . . nor shall the [46]
purchaser,[4] and his sureties, and his estates as
securities, be freer from liabilities, and the quaestor
who shall have the treasury as his department shall
have the names of the said purchasers . . . entered
in writing in the public records, . . . nor [5] shall [47]
any person who has bought such land from a Roman
magistrate pay money or grant sureties, or estates
as securities, to the people on account of such land or
ground . . . nor shall any person be bound in

----

[3] In 122 Gaius Gracchus had passed a plebiscite (Lex
Rubria) founding a colony, to be called Junonia, on the site
of Carthage.   The law was annulled and the scheme abandoned,
but a certain number of settlers had by then been established.
They were not really colonists after the annulment, but their
rights were confirmed.

[4] from the state at a public auction or in some other way.
Cf. the *Lex Parieti Faciendo*, at the end, pp. 278-9; cf. 180-3.

[5] The gaps in these portions of the law are very large.

⁴⁸ praes factus est, populo obligatus est[o . | . . .
quei ob eu]m agrum locum manceps praesve
factus est, quodque [*pr*]aedium ob [*eam rem in*
⁴⁹ *publico obligatum est . . . q*]uei ager locus in
Africa est, quei Romae publice . | . . eius esto,
isque ager locus privatus vectigalisque u . . . tus
erit; quod eius agri locei extra terra Italia est
⁵⁰ [. | . . *socium nominisve Latini, quibus ex formula*
t]ogatorum milites in terra Italia inperare solent,
eis po[*puleis*, . . .]ve agrum locum quei quomque
⁵¹ habebit possidebit [*fruetur*, . | . . *eiusv*]e rei pro-
curandae causa erit, in eum agrum locum,
in[*mittito . . . se dolo m*]alo. |

⁵² Quei ager locus in Africa est, quod eius agri
[. . . *habeat pos*]sideat fruaturque item, utei sei
is ager locus publi[*ce . . .*

IIvir, quei ex h. l. factus creatusve erit,] in biduo
⁵³ proxsumo, quo factus creatusve erit, edici[*to* . | . .
in diebus] XXV proxsumeis, quibus id edictum
erit [. . . *datu*]m adsignatum siet, idque quom
⁵⁴ profitebitur cognito[*res* . | . .]mum emptor siet

⁵⁸ EIICI

---

¹ nominal, apparently; this seems to have applied to all
small allotments made by the state to which a very small sum
was paid by the owner in token of the fact that the people as
a whole still had claims on the allotted land. This condition
of ownership was abolished for Italy by this law (pp. 374 ff.).
² at Rome.
³ Instead of III, sc. *agris dandis adsignandis iudicandis,*
probably one for Africa, one for Achaia (Corinth; p. 437).

pledge to the people, in regard to the said matter, on account of having become a surety . . . any [48] person who has become a purchaser or surety in regard to the said land or ground, and any security in estates which has been bound in pledge to the public in regard to the said matter, . . . in regard to the land or ground which, situated in Africa, has been bought from the people at Rome, . . . shall [49] belong to him, and the said land or ground shall be private under a rent [1] . . ., any part of the said land which, situated outside the country of Italy, . . . member of the allies or of the Latin name, from [50] whom the government is accustomed to recruit soldiers in the country of Italy according to the Roll of Gowned Men, to the said peoples . . . . . . or any land or ground which any person whatever shall hold possess and enjoy, . . . or shall be . . . [51] into the said ground for the purpose of managing the said matter, he shall install the same . . . without wrongful intent.

In regard to the public land or ground in Africa, [52] any part of the said land which . . . he may hold, possess and enjoy, in the same manner as though the said land or ground had been sold by the public.[2]

The member of the Board of Two [3] who shall have been appointed or created under this law shall within the next two days after he shall have been appointed or created make edict that [any claimant [53] to land] which has been granted or assigned [must state his claim] within the next 25 days after the said edict has been made . . . and at the time when he shall make declaration of such claim, he shall furnish vouchers . . . is a purchaser from another person [54]

ab eo quoius homin[*is privatei eius agri venditio
fuerit . . . L.*] Calpurni. cos. facta siet, quod
55 eius postea *ne*que ipse n[*eque .* | *. .*] praefectus
milesve in provinciam er[*it . . . colono eive, quei
in colonei nu*]mero scriptus est, datus adsignatus
56 est, quodve eiu[*s . . .*] ag[*.* | *. . u*]tei curator eius
profiteatur, item ute[*i . . . ex e*]o edicto, utei
is, quei ab bonorum emptore magistro curato[*reve
57 emerit, .* | *. . Sei quem quid edicto IIvirei ex h. l.
profiteri oportuer*]it, quod edicto IIvir. professus
ex h. l. n[*on erit, . . . ei eum agrum lo*[cum neive
emptum neive adsignatum esse neive fuise iudi-
58 cato. Q.[*.* | *. .*]ro, ei ceivi Romano tantundem
mod[*m agri loci . . .*] quei ager publice non
venieit, dare reddere commutareve liceto.
59 IIvir, q[*uei ex h. l. factus creatusve erit .* | *. . de*]
eis agreis ita rationem inito, itaque h . . . et,
neive unius hominis nomine, quoi ex lege Rubria
quae fuit colono eive, quei [*in colonei numero
scriptus est, agrum, quei in Africa est, dare oportuit
60 lici.itve .* | *. . data adsign*]ata fuise iudicato; neive

54 C ? · CALPVRNI   IQVE · IPSE
59 INITIO   EIVS QVEI ?

---

[1] in 111 B.C.
[2] or: 'of the said person.'
[3] *sc.* of a colonist or purchaser who had become bankrupt.
[4] see note 3, p. 407.

who shall have exercised the right of private sale of
the said land . . . the sale was completed in the
consulship[1] of [Publius Cornelius and] Lucius Calpurnius, any part of which since that time neither the
person himself nor . . . shall have been . . . to
the province as officer or soldier . . . or whatever [55]
part of such land has been granted and assigned
to a colonist or a person who has been registered
in the roll of colonists, or any part of the said land
. . . that the manager of the said land[2] shall make [56]
declaration in the same manner as . . . under the said
edict, that the person who has purchased the land
from the purchaser receiver or manager of assets,[3] . . .
If any person shall have been required to make any [57]
declaration by edict of a member of the Board of
Two under this law, which declaration he shall not
have made by edict of a member of the Board of Two
under this law, . . . the member of the Board of
Two shall deliver judgment to the effect that the
said land or ground has not been bought by or
assigned to, or belonged to the said person . . . it
shall be legally permissible to give, restore, or grant [58]
in compensation to the said Roman citizen a measure
of land or ground of equal amount . . . land which
has not been sold by the public. . . .

The member of the Board of Two who shall have [59]
been appointed or created under this law . . . shall
so set up an investigation regarding the said lands,
and so . . . nor, in regard to land which, situated
in Africa, it was rightfully and permissibly allowed
under the Rubrian[4] law, since annulled, to grant
individually to any one man the same being a
colonist or person registered in the roll of colonists,
. . . shall he adjudge such properties to have been [60]

unius hominus [*nomine, quoi . . . colono eive, quei
in colonei nu*]mero scriptus est, agrum quei in
Africa est, dare oportuit licuitve, amplius iug.
CC in [*singulos homines data adsignata esse fuiseve*
61 *iudicato* . | . . *neive maiorem numerum in Africa
hominum in coloniam coloniasve deductum esse
fu*]iseve iudicato quam quantum numer[*um ex
lege Rubria quae fuit . . . a IIIviris coloniae
dedu*]cendae in Africa hominum in coloniam
coloniasve deduci oportuit licuitve.

62   IIvir, quei [*ex h. l. factus creatusve erit* . | . .] re
Rom . . . agri[. . . *d*]atus ads[*ignatus . . . quod
eiu*]s agri ex h. lege adioudicari licebit, quod ita
comperietur, id ei heredeive eius adsignat*um*
63 esse iudicato [. | . . *quod quand*]oque eius agri
locei ante kal. I[. . . *quoiei emptum*] est ab eo,
quoius eius agri locei hominus privati venditio
fuit tum, quom is eum agrum locum emit, quei
64 [. | . . *et eum agrum locum, quem ita emit emer*]it,
planum faciet feceritve emptum esse, q[*uem agrum
locum neque ipse*] neque heres eius neque quoi is
heres erit abalienaverit, quod eius agri locei ita

60 DARE · OPORTEBIT
62 ADSIGNATO

granted and assigned; nor in regard to land which, situated in Africa, it was rightfully and permissibly allowed [under the Rubrian law, since annulled], to grant individually to any one man, the same being a colonist or person who has been registered in the roll of colonists, shall he adjudge more than 200 Roman acres to be or to have been granted and assigned for each separate person . . . nor shall he [61] adjudge a larger number of persons to be or to have been conducted to the colony or colonies in Africa than the number of persons which under the Rubrian law, since annulled, . . . was laid down as rightful and permissible to be conducted to the colony or colonies in Africa by the Board of Three for conducting a colony.

A member of the Board of Two who shall have been appointed or created under this law . . ., in [62] regard to land which has been granted and assigned . . . any part of the said land which may henceforth be rightfully adjudged under this law, provided that the title thereto on inquiry be found flawless, he shall adjudge the same to be assigned to the said person or his heir . . . provided that at some time before the first [63] day of . . . that part of the said land or ground which was purchased by one person from another who exercised the right of private sale of the said land or ground at the time when the said buyer made his purchase of the said land or ground, who . . . and [64] shall make or shall have made it clearly proved that the land which he has or shall have so purchased, has been purchased, provided that neither he himself nor his heir nor the person whose successor the purchaser shall be shall have alienated the said land or ground, a member of the Board of Two shall so

⁶⁵ planum factum erit, IIvir ita [. | . . *dato re*]ddito,
quod is emptum habuerit quod eius publice non
veniei[*t. Item IIvir, sei is*] ager locus, quei ei
emptus fuerit, publice venieit, tantundem modum
agri locei de eo agro loco, quei ager lo[*cus in
Africa est, quei publice non venieit, ei quei ita emptum*
⁶⁶ *habuerit, dato reddito* . | . . *Queique ager locus ita
ex h. l. datus redditus erit, ei, quoius ex h. l. f*]actus
erit, HS n. I emptus esto, isque ager locus
privatus vectigalisque ita, [*utei in h. l. supra*]
scriptum est, esto.

Quoi colono eive, quei in colonei numero
scriptus est, ager locus in ea centuria subsicivov[*e
de eo agro, quei ager in Africa est, datus adsignatus
est, quae centuria quodve supsicivom Romae publice*
⁶⁷ *venieit venieritve* . | . . *si quid eius agri IIvir, quei
ex h. l. factus creatusve erit, ei colono heredeive eius
minus adiudicaverit, tum tantundem modum agri
locei pro eo agro loco de eo a*]gro loco, quei ager
locus in Africa est, quod eius publice non venieit,
ei he[*redeive ei*]us IIvir, quei ex h. l. factus
creatusve erit, reddito.

⁶⁵ VENIᵢ . . . VENIET

---

¹ *sc.* by the Roman state to another purchaser already.
² a nominal sum which would give the owner title by lawful
sale and not simply by gift of a land-commissioner. Compare
' peppercorn rent.'

grant or restore any part of the said land which shall have been so cleared of doubt, . . . which the said [65] person shall have purchased, such portion thereof as has not been sold by the public.[1] Likewise, if the said land or ground, which shall have been purchased by the said person, has been sold by the public, a member of the Board of Two shall grant and restore, to the person who shall hold the said land by purchase under the said conditions, an equal measure of land or ground out of that land or ground which, situated in Africa, has not been sold by the public . . . and any land or ground which shall have been [66] so granted and restored under this law to the person whose possession it shall have become under this law, shall be bought by the said person for 1 sesterce [2] in money, and the said land or ground shall be private land under a rent, as recorded above in this law.

With regard to land or ground which has been granted and assigned, out of the land which is situated in Africa, to a colonist or to a person who has been entered in the roll of colonists, within a hundred or surplus-plot, which hundred or surplus-plot has or shall have been sold by the public at Rome, . . . if a member of the Board of Two who shall [67] have been appointed or created under this law shall have failed to adjudge any part of such land in secure title to the said colonist or his heir, then a member of the Board of Two who shall have been appointed or created under this law shall render unto the said person or his heir, by way of compensation for the said land or ground, a measure of land of equal amount out of that land or ground which, situated in Africa, has not been sold by the Roman public.

Quoi colono eive, quei in colonei numero
68 scriptus est fuitve, [*ager in ea centuria | supsicivove
*de eo agro, quei in Africa est, datus adsignatus est,
*quae centuria quodve supsicivom Romae publice
*venieit venieritve, si quid eius agri IIvir, quei ex h. l.
*factus creatusve erit, ei quei ab eo colono heredeve
*eius emit habuitve minus adiudicaverit, tum tan-
tundem modum agri ei, quem ita emise habui]seve
comperietur, heredeive eius de agro, quei ager in
Africa est, pro eo agro [*IIvir reddi*]to, quoieique
ita reddiderit, ei adsignatum fuisse iudicato.

Quoi agrum de eo agro, quei ager in Africa est,
quei colono e[*ive, quei in colonei numero scriptus
*est fuitve datus adsignatus est, magistratus Romae
*69 publice vendiderit . | . . seiquid eius agri IIvir quei
*ex h. l. factus creatusve erit ei, quoi ita emptum esse
*comperietur, emptorive eius pro curatoreve eius
heredive quoius eorum minu]s adiudicaverit: tum
tantundem modum agri ei, quoi ita emptum
esse comperiet[*ur, emptorive ei*]us pro curatoreve

---

¹ For these, see pp. 160, 163.

With regard to land or ground which has been **68** granted and assigned, out of the land which is situated in Africa, to a colonist or to a person who has been entered in and has functioned in the roll of colonists, within a hundred or surplus-plot,[1] which hundred or surplus-plot has or shall have been sold by the public at Rome, if a member of the Board of Two who shall have been appointed or created under this law shall have failed to adjudge any part of such land in secure title to the person who has purchased or acquired the same from the said colonist or his heir, then a member of the Board of Two shall render to the person who shall be found and proved to have thus purchased and acquired the same, or to his heir, by way of compensation for the said land, a measure of land of equal amount out of that land which is situated in Africa, and shall judge the said land to have been assigned to the person to whom he shall have thus rendered the same.

Should a magistrate have sold publicly in Rome to any person land out of that land which, situated **69** in Africa, has been granted and assigned to a colonist or to a person who has been entered in and has functioned in the roll of colonists, . . . if the member of the Board of Two who shall have been appointed or created under this law shall have failed to adjudge any part of such land in secure title to the person who shall be found and proved to have thus purchased such land or to a purchaser from him or to the managers or heirs of any of the parties, then the member of the Board of Two shall render to the person who shall be found and proved to have thus purchased the same, or to a purchaser from him or to the managers or heirs of either party, by way of com-

eius heredive quoius eorum de eo agro, quei ager
in Africa est, pro eo agro IIvir reddito ; quoi ita
70 reddiderit, [*ei adsignatum* | *fuisse iudicato. Quantae*
quis pequniae ab populo mercassitur quam pequniam
qui agrum locum publicum in Africa emerunt emerintve
pro eo agro loco populo dare debent debebuntve, . . .
quod eius p]equniae adsignatum discriptum adsig-
natumve in tabuleis publiceis est eritv[*e : tantam*
pequ]niam populo ex eid. Mart., quae, post ea
quam vectigalia consistent, quae post h. l. r.
primum consistent, primae erunt, in[*ferto.* |

71   *Quam pequniam quei agrum locum publicum in*
Africa emit emeritve pro eo agro loco populo dare
debet debebitve, ab eo quei eam pequniam ab populo
mercassitur ex eidibus Martis eisdem exigito . . .
neive quis eam pequniam propiore die exigito, atque]
uteique in h. l. s. e.; neive, quod pequniae ob
eam rem propiore die exactum er[*it, atque uteiqu*]e
in h. l. s. e., is quei pequniam populo dare debebit
ei, quei eo nomine ab populo mercassitur, ob
72 eam rem pequniam ei nei [*minus solvito .* | . .
pla]num fiat; neive quis mag. neive pro mag.
facito neive quis senator decernito, q[*uo ea*
pequnia,] quae pro agreis loceis aedificieis, quei

71 PROPIOREM

---

¹ *sc.* a *publicanus* who intervenes and buys up the debts
owed to the state by persons who have not yet paid for land
bought by them in Rome.
² *mercassitur* is an archaic form for *mercatus fuerit.*

pensation for the said land, a measure of land of equal amount out of that land which is situated in Africa; he shall judge the said land to have been assigned to the person to whom he shall thus have rendered the same.

With regard to the amount of money for which [70] any person [1] has purchased [2] from the people the money-debts which persons who have or shall have bought public land or ground in Africa owe or shall owe to the people for the said land or ground, . . . any part of such money which has or shall have been entered as assigned or apportioned in the public records he shall pay in to the people such money to the full amount, from the fifteenth day of March next following the time when imposts shall fall due, which shall have first fallen due after the introduction of this law.

Any money which any person who has or shall [71] have bought public land or ground in Africa owes or shall owe to the people for the said land or ground shall be exacted from the said fifteenth day of March from the said person by the person who has purchased from the people the said money-debt . . . nor shall any person exact the said money on an earlier day than is prescribed in this law; nor, in regard to any sum of money which shall have been exacted on account of the said matter on an earlier day than is prescribed in this law, shall the person who shall owe money to the people be exempted in view of such act from paying money due to the person who has made a purchase under the said category . . . be proved; nor shall any magistrate or pro- [72] magistrate so act or senator so decree whereby the money, which is or shall be owed to the people for

s. s. sunt, populo debetur debebiturve, aliter exsigatur atque uteique in h. l. s. est.

[*Quei agrum locum publicum in Africa emit*
73 *emeritve .* | . . *sei ea pequnia, quam eo nomine populo debet debebitve, in diebus* . . . *proxsumeis, quibus is ager locus Romae publice venieit*] venierit, populo soluta non erit: is pro eo agro loco in diebus CXX proxsumeis ea[*rum summarum nomine*] quae s. s. s., arb. pr., quei inter ceives tum Romae ious deicet, satis subsignato.

74 Pr., quei inter ceives Romae ious de[*icet .* | . . *nisei*] praedium ante ea ob eum agrum locum in publico obligatum erit in publicu[*mve praes datus erit*], agrum locum, quo pro agro loco satis ex h. l. arb. pr. supsignatum non erit, pequnia
75 praesenti vendito. Que[*i . .* | .

Que]i ager locus in Africa est, quei Romae publice veniei[*t*] venieritve, quod eius agri [*locei, quei popul*]eis libereis in Africa sunt, quei eorum *in* ameicitiam populi Romanei bello Poenicio proxsumo manserunt, queive a[*d imperatorem populi Romanei bello Poenicio proxsumo ex hostibus perfugerunt, quibus propterea ager datus adsignatus*
76 *est d. s. s.*, eorum quisque habuerunt, . | . . pro eo agro loco IIvir in diebus . . . proxsumeis, qu]ibus

73 INTE · CEIVES · TVM   74 OBLIGAIVM
75 VENIEII

---

[1] the *praetor urbanus*.   [2] Here undoubtedly should come line 84, with the last part of line 83, pp. 426–9.

[3] the Third Punic War, 149–146, ending with the destruction of Carthage.

[4] These were Utica and six others—see below, p. 425.

[5] particularly the light cavalry of the Carthaginian officer Himilco Phameas who deserted to Scipio Aemilianus in 148 B.C.

the lands grounds or buildings which are above recorded, is exacted in a manner different from that which is prescribed in this law.

Any person who has or shall have bought public land or ground in Africa . . . if the said money [73] which he owes or shall owe to the people under the said category shall not have been paid to the people within the next . . . days after the said land or ground has been or shall be sold by the public at Rome, the said person shall on behalf of the said land or ground, at the will and pleasure of the praetor [1] who shall at that time have jurisdiction among citizens at Rome, pledge by signature within the next 120 days sufficient securities under the category of the said sums, which are above recorded.

The praetor who shall have jurisdiction among the citizens at Rome . . ., unless beforehand security [74] in estates shall have been given in pledge to the state on account of the said land or ground or a surety provided to the state, shall sell for ready money any land or ground for which satisfactory security, at the will and pleasure of the praetor, has not been pledged by signature under this law. . . . [2]   [75]

In regard to land or ground in Africa which has or shall have been sold by the public at Rome, any such land or ground as has been held by such peoples as are free states in Africa to wit any of the said peoples who in the last [3] Punic War remained [4] firm in the friendship of the Roman people or any [5] who deserted from the enemy to a Roman commander in the last Punic War, to whom for that reason land has been granted and assigned by a vote of the Senate, . . . a member of the Board of [76] Two shall, within the next . . . days after he has

IIvir ex h. [*l. fact*]us creatusve erit, facito,
quantum agri loci quoiusque in populi leiberei
inve eo agr[*o loco, quei ager l*]ocus perfugis datus
adsignatusve est, ceivis Romanei ex h. l. factum
erit, quo pro agro loco ager lo[*cus ceivi Ro*]mano
77 ex h. l. | [*commutatus redditusve non erit, tantundem
modum agri loci quoieique populo leibero perfugeisve
det adsignetve* . . .

II]vir quei ex h. l. factus creatusve erit, is in
diebus CL proxsumeis quibus factus creatusve
erit, facito, quan[*do Xvirei, quei ex*] lege Livia
factei createive sunt fueruntve, eis hominibus
agrum in Africa dederunt adsignaverun[*ntv*]e,
78 quos stipendium | [*pro eo agro populo Romano
pendere oportet, sei quid eius agri ex h. l. ceivis
Romanei esse oportet oportebitve,* . . . *de agro, quei
publicus populi Romanei in Africa est, tantundem,
quantum de agro stipendiario ex h. l. ceivis*] Romanei
esse oportet oportebitve, is stipendiarie*s* det
adsignetve idque in formas publicas facito ute[*i
referatur i. u. e r. p. f.*] q. e. e. v.

IIvir, quei ex h. l. factus creatusve erit, is facito
in diebus CCL proxsumeis, quibus h. [*l.*] populus
79 plebesve iuserit | *utei extra eum agrum locum, quei*

---

¹ *sc.* which, belonging to a free people, has been sold to a
Roman citizen.

² Passed soon after the Third Punic War. Cf.line 81.

³ *forma* was one of the words for the completed chart of
a land-surveyor. See pp. 159, 166–7.

⁴ The first clause in the Latin, line 78 (*IIvir, quei* . . .
iuserit) appears, in the translation, considerably below (p.
427), after the words 'assigned to the people of Utica . . . in
Africa.'

been appointed or created member of the Board of Two under this law, in lieu of the said [1] land or ground, see to it that he grant or assign to every free people or deserters from the enemy a measure of land or ground equal in amount with the land or ground which under this law shall have been made the property of a Roman citizen within the bounds of land owned by any free people or of that land or ground, which has been granted or assigned to deserters, in exchange for which land or ground [77] no land or ground has been given in compensation under this law or restored to the Roman citizen. . . .

Seeing that the members of the Board of Ten who were appointed and created and functioned under the Livian [2] law granted or assigned land in Africa to those persons who are required to pay [78] tribute to the Roman people for the said land, a member of the Board of Two who shall have been appointed or created under this law shall, within the next 150 days after he shall have been appointed or created under this law, see to it that any of the said land which rightfully belongs or shall rightfully belong to a Roman citizen under this law . . . and the same shall, out of land which is public land of the Roman people in Africa, grant or assign to the payers of tribute a measure of land of equal amount with the land which out of tributary land rightfully belongs or shall rightfully belong to a Roman citizen under this law, and shall cause the land to be entered on the public plans [3] according as it shall appear to him to be consistent with the advantage and good faith of the commonwealth.

In regard to the land which is situated in Africa,[4] not including that land or ground which was [79]

*ex lege Rubria quae fuit colono eive, quei in colonei numero scriptus est, datus adsignatus est . . . quo pro agro loco ager locus com]*mutatus redditusve non erit; extraque eum agrum, quei ager intra finis populorum leiberorum Uticensium H[*adrumetinorum T*]ampsitanorum Leptitanorum Aquillitanorum Usalitanorum Teudalensium, quom
80 in ameicitiam populei Romani proxumum | [*venerunt, fuit; extraque eum agrum locum, quei ager locus eis hominibus, quei ad imperatorem populi Romani bello Poenicio proxsumo ex hostibus perfugerunt, . . . datus adsignatusve est de s.*] s.; extra*que* eum agrum, quei ager ex h. l. privatus factus erit, quo pro agro loco ager locus redditus commutatusve [*non erit; extra*]que eum agrum locum, quem IIvir ex h. l. stipendiarieis dederit adsignaveritve, quod eius ex h. l. in *f*ormam
81 publicam rellatum | [*erit; extraque eum agrum, quem agrum . . . P. Cornelius imperator leib*]ereis regis Massinissae dedit, haberee fruive iusit; extraque eum agrum locum ubei oppodum Char[*tago*] fuit qu[*ondam; extraqu*]e eum agrum locum, quem Xvirei, quei ex [*lege*] Livia factei createive fuerunt, Uticensibus reliquerunt ad-
82 signaverunt: ceterum | [*agrum omnem, quei in*

79 LEIBERL · RVM   80 EXPRA *pro* extraque
81 IVSII   EX · H · L · LIVIA?

---

[1] see p. 407, note. 3.
[2] Scipio Aemilianus. For *forma*, see p. 422, n. 3.
[3] of Numidia; he had been an ally of Rome at the end of the Second Punic War and by his aggressions on Carthaginian territory helped to precipitate the Third Punic War. His

granted or assigned under the Rubrian [1] law, since
annulled, to a colonist or to any person who has
been registered on the roll of colonists . . . in
exchange for which land or ground no land or ground
shall have been given in compensation or restored;
and not including that land or ground which was
situated within the boundaries of the free peoples
of Utica, Hadrumetum, Tampsus, Leptis, Aquilla,
Usalis, and Teudalis, at the time when they lately
entered into friendship with the Roman people; [80]
and not including that land or ground which . . .
was granted or assigned by a vote of the Senate to
those persons who in the last Punic War deserted
from the enemy to a Roman commander; and not
including that land which shall have been made
private under this law, in exchange for which land
or ground no land or ground shall have been given
in compensation or restored; and not including that
land or ground which a member of a Board of Two
shall have granted or assigned under this law to
payers of tribute in so far as the said land shall have [81]
been entered on a public plan; and not including
that land which Publius Cornelius [2] the commander
. . . granted to the children of King Massinissa [3]
and gave orders that they should hold and enjoy;
and not including that land or ground where the
town of Carthage at one time stood; and not
including that land or ground which the members
of the Board of Ten who were appointed or created
and functioned under the Livian law left and assigned
to the people of Utica;—in regard to all other land [82]

sons, Micipsa, Gulussa, and Mastanabal had been granted
land within the Roman province of Africa which was kept
separate from Numidia.

Africa est, quei de eo agro vectigal decumas scrip-
turamve pro pecore populo aut publicano dare debe-
bunt, quei ager eis ex h. l. datus redditus commutatus
erit, habeant possideant fruanturve et pro eo agro
loco vectigal decumas scripturamve, quod post h. l.
fruetur, populo aut publicano dent . . .

Quei quomque de eo agro vectigal decumas scrip-
turamve pr]o pecore ex lege Sempronia dare non
solitei sunt, quei ager eis ex h. l. datus redditus
commutatus eri[t, quei eor]u[m eum agrum habebit]
possidebit frueturve : pro eo agro loco nei vectigal
neive decumas nei[ve] scripturam, quod post
h. l. r. fruetur, dare debeto. |

83   [*Quem agrum locum populus Romanus ex h. l.*
locabit, quem agrum locum Latinus peregrinusve ex
h. l. possidebit, is de eo agro loco . . . vectigal
decumas] scripturam populo aut publicano item
dare debeto, utei pro eo agro loco, quem agrum
locum populu[*s Romanus ex h. l. locabit, que*]m
agrum locum ceivis Romanus ex h. l. possidebit,
dare oportebit.

Pr., quoius arb. pro agro loco, quei Romae

---

[1] Here the translation takes up the Latin clause in line 78
above, p. 422,—*IIvir, quei . . . iuserit.*

[2] About lines 82ff. consult Hardy, *Six Roman Laws,* pp.
79, 86ff.

[3] apparently in special cases of public disaster.

[4] C. Gracchus' *Lex Sempronia de vectigalibus Asiae,* whereby
in 123 B.C. the taxes of Asia were given to the *equites.* It
probably gave remission to tenants after local public disasters,
and could naturally be applied outside Asia.

[5] Undoubtedly this clause should come soon after the clause
in line 74.

which is situated in Africa, a[1] member of the Board of Two, who shall have been appointed or created under this law, the same shall, within the next 250 days after the people or plebs have ratified this law, see to it that those persons, who with respect to the said land shall be bound to pay impost tithes or pasture-tax for cattle to people or tax-farmer, hold possess or enjoy land which shall have been granted confirmed or given in compensation under this law, and that on account of the said land or ground for enjoyment thereof after the passing of this law, they pay to the people or tax-farmer impost tithes or pasture-tax. . . .[2]

All persons whatever who have not,[3] under a Sempronian[4] law, been accustomed to pay impost tithes or pasture-tax for cattle, with respect to that land which shall have been granted confirmed or given to them in compensation, none of the said persons who shall hold possess or enjoy the said land shall be bound to pay impost tithes or pasture-tax on behalf of the said land or ground for enjoyment thereof after the passing of this law.

In regard to land or ground which the Roman [83] people shall lease out under this law, a Latin or other non-citizen who shall possess such land or ground under this law, the same shall . . . in regard to the said land or ground, be bound to pay impost tithes or pasture-tax to people or tax-farmer in the same manner as a Roman citizen shall be required to pay for such land or ground, which land or ground the Roman people shall lease out under this law and the said person shall possess under this law.

The praetor[5] at whose discretion sufficient

84 publice venierit, e h. l. | [*satis supsignari oportet
. . . praedia emptor*]ris ter tanti invito eo quei
dabit accipito, facitoque, quei ex h. l. praedia
dederit, utei ei satis supsig[*netur neive quis quid
fax*]sit, quo minus ex h. l. praedium quei quomque
velit supsignet pequniamve solvat praesque, quei
quomque ex h. l. fieri volet, fiat. |

85 [*Quantum vectigal decumas scripturamve pecoris
eum, quei agrum locum aedificium in Africa possidebit, . . . quei ager*] locus populorum leiberorum,
perfugarum non fuerit, pro eo agro aedificio
locoque ex l. dicta, q[*uam L. Caecilius Cn. Domitius
cen*]s. agri aedifici loci vectigalibusve publiceis
fruendeis locandeis vendundeis legem deixerunt,

86 publicano dare oportuit : | [*tantundem post h. l.
rog. quei agrum locum aedificium in Africa possidet,
possidebit . . . publicano vectigal decumas scriptura*]mque pecoris dare debeto, neive amplius ea
aliubeive aliterve dare debeto, pequsque ne[*i
aliter alieisve legibus*] in eo agro pascito.

---

¹ *sc.* in case of payment not being made.
² in 115 B.C.

security is required to be pledged by signature [84] under this law on behalf of land or ground which shall have been sold by the public at Rome . . . shall[1] accept estates of the purchaser as securities, without the consent of the person who shall give them, to the value of three times the amount, and shall see to it that, by the person who shall have given estates as securities under this law, sufficient pledge by signature shall be registered, and that no person shall so act as to prevent any person whatever who shall be so minded from entering by signature such estates as security under this law or from paying the money and becoming a surety, if any person shall be minded to become the same under this law.

In regard to the amount of impost tithes or [85] pasture-tax on cattle which any person who shall be possessor of land ground or building in Africa, . . . which land ground or building shall not have belonged to free peoples or deserters from the enemy, was required to pay to a tax-farmer on account of the said land building or ground on the conditions which were laid down[2] by the censors Lucius Caecilius and Gnaeus Domitius for the lease of land building or ground or for the usu-fruct lease or sale of the public revenues: any person who possesses or shall possess land ground [86] or building in Africa after the introduction of this law . . . shall be bound to pay to a tax-farmer the same amount of impost tithes or pasture-tax for cattle; nor shall he be bound to pay thereof more or elsewhere or otherwise, nor shall he pasture cattle otherwise or on other conditions on the said land.

429

Quae vectigalia in Africa publica populi Romani sunt, quae L. Caecilius Cn. Domiti. cens.

87 fruenda | [*locaverunt vendideruntve, quei quomque mag. post h. l. rog. ea vectigalia locabit vendetve, quominus publicano eam legem dicat . . . quo pl*]us populo dare debeat solvatque, e. h. l. n. r.

Mag. prove mag., queive pro eo inperio iudicio [*potestateve erit, . . . quei quomque, quae*] publica populi Romani in Africa sunt eruntve, vectigalia fruenda locabit vendetve, quom ea vectigalia

88 fruenda locabit vendetve, | [*nei eis vectigalibus legem deicito, quo inviteis ieis, quei eum agrum possidebunt, publicano quid facere liceat, . . . quod ei non licuit facer*]e ex lege dicta, quam L. Caeci. Cn. Dom. cens., quom eorum agrorum vectigalia fruenda locaverunt [*vendideruntve . . . eis agris lege*]m deixerunt; neive quod in eis agris pequs [*pas*]cetur, scripturae pecoris legem de[*i*]cito, quo inviteis eis, quei eum agrum possidebunt, |

89 [*aliter pascatur quam pastum est ex lege dicta, quam L. Caecilius Cn. Domitius censores, quom eorum agrorum vectigalia fruenda locaverunt vendideruntve, legem deixerunt.*

88 DEIXERINT . NEIVE . QVOI   LEGE

---

[1] a censor, in years when censors were in office; otherwise a consul.

LAWS AND OTHER DOCUMENTS

In regard to the public revenues in Africa which belong to the Roman people and of which the censors Lucius Caecilius and Gnaeus Domitius leased out or [87] sold the usufruct, it is not intended by this law to prevent any magistrate [1] whatever, who shall lease out or sell the said public revenues after the passing of this bill into law, from laying down such conditions for the tax-farmer . . . whereby he must be bound to pay and render a larger sum to the public.

No magistrate whatever, or promagistrate, or any person who shall be entrusted with the state authority jurisdiction or rightful competence of such who shall lease out or sell the usufruct of the present or future public revenues of the Roman people in Africa, at the time when he shall lease out or sell the said usufruct of the said revenues, lay down for the [88] said public revenues conditions whereby the tax-farmer is permitted to perform, without the consent of those who shall possess the said land, any act . . . which he was not permitted to perform on the conditions which were proclaimed by the censors Lucius Caecilius and Gnaeus Domitius for the said lands . . . at the time when they leased out or sold the usufruct of the imposts of the said lands; nor shall the said official, in regard to any cattle that shall be pastured on the said lands, proclaim conditions of pasture-tax on cattle whereby, without the consent of those who shall possess the said land, cattle shall be pastured otherwise than they [89] were pastured on the conditions which were proclaimed by the censors Lucius Caecilius and Gnaeus Domitius at the time when they leased out or sold the usufruct of the imposts of the said lands.

431

*Quae vectigalia fruenda in Africa Cn. Paperius
cos. vendidit locavitve, qu]*ominus ea lege sient
pareantque, quam legem Cn. Paperius cos. eis
vendundeis [*locandeis deixit*] e. h. [*l.*] n. r.

Quei [*ager in Africa est, . . . quae viae in eo*]
agro ante quam Cartago capta est fuerunt : eae
omnes publicae sunto limitesque inter cen-
90 turia*s* [. . | .

*IIvir, quei ex h. l. factus creatusve erit, sei apud
eum, quoi ager in Africa adsignatus est, eum agrum
professus erit, ei eum agrum, quem a]*grum in eo
numero agri professus erit, quo in numero eum
agrum, quem is, quoi adsigna[*tus est, professus
erit, profiteri non oportuit, . . . nei dato*] neive
reddito neive adiudicato. Quei eam rem [*ita*]
indicio fuerit, ei eius agri, quod is indicio eius, |
91 [*quei eam rem ita indicaverit, in eo numero agri,
quo non oportuit, professus esse iudicatus erit, . . .
partem . . . magistratus, qui de ea re iudicaverit,
dato adsignato.*

*Quibuscum tran]*sactum est, utei bona, quae
habuisent, agrumque, quei eis publice adsignatus

---

[1] in 113 B.C. We have no details of Papirius' lease-contract.
It supplemented that of the censors of 115 B.C. See also
preceding note.

[2] On boundary-paths or balks, and hundreds, see above,
pp. 158 ff.

[3] *sc.* when their *professio* had been accepted.

In regard to the usufruct of the public revenues in Africa which the consul [1] Gnaeus Papirius sold or leased out, it is not intended by this law to prevent such revenues from being and remaining subject to the conditions which the consul Gnaeus Papirius proclaimed for the sale or leasing of the same.

In regard to the land in Africa . . . all roads which existed on the said land before the capture of Carthage, the same shall be public and also the boundary-paths between the hundreds [2] . . . 90

A member of the Board of Two who shall have been appointed or created under this law, if any person, to whom land has been assigned in Africa, shall have made declaration, in his presence, of the said land, . . . shall not grant or confirm or adjudge to the said person any such land as the said person shall have declared under that category of land under which category it was not rightfully permitted the person, to whom it was assigned, to declare the same as he shall have declared it. To any person who shall have given information on the [91] said matter to that effect, the magistrate . . . who shall have delivered judgment on the said matter shall grant or assign to him a . . . part of the said land to the said person, in the event of the other party being adjudged guilty, on the information of the person who shall have given information on the said matter to that effect, of having made declaration of land under that category of land under which he was not permitted to declare the same.

To all persons with whom official settlement [3] has been made to the effect that they should hold possess and enjoy the possessions which they had formerly held and also the land which had been

433

esset, haberent [*possiderent fruerentur, eis . . .
quantus*] modus agri de eo agro, quei eis publice
[*datus adsign*]atus fuit, publice venieit, tan-
92 tundem modum | [*agri de eo agro, quei publicus
populi Romani in Africa est, quei ager publice non
venieit, . . . magistratus commutato.*

*Quei in Africa agrum possesionemve agrive pos-
sesionisve superficium habet possidetv*]e fruiturve,
quem agrum possesionemve quoiusve agri pos-
sesionisve superficium q. pr.ve pu[*blice vendi-
derit . . . o*]b eum agrum locum possessione[*m
agrive superfic*]ium scripturam pecoris nei dato
93 neive | [*vectigal solvito . . .*] is ager ex s. c. datus
adsignatus est, ei agrei, quei s. s. s., possesion-
esque, ea omnia eorum h[*ominum . . . dum
magistratus quo de ea*] re in ious aditum erit, [*ita
de ea re iudicium de*]t, utei de rea re in h. l. s.
94 est, neive | [. . .]uos comportent, quibus ex h. l.
ager locus datus redditus commutatus adsignatus
[*est . . . agrum locum ex h. l.*] dari reddi adsig-
nar[*i . . . e*]um agrum locum ceivis R[*omanus
95 . .* | *. qui fructus in eo agro loco natei erunt*] quodque
in eo agro loco vinei oleive fiet, quae messis
vindemiaque P. Cornelio L. C[*alpurnio cos. pos-*

---

[1] *superficium* = a farm-house cottage or building 'made
above,' built on, the ground; usually *superficies*.

[2] in cases where securities were not provided within the
time allowed. See line 74.

[3] The gaps now become too great to allow a connected
restoration.

[4] in 111 B.C.

assigned to them by the people . . . according to the measure of land which has been sold by the public out of that land which was granted or assigned to them by the public . . . the magistrate shall grant in exchange a measure, to an equal amount, [92] out of that land which is public land belonging to the Roman people in Africa and has not been sold by the public.

Any person who occupies possesses or enjoys in Africa land or holding, or messuage [1] appertaining to land or holding, in the event of a quaestor or praetor having publicly sold [2] any such land or holding or messuage appertaining to such land or holding . . . the said person shall not render pasture-tax on cattle or pay impost on account of [93] the said land ground holding or messuage appertaining to land [3] . . . the said land has been granted or assigned by decree of the Senate, the said lands, which are above recorded, and holdings, all the said possessions shall belong to those persons . . . provided that the magistrate before whom appeal shall have been made to court deliver judgment on the said matter according to the principles laid down in this law on the said matter, nor shall . . . [94] convey . . ., to whom under this law land or ground has been granted confirmed given in exchange or assigned . . . land or ground to be granted confirmed or assigned under this law . . . the said land or ground a Roman citizen . . . all fruits [95] which shall have grown on the said land or ground and any wine or oil that shall be produced on the said land or ground, and the harvest and vintage which shall be gathered in the consulship [4] of **Publius Cornelius and Lucius Calpurnius** or after-

teave fiet . . . eo]s fructus [*. . . q*]uei eum agrum
96 tum . | . .

[*Quei ex h. l. IIvir factus creatusve erit, is in*
diebus . . . proxsume]is, quibus ex h. l. IIvir
factus creatusve erit ag[*ru*]m locum, quei Corin-
97 thiorum [*fuit . . . e*]xtra eum ag[*rum locum .* | *. .*
agrum locum,] quem ex | h. l. venire oportebit,
omnem me[*tiun*]dum terminosque statui [*curato*
98 *. . . eu*]m a[*grum .* | *. . opu*]sque loc[*at*]o eique
operei diem deicito, u[*bei perf*]ectum siet; faci-
99 toque . | . . [*quod eius*] agri loci aedifici quoieiqu[*e*
100 *emptum*] erit, is eius pequniae, q[*uam .* | *. . man-*
ceps prae]videsque nei magis solutei sun[*to ;*
eaque] nomina mancupu[*m praevidum is quaestor,*
quei aerarium provinciam optinebit, in tabuleis pub-
101 *liceis scripta habeto .* | *. . ab ipsis here*]dibusque
eorum persequtio e[*sto.*

102 105 *Quei*] ager locus aedif[*icium .* | *. . populo*] dare
damnas esto. Pr. [*prove pr. quo de ea*] re in
ious adi[*tum erit*] . | . . i venierit n . . . iei . | . .
possesi[*ones*] . . . | . . . pli . . .

wards . . . the said fruits . . . the person who
then . . . the said land . . .   96

A [1] member of the Board of Two who shall
have been appointed or created under this law
shall. within the next . . . days after he shall have
been appointed or created member of the Board
of Two under this law . . . the land or ground
which belonging once to the Corinthians [2] . . .
not including that land or ground . . . shall [97]
take care that all land or ground which shall rightfully be sold under this law is measured and that
boundary-marks are set up . . the said land . . . [98]
shall lease out the work and appoint for the said
work a day when it shall be completed.[3] and shall
cause . . . whatever part of the said land ground [99]
or building shall have been bought by any person,
the said person . . . of that money, which. . . the [100]
purchaser and his sureties shall not thereby be
freed in the least from obligation: and a quaestor
who shall have the treasury as his department
shall have the names of the said purchasers and
sureties entered in writing in the public registers
. . . claim shall be made from themselves or their [101]
heirs.

In regard to land ground or building . . . shall [102-105]
be condemned to pay to the people. The praetor
or propraetor, before whom appeal shall have been
made to the court on the said matter . . . shall
have been sold . . . holdings . . .

---

[1] The remaining fragments deal with the Corinthian land.
The commissioner here mentioned is separate from the
official connected with the land in Africa.

[2] Corinth was, like Carthage, destroyed in 146 B.C.

[3] See the *Lex Parieti Faciendo*, pp. 278–9.

61

Constitution granted ('Lex data') by specially appointed commissioners to Tarentum which received, as a municipium (borough), Roman citizenship after the grant of the Roman franchise to the Italians in 90 and 89 B.C. The 'Lex rogata'

VIIII

590 . . . . .]ne esse liceat neive qu[*is*] quod eius
municipi pequniae publicae sacrae | religiossae
est erit fra[*u*]dato neive av[*o*]rtito neive facito
quo eorum | quid fiat neive per litteras publicas
fraudemve publicum peius | facito d. m. Quei
faxit, quant[*i*] ea res erit, quadruplum multae

5 esto | eamque pequniam mu[*n*]icipio dare damnas
esto eiusque pequniae | magistratus, quei quomque
inmunicipio erit, petitio exactioque esto. |

IIII vir. aedilesque quei h. l. primei erunt, quei
eorum Tarentum venerit, | is in diebus XX
proxumeis quibus post h. l. datam primum
Tarentum venerit, | facito quei pro se praes stat

10 praedes praediaque ad IIII vir. det quod satis | sit,
quae pequnia public[*a sa*]cra religiosa eius
municipi ad se insuo magistratu | pervenerit,
eam pequni[*a*]m municipio Tarentino salvam
recte esse futur[*a*]m | eiusque rei rationem r[*ed*]-

³ fraudemve [aurum argentum aes] publicum, Scialoja

---

¹ E. Hardy, *Six Roman Laws*, 102 ff., 161–2.
² The ninth tabula of the law. The beginnings of the lines of the tenth tabula are also preserved.
³ As with other *municipia*, these were the chief magistrates; they included the aediles as well as the two superior *duoviri iure dicundo*, so that the addition of *aedilesque* is a mistake, or a careless way of saying: 'including the aediles.' For boards of chief magistrates, see also pp. xxxviii ff.

which authorised the commission to ' give ' this law may have
followed the Lex Julia of 90 B.C. *(see p. 272) immediately, but*
style and spelling suggest a later date.[1] *Tablet of brass found at*
Tarentum; now at Naples. Cf. C.I.L., I, 2, 2. Fasc. III,
p. 833.

9 [2]

. . . nor shall he be allowed to be . . . nor shall
anyone seize by fraud or misappropriate any money,
public sacred or employed in religion, which belongs
or shall belong to the said borough, or commit any
act whereby any of such malpractices may ensue;
nor shall he with wrongful intent impair public funds
by mishandling the state's accounts or by fraud.
Whoever shall so act shall incur a fine of four times
the sum embezzled, and shall be condemned to pay
the said money to the borough, and the demand for
and exaction of the said money shall rest with
whoever shall be any magistrate for the time being
in the borough.

With regard to the magisterial Board of Four [3]
and the aediles who shall be the first in office under
this law, whoever of them shall have come to Tarentum, shall, within the next twenty days following his
first coming to Tarentum after the granting [4] of this
law, take steps whereby he shall stand as surety
for himself and present sureties, and estates as
securities, before the members of the Board of Four,
sufficient to guarantee that money, public sacred
or employed in religion, belonging to the said
borough, coming into his hands during his magistracy,
shall be well and duly secured to the borough of
Tarentum, and that he will render an account of the

[4] By officials specially empowered to do so by a *lex rogata* of
the Roman people or by a decree of the Roman Senate.

diturum, ita utei senatus censuerit, isque IIII
vir | quoi ita praes dabitur ac[c]ipito, idque in
tabu[leis p]ubliceis scriptum sit | facito, quique
quomqu[e] comitia duovireis a[ed]ilibusve rogan-
15 deis | habebit, is antequam maior pars curiarum
quemque eorum, quei magistratum eis comitieis
petent, renuntiabit, ab eis quei petent praedes |
quod satis sit accipito, [q]uae pequnia publica
sacra religiosa eius municipi | [ad] quemque
eorum in eo magistratu pervenerit, eam pequniam
municipio | Tarentino salvam rec[te] ess[e futu]ra[m
20 ei]usque rei ration[e]m redditurum, | ita utei
senatus ce[nsu]erit [i]dque in [tabul]eis publiceis
scriptum sit facito | quodque [quoi]que neg[oti
pub]lice inm[unicipi]o de s. s. datum erit negotive[1] |
publicei gesserit pequniamque publica[m deder]it
exegerit, is quoi ita negotium | datum erit
negotive quid publice gesser[it] pequniamve
publicam dederit | exegerit, eius rei rationem
senatui reddito refertoque in di[eb]us X proxum-
25 e[is] | quibus senatus eius municipi censuer[i]t
sine d. m.

  Quei decurio municipi Tarentinei est erit
queive in municipio Tarenti[no in] | senatu sen-
tentiam deixerit, is in o[pp]ido Tarentei aut intra
eius muni[cipi] | fineis aedificium, quod non

19 *post* rei *vel* rationem *add.* se?
21 *post* negotive *add.* quid?

---

[1] Each of which formed a voting unit. *Curiae* or geographical unions of *gentes* for worship, etc., were used in
primitive times in Latin towns, Rome included, in organising
the assembly. In Rome they were superseded (except in the
comitia curiata) by centuries and tribes, but survived elsewhere.
[2] For *decurio* see p. xxxix.

said matter in such a manner as the senate may decide. And of the said Board of Four he to whom surety shall be presented as above shall accept it and shall cause the fact to be entered in the public records; and whoever shall hold a meeting of the Assembly for proposing the election of the members of the Board of Two or of aediles, that same shall, before a majority of the wards [1] returns the name of any of those who shall be seeking a magistracy at the said assembly, accept from the candidates sureties such as are sufficient to guarantee that money, public sacred or employed in religion, belonging to the said borough, coming into the hands of any of the said candidates during the said magistracy, shall be well and duly secured to the borough of Tarentum, and that he will render an account of the said matter in such a manner as the senate may decide, and he shall cause the fact to be entered in the public records; and with regard to each person to whom any business in the borough shall be publicly given by a vote of the senate, or who shall have performed public business, and shall have paid out or exacted public money, he to whom public business as above shall have been given, or shall have performed some public business or shall have paid out or exacted public money, shall render and present an account of the said matter to the senate in good faith within ten days following the decision of the senate of the said borough.

Any man who is or shall be a councillor [2] of the borough of Tarentum, or shall have given a vote in the senate in the borough of Tarentum, the same shall in good faith possess, in the town of Tarentum or within the boundaries of the said borough, a

minu[s]MD tegularum tectum sit, habeto [*sine*] |
d. m. Quei eorum ita aedificium suom non habebit
[30] seive quis eorum [*eo*] | aedificium emerit man-
cupiove acceperit, quo hoic legi fraudem f[*aceret*],|
is in annos singulos HS n. IƆƆ municipio Tarentino
dare damnas esto. |

Neiquis inoppido, quod eius municipi e[*r*]it,
aedificium detegito neive dem[*olito*] | neive dis-
turbato, nisei quod non deterius restituturus erit,
nisei d. s. s. | Seiquis adversus ea faxit, quant[*i*] id
[35] aedificium f[*u*]erit, tantam pequni[*a*]m | muni-
cipio dare damnas esto, eiusque pequniae [*que*]i
vol[*e*]t peteti[*o*] esto. | Magi. quei exegerit di-
midium in [*p*]ublicum referto, dimidium in
l[*u*]deis, quos | publice in eo magistratu facie[*t*]
consumito, seive ad monumentum suom | in
publico consumere volet, l[*icet*]o idque ei s. f. s.
facere liceto. |

Seiquas vias fossas clouacas IIII vir II vir
[40] aedilisve eius municipi caussa | publice facere
immittere commutare aedificare munire volet
intra | eos fineis, quei eius municipi erun[*t*], quod
eius sine iniuria fiat, id ei facere | liceto.

Quei pequniam municipio Tarentin[*o*] non

[41] *post* iniuria *add.* privatorum ?

---

[1] On this careless expression, see above. The meaning
intended is ' if any member of the Board of Four—whether
one of the two *duoviri* or one of the two aediles.'

house which shall be roofed with not less than 1,500 tiles. Any of the said councillors who fails to possess as above a house of his own, anyone of them likewise who shall have bought a house or received it by formal transfer in such a way that he would fraudulently evade this law, the same shall be condemned to pay to the borough of Tarentum 5,000 sesterces in money for each separate year of offence.

No one in the town which belongs to the borough of Tarentum shall unroof or demolish or dismantle a house unless it be by a vote of the senate or he be ready to restore the building to a condition no worse than before. If anyone acts contrary to the said ordinance, he shall be condemned to pay to the borough money of value equal to that of the said house, and the power of suing for the said money shall belong to anyone who shall be so minded. The magistrate who shall have exacted the money shall pay one half into the public treasury, and spend one half on the games which he shall give publicly during the said magistracy, or, if he shall desire to spend the money on a public memorial of himself, he shall be allowed to do so, and he shall be so allowed without liability to personal penalty.

If any member of a Board of Four or a Board of Two or an aedile [1] shall be minded, for the sake of the said borough, to make, lay down, alter, construct, or pave any roads, ditches or sewers within those boundaries which belong to the said borough the said person shall be allowed to do the same, provided that none of it shall be done with damage to any person.

In regard to any who shall owe no money to the borough of Tarentum, if any of the said persons (who

443

debebit, sei quis eorum quei | municeps **erit**
neque eo sexennio [*p*]roxumo, quo exeire volet,
duovirum | a[*edilisve fuerit, ex municipio Tarentino
exeire volet, id ei s. f. s. facere liceto* . . . . .]

62

*Decree of the Roman Senate concerning Asclepiades, Poly-
stratus, and Meniscus, 78* B.C. (For other senatorial decrees
known in Greek translation only, see Bruns, *Fontes*, ed. VII,
166 ff.) Cf. *L. Gallet, ' Rev. Hist. de Droit,'* XVI, 242 ff., 387 ff.
*Tablet of bronze found at Rome ; now at Naples. Bilingual.
Of the Latin only parts are preserved, but the rest is supplied from
the Greek translation, which is almost complete. This inscription
is to be classed with Senatus consulta like that given on pp. 252-5,
but I have put it near the end of this book because not much
of the actual Latin is preserved, and because the date is at the
very end of the archaic period, if not beyond it. The restoration
of lost Latin from the extant Greek is fairly certain ; the following*

588 [*Cos. Q. Lutatio Q. f. Catulo et M. Aemilio Q. f. M. n.
Lepido, pr. urbano et inter peregrinos L. Cornelio
. . . . . f. Sisenna, mense Maio.*

*Q. Lutatius Q. f. Catulus cos. senatum consuluit
a. d. XI K. Iun. in comitio. Scribendo adfuerunt
L. Faberius L. f. Ser., C. . . . L. f. Pop., Q.
Petillius T. f. Ser.*

*Quod Q. Lutatius Q. f. Catulus cos. verba fecit
Asclepiadem Philini f. Clazomenium, Polystratum*

---

[1] A few fragments, chiefly syllables, remain. Even part
of the last sentence given here is conjectural.

[2] That is, Sisenna was both urban *praetor* and *p. peregrinus.*
Usually these praetorships were separate departments managed
by separate men.

[3] *i.e.,* in the Curia Hostilia which was in the Comitium.

shall be a citizen of the borough, and has not, during the six years previous to his desire to move his residence, been a member of the Board of Two or aedile) desire to move his residence from the borough of Tarentum, the said person shall be allowed to do the same without liability to personal penalty. . . .[1]

62

*are perhaps to be preferred to the words given in the Latin text :
'nauarchos' for 'magistros' (the Greek has ναυάρχους); 'in-
cipiente' for 'coepto' (ἐξαρχομένου); 'in patrias dimittere . . .
sei sibi' for 'domos dimissos . . . sei ei' (εἰς τὰς πατρίδας
ἀπολῦσαι . . . ἐὰν αὐτῷ φαίνηται); and later : 'e re publica
nostra' for 'rei publicae nostrae' (τοῖς δημοσίοις πράγμασιν
τοῖς ἡμετέροις); 'vacui omnium rerum et tributorum immunes'
for 'omnium rerum leiberei et immunes' (ἀλειτούργοι πάντων
τῶν πραγμάτων καὶ ἀνείσφοροι); 'e patria' thrice for 'domo'
(ἐκ τῆς πατρίδος); 'et si qui dies constitutus exierit' for 'seique
quae dies exiit' (εἴ τέ τις προθεσμία παρελήλυθεν); and 'in
patria' for 'domi' (ἐν ταῖς πατρίσιν).*

In the consulship of Quintus Lutatius Catulus son of Quintus, and Marcus Aemilius Lepidus, son of Quintus, grandson of Marcus; and the urban praetorship, and the praetorship for aliens,[2] of Lucius Cornelius Sisenna, son of . . . in the month of May.

Quintus Lutatius Catulus, consul, son of Quintus, consulted the Senate in the Meeting-place [3] on the 22nd of May.

Present to sign as witnesses to the record: Lucius Faberius son of Lucius, of the Sergian tribe, Gaius . . . son of Lucius, of the Poblilian tribe, and Quintus Petillius son of Titus, of the Sergian tribe.

With regard to the matter on which Quintus Lutatius, consul, son of Quintus, made verbal report, to wit that Asclepiades of Clazomenae son of Philinus,

INSTRUMENTA

Polyarci f. Carystium, Meniscum Irenaei, Meniscus Thargelii¹ qui fuit, filium Milesium magistros in navibus adfuisse bello Italico coepto,² eos operam fortem et fidelem rei publicae nostrae navasse, eos se ex senatus consulto domos dimissos velle, sei ei videretur utei pro rebus bene gestis ab eis fortiterque factis in rem publicam nostram honor eis haberetur : de ea re ita censuerunt :

 Asclepiadem Philini f. Clazomenium, Polystratum Polyarci filium Carystium, Meniscum Irenaei, qui fuit ante Meniscus Thargelii, filium Milesium, viros bonos et ameicos appellari ; senatum populumque Romanum existumare operam eorum bonam et fortem et fidelem rei publicae nostrae fuisse ; quam ob rem senatum censere, uti iei leiberei postereique eorum in patrieis sueis omnium rerum leiberei et immunes sint. Sei qua tributa ex boneis eorum exacta sunt, postquam rei publicae nostrae causa profectei sunt, utei ea eis reddantur restituantur, seique quei agrei aedificia bona eorum venierunt, postquam domo rei publicae nostrae caussa profectei sunt, utei ea omnia eis in integrum restituantur ; seique quae dies exit, ex quo domo rei publicae nostrae caussa profectei sunt, neiquid ea res eis noceat neive quid eis ob eam

---

¹ *i.e.*, Meniscus was true son of Thargelius, but had been adopted by Irenaeus.

² The ' Social ' War of 91–88 B.C., or possibly Sulla's war of 83–82.

³ *sei ei* (or *sibei*) *videretur*, sc. *consuli*; the Greek has ἐὰν αὐτῷ φαίνηται; Goettling would alter αὐτῷ to αὐτῇ, sc. τῇ συγκλήτῳ, the senate. For *honor* the Greek has καταλογή, which here means ' respect,' ' regard ' (as in Polyb. XXIII, 12, 10), not ' enrolment.'

Polystratus of Carystus, son of Polyarces, and
Meniscus of Miletus, son of Irenaeus (who was at
one time known as Meniscus [1] son of Thargelius)
were present on our side as captains in their ships
at the beginning of the Italic [2] War; that they had
staunchly rendered valiant and trusty aid to our
commonwealth; that he wished that they might be
dismissed to their homes by decree of the Senate
should it seem good to him that such honour [3] be
accorded them in return for successful campaigns
accomplished by them and for valiant deeds done
by them in favour of our commonwealth: on this
matter the Senators passed the following resolution:—

' That Asclepiades of Clazomenae son of Philinus,
Polystratus of Carystus son of Polyarces, and
Meniscus of Miletus son of Irenaeus (who was
formerly known as Meniscus son of Thargelius) be
called " good friends and fighters true "; that the
Senate and the Roman people believed that their
aid rendered had been noble valiant and trusty
towards our commonwealth; wherefore the resolution of the Senate is, that they, their children, and
their descendants be free and exempt from all
dues and services in their native countries; that
any tributes, that have been exacted from their
estates after their departure in the service of our
commonwealth, be returned and restored to them,
and any lands buildings or estates of theirs sold
up after their departure from home in the cause of
our commonwealth, all of the same be restored to
them in entirety; and that, if any time-limit has
run out after their departure from home n the
cause of our commonwealth, the fact do no harm to
their interests, and that no debt owed them be for

causam minus debeatur, neive quid minus eis per-
[1] *sequi exigere liceat, quaeque hereditates]* || eis leibe-
reisve eor[*um obvenerunt, utei eas habeant possi-*
[2] *deant fruanturque ; quaeque | ei leiberei posterei
uxoresve eorum ab altero persequentur seive quid ab]*
eis leibereis postereis ux[*oribus eorum aliei perse-*
[3] *quentur, utei eis leiberei postereis uxoribusve | eorum
ius potestasque sit, seive domi legibus sueis velint]*
iudicio certare seive apud magistratus [*nostros*
[4] *Italicis iudicibus seive in civitate libera | aliqua
earum, quae semper in amicitia p. R. mansueru]*nt,
ubei velint utei ibei iudicium deeis rebus fiat.
Seiqua [*iudicia eis absentibus postquam domo*
[5] *profectei sunt | facta sunt, ea utei in integrum
restitu]*antur et de integro iudicium ex s. c. fiat.
Seiquas pecunias c[*ivitates eorum publice debeant,*
[6] *in eas pecunias nei | quid dare debeant.   Magistrat]*us
nostri queiquomque Asiam Euboeam locabunt
vectigalve Asiae [*Euboeae imponent, curent ne quid*
[7] *ei dare debeant. | Uteique Q. Lutatius M.]* Aemilius
cos. a. a. s. e. v. eos inameicorum formulam
re[*fe*]rundos curarent, eis[*que tabulam aheneam*
[8] *Amicitiae in Capitolio ponere | sacrificiumque]* facere
liceret, munusque eis exformula locum lautiaque

---

[1] EIS · LEIBERISI VĪTO   [7] COS · AA · SE · V · EOS

---

[1] added because Carystus, Polystratus' city, was in Euboea.
Locabunt here means ' shall lease out the public land in ';
cf. Hardy, *Six Roman Laws*, 86–93.
[2] *a. a. s. e. v.* = *alter ambove sei eis videretur* (in line 10
videatur).

448

that reason less valid, and that they be no whit the
less permitted to assert a claim thereto and exact
the same; and that all inheritances that have fallen
to them or their children, they may have, possess,
and enjoy; and that in all claims which themselves
their children their descendants or their wives shall
assert from a second party, or in any which other
parties shall assert from them their children their
descendants or their wives,—they their children
their descendants or their wives shall have legal right
and free power to contest the same in court at home
according to their own laws or in courts of our
own magistrates, Italians to be judges, or in some
free state of those who have at all times stayed firm
in friendship with the Roman people; that, wherever
they may wish, there the law-court be held on the
said matters; that any judgments at law that were
delivered on them in their absence after their
departure from home be made entirely null and
void, and judgment be delivered afresh in entirety
by decree of the Senate. If there be any moneys
publicly owed by their states, they shall not be
required to pay anything towards the said moneys.
Any magistrate of ours, whatever, who shall lease
out Asia and Euboea [1] or shall impose revenue-taxes
on Asia and Euboea must take care that the said
persons be not required to pay anything. And that
the consuls Quintus Lutatius and Marcus Aemilius,
either, or both, if they think fit,[2] must superintend
the entering of the said persons on the official roll
of friends; and that they be permitted to put up a
bronze tablet to Friendship and make a sacrifice;
and that for them they order the quaestor of the
city to despatch a contribution according to official

q. urb. eis locare mitte[*reque i*]uber[*ent. Seique*

⁹ *de rebus sueis legatos ad senatum | mittere legateive*]
veneire vellent, uti [*e*]is leibereis postereisque
eorum legatos venire mittereque liceret.||||||

¹⁰ Utei[*que Q. Lutatius M. Aemilius cos. a. a.*] | sei
v. e. litteras ad magistratus nostros, quei Asiam
Macedoniam provincias optinent, et ad magi-

¹¹ stratus eorum mitt[*ant senatum velle et*] | aequom
censere ea ita fierei, i. u. e. e r. p. f. s. v. C.

[*Sequitur textus Graecus.*]

63
Tabula Fastorum

Notiz. d. Sc., 1921, 73ff.

There have long been known examples of Roman urban
calendars or almanacs belonging to times later than Julius
Caesar's calendar-reform, and for this reason known as *Fasti
Anni Iuliani*. But in 1915 there were discovered at Antium
(*Anzio*) pieces which when reconstructed revealed an urban
calendar of an earlier period. In it the month *Augustus*,
August, first so-called in honour of the emperor Augustus, is
called *Sextilis*, being the sixth (*sextus*) month of the earlier
Republican calendar; and the month *Iulius*, July, first
so-called in honour of Julius Caesar, was called *Quintilis*,
being the fifth (*quintus*) month, though the name is not on a
surviving part of this calendar; it also shows the normal
Republican year of 355 days, has months of pre-Julian
length, and also includes the intercalary month abolished by

---

⁸ VRBEIS · LOCARE   ⁹ VTI FIS
¹⁰ SEIVE LITTERAS

formula, and to contract for free quarters and all necessaries. And that, if they should wish to send ambassadors, or to come as ambassadors, to the Senate about their personal affairs, they, their children, and their descendants be permitted to come as ambassadors or to send the same. And that the consuls Quintus Lutatius and Marcus Aemilius, either, or both, if they think fit, send a letter to our magistrates who hold Asia and Macedonia [1] as provinces, and to their magistrates to the effect that the Senate wishes and thinks it right that these matters hold good in such a way as seems to them advantageous to the commonwealth and consistent with their personal honour.' Passed.[2]

[*The Greek translation follows, but is omitted here.*]

63

A Pre-Julian Calendar

Caesar. Nevertheless the year in this calendar begins on the 1st of January, which shows that Caesar had local as well as official precedent when he made such a beginning to his normal year of 365 days a universal rule; the custom probably arose locally after 153 B.C. when the Roman consuls began to enter office on the 1st of January. The spelling and style of this calendar point to a date early in the first century B.C. It was published by G. Mancini in *Notiz. d. Sc.*, 1921, pp. 73 ff. (see folder there facing p. 140). The urban calendars are quite distinct from the extant epigraphic lists (*Fasti consulares*) of higher magistrates (except praetors), and of course from the lists of magistrates and promagistrates who had been granted triumphs (*Fasti triumphales* or *Acta triumphorum*); they are distinct also from the rustic calendars

---

[1] Greece was not yet a province, but was under the watchful eye of the governor of Macedonia, which *was* a province.

[2] *C.* = *Censuere.* The letters *i. u. e. e r. p. f. s. v.* stand for *ita utei eis e re publica fideque sua videatur.*

INSTRUMENTA

called *Menologia rustica*. The urban calendars are each a list of *Fasti sacri* or *F. kalendares ;* their object was to ensure due observance of religious ceremonies by reminding people (i) of the days which were *dies fasti* on which it was religiously right or harmless to do business in assembly or law-courts by word of mouth (*fari*, to speak) and of the *dies nefasti* on which it was not right; (ii) of the fixed festivals (*feriae stativae*) of which some (the name ending normally in *-alia*) were the very old festivals having no specific reference to the dedications of temples, because their origins took place at undateable periods much earlier than the building of temples proper, others (shown by the deity's name in the dative case) celebrated ' *dies natales* ' ' birthdays ' commemorating the anniversary of the dedication of a later temple. The building of temples had begun not long before the end of the monarchic period near the end of the sixth century B.C. The latter, the temple-*feriae*, lasted always one day only; probably all the old festivals also lasted one day, not excepting even the Saturnalia and such as were marked by *ludi* or games; some were ceasing to have much meaning even in Cicero's time. All older festivals, except one or two, and most of the dedications of later temples for superstitious reasons took place on odd-numbered days. Again, in these calenders each day (*dies nundinalis*) of the eight-day week (*nundinum*) received letters A to H repeated in succession (so that the first day of each month did not necessarily begin with A); the Kalends, Nones, and Ides are always named; some calendars also date fully every day. Every day received also an epithet shown by one or other of the following initials. F = ' *fas est ius dicere* ' ' it is permitted to pronounce justice '; and a day so marked is *fastus*, a ' speechable ' day (if I may so put it) on which at any hour the praetor urbanus may decide legal cases in his court; but assemblies of the people (*comitia*) must not be held on it. FP = (Aug. 19th only) probably *fastus principio*, a day on which legal business was allowed only in the morning (*principium* ' beginning '). C = *comitialis*, an ' assembly-day ' on which the *comitia* may meet; if no *comitia* met, the day was *fastus*. N = *nefas*, and a day so marked is a ' not-speechable ' day; on it, because of some bad omen associated with the day, neither could legal business be done nor could the *comitia* meet. N A disputed sign, but probably a monogram for NFP *nefas(tus), feriae*

452

publicae, ' not-speechable; public holiday,' *nefastus* indeed,
but of a cheerful nature, when freemen were exempt from
public work and slaves had relief. EN = *endotercisus*, old
Latin for *intercisus*, ' midsplit day,' ' day cut into two parts,'
a day which was *fastus* in the middle hours, *nefastus* in the
early morning and in the evening. There were only a few
of such days. QRCF = (March 24th, May 24th only) *quando
rex comitiavit, fas* ' when the king (of the sacrifices) has
finished his duties in the meeting-place, the day is speechable '.
These duties were performed before and at meetings of the
comitia curiata in the *comitium* in the Forum for the sacred
purpose of giving sanction to wills. QSDF = (June 15th
only) *quando stercus delatum, fas* ' when refuse has been carried
off, the day is speechable,' that is when, at the end of Vesta's
festival beginning on the 7th of June, her temple has been
cleaned and all sweepings have been carried away. Note
that days marked EN or QRCF or QSDF are all *dies fissi*
' cleft days.'

The calendar of Antium is a true Roman urban calendar,
like the other surviving urban calendars. Like them it was
for the use primarily of Roman citizens (true Romans and
others), who lived near enough to Rome to come to that city
for political business and religious celebrations. But citizens
even in remote regions of Italy might like to travel to Rome
when it suited them or to take local notice of Roman celebrations; so we have a calendar of Venusia (known from
copies only) and even of a place in Cisalpine Gaul. After
89 B.C. all adults in Italy were Roman citizens. As regards
this particular calendar, Antium was a Roman colony on the
coast of Latium and after the Marian troubles was also a place
of resort for the rich. This calendar belongs further to the
kind in which, though all the days of each month are marked
A to H according to the Roman eight-day week, the date is
not otherwise marked except Kalends, Nones, and Ides.
The ' week '-days (except each A-day), the Kalends, Nones
and Ides, and the fixed festivals not connected with dedication of temples, are written in black; A-days (each of which
the Romans called *nundinae*)—that is, market-days, the
character-signs of days placed after the abbreviations for
Kalends, Nones and Ides, and after any festivals mentioned,
are written in red; so are the notices of temple-birthdays.
All other characterisations of days are in black. The sum-

totals of days in each month are added in black and red in alternate months. The gaps in this calendar, especially since the surviving bits are scattered over pretty well the whole year, can be restored extensively from the later ones or copies where they are lost (most are in *C.I.L.*, I, part 1, ed. 2; cf. '*Fasti Vaticani*' *C.I.L.*, VI, 32433, '*Suburani minores*' VI, 32496, '*Oppiani minores*' VI, 32494, and an Ostian in *Notiz. d. Sc.*, 1921, 251 ff.). It was written on rough-cast as part of a wall on which it was displayed. I give here the details of

	(*Aprilis*)			(*Sextilis*)	
A	[*K. Ap*]r.	F	A	K. Se[*xt*.]	
				Spei Victor. II	
B	F		B	F	
C	C		[*C*]	[*C*] (?)	
D	C		[*D*]	[*C*] (?)	
E	Non.	N	[*E*]	Non.	[N˙](?)
	Fort. Publ.			Salu.	
F	N		F	F	
[*G*]	N		G	C	
[*H*]	[*N*] (?)		H	C	
A	[*N*] (?)		[*A*]	[*F*] (?)	
B	N		[*B*]	[*C*] (?)	
C	N	M.D.M.I.	C	C	

the text for April and for August (which of course are not adjacent in the calendar), and add a translation which will make clearer the nature of the reminders given to any who consulted the calendar. It should be noted that up to a point it was a matter of arbitrary taste as to what notices of celebrations should be shown on any calendar, so that our extant examples are not alike, but vary in their completeness. In the commentary on pp. 460 ff. I have not given any details of deliberate omissions by this calendar.

	(April)		(August)
A	Kalends of April. Business in Court.	A	Kalends of August. To Hope; To the two Victories.
B	Business in Court.	B	Business in Court.
C	Business in Assembly.	C	Business in Assembly (?).
D	Business in Assembly.	D	Business in Assembly (?).
(5th) E	Nones. No Business. To Fortune of the State.	E	Nones. No Business; Public Holiday (?). To Safety.
F	No Business.	F	Business in Court.
G	No Business.	G	Business in Assembly.
H	No Business (?).	H	Business in Assembly.
A	No Business (?).	A	Business in Court (?).
(0th) B	No Business.	B	Business in Assembly (?).
C	No Business. To Mighty Idaean Mother of the Gods.	C	Business in Assembly.

455

	(Aprilis)			*(Sextilis)*	
D	N		D	C	
E	Eidus N͡		E	[*Eidus*] N͡	
	Iovi. Victor.			Dianae. Vortu. |	
	Iov. | Leibert.			Fort. Equ. Her.	
				Vic. | [*Cas*]t.	
				Poll. Came.	
F	N		F	F	
G	Fordi. N͡		G	C	
H	N		H	C	
A	N		A	Port.	[N͡] (?)
B	N		[*B*]	[*C*] (?)	
C	Ceria. N͡		[*C*]	Vina.	
	Cereri Lib.			Venere **FP**	
	L[*ib.*]				
D	N		D	[*C*] (?)	

456

	(*April*)		(*August*)
D	No Business.	D	Business in Assembly.
E	Ides. No Business; Public Holiday. To Jupiter Conqueror; To Jupiter Liberty.	E	Ides. No Business; Public Holiday. To Diana, Vortumnus, Fortune H o r s e - r i d e r, Hercules Conqueror, Castor, Pollux, Goddesses of Song.
F	No Business.	F	Business in Court.
(15th) G	Festival: Sacrifice of Cows in calf. No Business; Public Holiday.	G	Business in Assembly.
H	No Business.	H	Business in Assembly.
A	No Business.	A	Festival: of God of our Harbour. No Business; Public Holiday (?).
B	No Business.	B	Business in Assembly (?).
C	Festival: of Ceres. No Business; Public Holiday. To Ceres, Liber, and Libera.	C	Festival: of Vintage. Business in Court in the morning. To Venus.
(20th) D	No Business.	D	Business in Assembly (?).

457

	(Aprilis)				(Sextilis)	
E	Paril.	N⌐		E	C[o]ns.	N⌐
	Roma Cond.					
F	N			F	En.	
G	Vinal.			G	V[olk.]	N⌐
	Vener.				V[olk.	H]orae
	Eruc.	F			Qu[i.	Maiae?
					s]upr. com[i.]	
H	C			H	C	
A	Robig.	N⌐		A	O[pic.]	[N⌐](?)
[B]	C			B	[C](?)	
[C]	[C](?)			C	[Volt]u.	N⌐
D	C			D	[C](?)	
E	C			[E]	[C](?)	

XXIX	XXIX

	(April)		*(August)*
E	Festival: of Pales. No Business; Public Holiday. Foundation of Rome	E	Festival: of God of Sowing. No Business; Public Holiday.
F	No Business.	F	Midsplit.
G	Festival: of Vintage. Business in Court. To Venus of Eryx.	G	Festival: of Vulcan. No Business; Public Holiday. To Vulcan, Hora, Quirinus, Maia above the Meeting-place.
H	Business in Assembly.	H	Business in Assembly.
(25th) A	Festival: of God of Mildew. No Business; Public Holiday.	A	Festival: of Goddess of Good Sowing. No Business; Public Holiday (?).
B	Business in Assembly.	B	Business in Assembly (?)
C	Business in Assembly (?).	C	Festival: of Volturnus. No Business; Public Holiday.
D	Business in Assembly.	D	Business in Assembly (?)
E	Business in Assembly.	E	Business in Assembly (?)

INSTRUMENTA

Notes on April : 1st : *Apr.* = *Apriles.* 5th : *Fort(unae)
Publ(icae).* The dative case means that the day is dedicated
to the divinity. Of three temples of Fortune close together
on the Quirinal Hill, one was dedicated in 194 B.C. But
which one is unknown. 8th : [*N*] I supply these bracketed
signs from later calendars, but the supplements are, as applicable to this calendar, mere guesswork. 11th : *M(atri) D(eum)
M(agnae) I(daeae).* The temple of the Phrygian Magna Mater
or Cybele was dedicated on the Palatine in 192 B.C., 12 years
after her fetish-stone was brought from Pessinus. 13th :
Iovi Victor(i); his temple was ' vowed ' in 295 B.C. *Iuppiter
Libertas* had a temple on the Aventine, year of dedication
unknown. 15th : *Fordi(cidia)*, festival (to Tellus ?) at which
boves fordae or *hordae*, pregnant cows, were sacrificed by
priests and Vestals. 19th : *Ceria(lia)*. *Cereri Lib(ero) Lib-
(erae).* Liber was a son, Libera a daughter, of Ceres. A
temple was, according to tradition, dedicated to all three in
493 B.C. The *Cerealia* was a festival of Ceres which marked
the last day of the plebeian *Ludi Cereales* beginning or the
12th of April. 21st : *Paril(ia)* a festival (probably to Pales,
goddess of flocks) of the first day of the shepherds' spring,
with purification of fields. *Roma cond(ita).* The 21st of
April was the traditional day of Rome's foundation. 23rd :
Vinal(ia), that is *V. priora*, when there was libation to Jupiter
and tasting of wine pressed during the previous year. See
also Aug. 19th. *Vener(i) Eruc(inae).* The cult of Aphrodite
of Eryx in Sicily was brought thence by soldiers of the 1st
Punic War (264–241 B.C.), and Aphrodite was identified with
Venus; her temple was dedicated outside the Colline gate in
181 B.C. 25th : *Robig(alia)*, festival of *Robigus* the god of
' red rust ' or ' mildew,' celebrated in a grove at the 5th milestone on the *Via Claudia*. *Notes on August* : 1st : *Sext.* =
Sextiles. Spei Victor(iis) duabus. This Hope's temple was
dedicated in 257 B.C.; one temple of Victory was dedicated
in 294 B.C., the other (to Victoria Virgo) in 193 near the
first. 5th : *Salu(ti).* The temple to Salus was dedicated in
302 B.C. 13th : *Dianae Vortu(mno) Fort(unae) Equ(estri)
Her(culi) Vic(tori) Casto(ri) Poll(uci) Came(nis).* There was
on the Aventine a very old temple of Diana and one dedicated
by M. Fulvius Flaccus in 264 B.C. to Vortumnus; one to
Fortuna Equestris was vowed by C. Fulvius Flaccus in 180 in
a successful battle with the Celtiberi where his cavalry played

460

LAWS AND OTHER DOCUMENTS

an important part. Of Hercules Victor there was a temple near the Circus Maximus and another near the Porta Trigemina; the latter is the one alluded to here. The Camenae were prophetic nymphs of the country and were identified by the Romans with the Greek Muses. They had a small shrine at the foot of the Aventine. 17th : *Port(unalia)*. Portunus was perhaps protector of the port of Ostia, and the mercantile stores of Rome and Ostia. His festival was held at the Pons Aemilius of unknown site. 19th : *Vina(lia)*, that is *V. rustica*. Most probably marked by offering of unripe grapes in hopes of a good ripe crop after a month had gone by. See also April 23rd. *Venere* is a dative for *Veneri*. The temple here meant was dedicated in 295 B.C. near the Circus Maximus. 21st : *Cons(ualia)*, festival of Consus, the god of 'stored up harvest.' 23rd : *Volk(analia)*. *Vol(kano) Horae Qui(rino) Maiae supr(a) comi(tium)*. Vulcan had a temple of unknown date before 215 B.C. in the Circus Flaminius. After Romulus had become the god Quirinus, his bereaved wife Hersilia according to one story was allowed to become the goddess Hora. It looks as though *Hora Quirini* ' Hora consort of Quirinus ' might be the meaning here, especially since the dedication of Quirinus' own temple was celebrated on 17th Feb. But the Arval records give Aug. 23rd, as a day for Quirinus himself *in colle*. This latter would probably refer to a reconstruction and rededication. Maia was closely connected with Vulcan. 25th : *Opic(onsivia)* a festival of *Ops Consiva* ' Lady bountiful of Seed-sowing ' (but she is so closely related to Consus as well as to Saturnus, that it may mean ' of stored harvest '), to whom sacrifices were made in her shrine in the Regia or ' King's House.' 27th : *Voltu(rnalia)*. This festival was sacred to the god Volturnus, perhaps an old name (' Winding ') of the Tiber as it was the permanent name of a river in Campania. Of course, on the 1st of both months K = *Kalendae*, on the 5th *Non.* = *Nonae*.

Other than the usual single signs, and other than single names, the remaining months include the following: February 5th : Concord(iae) in Capit(olio). To Concord on the Capitol. Her temple was begun in 216 B.C. March 7th : [*N*]on(ae). F. Vedi(ovi) in Ca[*p*]itol(io.) Nones. Business in Court. To Vediovis on the Capitol.

461

INSTRUMENTA

In 200 B.C. the praetor L. Furius Purpureo vowed a temple to Vediovis; it was built on Tiber Island and dedicated on Jan. 1st, 194 (this calendar for Jan. 1st has *Vediove* = dative Vediovi); when consul in 196, Furius vowed another which was built between the Capitol and the Arx Capitolina, and dedicated in 192. This second is here meant. 19th: [Q]uin(quatrūs). ℕ Minervae. **Fifth-day Festival. No business; public holiday. To Minerva.** Minerva was protectress of artists. The date of her Temple is unknown. The Quinquatrūs (5th day after the Ides) lasted five days in the later Republic and under the Empire. The festival was sacred to Mars, then to Minerva, and included a review of the *ancilia* or sacred shields. 23rd: Tubil(*ustrium*). ℕ **Review of trumpets;** *etc.* The trumpets used in sacrificial ceremonies and in calling the assemblies were purified. This was the last day of the Quinquatrus. 24th: Q(uando) r(ex) c(omitiavit), f(as). **When the king has finished in the Meeting-place, Business in Court.** May 25th: For[*t*](unae) P(opuli) R(omani) Q(uiritium). **To Fortune of the Roman Commonwealth of Quirites.** This refers to another of Fortune's 3 temples on the Quirinal—see above. Dedication or rededication of the temple of Fortuna Primigenia (see below) is recorded for this day; but on this calendar it was not shown. June 1st: E K(alendae) Iun(iae). [*N*](efastus). | Marti in cl[*ivo Iuno*]-n(i) in [*arce*(?)]. **Fifth week-day. Kalends of June. No business. To Mars on the Slope. To Juno on the Stronghold.** There was a temple of Mars on the rising ground beyond the first milestone on the Appian Way, probably the one vowed in 388 B.C. On the *arx* was a very old altar or shrine of Juno, which is doubtless the one here alluded to; but the temple of Juno Moneta was finally dedicated in 344 B.C. probably on Oct. 10th, as mentioned in this calendar under that day; though sometimes the 1st of June was given as Juno Moneta's birthday. 15th: Q(uando) st(ercus) d(elatum), [*f*](as). **When refuse has been carried off, legal business.** July 7th: Palibus II. **To the two Paleses.** Two temples of Pales, doubtless close together,

462

are mentioned here only. 13th: Loed(i) Apol(linis).
Games of Apollo. The Ludi Apollinares were instituted in
212 B.C.; originally lasting one day, they were in the end
spread back over 8 days from July 6th to the 13th. 18th:
[*Al*]liens(i) die. To the day of Allia. This was in memory
of the defeat of Rome by the Gauls at the river Allia in 390
B.C. Nov. 13th: [*Fer*]on(iae) Fort(unae) Prim(igeniae)
[*Pie*?]tati. To Feronia, to Fortune, Jupiter's first-
born, to Loyalty. Feronia, famed in Latium and central
Italy, was less so in Rome, but had a shrine in the Campus
Martius; the temple of fortune Primigenia (see inscriptions
above pp. 60, 120–3) was one of the 3 on the Quirinal, perhaps the one dedicated in 194 B.C. See above. There was a
famous temple of this Fortuna at Praeneste, and another at
Antium; both temples were oracular seats for ascertaining
the future. The Romans came to believe that this Fortune
was the first-born (*primogenia*) daughter of Jupiter. Pietas
is uncertain here, but a temple was dedicated to her in 181
B.C. Dec. 8th: Tiberino, Gaiae. To Tiberinus, to
Gaia. The temple to the river-god Tiberinus, of unknown
date, was on Tiber Island. Here we have the only mention,
in any calendar, of Gaia Taracia who in one story takes
the place of Tarquinia, wife of Tarquinius Priscus. 17th:
Satur(nalia). En. | Saturno. Festival: of Saturn.
Midsplit. To Saturn. Saturn's festival, lasting originally
3 days, then 5, and, under the Empire, 7, was marked by
great celebrations, exchange of gifts, and relaxation for slaves.
Saturn's temple was built in the monarchic period. 22nd:
L[*a*]r(ibus) Perm(arinis). Household Gods of the Sea.
Their temple was vowed by L. Aemilius Regillus in 190 B.C.
after a naval victory over Antiochus III, and dedicated in
the Campus Martius in 197 B.C. 23rd: Lare(ntalia). N
Dian(ae) Iunon(i) R(eginae) in Camp. Tempe(stati-
bus). Festival: of Larentia . . . To Diana; to
Iuno Queen in the Field. To the Weathers.
The festival was in honour of Acca Larentia (who was,
according to one story, wife of Faustulus, and nurse of
Romulus and Remus), with sacrifices for fertility of fields.

INSTRUMENTA

The temples to Diana and Juno here meant were vowed by Aemilius Lepidus in 187 and dedicated in 179. A temple to the goddesses of weather was vowed by L. Scipio son of Barbatus during a storm on his return from Sardinia in 259 B.C. See the inscription on his tomb, pp. 4–5. The temple was built by the Via Appia outside the porta Capena. *Intercalary month.* This is placed after December in this calendar; but when this month was actually inserted into the year, it was put between February and March—see p. 108. So little of it has survived in this calendar that we cannot tell whether the alleged name *Mercedonius,* ‘ pay-month,’ supposed to rest on a mistake in Plutarch, is true or not, because the part giving the month’s name is lost.

LAWS AND OTHER DOCUMENTS

Note lastly that this calendar records the following anniversaries of temple-dedications not mentioned in other extant calendars, though alluded to or mentioned in literary works : Iuturna (11th Jan.), Iuno Sospita Mater Regina (1st Feb.), Iuppiter Victor (13th Apr.), Mars in Clivo (1st June), Fortuna (11th June), Lares (27th June) ; and the following mentioned neither in other extant calendars nor in literary works : Vica Pota (5th Jan.), Iuppiter Leibertas (13th Apr.), Mania ? (11th May), Pales two temples (7th July), Honos (17th July), Fortuna Equestris, Camenae (13th Aug.), Hora, Maia ? supra Comitium (23rd Aug.), Iuppiter Stator (5th Sept.), Pietas ? (13th Nov.), Gaia (8th Dec.), Diana, Iuno Regina in Campo, Tempestates (23rd Dec.).

LIST OF INSCRIPTIONS

Lists of the sources from which each inscription in this book has been taken, and of the pages of this book on which the inscription is found or begins.

LIST OF INSCRIPTIONS

LIST OF INSCRIPTIONS

LIST OF INSCRIPTIONS

LIST OF INSCRIPTIONS

LIST OF INSCRIPTIONS

LIST OF INSCRIPTIONS

LIST OF INSCRIPTIONS

473

LIST OF INSCRIPTIONS

INDEX OF PROPER NAMES

(The numbers refer to pages)

INDEX OF PROPER NAMES

INDEX OF PROPER NAMES

477

INDEX OF PROPER NAMES

INDEX OF PROPER NAMES

479

INDEX OF PROPER NAMES

480

INDEX OF PROPER NAMES

INDEX OF PROPER NAMES

INDEX OF PROPER NAMES

INDEX OF PROPER NAMES

INDEX OF PROPER NAMES

INDEX OF PROPER NAMES

INDEX OF PROPER NAMES

SURVEYED LAND

The plan on the next page shows a small imaginary area of ground divided up by a Roman surveyor into square centuries. The surveyor is presumed to stand in the centre.
$+$ = surveyor's central *groma*; $\longrightarrow$ = his orientation.

The surveyor is presumed to use an orientation facing eastwards. The width of the *decumanus maximus* and the *kardo maximus* is much exaggerated. The thick black lines represent *quintarii*.

· marks a boundary-stone.

⌐ ⌐ ⌐ ⌐ mark each an *angulus clusaris* with boundary-stone.

Every similar corner of every similar century on an area like this would have its boundary-stone.

:: shows the possible position of stones on the *dec. max.* or on the *kardo max.* or on both.

a shows where four stones marked SDIKM might be placed (see p. 164).

b shows where four stones marked DMKKIII might be placed (see p. 164).

||||||| indicates the century which the imaginary stone marked DDVIIVKIX would indicate in this area (see p. 165).

\\\\\ indicates a century in which the stone in *C.I.L.*, I, 2, 639 (see p. 168 of this book, number 24, presumed to be DMVKVII) might be placed in this area. It would be placed in the north-eastern corner of the century.

⌐ ⌐ ⌐ indicate the other possible positions of stones so marked.

//// indicates the century which the stone in *C.I.L.*, I, 2, 640 (SDIKKXI, see p. 170 of this book, number 25) would indicate in this area.

C shows a century (which would be marked SDVVKIV) divided into six plots each of thirty *iugera* = 10 × 6 *actus*, with a spare patch (shown in black) which would belong to another plot overlapping on to another century.

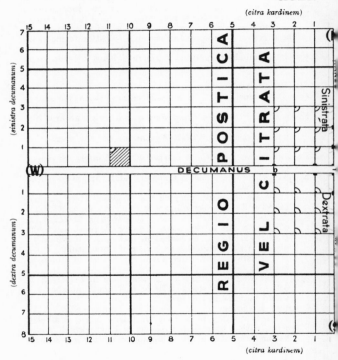

AGER

(citra kardinem)

(citra kardinem)

LIMITATUS

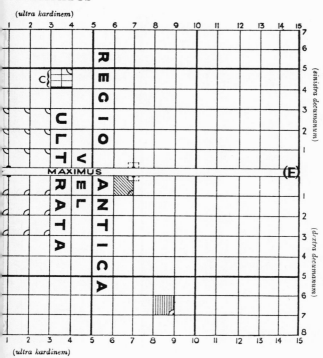

(ultra kardinem)

(sinistra decumanum)

(dextra decumanum)

(ultra kardinem)